The origins of the South African War

South Africa at the outbreak of war, 1899

—.—.—.— *political boundaries*
++++++++ *principal railways*

The origins of the South African War

JOSEPH CHAMBERLAIN AND THE DIPLOMACY OF IMPERIALISM 1895–99

A. N. Porter

ST. MARTIN'S PRESS   New York

All rights reserved. For information write:
St. Martin's Press, Inc., 175 Fifth Avenue, New York, N.Y. 10010
Printed in Great Britain
First published in the United States of America in 1980

ISBN 0-312-58874-7

Library of Congress Cataloging in Publication Data

Porter, Andrew N
    The origins of the South African War.

    Bibliography: p. 307
    Includes index.
    1. South African War, 1899–1902—Causes.
2. Chamberlain, Joseph, 1836–1914. 3. Great Britain—
Colonies—Africa—Administration. 4. Great Britain—
Foreign relations—1837–1901. I. Title.
DT930.A35P67 1980   968.04'8   79-28491
ISBN 0-312-58874-7

Contents

Abbreviations

Af.(S)   Colonial Office Confidential Print, series African (South).

AYB   *Archives Year Book for South African History*

BP   Balfour Papers

BIHR   *Bulletin of the Institute of Historical Research*

BDI   G. P. Gooch and H. Temperley, eds., *British Documents on the origins of the War, 1898–1914* (11 vols, 1926–38), vol 1

CHBE   *The Cambridge History of the British Empire*

CO   Colonial Office

EHR   *The English Historical Review*

FO   Foreign Office

FOP   Foreign Office Confidential Print

HJ   *The Historical Journal*

HPD   *Hansard Parliamentary Debates*

ISAA   Imperial South African Association

JAH   *The Journal of African History*

JC   Joseph Chamberlain Papers

JICH   *The Journal of Imperial and Commonwealth History*

JSAS   *The Journal of Southern African Studies*

MP   Milner Papers

MSP   Salisbury Papers

PP   *Parliamentary Accounts and Papers*

QVL 3rd   G. E. Buckle, ed., *Letters of Queen Victoria*, 3rd series (3 vols, 1930–2)

SP   Selborne Papers

The place of publication of all books is London unless otherwise stated. Works listed in the select bibliography when cited in the notes appear in abbreviated form.

Preface

In recent years, much has been written about British policy towards southern Africa in the two decades after 1890, on the history of southern Africa itself, upon the gradual transition from Empire to Commonwealth of Nations, and on issues in the debate about the nature of late-nineteenth-century imperialism. Paralleling these studies of policy, contemporary beliefs in, and justifications of, the nature and purpose of imperial rule and expansion have found their analysts; the highly critical Radical contribution to the thinking behind colonial policy has also been clearly portrayed.   There are, however reasons for feeling that perspectives on Anglo-South African relations have been in some respects at once too broad and too narrow, too frequently bent with the purpose of passing moral judgements on those responsible for charting the course of British policy. Studies on the imperial theme, or of the question of personal responsibility for the drift into war, have neither fully explained the contemporary significance of the South African question, nor really considered the circumstances within which official policy evolved in the years 1895–9. One factor in particular, that of 'public opinion', was important for the effects which it had upon the formulation and development of British policy, but has been given scant consideration by historians. There are good reasons for this, not least those involving problems of definition and lack of adequate source materials. Yet there is still much evidence to suggest that among the obstacles understood by policy-makers to stand in the way of any foreign or imperial policy, the factor of 'public opinion' was, during the 1890s, felt to loom very large. While always remaining by the standards of any modern political scientist extremely ill-defined, the importance of 'public opinion', usually (as far as politicians or policy-makers were concerned) in the shape of 'parliament' or 'the electorate', was none the less considerable. Such evidence as there is seems to point to the growth of the feeling amongst British statesmen, officials, and imperialists in general, that they were being increasingly bound or restricted in their actions, particularly by the extra-governmental or extra-diplomatic factor of 'public opinion'. The rise of 'public opinion' to importance in the policy-making process was associated by those concerned with the problem with the extension of democratic forms of government. Concern appears to have reached a peak in the last two decades of the century, and of the many who shared this conviction, Joseph Chamberlain and Alfred Milner were among the most notable. 'Political power has passed from the few to the many. With its passing, as Lord Milner was one of the first to urge, the only sure foundation of public policy must, in future, rest upon public opinion. Democracy must formulate for itself the principle upon which it desires not only domestic affairs, but also international relations to be conducted by those who represent it. In order to do so, the People must be furnished with the necessary knowledge, and the evidence upon which they must determine their verdict upon the past, and address themselves to the problems of the future in the light of old experiences.' Not for nothing did Cecil Headlam write this in the Preface to his edition of the Milner Papers, even though his presentation of the papers themselves was sometimes no less partial than Milner's own attempts to 'inform' the public on what he felt to be the vitally important question of South Africa.

Given the facts that there existed widespread concern as to the difficulties of conducting a coherent foreign and imperial policy inside a democratic political system, and that this concern was not only shared by but markedly affected the activities of those British policy-makers most concerned with South African affairs after 1895, it became clear that here was a framework of reference, both wide and neglected, and important to any re-examination or deeper understanding of the origins of the South African War of 1899. However, before proceeding further to outline the scope of this book, it is necessary to consider briefly this concept of 'public opinion' as used by democratic politicians.

Among historians it is possible to discern at least two approaches to the study of 'public opinion'. There is first the study of 'public opinion' as an objective entity, as the sum total of certain beliefs and ideas held by the 'public' which can be understood by reading the newspapers and other recorded expressions of opinion, and then taking their highest common denominator. Very often 'public opinion' has been sub-divided, historians detecting 'liberal' or 'conservative' public opinion, and so on. The problems attached to finding truly satisfactory definitions in this way are akin to those met in attempts to pinpoint the meaning of 'class', the diversity of sources and the complexity of opinions held paralleling varieties of, for example, occupation, status, and income. To try and pick out 'working-class' or 'middle-class' opinion only compounds the difficulties still further.

Other historians have preferred to concentrate on those who have used the term 'public opinion' or have appeared to try and capture public attention, attempting to assess either their meaning or the practical implications of the importance which they attached to it; in so far as it refers to 'public opinion', it is to this camp that the present work primarily belongs. The references to and usage of the term by politicians may only too often have been full of sound and fury, all the while signifying nothing, yet it is inevitable that the conceptual debate and attempts at definition will continue, certainly for as long as politicians are thought to be rational men and their language felt to merit dissection.

One major problem faced here is that politicians in particular have been liable to use the phrase while having very little idea what it meant. Periodically, in an effort to escape the uncertainties of their situation or to claim an ultimate authority for their own arguments, politicians have tried pinning the omnibus label to certain segments of the population – segments which, while clearly partial in themselves, might plausibly be presented as representing a 'national', rather than a purely selfish, interest in a particular context. In the nineteenth century, the middle classes, London society and Clubland, and the readers of The Times all at one time or another acquired such recognition.[1] On the ideological plane, politicians were in fact confronted then with the same kind of uncertainty as has plagued historians at a later date. The opinions expressed in newspapers or journals might or might not reflect those either of reader or proprietor, but in what proportion it was difficult to know. The kindred problems of assessing election results, of estimating the representative nature of letters or deputations, have also long been appreciated by both practising politicians and analysts of the political scene.

However, if they were often unsure as to what 'public opinion' actually was, or what group actually embodied it, politicians always knew what from their own point of view it ought to be, and well understood the kind of occasion on which they needed to invoke it. If one is concerned with politicians and what they meant by 'public opinion' it is necessary to recognise that the relevance of ideas, beliefs, or desires, to that 'public opinion' with which politicians affect to concern themselves is only of a secondary kind. 'Public opinion' is primarily important as something affecting the possibility of *action* rather than as something related to ideas of moral worth and impartial representation. For the politician 'public opinion' is only that opinion which, regardless of its limitations or extent, can make itself *politically effective*. Of fundamental importance or concern to any politician is his knowledge of those individuals or groups which have the political power to hinder him, to thwart his policy, cut short his tenure of office, and promote the interests of his rivals; if he can neutralise them, or, better still, win them round to his way of thinking, his position will be secure. Either course necessitates something in the nature of a propaganda campaign, the publication of carefully-chosen arguments intended to consolidate his support. This support may be looked for in different places at different times, within his constituency, from the electorate as a whole, within the ranks of fellow MPs, or from a national interest group, be they butchers, bakers, or merchants engaged in the South American trade. Alternatively, support may be sought, through the use of a different appeal, from all these groups at the very same moment. But the fact remains that opinions are only rarely felt to be anything but insignificant, the exception being when they incline those who hold them to action. If a man is likely to vote or air his views publicly with the possibility of blocking or promoting definite policies through the lobby or ballot box, or of persuading others to do so, only then is he really worth worrying about. Bagehot, for example, was expressing the politician-cum-policy-maker's viewpoint when he observed that under 'free institutions it is necessary occasionally to defer to the opinions of other people; and as other people are obviously wrong, this is a great hindrance to the improvement of our political system and the progress of our species'. Politics may well be the art of the possible; it is also the art of self-defence and self-promotion, with the result that each politician necessarily has his own flexible working definition of what at any one time constitutes 'public opinion'. Generally speaking, success in the promotion of policy comes to the man able to call the biggest battalions into play when contentious issues are debated, the nature of his forces being governed by the nature of timing of questions under discussion, by the political framework and conventions of the day, and his own temperament or abilities.

In the course of the nineteenth century, this functional concept of 'public opinion' was extended into almost every sphere of government activity. Ministerial insecurity in the Commons combined with pressure from outside Parliament led, via a series of Reform Acts, to the progressive creation of an ever larger body of opinion which could normally make itself politically effective. Politicians of all shades, concerned as always with promoting particular courses of action and with preserving their freedom of action or manoeuvre, were forced to adapt both their ideas about 'public opinion' and their tactical methods to this change. In some respects their independence was protected by parallel developments – the decline in the fear of revolution, the growth of tighter party discipline, respect for the idea of 'the expert', and the sheer complexity of certain issues. However, at least in the second half of the century, the extension of representative government was the dominant element in the situation and inevitably bred conflicts as to the nature and degree of publicity or prior commitment to be given to individual policies. Foreign and imperial policies were in no way exempt from these changes, especially as the size of, and multiplicity of views represented within, the electorate increased out of all recognition. It was eventually the electorate as a whole rather than any subordinate group whose opinions, or lack of them, frequently seemed to stand in the way of the successful protection of Britain's overseas interests.

It has therefore been felt necessary in Chapter I to provide a brief survey of the development amongst leading foreign policy makers of the feeling that 'public opinion' in one form or another had increasingly to be taken into account as a factor in their diplomacy. Lack of space prevents any detailed analysis of individual attitudes or policies, of what at any one moment they chose to call 'public opinion'; such an exercise would alone require several separate monographs. But from a reading mainly of secondary sources, it seems possible to point to the steady growth of official concern with the views of an ever-wider audience. Initially some statesmen actively encouraged this development as a source of strength to their own diplomacy. Others never had anything but reservations, and in the later years of the century the fear spread that the nature of parliamentary and particularly electoral opinion more often than not made the diplomatists' task well nigh impossible. Chapter II sets out to show how Chamberlain, atuned to the problems of democratic politics and increasingly committed to an active imperial policy, developed an analysis of Britain's needs and of his own domestic political position which required the involvement of parliamentary and electoral opinion in the pursuit of imperial greatness.

The remainder of the book, based above all on the private and official papers of Chamberlain, Milner, and the Colonial Office, is devoted to a study of how Chamberlain's vision affected his handling of South African affairs between 1895 and 1899. Inevitably it covers afresh much well-trodden ground, but offers revised interpretations or produces fresh material on a number of subjects, including Chamberlain's role in the events leading up to the Jameson Raid, Cabinet discussions of South African affairs, and the relations between Chamberlain and Milner, the Colonial Office officials and imperial officials on the spot, the gold-mining magnates, the Uitlanders and the press. More generally, it seeks to reinterpret the nature of, and to provide a new explanation for the breakdown of, the diplomacy which led to war in October 1899. It tries to remedy the failure of other accounts to consider how important were certain conditions of Britain's domestic politics as perceived by the policy-makers in affecting the nature and outcome of the pre-war diplomacy.

There are of course other angles from which the origins of the war might be profitably examined. While touching on the role of the Uitlanders and their leaders, I have not sought to enter directly into the debate on the nature of the economic considerations which may underlie imperial policy.[2] So too, analysis of, for example, German and Afrikaner diplomatic material has purposely been avoided; questions as to how justified were British fears of foreign interference in South Africa, or the role given to South Africa as an issue in Germany's own *Weltpolitik*, need further investigation, but are not especially relevant to a study of policy decisions as affected by British public figures' beliefs and assumptions about the practice of politics and imperial affairs.

One final point is worth making by way of introduction. South Africa could no more than many other questions be dealt with in isolation as an 'imperial' question. At the close of the nineteenth century, the distinction between 'imperial' and 'foreign' often serves to confuse rather than illuminate, for though questions had to be formally dealt with through either the Foreign or the Colonial Office, contact between the two and Cabinet discussions of issues with which both were concerned was frequent. South Africa was equally a foreign and an imperial question. Instability within South Africa was regarded as a threat to schemes for eventual federation of the states under British auspices, as well as to grander schemes of imperial consolidation; at the same time, British weakness there was felt to encourage continental rivals intent on undermining British influence anywhere in the world, thus making it a source of friction between the Great Powers. The fact that imperial consolidation was itself intended to strengthen Britain in a world where Great Power rivalries were growing, only completes the circle. Yet the key to British weakness and the general instability of the region lay in the handling of British relations with the Transvaal, and the formal channel for dealing with such matters was the Colonial Office. Thus a question with 'foreign' and 'imperial' implications came to be dealt with by Chamberlain, a man whose ideas on the necessary relations between policy-makers and the electorate were to govern his handling of South African affairs.

Many of the views expressed here on questions of responsibility for the catastrophe that was the second Boer War differ from those argued elsewhere; but no historian concerned with South African questions at the end of the nineteenth century can now fail to be conscious of numerous debts to previous scholars. This applies both to the way in which a vast bulk of original source material has been made infinitely more manageable, and to the insights or questions which they have offered and provoked. I hope that I have acknowledged my obligations fully, whether in references or in my list of sources. For permission to consult and use material from papers in their possession, I am most grateful to the Marquess of Salisbury and to the Governing Body of Christ Church, Oxford; to the Warden and Fellows of New College, Oxford; to the Librarian of Birmingham University; to Earl St Aldwyn and the County Archivist in Gloucester; to the Earl of Selborne; to the Editor of *The Times*; to Mr A. J. P. Taylor; to Commander Charles H. Drage, and the late Lt. Col. P. V. W. Gell. I would also like to thank Mr W. R. A. Easthope and the late Mr John Maywood for their help with the archives at the old Printing House Square; Mr D. C. L. Holland, formerly Librarian of the House of Commons; Dr J. M. Fewster for his help in making the Grey Papers available, and the staffs of the Public Record Office and the many libraries where I have had occasion to work. I am grateful to the editors of both *The Historical Journal* and *The Journal of Imperial and Commonwealth History* for allowing me to use material from articles of mine which have appeared in their pages.

Prefatory tributes are in appearance conventional things, but I hope the form will not obscure the real substance. This book could not have been written without considerable financial assistance. Much of it began life as a Ph.D. thesis, and I am most grateful to the Master and Fellows of St John's College, Cambridge, to the Board of Graduate Studies, and to the Department of Education and Science for their aid. Their generosity was subsequently matched by a grant from the Central Research Fund of the University of London and by a grant towards the cost of publication from the Isobel Thornley Bequest. Many people have, often perhaps unwittingly, given me help and encouragement; my thanks goes to all of them. In particular, Mrs Z. Steiner, who first awoke my interest in nineteenth-century history, and the two examiners of the original thesis, Dr R. Hyam and Professor G. H. L. Le May, made many helpful criticisms. At the same time, the kindness and inspiration which I received from my Cambridge supervisor, Professor F. H. Hinsley, cannot be exaggerated. Latterly, my colleagues at King's have helped me a great deal, and been most generous with their time and energies in reading and criticising the manuscript. My wife joined me when much of the research was complete, but has more than made up for lost time by her ministrations as the book was hammered into shape. Those blemishes and blunders which remain are therefore mine.

Andrew Porter   University of London King's College   1979

Notes to Preface
[1] A. Briggs, 'The language of 'class' in early nineteenth-century England', in A. Briggs and J. Saville, eds., *Essays in Labour History* (1960), 54–7; P. Fraser, 'Public petitioning and Parliament before 1832', *History* XLIV (1961), 195–200; F. Bamford and The Duke of Wellington, eds., *The Journal of Mrs Arbuthnot* (2 vols, 1950), II, 83, 'The clubs & the public (that is to say the newspapers) settle that Mr Canning is to be Prime Minister. . . .'
[2] For a recent statement A. Atmore and S. Marks, 'The imperial factor in South Africa in the nineteenth century: towards a reassessment', in E. F. Penrose ed., *European Imperialism and the Partition of Africa* (1975), 105–39.

I

CANNING, PALMERSTON AND SALISBURY: THE GROWTH OF A PROBLEM

I

'Memorable and deserving of study for many reasons, the last thirty years of the nineteenth century will in no respect demand closer examination from future historians than with regard to the light which they throw upon the working of democratic forms of government in the sphere of foreign affairs.' With these words, in January 1899, a writer in the *Quarterly Review* opened the article which he had entitled 'Democracy and Foreign Affairs'.[1] He was undoubtedly voicing the opinion of many contemporaries, and, although more recent students of that period have rarely shared his concern, historians too were at that time prepared to place discussion of the role of public opinion in the conduct of foreign affairs amongst 'the burning questions of the day'.[2] For politically-conscious Victorians, whether eminent or unknown, early or late, events in their lifetime had shown that foreign affairs were frequently capable of arousing extremes of enthusiasm in very large numbers of people. The focus of popular attention wandered from Bulgaria to Uganda, opinions were expressed with varying degrees of spontaneity, and the effects of such outbursts differed, usually according to the particular standpoint from which contemporaries viewed them. Yet whether or not one agreed with Mr Gladstone that the masses might possess an instinctive righteousness on such occasions, there could be no doubt that outbursts of enthusiasm – whether friendly or hostile – were able temporarily to embarrass statesmen, while their alternation with spells of total indifference seemed likely to threaten any practical consistency of policy. By the last decade of the century, when Britain's international position was widely felt to be threatened by the growth and policies of rival powers, it was natural that the role of public opinion in the conduct of foreign affairs should become the subject of frequent discussions, particularly among those with strong imperial sympathies and whose allegiance lay generally to the right in English politics.

To a generation of statesmen who lacked ready confidence in Britain's position and were attempting to plan for the future, outbursts of public feeling were a menace because of their apparent irrationality. A peculiar waywardness characterised public opinion, and its effects appeared to have been aggravated by successive Reform Acts which had enabled such irrationality to be given political effect, not only at elections but in the subsequent behaviour of the elected. Some felt that 'the experience of recent years would seem to show that among the newly enfranchised classes the very poor give a fitful and almost unreasoning adherence to either party, and cause those swift and apparently unaccountable vacillations which are the despair of responsible politicians and the joy of "wreckers"'.[3] Others felt that the situation was still deteriorating, and that the swing of the party pendulum was not even the greatest of the evils that had come upon them. A director of the British South Africa Company regretted that 'Party Government run by Demagogues and speech-makers has left us without any School of Imperial Statesmen'.[4] Worse still, vacillation was by no means the prerogative of the recently enfranchised; if anything, sections of the contemporary upper classes were even more fickle, a prey to passions for novelty and swept by the tides of fashion despite the fact that they should know better. That same director's scorn for what he called 'the wobbly rush-and-gush of upper-class London' was unlimited.[5] Although such things might have to be tolerated in home politics, in foreign affairs it was the surest way to ruin when Britain stood challenged at every turn by Germans, Russians, and Frenchmen.

While active expressions of public opinion – decisions made at elections, spates of agitation, of organised meetings and petitioning, or volumes of wild press commentary – might create difficulties, lethargy could be equally problematical. Indifference by the majority to foreign and imperial affairs in between these bouts of enthusiasm was felt no less likely to threaten coherent policy. The result of such indifference, for Lord Salisbury, was 'that the Members of the House of Commons are each like a ship without an anchor. . . . Yet the combined resultant of their many drifting wills is omnipotent and without appeal.'[6] Politicians and imperialists wanted neither isolated outbursts of ill-directed heady enthusiasm nor apathetic unconcern, whether from fellow MPs or members of the electorate at large. A consistent, interested, and even informed concern was preferred, but, failing that, it was felt that there ought to exist in everybody's mind at least a general awareness that the world was a hostile one, that the empire had to be strengthened if Britain's power and prestige were to survive. Unpredictable outbursts of enthusiasm were tiresome, but in time they came to be regarded as symptoms of the disease not the malady itself. They came to be looked upon as the natural corollary of lethargy and indifference, and both kinds of behaviour were felt to have their roots in the common ignorance of the majority. It was, in fact, the absence of sound views when and where they were required, what one might call 'negative' public opinion, that was felt to be peculiarly the problem of the late nineteenth century. As foreign and imperial affairs became inextricably intertwined, many people came to fear that unless something was done, the behaviour of the electorate and its representatives would lead to imperial disintegration and the end of Britain's world-wide influence. A collapse of British power and prosperity would inevitably be followed by social upheaval at home.

When they asked themselves whether such characteristics and problems were an unavoidable or permanent attribute of a democratic system, critics were less certain. The view was widely held that one could hardly judge a system adequately which was dependent upon such a recently enlarged and inexperienced electorate. To some extent one's sanity depended upon the conviction that time, experience, and education would remedy the democracy's defects; the politician after all was presumably faced with an electorate of rational people amenable to reasoned argument who would, given the facts, come to the same conclusions as himself. Rarely does the historian find 'the people' as a whole castigated, and even then external circumstances rather than an innate incapacity were invoked as explanation enough for popular behaviour.[7] Real disillusionment was long in coming to even the most illiberal mind. Far more frequently the chief cause of popular failures either to understand or to take an interest was seen to lie in a general failure of leadership, or even in positive misguidance; such failures had in their turn encouraged the malfunctioning of already imperfect political institutions. In 1891, for example, Cromer expressed in just these terms the widespread concern which he felt existed.

It is so difficult to forecast what the present enormous electorate will do. ... Foreign policy is pre-eminently a matter about which the crowd not only should, but may be guided. Ever since Lord Palmerston's death they have been steadily guided by Gladstone and Co. in the wrong direction, and it is much to be feared that they will not wake up to the enormous importance of foreign, Indian and colonial policy to the working classes until some catastrophe has taken place.[8]

Some critics not simply saw a lack of capacity in the country's leaders, above all amongst the politicians, but also deplored what they thought was a failure, human and institutional, to use existing energies and enthusiasm to the full. Sir Alfred – later Viscount – Milner was perhaps the most notable exponent of these views, and was only confirmed in them as a result of his South African experiences. Early in his career, he foresaw the need for a great effort by Britain if she was to survive as a force in the world.

The courage of our troops, the forwardness of the Colonists to help, all show that the stuff is there. But the stuff is not enough. We want the prescient mind and resolute will – and where are they? More or less, I think, they are present in many quarters, obscure and otherwise. There is only one quarter where they are absolutely lacking – in the rulers of the realm.[9]

By the end of the century, similar views were more widely held, and the ordinary Member of Parliament in particular met heavy denunciation for his ineffectiveness and narrow vision. Milner also stressed the institutional failure. His solution to the Irish question had once been to suggest closing the House of Commons for ten years, and he was pressing the same point years later. On leave in Britain from South Africa, he had felt cheered by

the unmistakeable evidence of support and goodwill from the mass of the people. I am strongly impressed by two things: one, that the heart of the nation is sound, as I believe is also that of the British Colonials everywhere, and, secondly, that our Constitution and methods are antiquated and bad, and the real sound feeling of the nation does not get a chance of making itself effective. I would rather not say what I think of the House of Commons as an Imperial Council or of the effect of our wretched Party system on national affairs. ... The existing Parliaments ... are too small, and so are the Statesmen they produce (except in accidental cases, like Chamberlain) for such big issues.[10]

Of course, democratic forms of government had always found their critics, particularly outside the House of Commons, and in this the 1890s marked no exception. The novelty lay in the fact that the old saws – inefficient institutions, lack of capacity in the electorate, partisan politicians – were being newly sharpened, and those who wielded them were focusing almost exclusively on questions of foreign affairs, on the problems attaching to the conduct of a coherent and successful foreign policy within a democratic system of politics. At times in the past these questions had been taken up in criticism of other people's foreign policies when they had seemed inimical to British interests, but it was not until the late 1870s that this became of any importance to Englishmen in respect of their own diplomacy.[11] From then on, the growing competition which Britain was facing, the decline in her relative pre-eminence among states, combined with reservations about democracy or unfamiliarity with new political practices to make many wonder whether national survival was possible.

In the historiography of nineteenth-century British foreign policy, it has for long been agreed that the conduct of relations with the outside world then showed a remarkable continuity of ideas and objectives. More recently a similar degree of consistency has been discerned in respect of imperial policy, in the concerns of the 'official mind' such as strategy and defence, in ideas as to the structure of empire and the purpose of imperial rule.[12] However, in the successful execution of foreign and imperial policy, of equal importance with clearly defined objectives are the actual means by which such goals are to be achieved; here, evidence such as that related to the late-century debate on democracy, public opinion, and foreign policy, suggests that concepts of continuity are much less helpful. This is not simply to suggest that the personal style of particular Foreign or Colonial Secretaries was inevitably of great importance; historically speaking, this would in any case be untrue. It is rather to emphasise that the methods by which policies were promoted were necessarily altered to meet the changing conditions not just of the international situation but also of domestic politics; in different circumstances, new methods were required to further long-established intentions and attempts were made to change old procedures. This point may verge on the platitudinous, but it has not always been remembered. While on the broadest level British aims remained constant, the Foreign

Office had increasingly to have recourse to new methods for the protection of trade after 1880, in the face of changing foreign attitudes and hostile practices.[13] It will be shown in what follows that other more narrowly diplomatic practices were also altered, not in response to analyses of foreign powers' behaviour so much as to cope with fundamental changes taking place at home; these alterations in practice were exaggerated by the fact that fears generated by overseas events both reinforced and were reinforced by apprehensions on the domestic front.

Although late-century fears about the damaging effects of democracy acted as the spur to experiments in diplomatic method, it would be a mistake to think that statesmen had previously always felt able to ignore outbursts of popular feeling on questions of foreign policy, or to forget entirely anything calling itself 'public opinion'. What is true is that men like Canning or Palmerston did not feel them a source of worry and inhibition to the extent that late-nineteenth-century diplomatists did, and, therefore, they evolved very different patterns of diplomatic activity designed to reassert their own control of events from those which became characteristic of Lord Salisbury and, above all, Joseph Chamberlain. It was public opinion in the nebulous form of the electorate which lay at the heart of the late-century policy-makers' concern. As the Reform Acts transformed the number of voters out of all recognition, as old forms of influence declined and the channels of influence and opinion multiplied almost beyond the ken of politicians let alone their control, it was impossible for many to feel sure of the future. The swing of the electoral pendulum was, by the 1890s, almost being taken for granted; yet if this was to be so and the gulf between the parties on foreign and imperial questions was not bridged, then it was impossible to plan ahead. This may to twentieth-century minds appear naive and needlessly pessimistic, but such ideas were firmly held. It is too easy to forget that 1867 was a 'leap in the dark' and that the reforms of the 1880s were no less so. The political habits and assumptions of large numbers of Britain's rulers had been formed before 1870, and certainly changed more slowly than the institutions with which from then on they were forced to live. With the old unsure of their guidelines, the young had no mentors and had to learn their own way. In other words, more than one generation of leaders had to learn to live with and operate the new 'democratic' system. Earlier in the century, it seemed to them, life had been much simpler.

II

It was a persistent British belief common to ruling-class Whig or Tory that the conduct of foreign policy was an aristocratic pursuit, with which it was unfitting for any but the initiated, and certainly not the mass of the people, to concern themselves.[14] However, while the personnel of the Foreign Office long remained an upper class apart, it became increasingly difficult for Foreign Secretaries to avoid public scrutiny of their policies. The return of peace in 1815 and the weakened position of Governments in the House of Commons forced Ministers to adopt an unaccustomed responsiveness to parliamentary and public criticism.[15] Already, during the Napoleonic Wars, successive governments had attempted to smooth their parliamentary passage by producing plenty of documentary material for MPs' consumption, and interest in foreign affairs did not fall off with the signing of the Treaty of Vienna. By 1820 it was clear that the growth of public interest in, and knowledge of, foreign policy had been such that it was now a factor almost equal with any other in affecting the general popularity of Governments. This was a fact the importance of which was not lost on Canning when he became Foreign Secretary in 1822. Contemporaries undoubtedly felt that Canning's methods in conducting foreign affairs were novel, and although later historians' illustrations of this have been shown to be incorrect,[16] there remains considerable truth in the suggestion of novelty itself.

The key to Canning's methods lies in the nature of his ministerial position, so different from that of Castlereagh his predecessor. At first heartily disliked by the King, the focus of strained relations inside the Cabinet, possessing only a small Parliamentary following, widely detested and heavily dependent on his own personal brilliance, Canning's position was far from secure. As Canning himself understood it, this situation could not be resolved within the limits of Westminster, with the result that he took great care to nurture local support in his Liverpool constituency.[17] This he combined with a careful attention to British trading interests and the habit of making periodic speeches outside Parliament, both activities aimed at securing the attention and support of substantial local businessmen and commercial interests throughout the country.[18] Such groups were at this time increasingly critical of their lack of direct and effective parliamentary representation, and so were only too glad to welcome such a champion.

Here was the 'public opinion' that mattered for the time being, a group limited in relation to the country or even the electorate as a whole, but sufficient to sustain him, especially when few politicians – least of all his colleagues – saw anything to be gained by an appeal to still more diverse sections of the population. This manner of courting popularity provided the basis of Canning's position and no more; it helped to keep him in office, and therefore indirectly aided all his activities, even those unconnected with foreign policy. There was no question at this time of success in the conduct of foreign policy being felt to necessitate the prior cultivation of public understanding and support; this was as true for Canning as for any other prominent politician of the day. His extra-parliamentary speeches were therefore few in number, often made on formal occasions and so rarely more than fortuitous events from the point of view of timing in relation to particular diplomatic exchanges.[19] Canning's enemies, just as much as he himself, realised the limitations of these pronouncements. The comments passed by Wellington and his friends, 'the sighers after the Continental School', on this unconventional behaviour were therefore characterised by little more than jealousy and scorn.[20] What really provoked their anger was the actual publication of despatches in Parliament, or the apparent writing of despatches with such publication in mind.

Many of these publications were customary and unexceptionable. As a rule, Canning had little wish to break with precedent, but on occasion he felt it necessary to be less than orthodox, either to prevent deception or a *volte face* on the part of another Power, or to put pressure on colleagues doing their utmost to undermine his policy. Sometimes he simply hinted at the possible effects of publicity in order to achieve his wishes.[21] In particular, the publication of his despatch to Chateaubriand in April 1823, and of the Polignac Memorandum almost a year later, are cases in point. After the former episode, Canning wrote to one of his friends with the news that since April 'I have had pretty much my own way; and I believe you may now consider my politicks as those of the Government, as well as of the Country'.[22] Canning felt that the tactics of Wellington and Metternich, their secrecy and intrigue, involved an attempt to carry '*their* decisions into effect by throwing a little dust in the eyes of the House of Commons'. For any Minister such a policy 'would be a perilous enterprise, and as fruitless; fatal to his own power, and treacherous (in effect) to the hopes of his allies'. Metternich had to understand that 'we are such as we *seem*, such as we profess ourselves to parliament and to the world'.[23] His own policy was, by contrast, one which he felt was wholeheartedly approved by the middle-class opinion he cultivated, and he had no doubt as to his support in the event of a clash with the Holy Alliance.[24] Secure in this conviction, he had no need as a rule to indulge in continuous educative publicity – hence his relative reticence in contacts with the press.[25] The threats to his policy, Canning felt, came not from apathy or hostility in the country but from the backstairs manoeuvres of cliques and courts. On occasion when these were at a height, he therefore published in order, on the one hand, to prevent departure from previously private statements of intent, and, on the other, to remind his opponents of their lack of support.

Public opinion had therefore established under Canning somewhat tenuous links with methods of conducting foreign policy, chiefly as a prop to the personal position of a Foreign Secretary unpopular with, if unfortunately necessary to, a number of other leading politicians. A stronger Government, and greater personal harmony among ministers could easily have rendered Canning's tactics more or less superfluous. Evidence that a public opinion existed which was concerned with foreign affairs had been provided in a variety of ways by 1822; that being so, Canning was prepared to take it into account and where possible turn its interest to his own ends. However, neither he nor his contemporaries ever doubted for one moment that they were wholly in control of the circumstances at home in which they found themselves called upon to formulate a foreign policy.

III

Canningite practice was preserved as Palmerstonian tradition, but the relationship between the two men is not simply that of a disciple building on the ground of his master's teaching. Palmerston, while sharing Canning's conviction that commercial prosperity was the basis of Britain's standing in the eyes of the world, yet felt that alone this was insufficient. Of equal importance was the political weight and prestige of a nation, which in its turn depended upon a people's idea of its own greatness and achievement. He rejected the view of those 'who see in the relations of countries nothing but the intercourse of Cabinets', and felt that no statesman should overlook the power of the imagination of his countrymen.[26] He therefore believed in boosting a little the conscious image which the British had of themselves, in trying to counter the short memory of the public to ensure that mental attitudes paralleled the commercial supremacy he felt was already Britain's own.[27] It was an old view newly applied, that achievement largely reflects determination.

While such views may reflect a predisposition to diplomatic publicity, Palmerston's behaviour was as closely linked as Canning's to the necessities of his own personal political position. In 1827 he realised the necessity of widening the political support of the Canningites if they were to survive,[28] and the same was always to hold true for his own position. He only became at all certain of his parliamentary seat when elected at Tiverton in 1835, and as a member of no particularly privileged family, he always remained something of an outsider in Whig circles.[29] Even before he became Foreign Secretary, Palmerston had tried to increase the Wellington Ministry's unpopularity by bringing its foreign policy into disrepute. Speaking as one of the weak Canningite group on 1 June 1829 to a small number in the Commons, Palmerston took the trouble to have his speech, critical of the Government's Greek and Portuguese policy, printed and distributed to the press, other Members of Parliament and the Hansard reporters.[30] As he explained to his brother,

> My objects were, first, to put on record my own opinions, both now and when I was in the Cabinet; secondly, to excite public attention to these matters a little; and, thirdly, to let the Government see that they were not to suppose that they could have their own way entirely in foreign affairs; and that, however incompetent the individual might be who broached the subject, yet when once the stone was set a rolling, it would acquire a force which did not belong to the first mover. . . . Public opinion has not touched foreign affairs, but these

have hitherto been left as *carte blanche* to the unscrutinized discretion of the Government.

Whenever public opinion applies itself to foreign affairs – which it will certainly do next session – the Duke will give way upon that point also, and by so doing will retain his power.

I am sorry there has been so much abstinence and apathy on these topics this session, because if the screw had been strongly applied this spring, it would have had its effect upon the policy of our Government about Russia, Turkey, Greece, and Portugal in the course of this summer; and might have prevented them doing things which when done become irrevocable, and have impelled them to do others which, when the opportunity is gone by, can never afterwards be done.[31]

Aware in opposition of the effects that such an attack on policy in the House might have, it was hardly surprising that Palmerston when he came to power adopted tactics designed to remove just such opportunities. In the House of Commons Tories and Radicals were exceedingly critical of Palmerston's foreign policy in the 1830s, while in the Cabinet he faced either considerable opposition or, on other occasions, apathy and indecision.[32] Palmerston at first did his best to inform his Cabinet colleagues on major questions, and was prepared to debate his proposals and give way to reasonable objections, but this was often insufficient to overcome his critics.[33] Hankering after the style of an older generation, he was also aware that changing times necessitated new methods.[34] He therefore concluded that, for reasons clearly similar to Canning's, he would have to give the impression of commanding forces beyond those at Westminster in order to overcome opposition at the political centre, and so promote the foreign policy of his own devising.

In the 1830s, as before, carefully controlled publicity was the answer. Palmerston was no more prolific than Canning with public speeches; outside Parliament, only election speeches in his constituency or the occasional formal dinner were used to expound views on policy. Inside Parliament he avoided speaking either at length or in detail except at moments of his own choosing; he did not expect to be called constantly to account, and made this clear to the Commons.[35] He would explain – it was constitutionally and politically necessary – but in his own time. Timing was in turn dictated chiefly by Palmerston's own awareness of the quarter from which effective interference might come – from the Court, the

Cabinet, vociferous or interested parties in Parliament, the press, or even moves by foreign governments. Certainly Palmerston, unlike Canning, kept close and constant contact with newspapers. The *Observer, Morning Chronicle, Courier* and *Globe* above all were at one time or another strongly influenced by Palmerston, who not only contributed information but wrote a large number of articles, whether in or out of office.[36] This is to be explained by Palmerston's awareness of changing circumstances, rather than by attributing to him different goals. The growth of the press, and of its readers, especially, it was thought, among those given political weight in 1832, made it important that one's own views be represented in it. Palmerston believed that the press was responsible for the opinions of its readers, and so ensured that a general defence of his policy was regularly made. His influence with the press was directed towards people who, Palmerston believed, thought as he did, but did not have sufficient acquaintance with the outlines of the foreign scene. If they were well informed, their known opinions would be a useful check on the jealousies and factions which so often thwarted a Government's or a Minister's policy.

To cope with the Parliamentary audience, Blue Books were published in abundance – again a justification of the Government's policy, again with the aim of forestalling or nullifying wrong-headed or spiteful criticism. While publishing far more than Canning, Palmerston's wish to enlighten the public was identical.[37] Moreover, what Temperley has stressed in respect of Canning is equally true of Palmerston – that he intended there should be no difference, except in small details, between diplomacy as conducted in private and diplomacy publicly understood.[38] His aim was always to show the country that he really was doing something with which they sympathised. There is much to the point in this letter to Russell.

> I pretend to guide nobody, except as far as reasons which I may give in Parliament, and arguments which I may there employ, may influence the minds of fair and impartial men. All that I can claim for myself is freedom of action according to the best judgement I can form of the interests of my country; and that freedom I shall always exercise as long as it may please Heaven to continue to me my faculties, whether Radicals or old Whigs are pleased or displeased with the line I may think it my duty to take. If I am right, I am quite sure that my arguments and reasonings will have weight in the

country, even if not in the House of Commons.[39]

Such an approach to foreign policy could, however, create its own necessities and problems. Palmerston's colleagues, feeling their hands forced either by Palmerston's tactic of setting certain moves in motion before informing them or by his support in the press, resented the fact and became more obstructive. This in turn sometimes made it more difficult for Palmerston to get his way, and therefore increased his tendency to look beyond Westminster. At times the Cabinet's internal strife was transferred to the press for all to see, as was the case over the Eastern Question in 1840.[40] Moreover, what began as expediency became almost habit through frequent repetition, Palmerston considering the feeling of the House of Commons automatically and almost regardless of the possibilities of a situation.[41] The more frequently Palmerston felt the need for publication, the more it was taken for granted by those at whom it was directed and the greater the suspicions if the flow of information ceased. Almost inevitably, the practice which Canning had promoted was increasing under its own momentum.

Not only did Palmerston's style of diplomacy, especially his preference for decisive action, and his publicity constantly excite attention, but for a variety of reasons public interest in foreign affairs increased, especially from the mid-1840s onwards. Debates on the merits of Free Trade, discussion of possible solutions to domestic agitation and economic crisis, all drew people's attention to questions of foreign policy, especially when those often most interested – the commercial and manufacturing interests – were those whom Canning and Palmerston had largely cultivated. Some traced this growing interest way back into the 'forties,[42] but the comparative lull in domestic preoccupations after 1850, the provocations of other powers,[43] and the Crimean War, made foreign policy the chief interest of many. The fact that this coincided with a period of weak and unstable ministries created a situation where expressions of opinion in the country, but above all in Parliament, had to be taken into account as an element almost equal with any other external question in the determining of diplomatic policy. Circumstances were such that Ministers felt obliged to look ahead to the possible repercussions of policy on opinion at home far more than ever before. When they foresaw the possibility of problems created by popular feeling they attempted to meet them, more often than not by some form of publication, but on occasion by abandoning a certain line of action as potentially too unpopular.

The difficulties Ministers faced at this time have been admirably analysed elsewhere.[44] Nevertheless, it needs to be emphasised that Governments were now faced only with an exaggerated form of the situation which Canning had understood and with which Palmerston had long been familiar. A fluid party situation, with bitter personal rivalries, weak and divided ministries sniped at from all sides, not to mention from within, all made successful continuity in foreign policy very difficult. In these circumstances it was the politician able to widen the bases of his support, both within Parliament and outside, especially amongst the electorate, who could come out on top. The key to such success was the willingness and ability to publish information, to make one's broad views and intentions clear, to make the arguments of opponents look absurd, and to convince waverers that foreign policy was in the best of hands. Palmerston was, by the late 1840s, a past master in the art of cultivating journalists and at appealing to wider opinion groups than those from which the attacks on his policy came.[45]

From a personal point of view, his problems during his third term at the Foreign Office were worse than ever, largely the result of his conflict with the Queen and her spouse. Matters soon came to a head,[46] and in response Palmerston publicly defended his Portuguese policy at Tiverton in July 1847. Spain, Greece, Italy, France and Schleswig-Holstein all produced further friction. Palmerston combined obstinate resistance in private with occasional general justifications for the world at large. These appeals for public support culminated in the famous 'Civis Romanus' speech of 1850, in which he openly attributed the attacks on his policy to a mixture of foreign conspiracy and domestic intrigue.[47] Some observers felt that he was trying to build up Radical support at Westminster, but although Palmerston was gratified at the Parliamentary majority which he had secured, he was still fully conscious that his difficulties in London were only to be resolved by evidence of support outside.[48] Where that support came from was of much less importance than its volume. This it was which would go some way to check party faction, and his critics would realise the impossibility of forcing him into opposition. While Palmerston's speeches and publications often had at least half an eye on foreign reactions[49] – foreigners too had to recognise that his despatches represented more than just private unsupported bluff – his outlook was directed chiefly towards support at home.

Politicians of all shades, faced with the need to conduct foreign policy effectively, had to adopt certain Palmerstonian methods. None however went to the same lengths as Palmerston before he became Prime Minister, a difference for which the latter's own blunt obstinacy and self-righteousness were ultimately responsible. After all, the limitations on the powers of the House of Commons, whose members were also reluctant to bear the cost of frequent elections, were still formidable.[50] Diagnosis of the situation and the decision to publish were still very much a personal matter; it appears that the Queen hardly ever, and the Cabinet as a whole never, considered questions of publicity.[51] Even Palmerston, once his own political supremacy was assured by the 1857 election, thought far more in terms of managing 'the present anarchical state of the House of Commons'[52] within the framework which Westminster itself provided. For him Parliament had proved its absurdity in 1857, something the soundness of the voters had emphasised when they had proceeded handsomely to reverse his Parliamentary defeat; his distinction between Parliamentary and public opinion was confirmed.[53] Nevertheless, it had always to be Parliament whom one should try to manage first of all. He and Russell therefore devoted great care to the production of Blue Books after 1859, while the latter paid increasing attention to the advice of his Parliamentary Under-Secretary on their construction. While Palmerston remained newspaper-conscious to the end,[54] relations were put on a new footing by Russell's practice of using selected papers for the official release of information, especially when Parliament was in recess.[55] With Palmerston's leadership settled and the Peelites at least contained, the House of Commons became more controllable. At the same time, the declining influence of Cobden and Bright, and Palmerston's achievement of relative security in old age, meant that those hitherto most active in stimulating public feeling in the country as a means to influence foreign policy, were now directing their energies elsewhere; they felt it no longer either so necessary or so feasible to control the conduct of foreign affairs via the impact which widespread evidence of popular feeling might make on the ordinary Member of Parliament, or which fear of defeat in the Commons might have on otherwise critical Cabinet colleagues. Stronger Ministers, looking only to Parliament, began once more to draw a veil over their affairs.

IV

Although equilibrium appeared to have been achieved, the peace it brought was not to last. Politicians, not least Palmerston, only wanted the support they looked for. There were occasions, said Aberdeen, when he dreaded it, feeling like Alciabiades who 'on some occasion, when the Athenian assembly vehemently applauded ... asked if he had said anything particularly foolish'.[56] Far more, however, it was the press which increasingly worried politicians. Malmesbury, for example, talked of competition between the newspapers and those who produced Blue Books, for the opinion of the House of Commons.[57] Russell's new use of the press for disseminating selected snippets of official information can similarly be seen as implying that 'the press' – particularly perhaps The Times – was to be set at a distance, that it was seen as something which, with its great expansion, now possessed a power of its own. The feeling grew that the old-style unofficial contacts between Ministers and editors had rather less place than before. Most explicit in his denunciations – despite his own indiscretions and contacts with The Times – was Clarendon, for whom the press and 'public opinion' were practically synonomous.[58] It was the press, and so public opinion, which, given the disorganised state of the Commons, made the conduct of business by the Government so extraordinarily difficult.[59] Shortly after the Crimean War, he expressed the view that British newspapers 'are incurably blackguard, and they are so accustomed to deal with home matters in the strongest language, that it would not suit their customers (which is all they care about) if they dealt differently with foreign affairs. It is useless to attempt any check upon them, for there are but one or two that will receive an occasional hint.'[60] The only remedy for Clarendon lay not with the House of Commons, but in governments openly contradicting editorial falsehoods. Others, however, felt that anything approaching actual warfare with reporters was to be avoided at all costs.[61] Nevertheless, as long as the remedy for press calumnies and misplaced criticisms lay through the press itself, while it was also generally assumed that 'the habit of most people is to believe what they read in the newspapers',[62] so a more or less uneasy relationship between statesmen and the press was bound to endure.

That the press could still do considerable harm was something on which all were agreed, especially as foreigners often tended to assume that English newspapers were inspired in the same way as their own. The tendency to sensationalism was regretted, and party agents worried about the rapid growth of a provincial press far less dependent than before on London for its news and opinions.[63] Politicians at the centre felt there was little they could do in the circumstances. This was due partly to inertia, but also to a recognition that in many respects the sheer volume and variety of newspapers ensured that in most situations numerous conflicting opinions were likely to be expressed. The sheer impracticality of influencing the press encouraged politicians to accept the facts of life. 'I have always felt that while for domestic purposes our press is admirable we have no security whatever from it against even the most outrageous follies in matters of foreign policy', wrote Gladstone.[64] In these circumstances, the most a politician might expect to do was to keep on friendly terms with one or two individuals,[65] to try and soothe others at times of crisis lest they in any way embarrass the Government,[66] occasionally encourage unexpected signs of support,[67] and otherwise hope for the best. The combination of time, aptitude and inclination for cultivating relations with the press was clearly rare in a politician,[68] and in coming to terms with the growing volume of newspapers it appears that most activity occurred at a purely official level. The number of recipients of Parliamentary Papers and Foreign Office communications almost doubled in the period between the mid-1860s and mid-1880s, and by 1889 included several press agencies as well as individual newspapers.[69] It also became standard practice to send copies of every Parliamentary answer given in the Commons by the Under-Secretary of State for Foreign Affairs to the Reporters' Gallery of the House, one each to those papers on the Foreign Office list and a general copy for other papers whose reporters happened to be present.[70]

Of even greater significance, however, than the behaviour of the press were the large and rapid changes which took place in the political world after Palmerston's death. The Reform Acts of 1867 and 1884, the redistribution of seats, the changing nature of constituencies, and the changes in party organisation, completely altered Britain's political appearance in only two decades. The Cave of Adullam provided only a temporary and deceptive refuge, preserving its occupants for a worse fate in which the relatively cosy, exclusive, Palmerstonian world was destroyed. When men like Canning and Palmerston had made their public appeals in the face of a varying opposition in London, they expected an answering shout in a familiar voice. They had directed their message to groups of upper- and middle-class supporters, substantial and respectable men whose thinking and habits were both familiar and predictable, men with votes and voices in the press, at Westminster and amongst the electorate. After 1867 the electorate became progressively larger and old-style influence decreased. The new electorate was composed, it was felt, of people who not only thought and acted differently, but were also mostly unacquainted with such things as Blue Books and influential newspapers, in other words almost wholly out of reach. In an uncertain situation, old rulers still in power sought new guidelines. It became fashionable to distinguish somewhat more clearly between London society and that of the provinces.[71] In 1877, Sir Philip Rose reminded Montagu Corry that 'we must remember that things are now much changed and that it is not the opinion of the Clubs that influences public opinion. The real voting power of the country is several degrees lower and it is this power which must now be consulted.'[72] Of course, it had always been the holders of possibly effective political power who required consultation and flattery, but a new electorate required new methods of doing so. Thus even Lord Salisbury eventually rejected the usual sources of intelligence open to him and went off to stump the country, in order that he might study opinion.[73] Many years later he still felt himself little the wiser. 'When the great oracle speaks, we are never quite certain what the great oracle said'; while it might be abundantly clear that the country was excited, the confusion of voices and views which had now to be consulted made it very difficult to draw any practical conclusions.[74]

If consulting the oracle produced worse than Delphic obscurity, the nature and influence of the oracle rapidly became clear. The decade 1876–86 appeared to confirm the disastrous effect of democratic party politics in the sphere of foreign affairs, and awoke in statesmen, particularly conservative ones, an abiding fear of public opinion's unpredictability, of its fits of irrationality rather than its ultimate reasonableness. Derby and Disraeli found the 'Bulgarian atrocities' agitation in 1876 extraordinarily inconvenient, and periodic outbursts of feeling on into 1878 created many difficulties, acting as they did on a divided cabinet.[75] Lord Salisbury's reactions at that time are of particular interest in view of his subsequent tenure of the Foreign Secretaryship. He criticised the general policy of drift and the lack of bold initiatives, attributing it to the fact that too many people were pulling at the strings of foreign policy, and to the extraordinarily violent divisions of opinion which made reasonable decisions impossible.[76] The agitation itself he, like many others, saw as a fit of national madness, and was conscious as well of the danger of jingoistic demonstrations at home when it came to the details of negotiations at the Berlin Congress.[77] In the immediate circumstances of the Eastern Question, it was Lord Derby – somewhat less than mindful of his own role – who expressed most clearly the fundamental worry that was to afflict many others before the century was out.

> If I could from this place address the English people [it is interesting that he felt this impossible] I would venture to ask them how they can expect to have a foreign policy – I do not say farsighted, but even consistent and intelligent – if, within eighteen months, the great majority of them are found asking for things directly contradictory?[78]

It was this same theme that Salisbury elaborated to the Queen at the end of the decade, when he diagnosed the weakness of British diplomacy: 'our shifting foreign policy during the last ten years – our precarious Governments – the necessity of adapting our foreign policy to the views of a Cabinet of fourteen or sixteen men, usually ignorant of it, and seldom united in their views . . . [in other words the need to rely upon] an insecure tenure of power, and an ineffective agency',[79] were the things at fault. In part of course they had been present at times in the past, but were now felt to be far worse, for Salisbury publicly rejected the old liberal belief that 'there would be no more wars in the world but for the rulers – that the people would always be for peace. . . . the reverse of that fact is true at the present time. . . . If there is any possible danger in the future, it rather arises from another cause – from possible gusts of passionate and often ill-informed feeling arising from great masses of population.'[80]

Such was now the size of the electorate, such its partial knowledge of foreign affairs, that politicians could no longer play the Palmerstonian game of *temporarily* calling in a larger weight of opinion to resolve disputes over policy in their favour. Even Palmerston's appeals to the public at large were always selective, as his behaviour in 1857 and 1858 shows. But as Palmerston's biographer sensed even in the early 1870s, the British political world had changed,[81] and Salisbury felt that outbursts of feeling could no longer be predicted or manufactured to suit one's own purpose. They occurred willy-nilly,[82] and were certain to have considerable political effect, above all at election time when less scrupulous politicians inevitably exploited them. For Salisbury nothing was illustrated more clearly than this by Gladstone's Midlothian campaigns, and the Conservative defeat in 1880. On this occasion, even Disraeli declared that there would now be no holding the democrats of Europe in check. Queen Victoria may have cried that she would not be the Queen of a democratic monarchy, but it was naturally of little avail. Liberal handling of the Boers, of the Egyptian question and its sequel, and Gladstone's tactics in committing the party to Home Rule only confirmed the gloomy outlook.

The debate on democracy and foreign policy really dates from this time, originating, it would seem, in Liberal criticisms of Disraelian policies at the time of the Bulgarian agitation.[83] Liberal leaders themselves were then hardly less perplexed than their opponents by the oscillations of public feeling, and after 1880 all saw similar threats to any continuity of policy in a variety of guises, 'jingoism', 'the rot of Forsterism', 'F.O. annexationism', and the antics of the press.[84] On the right of the political spectrum alarm was far stronger, for criticisms of democracy, there always more explicit, were joined to a growing distrust of Gladstone's lack of realism and apparent perversity, the whole attack given greater weight through the steady conversion of intellectuals to conservative causes. Gladstone was the evil genius whose abandonment of all restraints had given full rein to a process – Salisbury called it 'disintegration'[85] – which would continue long after he himself had disappeared. However, with whatever literary elegance criticisms of the system were penned, it remained for politicians themselves to find a solution to the problem on which so many expatiated.

V

The Liberals' practice – or at least Mr Gladstone's – of enunciating general principles and statements of intent with which their subsequent actions squared badly had been largely discredited by 1885. But this had in any case never really been Salisbury's method, despite accusations to the contrary, any more than he had shared their principles. With an assured political position after succeeding Derby at the Foreign Office, Salisbury had little need to win wider support at Westminster; later on, as a member of the House of Lords and leader of his party, his position was unchallenged. To some extent then, Salisbury was in any case free to indulge his strong temperamental dislike of public attention. It was also his settled conviction that publicity in any form was almost always a potential threat to successful diplomatic negotiation.[86] Far from being more than 'the intercourse of Cabinets' as Palmerston had claimed, foreign affairs Salisbury felt should be left as far as possible to the sole and undisturbed care of Foreign Ministers aided by their aristocratic, yet professional, go-betweens. With only rare exceptions, Salisbury attempted to preserve his own freedom of initiative by limiting parliamentary scrutiny and public discussion of his foreign policy. This was a question not of any 'secret diplomacy', but of a general diplomatic method, based on the conviction that now, far more than had ever previously been the case, it was positively dangerous to give people factual food for thought, let alone purposely to attract their attention.

Shortly after the beginning of his career at the Foreign Office he denied that the Government had any wish whatever to communicate with those outside the walls of Westminster. 'The members of the two Houses are the only people to whom Govt. is responsible & therefore the only people they want to reach',[87] was his rather gruff assertion. Yet even within this limited circle he clearly wished to avoid encouraging any discussion, provoking Granville to criticise his tactic of allowing large numbers of papers to accumulate before presenting them to the House.[88] Liberal wrath again freely poured forth on the matter of Salisbury's apparently undisclosed undertakings with regard to Cyprus, Tunis, and Egypt.[89] Not only did Salisbury believe in common with every diplomatist that a large element of secrecy was always necessary in the intimacies of diplomacy, but for him it was particularly necessary given the nature of Britain's political set-up. Not for him the manufacture of diplomatic crises to deflect attention from domestic troubles! The best diplomacy and that most likely to be successful was for him also the least spectacular. The more foreign affairs could be isolated, the greater the chances of satisfaction on all sides or at least of a peaceful outcome. Where firmness and continuity of affairs were essential to secure for Britain respect and consideration from rivals, foreign questions had perforce to be kept apart from the wranglings of parties; when, as in the 1870s and 1880s, there seemed little agreement on national interests and the means of achieving them, secrecy was the last resort of policy-makers such as Salisbury. It was this reasoning which partly explained his silence on the subject of the Mediterranean Agreements made in 1887, despite his conviction that the commitments involved were negligible.[90]

There is of course nothing new in suggesting that Salisbury disliked democracy or that he preferred a minimum of publicity in diplomatic negotiations. But Palmerston too was no democrat, and yet published or spoke far more on foreign affairs than Salisbury ever did. The point to be stressed is that Palmerston's publicity was a necessary part of his method, and that by and large the reverse is true of Lord Salisbury. The reason for this lies in a combination of three elements – individual temperament, personal political situation, and the changed political system, in which the last is by far the most important. It is insufficient to argue that Salisbury tended to be secretive because his policy was not 'striking', and that to draw attention to it would therefore not be profitable. Nor is it in fact paradoxical that the extension of democracy went hand in hand with restricted freedom to discuss foreign policy.[91] In an increasingly competitive world, with, it was felt, a large proportion of the population (including Members of Parliament) prone to act in exceedingly short-sighted or ignorant fashion, new methods were felt necessary to achieve often very traditional objectives. Many people did feel that the degree of democratic government which existed in Britain in the 1870s posed altogether new problems for policy-makers, at a time when the latter felt that national unanimity was of growing importance. Increasingly people – and not only Conservatives[92] – were coming to share Salisbury's view that popular enthusiasms and conflicts were undermining national interests in a way hitherto impossible. In a situation where the independence of MPs was being whittled away, both in their constituencies and at Westminster through the organisation of parliamentary business and procedure, it was possible, especially for Conservative Ministers, to rely to a greater degree on parliamentary majorities and so defeat the attacks of the Opposition in the Commons itself. Nevertheless, this was only the inner fortress secured and for a short period at that. Ultimately, there appeared to men of Salisbury's stamp no way of guarding against popular uproar, and well into the 1890s the possibility of replacement by a rival party intent on striking at the heart of imperial security and self-confidence was only too real. It was ten years before the spectre of Home Rule was temporarily laid, and after 1886 the Conservatives felt themselves heavily dependent on their partners in the Unionist coalition. This element of insecurity made the disarray and resulting factional bargaining within the Liberal party doubly worrying.

Salisbury's inborn scepticism and tolerance of imperfections, such an important part of his conservatism, enabled him at least to live with the system. In his exercise of power, his attempts to prevent foreign and imperial questions from being mishandled in the circus ring of party politics must be recognised for what they are – an endeavour to solve the problem of conducting foreign policy within a democratic system of politics. There was after all a challenge to be met in controlling that system to the best of his ability, so that it did not threaten the national interests he felt vital. The general character of Salisbury's approach is only highlighted further by those few instances when he deliberately used a certain degree of publicity to promote his own ends. When in opposition, he felt no qualms in using arguments concerning the duty of Cabinet Ministers to give full information,[93] although he would himself have had little time for such criticisms. While at the Foreign Office, on a few occasions when he felt the aggressive stance of foreign powers to be intolerable or perhaps a bluff, he published Blue Books presenting the British case and supported their widest possible circulation, rather than their distribution to the normal recipients of Parliamentary Papers on the Office's list.[94] The French Government he found particularly irritating, and in sanctioning a question by a backbencher in 1892, did so on the grounds that it 'will rather strengthen our hand with the French. They are always defending their worst proceedings by saying their Chamber won't stand this & won't stand that. It may be an advantage that we too should be able to flourish an inexorable Chamber in their faces.'[95]

Such instances were however rare, as indeed were his references to the business of the Foreign Office in his speeches outside Parliament. He often blamed Gladstone in the first place for the necessity of having to make such speeches,[96] and took care that only in those made at formal functions in the City of London should foreign affairs have much place.[97] The infrequency of such references gives them a particular importance in assessing Salisbury's attitudes to the relation between any public opinion and diplomacy. In his provincial speeches it was with reference to imperial issues that he tended to break his own rule of thinking a great deal and speaking but little in respect of foreign affairs. While on the one hand Salisbury frequently inveighed against jingoes and what he called 'the national, or acquisitional feeling',[98] it was his firmest conviction that the maintenance of the Empire Britain possessed was the surest guarantee of her future security and prosperity. Reluctant though he was to acquire new territory, once this was done there could be no shrinking from defence of the British position. That he tried to impress this upon his audiences from time to time reflects both the strength of his own belief,[99] and the importance which he attached to combating Liberal fallacies. Nevertheless, speechmaking of this sort could never, in Salisbury's eyes, be of more than very temporary and partial use. His consciousness of continuously changing circumstances, his pessimism about human nature and motives for action, his feeling that some form of class conflict was the most basic force in politics,[100] all led him to minimise the possibility of creating any lasting or desirable influence through one's personal efforts. 'Few people', he wrote, 'have memories for benefits received, still less for feelings or prejudices flattered', and this was particularly true in the world of international dealings.[101] For similar reasons he grew increasingly disdainful of the press and the worth of any links with the newspapers, claiming to follow 'Dizzy's sound rule, never to reply to the press except in correction of an evident misstatement'.[102] The populace at large was, in this respect, only slightly better than politicians as a breed. With such preconceptions, Salisbury was himself disinclined to woo the public. His paternalistic attitude, his general distaste for the platform, especially when so much other work had to be attended to that was heavy in its demands on both time and energy, led him to prefer business dealt with in the seclusion of his study at Hatfield, and to assume that such secrecy improved the likelihood of success.

There were people, however, unconvinced by Salisbury's reasoning, who felt that his methods were the product of personal judgements which had no necessary relevance to those with different perceptions and capabilities. Certainly Salisbury's general awareness of human limitations, not least his own, was keen. But it seems that his pessimism and reticence were increased by the apparent novelty of the political framework within which he was constrained to live. His judgement on the Unionist election victory in 1900 emphasises this only too well.

> I am not sure whether I can consider the omens as altogether favourable. The phenomenon is without example that a party should twice dissolve, at an interval of five years, and in each case bring back a majority of more than 130. What does it mean? I hope the causes are accidental and temporary. But it may mean that the Reform Bills, digging deeper and deeper into the population have come upon a layer of pure combativeness. If this is the case I am afraid the country has evil times before it. Of course I recognize the justice of the verdict the country has just given; but that the love of justice should have overborne the great law of the pendulum I confess puzzles and bewilders me.[103]

Salisbury lived with, but to the end was hardly happy with, the workings of the democratic constitution. Others, as illustrated above, were equally disturbed by the features of 'the new democracy', but they were also less tolerant of them. By the 1890s many had begun to look for solutions elsewhere. It was no use trying simply, as Salisbury tended to do, to avoid the potentially ruinous effects of popular behaviour on Britain's international standing, and, more particularly as the key to this, her imperial position. An alternative approach was conceived, in the shape of a positive educative onslaught on the irrational tendencies of the people. A definite programme was thought necessary – for example, by many of those worried at the growing power and restlessness of Germany – to overcome the dangerous indifference to foreign and imperial affairs which could be as much a threat to coherent policy as any sudden upsurge of feeling. Of course, such an educative programme depended on the use of real examples;

while some might be content simply to point out the moral implicit in a certain situation, other statesmen could equally well seize on any question and use it to illustrate the general principles of which they wished the public to be aware. This second approach carried with it the risk that the interpretation and handling of a complicated situation might be twisted to suit its presentation in a form which the public would respond to, a form not necessarily compatible with the successful solving of the initial difficulty. Dangers apart, however, the ability to show that a nation was united behind its leaders had always been reckoned a powerful weapon in the achievement of any foreign ambitions. Indeed, it was the very fact that extended democracy seemed in practice to preclude this which alarmed many people. In the context of the 1890s however, the Fashoda crisis was felt by people of various sympathies to confirm that such unity and strength were still possible. Similarly, an electorate actively interested in certain general policy aims was thought capable of forcing more recalcitrant leaders in the direction desired by a few. If Gladstone's activities could bring out the worst in the democracy, why should not a counter campaign stand an equal chance of success? Without widespread popular backing, some politicians, polemicists, and civil servants wondered whether their own aims and the protection of national prosperity or security could ever be achieved. Even Salisbury, it has been seen, could be momentarily attracted by this vision, and it was thought along these lines which produced in the last five years of the century a very determined attempt to arouse popular interest at last in the problems of a world-wide empire, to sustain that interest, and to indicate the necessity for a far-reaching, consistent foreign and imperial policy. The occasion for this was the arrival of Joseph Chamberlain at the Colonial Office, and the issue upon which it came to focus that of South Africa.

II

CHAMBERLAIN, DEMOCRACY AND THE EMPIRE, 1876–95

Further detailed studies of the work of Foreign Secretaries such as Canning or Palmerston would probably provide more specific information as to the membership at any particular time of the wider 'public' whose 'opinion' was being increasingly heeded, particular parliamentary groupings, interest groups in the constituencies, and the readership of certain newspapers. It might also be possible to throw light on the limitations of any one statesman's perception of his own situation and degree of success. Such investigations are not, however, central to the purpose of this work. The intention has been to stress the general point that attempts to cultivate extra-governmental opinion, both in Westminster and beyond its confines, as an aid to successful diplomacy were early adopted as temporary and specific expedients. A public speech, the publication of Parliamentary papers, and the influencing of the press were the principal means to this end. The cultivation of such wider interest and support was later, in the hands of Palmerston and within the context of weak ministries and divided parties, extended almost to the point of becoming settled habit. However, from the 1850s onwards, first the rapid expansion of the press along with the growing difficulties of influencing it, and then the enlargement of the electorate, changed the political framework within which foreign affairs had to be conducted. It has been shown how policy-makers began to fear and grew in the conviction that if the beast of 'public opinion' was to be disturbed by a diplomatic pin-prick in any one of its many joints, the whole might wake from its slumber with uncontrollable results. In reaction to this situation, two courses seemed to present themselves. On the one hand, one could try to restrict information and debate on foreign and imperial policy to an absolute minimum; alternatively, one might extend attempts to influence 'public opinion' to their logical limits, to the point where they embraced the electorate as a whole. Chamberlain was a man with the experience, self-confidence, and eventually the power to attempt this, and it is therefore necessary to examine in some detail the evolution of his own ideas about the methods of politics and the broad goals of political action, for assumptions arrived at early in his career frequently affected his handling of imperial affairs after 1895. This is above all true in that his ideas about political behaviour and method were the product of his youth, and remained largely unchanged; as he widened his interests and took up new causes, his manner of pursuing them owed as much to the persistence of long-formed political habits as to the suitability of those political methods to the achievement of the goal in question. In the case of South Africa his policies were presented in a way which sprang from his customary mode of political action, one concerned less with diplomacy than with winning over a large domestic following; policy twisted by method in the end contributed to its own undoing.

Although the points of difference between the head of Hatfield House and the son of the prosperous nonconformist shoemaker from Camberwell are at once very striking, it is not as absurd as it may at first appear to insist for a moment on considering certain features which Lord Salisbury and Joseph Chamberlain had in common. Born in 1830 and 1836, they were essentially members of the same generation, and their subsequent involvement in the world of national politics had made them both, by the early 1880s, dissatisfied men. The source of this discontent, viewed though it was from very different vantage points, consisted in what both men felt to be the malfunctioning of the political system. Their criticisms, given force by their experience as Cabinet Ministers, focused on the apparently uneasy relationship between Government policy, the House of Commons, and the behaviour and wishes of the electorate.

Chamberlain, an ambitious man, intolerant of opposition and having wielded power to considerable effect as Mayor of Birmingham, was not a little dismayed at what he felt, like many other new members of Parliament then and since, to be the ineffectiveness of the House of Commons. His experience at the Board of Trade further convinced him that it could be not only ineffective but obstructive of progress.[1] Even in 1880 he had felt that 'our free institutions are choked and neutralised by the forms intended to protect them',[2] and his conviction that large-scale constitutional reform would alone put things to rights steadily grew. Speaking in Birmingham early in 1882 he explained that the 'primary object of a parliamentary assembly is . . . to carry out the decisions at which the nation has arrived. . . . The House of Commons is the people's House, and public opinion can make it what it will; and if you will restore it to its ancient authority . . . the House of Commons will execute your decrees instead of as at present frustrating and postponing the decision of the constituencies.'[3] With its tilting at Whig and Irish yokes, this was the voice of opposition, of the radical hampered in office and vexed by many of his colleagues. But at the same time, Chamberlain, an emotional man possessed of practical ingenuity rather than sensitivity and imagination, was nothing if not an archetypal radical, and as such had a rather different view of real power in his own hands. Like most radicals, he was distinguished initially by his concern that political power was currently being either abused, or simply enjoyed and not used where necessary. This situation he was sure could be remedied by structural reforms in the constitution, reforms designed to preserve and make effective those principles according to which, in theory at least, the country's institutions already functioned. Practically speaking, this meant making government both more responsive and responsible, and – in Chamberlain's case – the extension of government powers and legislation where necessary to widen the extent of individual freedom. Such reforms would bring radical politicians of Chamberlain's own stamp into power, politicians into whose hands at last power could safely be put, since they alone were men who would be sure to use it aright. Thus it was that Chamberlain embodied the inverted whiggery of the late nineteenth century.

In the course of this process, the radical 'holier than thou' attitude tended to be redirected, away from old political opponents and towards the electorate on whose goodwill the radicals' new-found power would rest. As Chamberlain explained in conversation with Balfour

> Our misfortune is that we live under a system of government originally contrived to check the action of Kings and Ministers, and which meddles far too much with the Executive of the country. The problem is to give the democracy the whole power, but to induce them to do no more in the way of using it than to decide on the general principles which they wish to see carried out, and the men by whom they are to be carried out.[4]

This was no passing fancy, for a decade later Chamberlain was still suggesting that sooner or later 'we shall have to come to deal with the obstruction which paralyzes the House of Commons, and brings representative institutions into contempt, but I doubt if people are as yet prepared for the drastic changes which are necessary'.[5] For those out to secure a strong government with consistent policies which was also able to act without undue hindrance, the problem was much the same at whatever point on the political spectrum they stood. Salisbury recognised as much when this little interchange was relayed to him by his nephew.

> I am glad to see Chamberlain coming to the idea that a representative body interfering with every detail of executive Government is incompatible with strong government. But before you have a strong democratic Government, freed from this thorn in the flesh, you must follow the example of the U[nited]. S[tates]. and have 'fundamental laws', which could only be altered by special machinery. With us, the feebleness of our government is our security – the only one we have, – against revolutionary alterations of our laws.[6]

This fairly reflects the pessimistic thinking of Salisbury as examined above, but, had the exchange continued in this form, Chamberlain would have disagreed with the noble marquess. His political experiences, from which Salisbury as a peer was inevitably debarred in all but the mildest forms, had suggested an answer other than republicanism. Although written with Ireland in mind, the following letter gives the clue to Chamberlain's thinking: 'Ministers are only able to work through the instruments at their disposal. They cannot move much quicker or much in advance of those behind them, and English public opinion has to be educated quite as much as or more than English statesmen.'[7] The positive education of the electorate, of the country as a whole, was the answer. Chamberlain never lacked confidence in his own views, and always believed that if only they could be put to the country in the right way, people everywhere would agree and follow his lead in large numbers. Education for Chamberlain consisted in telling people the right answer, and this it was that would 'induce them to do no more ... than decide on the general principles ..., and the men' when it came to questions of government.

These of course represent two rather different beliefs, yet in both cases they are the convictions of the man with grand designs.

Chamberlain contrived to hold both, albeit in varying proportions, at the same time. Before 1886, he was acutely conscious of being either in opposition or occupied with a subordinate office, and felt himself undeservedly hampered first by Conservatives and latterly by ministerial colleagues; he therefore tended to emphasise the limitations on the will of the people as expressed, inevitably, by himself. Yet even in this earlier period – the case of the merchant shipping question for example – he was not unaware of the existence of popular restraints on ministerial action, although in this particular instance the fetters were imposed by the power of an interest group rather than by general popular ignorance. This consciousness of popular restrictions became more important to him after the Liberal split, as his reaction deepened against what he called 'socialism', as collaboration with the Conservatives was extended, and as the prospect of renewed and greater political influence became brighter.

He had on occasion defended his tactics against the complaints of his Liberal chief.

> Popular government is inconsistent with the reticence which official etiquette imposed on speakers, and which was easily borne as long as the electorate was a comparatively small and privileged class, and the necessity of consulting it at meetings infrequent and limited.
>
> Now, the Platform has become one of the most powerful and indispensable instruments of Government, and any Ministry which neglected the opportunities afforded by it would speedily lose the confidence of the People. A new public duty and personal labour has thus come into existence, which devolves to a great extent and as a matter of necessity, on those members of a Government who may be considered specially to represent the majority who are to be appealed to: and this duty cannot be performed at all if the men on whom it falls are to be confined within the narrow limits of a purely official programme.[8]

As shown by his constant speech-making, this 'educational' approach was the one Chamberlain favoured always, whether he was dealing with the Radical Programme, Home Rule, or Tariff Reform. For him the positive outward-going approach was the only one he felt likely to succeed. In some respects this was already a part of the Liberal tradition, having received after all Gladstone's own imprimatur in Midlothian. As even Salisbury occasionally acknowledged, the fact that the Gladstonians had selected the battlefield in this way and forced on the struggle after 1876, meant that some attempt at least had to be made to defeat them on their own ground. Where Chamberlain differed from Salisbury lay in the fact that he believed success in such a campaign to be perfectly possible, if one had the temperament and stamina enough to prosecute it. Sceptical of the possibility, and inwardly disinclined to fight the good fight in the country, Salisbury resorted to other expedients in his own field of foreign policy. Their starting points were of course very different. Salisbury, the conservative aristocrat, wanted strong government by himself and his class together with a minimum of interference or participation by outsiders. Chamberlain, born to business, was by temperament dictatorial, less class-conscious than concerned to get his own way, and exploited political forms and methods in a way which threatened to deprive 'politics' of any meaning. Yet both men resorted to their respective tactics in pursuit of aims which they largely shared — strength and consistency in government, freedom to manoeuvre as and when necessary and the avoidance of those embarrassing national fits of mania.

Chamberlain also felt that the end result of such campaigns, which he foresaw as bringing about a state of harmony between governors and governed, would be wholly beneficial. Unity of purpose would be achieved, and nowhere was this more important than in questions of foreign and imperial affairs. As he told Balfour, 'I think a democratic government should be the strongest government from a military and imperial point of view in the world, for it has the people behind it.'[9] The people were fundamentally pacific, but if 'the occasion should come to assert the authority of England, a democratic Government, resting on the confidence and support of the whole nation, and not on the favour of any limited class, would be very strong. It would know how to make itself respected, and how to maintain the honour and obligations of the country.'[10] Such solidarity could never be the end-product of Salisbury's less grandiose methods; at times like the Fashoda crisis, he only capitalised on a feeling already existing and made evident, whereas Chamberlain's policy in this respect was a creative one. The question for him presented itself simply as one of leadership, and here again at an early stage he came very close in his thinking to those who criticised democracy from a right-wing standpoint.[11] Of leaders, there was always a very real shortage; 'the rank and file are all right, but there is an awful lack of Generals, and even of noncommissioned officers'.[12] It is not simply the military language which makes this sound like a pre-echo of Alfred Milner. Chamberlain, although a politician by calling, had little liking for many of the compromises involved in parliamentary activity. One entered politics, and Parliament existed, to get things done; being a member of the House of Commons was no sinecure, and should certainly not be merely the final gloss on a position of local pre-eminence. Politics for him was the art of defeating an opponent, whether by gaining the latter's acceptance of his own viewpoint or by the simple expedient of forcing him into a minority position. The idea of arriving at a solution more or less mutually agreeable was one for which Chamberlain had little instinctive sympathy. No wonder, as Garvin tells us, he 'often sighed for the "democratic autocracy" of Birmingham'.[13]

While this militant outlook derives in Chamberlain's case from certain fundamental ideas about the nature of politics and political action, it was constantly reinforced by – and in its turn often increased – his comparative isolation at Westminster. Arriving in the House with a ready-made reputation and purpose, his tactic was never to roar his colleagues as gently as any sucking dove. Brisk from the beginning, he provoked Disraeli to alliteration. Chamberlain the cheesemonger[14] was never exactly an object of love. Even when he talked sense, his views were more often than not discounted because of the personal hatred which so many people appear to have had for him.[15] If this was true of Chamberlain as a Liberal before 1886, it was even truer in the following decade. Having little but his own talents on which to rely at Westminster, he had inevitably to cultivate his support in the country, above all in Birmingham, keeping himself constantly in the public eye while at the same time nurturing local affections and susceptibilities.[16] Chamberlain's position in national politics depended very largely on the conviction of other statesmen, especially Conservatives after 1886, that his presence within the fold brought considerable electoral strength to their party.

Such were the general assumptions that Chamberlain brought to bear on his political activities; their effect can be traced in connection with all the various causes he espoused. At certain points, his mode of procedure bears comparison with other politicians already mentioned. The appearance of considerable support, whether as something with which to bludgeon political opponents, win the acquiescence of doubtful colleagues, or to convey an impression of national solidarity to overseas rivals, was something which many occasionally tried to create or to exploit in the course of the century. As Chamberlain's acquaintance with foreign and imperial affairs grew, he too re-applied lessons learnt on the domestic front, and was to be found during the Penjdeh crisis urging his supporters to realise that the 'great security for peace lies in impressing the Russians with the conviction that they cannot do as they like and that English opinion is united'.[17] Nevertheless, the common tactics of politicians in tight corners were extended by Chamberlain and combined with certain novelties to produce a form of procedure which clearly sets him apart from earlier generations. His distinctiveness consists in a combination of three particular elements. Political changes, even before the reforms of the 1880s, had produced in Chamberlain's estimation an electorate far more independent, far less amenable to old forms of influence, than ever before. More and more seats were regularly contested, and the numbers of constituencies which seemed to be affected by national issues appeared to be increasing. Under such conditions, an electorate needed to be informed and organised in new ways, and, bearing this in mind, Chamberlain therefore set out to manipulate public opinion on the widest possible scale. Not only did this involve the careful definition of issues and presentation of programmes of action, but (and here is the second element) his ideas required constant and consistent reiteration to audiences all over the country. The growth of the provincial and lower-class press, the impossibility of influencing more than a very few press-men, the value people themselves put on personal appearances by politicians, all made public speech-making essential; Members of Parliament could be sure that their words would at least be locally reported or passed on by word of mouth. Earlier in the century not only had such speech-making campaigns been unconventional, but to carry this kind of verbal warfare into enemy camps would often have served very little purpose. The second and third Reform Acts however altered the framework of politics, whereupon conventions of all kinds had to be cast off and replaced by new. Finally, the need for continuity and repetition in this 'educative' process meant that Chamberlain pursued his course both in office and out, as a member of the governing party or in opposition, something again unprecedented and often causing his colleagues considerable embarrassment.

While it must necessarily be recognised that Chamberlain's political manners and abrasive style owed a great deal to the opposition which he frequently met, they were conditioned to a far greater degree by the emergence in the two decades after Palmerston's death of a new democratic system of politics. In company with many he realised that public opinion aroused on any really wide scale could be very effective, even if only negatively so. Confident in his ability to outbid and at least match in argument any political rival, Chamberlain intended to harness this power to his own chariot. Armed with his Radical Programme and looking to the completion of electoral alterations, Chamberlain confidently expected that 'next year, we shall for the first time have a full expression of the national will'.[18] A naive prophecy perhaps, and especially so in view of subsequent events under the impact of the Irish Home Rule debate. None the less, in Chamberlain's view the necessity for a campaign of this kind was now even greater, given the fundamental importance of the Irish Question. The Hawarden Kite, tail and all, had to be brought down and grounded for ever.

The events of 1885–6 and the ensuing lengthy fight to defeat Gladstone's Home Rule crusade were of course crucial in determining the career of the middle-aged and elderly Chamberlain. They prompted him to reconsider further his ideas on imperial and foreign subjects, and, in confirming his political habits, finally shaped the outlook of the man who was to become Colonial Secretary in 1895. Chamberlain had long confessed to a rather vague imperialism as part of his political credo. Commenting on the Conservative victory in the Commons' Debate on the Congress of Berlin, he felt that

> great harm has been done to the Liberal Party by its connection with those who are in favour of peace at any price, and those who measure everything by a pecuniary standard. It is our business to show that we are as keenly alive to the responsibilities and duties of a great nation as our opponents; that we also have 'Imperial instincts' but that we desire that these should be directed to worthy objects, and not used as the Prime Minister is doing, for ignoble party purposes.[19]

For a long time however Chamberlain's own 'imperial instincts' were dormant and very ill-defined, and the historian must be very wary both of imposing system where none existed, and of attributing to Chamberlain an intellectual subtlety which he did not possess. In fact, recent work has done little to shake the forty-year-old conclusion that Chamberlain had scarcely formulated any definite ideas prior to the Home Rule struggle.[20] Nevertheless, while Chamberlain's thoughts on empire consisted in hardly more than the sum of his reactions to a number of varied crises, he was accumulating a body of information and experience in the early 1880s which later proved of use. As a member of the Cabinet of 1880–5, with departmental responsibility for the Board of Trade, and as Commons spokesman for the Government on South African affairs, he acquired considerable knowledge as well as a number of new interests.

On the question of Britain's position in South Africa, Chamberlain showed that he was capable of acting both with generosity to the Boers and with determination in defence of British interests. He supported the British withdrawal from the Transvaal and the signing of the Pretoria Convention in 1881 as no more than realistic after Carnarvon's annexation and abortive attempt at federation in the late 1870s. He criticised only Gladstone's delay in making good promises to restore Boer independence, which had resulted in Boer rebellion, a British defeat at the Battle of Majuba, and Britain's giving the impression after this of retiring in despair, rather than appearing magnanimous by restoring self-government to the Transvaal. Later on, when the Boers broke their pledges, secured renegotiation of the Pretoria Convention, and then showed themselves disinclined to keep to the letter even of their second agreement with Britain – the London Convention of 1884 – he strongly urged the case for sending the Warren expedition to occupy Bechuanaland. It is difficult to draw any firm conclusions from his views at this time which shed light on his later thoughts on South Africa. He admitted that the South African question was one which greatly interested him and that he had followed the details carefully, something borne out by his appreciation even in 1880 that only a large immigration of Englishmen was likely to delay the return of the Boer's independence.[21] But although this clearly has a bearing on what happened after 1886, when gold was discovered in large quantities and immigration grew with the mining boom, Chamberlain was not gifted with foresight. He was then not apparently concerned that the Liberal policies he had supported in fact compressed into a period of only five years yet another cycle in the long history of recurrent British withdrawal and advance in South Africa. He expressed no particular sympathy with any ideas of federation, and did not see in the Warren expedition an attempt first and foremost to 'rationalise' or increase British holdings in South Africa; rather it was a strictly practical measure to restore stability in Bechuanaland, putting the Boers back where they belonged and illustrating that whatever had been the impression generated in 1881, Britain would keep to her agreements and not be pushed from pillar to post.

In fact, Chamberlain's expressed views show little beyond an implied and ill-defined wish to keep Englishmen within the Empire, and a desire to protect native rights, especially to their land. His reactions to South African difficulties while in office under Gladstone are indicative less of any deep thoughts about Britain's role there, than of his general attitude to foreign policy equally evident in his response to other crises between 1880 and 1886 – his desire to get away from the drift and aimlessness which he felt characterised so much Government behaviour, and his resentment of Britain's being pushed around by other powers, such as Germany or Russia. More significant than his acquaintance with South African details was the fact that along with many contemporaries, and in greater detail than most, he became increasingly aware of foreign rivalries and the stiffening competition which Britain was having to face to maintain her position of pre-eminence. Growth and expansion had been the key to past success, and to Chamberlain there appeared no reason for thinking the answer to the future any different. The idea that exclusive nationalism necessitated the existence of larger and larger states, that size was the answer to survival, inevitably made Englishmen look to their empire: Chamberlain, his imagination caught by both Dilke and Seeley,[22] and nourished with a dose of crude 'Darwinism',[23] was no exception. Yet when he considered the way in which Granville and Derby handled foreign and imperial affairs, he found cause for anything but satisfaction. 'If the Board of Trade or Local Government Board managed their business after the fashion of the Foreign Office and the Colonial Office, you and I would be deserve to be hung', he told Dilke.[24] Apart from the intrinsic interest of colonial problems, it was doubtless this feeling that he could manage such an office more successfully, plus the expectation that it was likely to grow in importance, that prompted

Chamberlain to suggest himself to Gladstone for the Colonial Secretaryship in January 1886.[25]

In the previous year he had already begun, under the pressure of German activity, to look to the resources of the whole Empire for the defence of its individual parts,[26] and this led him to consider how such co-operation could be arranged. His answer remained for some time a vision rather than a detailed scheme, but one which nevertheless encompassed his practical suggestions for Irish government. His thinking on imperial and Irish questions initially proceeded side by side, even though both were guided by the same basic conviction in the abiding importance of ultimately centralised control, in relation to which delegation of responsibility or functions was only a question of temporary expediency and efficiency. Chamberlain's ideas on democracy bear exactly the same hallmark. It was Gladstone's departure in the direction of Home Rule which fused the imperial and Irish strands in Chamberlain's mind, preservation of the structure of the Empire and therewith its power temporarily taking precedence over an improved organisation. As he wrote in May 1886,

> The hope, – it may be only a distant one, but it has infinite attractions – of drawing more closely together the great dependencies of the British Crown and welding them into a mighty and harmonious Empire rests on the determination to resist in their inception all separatist tendencies, and to maintain one central Parliament for the protection of the common interests of all who claim their part in the Imperial organization.[27]

The need for variation in order to avoid monotony while publicly reiterating the same basic theme, also aided its development. A little later, Chamberlain expressed his hope that 'we may be able sooner or later to federate, to bring together, all these great independencies of the British Empire into one supreme and Imperial Parliament, so that they should all be units of one body, that one should feel what the others feel, that all should be equally responsible, that all should have a share in the welfare, and sympathize with the welfare of every part'.[28] Again, the themes of strength in unanimity, and the desirability of complete harmony between the whole and its constituent parts were being spelt out.

The truth of his claim that 'my Radicalism ... desires to see established a strong government and an Imperial government'[29] was being clearly enunciated, and continued to be so in subsequent years. As a result of visits made to Canada, the United States of America and Egypt, he reflected on the problems of imperial defence and commerce – for him the two main routes towards the federation of which he spoke – and of rule over non-Europeans.[30] At the same time, however, Chamberlain never forgot that the ultimate reality of these growing convictions for him as a politician rested upon the possession of actual political power. It was all very well to declare his intention of being Colonial Secretary one day,[31] but the prospect in the late 1880s was none too bright. The way in which Chamberlain set to work to recoup his lost political fortune has been described very fully.[32] By reviving his social reform programme and linking it with his imperialism, he aimed to undermine the loyalty of the poorer voters to Mr Gladstone, and to convince them that reforms would now come from the party of the Right rather than the Left. This strategy seems to have paid increasing dividends after 1888, as Chamberlain managed to pose as the interpreter both of 'The People' to the Unionists and of reformism to the people. For a while at least the flow of Liberal by-election victories was reduced, and in the General Election of 1892 it was clear that Chamberlain's hold on the electorate, as distinct from that of the Unionists as a whole, had increased. It is important however to examine Chamberlain's changing presentation of the relationship between the two sides of his political programme, for this sheds more light on his understanding of the problems posed for imperial and foreign policy makers by a democratic system.

That the Empire needed protection against the ignorant whims of the democracy and unscrupulous politicians was pretty clear, especially after the raising of the Home Rule spectre, and the revelation of a popular tendency to vote for Gladstone and the Liberals as though most people had the wrong priorities, or even no opinion at all, on this matter of vital importance to Britain's future. To Chamberlain, as to many other imperialists in the mid-1890s, there seemed little ground for a belief in the steady growth of imperialist or jingoistic sentiment of the kind which caused Liberals to lose their sleep, and was later to be analysed by J. A. Hobson and L. T. Hobhouse in the light of the Boer War. Rather, he felt that there existed in the country a great pool of sentiment, potentially capable of being attached to the cause of empire but needing someone to harness it. Chamberlain, as argued above, favoured a positive educational approach to the problem of persuasion, whether on the subject of imperial policy or anything else. The fact that others concerned about the conduct of imperial policy in a democratic system were also coming to favour a grand propaganda campaign, brought him closer to an important current in upper-class thinking. There remained, however, the question in what form should such persuasion or education be cast. It would have suited Chamberlain to be able to argue that any active imperial policy was inseparable from social reform; such a case would have extended to the Empire that positive interest which he felt already existed in social reforms. On economic grounds, such an argument was even more difficult then than it was to prove when Chamberlain eventually endorsed it in the 1900s. Even more to the point was his own recent advocacy of extensive programmes of social reform before he emerged as a convinced imperialist. The only possibility open to him was to combine imperialism and social reform as two more or less distinct parts of a single programme. Meanwhile the tendency to amalgamation was always there, and whenever a chance arose for him to present 'forward' imperialist policies as promoting both welfare and prosperity, Chamberlain took it. Witness his defence of a British presence in Uganda and the building there of a railway.

> I firmly believe that the railway will . . . prove a good investment. If you spend this [money], the working classes of this country, and the people in the slums . . . will benefit, for the whole of the work will, of course, be done in this country, and the line will be engineered by natives of this country.[33]

Although so obviously crude, this was a common form of argument and superficially plausible. However, it raised problems with respect not only to the electorate, but also to the Conservative party. Many Tories had little sympathy with talk of the need for social reforms, whether or not they were tied to the apron-strings of an imperial policy. The basic conservative argument was put by Lord Salisbury, whose own record in trying to alleviate social hardship was not particularly black, in answer to Chamberlain himself:

> in short, the well-being of the working man shall be obtained by providing him with fresh material for his industry, and giving him an opportunity of finding in the wealth which that industry will create

ample satisfaction of all his wants. The Conservative points the working man forward to obtain wealth which is as yet uncreated.[34]

This being the case, Chamberlain tried to make the best of a difficult situation by bringing social reform and imperial policy, still not overtly connected,[35] under the new umbrella of his own 'National Party' which he hoped 'might include the more Liberal of the Tories as well as the Liberal Unionists, and to which the more moderate of the Gladstonians might be attracted'.[36] Based on the idea that it would defend and promote exclusively national interests, Chamberlain hoped that such a party would appeal to a wide spectrum of opinion. Although put forward by a politician, this suggestion fell in entirely with the ideas of those who criticised democracy for encouraging class warfare, for sacrificing national interests to personal or factional ends, and for producing 'politicians' of parochial outlook as opposed to 'statesmen' of vision. It was in conception a party to end politics, one which should win an overwhelming majority, thus condemning all diehards, factions, and faddists to impotence. It was also specifically designed to make a positive appeal, to avoid the negative cries which were proving attractive to more and more Liberals in the 1890s. The power of uninstructed public opinion and an unregulated electorate was, it was widely felt, essentially a negative one, encouraging weakness and timidity rather than positive aberrations; the latter were the inspirations of party hacks playing upon popular ignorance. Chamberlain's object was to secure continuous and heartfelt convictions, lasting devotion to a selection of causes among which the Empire loomed increasingly large. It was the 'acceptable face' of imperialism which he stressed, not the crudely xenophobic or narrowly self-interested. The people of this country were determined, he said, to 'take their full share in the disposition of these new lands [Uganda] and in the work of civilisation they have to carry out there . . . they are justified in that determination – justified by the spirit of the past, justified by that spirit . . . of . . . adventure and enterprise distinguishing the Anglo-Saxon race [which] has made us peculiarly fit to carry out the work of colonisation'. Just in case people had forgotten, he mentioned too that an earlier phase of expansion had been crucial to 'the condition in which at present a great part of our population live', his own convictions clearly securing him against the unintentional ambiguity of his language.[37]

It was then in this appeal constantly reiterated, in the image of his non-party man's party, that Joseph Chamberlain put his trust for the future. It would be the salvation of his own political career; it would put a stop to Gladstonianism; it would overcome the short-sightedness of Tory backwoodsmen, and it would enable Britain to hold her own against any challenge from the world outside. The limitations of democracy would be contained and contained moreover by mocking the sceptics with their own images. When Salisbury appealed to the working classes 'to give the lie to those who say there can be no consistency of purpose, no tenacity of resolution in a democratic Government',[38] he did so in spite of himself. Not so Chamberlain.

> Elections are carried by the shifting vote of a minority, who do not strictly belong to either party. The working classes are not divided on party lines as absolutely as the middle and upper classes, and my experience is that very large numbers do not actually make up their minds till the time of election comes round and are then very much influenced by the issues presented to them at the moment.[39]

Here lay the reasons for constant publicity. It would ultimately reach the widest possible audience, reaching those beyond whom there could be no appeal, and by force of conviction and repetition overcome transitory gusts of feeling, at least in important matters.

Of course, power was once again necessary to Chamberlain if his ideas were really to be put to the test, but before this was possible, three bridges had to be crossed. The Conservatives had finally to decide that they could work in harness with their erstwhile opponent; Chamberlain himself required convincing that he would not be forever champing at the bit if he became party to such an arrangement; and the Unionist alliance had to be returned at a General Election. It may be suggested that there was in a sense a fourth bridge which faced Chamberlain on the route to a Unionist alliance, namely his decision that reunion with the Liberals was impossible. In point of time, however, this had been the first to be crossed, and lay behind him even before his imperial ideas had been clearly elaborated. Chamberlain had decided after the Round Table Conference and in the early stages of Unionist co-operation that for him personally such a course was ruled out, except on his own terms, and these, he grew ever more confident, the

Gladstonians would never accept. Time simply confirmed the rift, and in 1894 Chamberlain was more concerned lest any initiative by Rosebery should reduce numbers upholding the Liberal Unionist standard than he was anxious to revive the Liberal party.[40] From the point of view of the Conservative leadership the answer to the question concerning their preparedness to work with Chamberlain was, by 1893, not a difficult one. Chamberlain was clearly here to stay while the organisation and votes which he commanded were of obvious value; he had kept his word in maintaining the Unionist alliance, and the Radicals were often felt to be more reliable and intelligible comrades than the Whigs.[41] Here again points of contact are apparent between Chamberlain and Salisbury. Neither man had much time for party as anything but the means by which particular causes might be furthered. In Salisbury's case 'the ethics which governed his conduct were those of war, not those of the cricket field',[42] with the result that any effective ally was welcome. As Rosebery's Ministry tottered towards its end, Salisbury's chief fear was not that he and his colleagues would have difficulty in working with Chamberlain, but that Chamberlain would refuse to work with the Conservatives. The root of the trouble here was the attitude of many rank-and-file Tories towards the apparently privileged position accorded to the Liberal Unionists by party headquarters, feelings which expressed themselves in a spate of press attacks and disputes over by-election candidates during 1894 and 1895.

This was seen by party leaders as a far greater problem than any ideological differences with the Birmingham set. Salisbury was characteristically candid in a letter to his son-in-law Lord Wolmer, the Liberal Unionist organiser. Unprepared for the protests of local Conservatives, he found his strategy for driving out the Liberals threatened by men who, having long worked loyally under their leaders' electoral compact, were no longer willing to watch the Liberal Unionists reap all the rewards of their efforts. 'It is a case in which the interests of the whole Unionist party are on one side, & the interest of parts of it are on the other. In such a conflict of interests the whole ought to prevail: but it very seldom does.'[43] That national interests should be thus dependent on local self-interest, however understandable it might be, was a major point in all criticisms of democratic politics, and on this occasion the Conservative leaders were able to count themselves lucky that the local conflicts were peacefully resolved. Whether Chamberlain was prepared to stand on such an unsure foundation was another matter. He appeared to Balfour and Lord Salisbury extraordinarily sensitive to the criticisms levelled at him,[44] and, whether these came from disgruntled party workers or the conservative press, the 'worst of it is that if Chamberlain forgives us this time, we cannot possibly promise not to offend again'.[45] Intervention in local party affairs was to be avoided where possible, and papers like the *Standard* or *New Review*, the chief offenders in their criticisms of Chamberlain, were not amenable to influence.

In fact, the matter was more serious than Salisbury knew. The Warwick and Leamington episode was almost the last straw because Chamberlain was seriously considering leaving politics altogether. Although he had appeared to have his plans well laid, Chamberlain, after the defeat of the second Home Rule Bill, was very unhappy about his position in the Unionist alliance. Turning his attention more to social questions he became, despite his optimism in 1892,[46] increasingly conscious of the differences between his own and his colleagues' attitudes. His approaches on various topics to Lord Salisbury late in 1894 were charmingly parried and Chamberlain felt compelled to try and exert pressure on the political leadership in a less direct but, he hoped, more effective way. Writing to Strachey, who had close links with the *Spectator*, he stressed the need for a positive Unionist social programme, and suggested that a constructive line adopted by the *Spectator* would be of immense value in the present situation, where Salisbury, Balfour and Devonshire, while avoiding all personal criticism of himself, put no alternatives to the social legislation which they criticised.[47] Finding Strachey sympathetic, he confided that even if Conservative leaders were to win at the next election and to show more interest in his ideas, '*between ourselves*, I am quite uncertain as to my own course. Personally I should prefer independence, with the full intention of giving loyal support to any Government that might be formed. There are difficulties about this – as indeed about every other course – & I do not know how it will eventually work out.'[48]

Chamberlain was clearly troubled by his position even in his less gloomy moments, when he paused to take stock after the best part of nine years spent battling against the odds. The depressing effect of the winter of 1894–5, his trouble with the Royal Commission on

Old Age Pensions, election disputes, and Tory criticisms were all quite as serious in shaking Chamberlain as his biographer, Garvin, made them out to be.[49] At the height of this trouble, moreover, Chamberlain showed himself in no mood to compromise, and voted with the Liberals on the second reading of the Welsh Disestablishment Bill. As Salisbury observed, if 'he wishes for a following . . . he has no choice now except to put as far into the shadow as he honestly can his anti-Church & anti-land opinions. . . . Undoubtedly, if he means to shape his political life on the Birmingham view of Church & squire, those two authorities will in the long run refuse to take him for one of their leaders.'[50] Chamberlain himself, less sure that Salisbury's example of Canning and Catholic Emancipation was one he wished to emulate, talked to a close friend of leaving politics altogether.

> It would take very little now to persuade me of this for I often think that my work has been accomplished, and that in helping to destroy the Home Rule Bill I have also destroyed my own prospects of important & beneficial influence on future politics. I have cut myself adrift from the Gladstonians, and I am not wholly in sympathy with the Conservatives in whose ranks there is still the [?] haven of the old reactionary Toryism.
>
> So far as the leaders are concerned, nothing could possibly be more cordial than our relations; and their loyalty to the alliance has made my task much easier than it would otherwise have been. But now the bugbear of Home Rule is removed I perceive trace in the rank and file of that jealousy of a stranger who was not born in the faith which might at any time lead to strained relations.
>
> So I am led often to reflect whether I should not be wise to leave the field of battle and 'to cultivate my own garden'.[51]

Letters to his wife at this time were very similar in tone, and more formally he told his nominal chief that 'unless I can see a clear public duty or a great public object – I am ready to and even desirous to be relieved of further responsibility'.[52]

Before Chamberlain could happily decide to serve under a Conservative Prime Minister it was necessary for him to reconcile his inclination to the Colonial Office with the general political conditions he knew that service would bring in its train. It is hardly possible to accept Garvin's claim that 'Our Joe's' ambition to be Colonial Secretary never wavered,[53] or to agree with the contemporary suggestion that Chamberlain, eventually convinced that his own ideas on social policy were those embodied in Conservative legislation before 1892, was on that score alone content to join a Unionist Cabinet.[54] Certainly he had not decided irrevocably on service with the Conservatives in 1892.[55] The question was again one which involved the relationship between imperialism and social reform in Chamberlain's own thinking. Depressed by the attitudes especially of provincial Conservatives towards local politics and social legislation, he sought to balance this in his mind by returning to his imperialism and the possible creation of a 'national party'. Encouraged somewhat by Salisbury's and Balfour's sympathy and support, and their ardent desire that he should be part of any future administration, Chamberlain was aware that he could occupy a position giving him considerable influence on Government policy. Given this, Chamberlain was able to see a way in which service under Salisbury might involve less possibility of personal frustration, and no compromise of principle.

Although it was on questions of social reform that the gap between Chamberlain and the Tories was widest, he had become far more aware in recent years of the importance for 'the condition of England' of imperial expansion and development. The successful promotion of this was at least a possibility with the Conservatives, whereas neither imperial policies nor social reform were, he felt, at all likely from traditional Liberals. If achieved, it might offset the need for intervention by the state to alleviate hardship, by bringing about a general increase in prosperity.[56] Moreover, with the proportionate increase in Government revenue, the refusal to spend at least a part of such income on social welfare could be made to seem even less morally defensible. By taking on the Colonial Secretaryship Chamberlain might thus be able to indulge his interest in imperial affairs, meanwhile promoting measures of social reform more effectively through the back door than by any frontal assault on Conservative prejudices. Thoughts of this kind certainly seemed to provide inspiration for the speeches he made in the run-up to the General Election in the summer of 1895.[57] There were also other reasons of a more purely tactical kind. For Chamberlain as the most powerful representative of Liberal Unionism, the presence of Liberal Unionists in the new Cabinet would proclaim the end of the days of uncertainty for the Unionist alliance. By taking the Colonial Office for himself he would certainly be taking that ground where he had most in common with the average Tory. Success in promoting imperial expansion might endear him to at least some erstwhile critics, and by enhancing his personal standing make them regard his other schemes rather more benevolently. Now that Ireland was less prominent in British politics, his presence anywhere but in the Colonial Office might only serve to aggravate the differences which existed. One other possibility which Chamberlain considered for a brief moment was the War Office, but, quite apart from its irrelevance to his domestic concerns, questions of imperial military organisation stood almost an equal chance of being dealt with by an active Colonial Secretary as by the Secretary of State for War. It was clear that the Colonial Office offered more scope for both his talents and his inclinations.

While Chamberlain was a man with few passions outside politics, and one therefore who would have found it extremely difficult to take the actual step of leaving public life, it must not be thought that this outline of his reasoning shows a man compromising principle simply for the sake of personal position. From the financial point of view, certain of his private reasons for wishing to abandon politics were stronger than they had ever been.[58] Instead, Chamberlain saw his decision to stay in politics as further affirmation of his belief in the need for a 'national party'. This concept no longer held the defensive implications which had attended its birth,[59] and Chamberlain now saw a new opportunity of bringing to reality the vision he had quietly sustained since 1886.[60] As suggested above, politics for Chamberlain were less a process of accepting and reconciling conflicting interests than of fighting and convincing others that his view was the right one. For him a properly functioning democracy was composed of voters who were encouraged to hold a particular view, rather than to have ideas of their own. Now that Home Rule had been laid low, and the Grand Old Man was at last in retirement, Chamberlain thought that such a national party might come into its own, and make the most of that victory. It was this theme that he made the central plank of his platform in the summer of 1895. Typical was the speech at Birmingham where he declared that 'we are the two wings of a greater party than ever, of a national party to which every patriotic man may be proud to belong, which is pledged, on the one hand, to maintain the greatness and the integrity of the Empire, and which is equally pledged to a policy of constructive social reform'.[61]

Imperialism and social reform were indisputably the permanent interests of the nation. Once Chamberlain saw his way to ensuring that Tory attention could be devoted to both, he was able to see his decision to join a Cabinet under Salisbury as a step towards the firm establishment of such a national party. Chamberlain the radical promoter of the caucus is widely remembered, but in these later ambitions a slightly different figure emerges. With the creation of what he called a 'national party', Chamberlain envisaged at the same time the widespread publication and popularisation of its policies. Such tactics were designed to guide and inform the electorate on the widest possible scale, to create a unanimity of opinion which would offset the instability then widely feared to be inseparable from democratic forms of government. Influencing policy at the highest level by his presence in the Cabinet, and opinion at the opposite extreme by his speech-making and propaganda (in which no colleague could match him), Chamberlain looked forward to a position of considerable strength. Although the habits of a long fight for political survival were as yet very deeply ingrained, and Chamberlain took care to retain the separate Liberal Unionist organisation as his ultimate pillar of strength,[62] the new position he hoped to occupy was one from which he might hope to render the powers of local party organisations, recently so troublesome, of far less account. The local bodies might be useful to him as to others at election times, or if his fight for political survival had to be renewed, but they were not to be allowed to dictate policy or mediate between Chamberlain and the electorate as a whole. At the same time, the continued existence of his own local associations served to emphasise that Chamberlain's national party was intended as a true centre party, attracting support from left as well as right. Working men unlikely ever to vote Conservative were still potential Liberal Unionist supporters, it was thought.[63] Such an image had become doubly important once Lord Rosebery emerged as Prime Minister in 1894, for talk of a 'third party' and expectations of the collapse of existing alignments had been current for some time in Liberal circles.[64] With aims of this kind, Chamberlain was also therefore a figure representative of the widespread uncertainty which underlay much of the political thinking of the 1880s and 1890s.

III

CHAMBERLAIN, THE CABINET, AND SOUTH AFRICA: THE EARLY MONTHS

I

When Lord Salisbury came to form his third Government after the Liberal's resignation in June 1895, Chamberlain caused some surprise by choosing the Colonial Office. Never considered one of the great offices of state, it had in the past acted as a stepping-stone for young men on the way to greater things, and as a haven for the second-rate or those on the verge of retirement. That a politician of his stature should choose to take the Colonial Office of his own accord was widely marvelled at. Although Chamberlain's record of interest in colonial affairs and his defence of Irish union in terms of the Empire were well known, Salisbury, by no means fully conversant with Chamberlain's reasoning, still tended like many others to interpret his new colleague's career largely in terms of domestic interests and rivalries. While he regretted his inability to offer his son-in-law other than the Colonial Under-Secretaryship, Salisbury felt able to provide some consolation. 'My impression', he wrote, 'is that Chamberlain's interest in the Colonies is entirely theoretic & that when he gets with the office he will leave the practical work entirely to you.'[1] The reality was to prove otherwise; although Chamberlain had had little opportunity for anything other than theorising for wellnigh ten years, the ideas which he had been developing were to govern practice in his new capacity. Chamberlain, the new Under-Secretary wrote many years afterwards, 'told me at once that he meant to make the office he held to be reckoned as highly as the Foreign Office, and that England had not yet realised what the British Empire really stood for or what a part it might play in the world or of what developments it was capable and that he meant to try and make England understand. He kept his word.'[2] Chamberlain was now clear in his own mind as to the kind of parliamentary party which he wished to see in existence, and was decided on the subordinate role which party organisations were to play in the relation between policy-makers and their public. Moreover, with his far wider outlook and experience than when he had first entered national politics twenty years before, Chamberlain's programme had broadened accordingly. Perhaps he remembered his Seeley – 'public understanding is necessarily guided by a few large, plain simple ideas. When great interests are plain . . . public opinion may be able to judge even in questions of vast magnitude.' In any case, having decided to take office with the Conservatives, and secured himself at the Colonial Office, he made his own views plain – imperialism and social reform promoted by a national party – to the public in the campaign following Salisbury's request for the dissolution of Parliament.

The Unionist victory, though scarcely unexpected, delighted the Government's supporters by the unforeseen size of the majority which it secured.[3] Chamberlain rejoiced, and drew the moral that his trust in 'the good-sense, in the courage, in the deep-seated patriotism of the masses of the people' was well placed.[4] He found it reinvigorating to be in office again, and was pleased with the reception which he was everywhere given. After a few months at his new post, his wife summed up the change in a letter to her mother. 'The newspapers far and wide, and on all sides, are ringing with praise of the new life infused into colonial affairs by the policy of the Secretary of State and it is a great encouragement after the years of abuse lavished on his devoted head. He feels the encouragement and it helps his interest and energy.'[5] The Colonial Office itself attracted attention from the fact that an established politician resided there, and Chamberlain's vigour and enthusiasms were apparent from the very start. He lost no time in making public certain of his ideas about imperial policy. Having remarked on the great importance of his speech in the Commons on 'the development of our estates' and his reply to a deputation concerned with West Indian railways,[6] The Times also noted approvingly that 'Mr Chamberlain has taken the first opportunity which presented itself of placing on record the views with which he has assumed the responsibility of his new office'.[7] Wherever interest in the Empire showed itself or might possibly be encouraged, Chamberlain did his best to nurse its growth. Public enthusiasm had in the past always ebbed and flowed as particular issues caught its attention and were then dropped; Uganda in 1892 had been the last to arouse any widespread feeling. Chamberlain's intention was to keep the Empire and its importance before all sections of the British public, to secure as far as possible its constant attention and increasing understanding of what the Empire stood for, of its importance for Britons at home and Britain abroad.

He believed, as has been seen, that democracy and imperial strength were reconcilable, less because there appeared to him to have been any overt 'rise' of specifically imperial sentiment among the bulk of the people, than because he felt that an electorate, in broad sympathy with its Government, would instinctively wish 'to maintain the honour and obligations of the country'.[8] To show that at this point in her history the honour and obligations of Britain, her very future, were bound up with the strengthening of the Empire, was his intention, because he himself had come to believe that this was so; to imbue the electorate with this same belief would be to produce that sympathy between governors and governed which would supply Britain with the strength and unity necessary in a hostile world. He was prepared to utilise any subject to further this end, so that if the Unionists were not returned at the next General Election, the commitment to empire which they had fostered would be sufficient to tie the hands of their successors. In this way would consistency and strength of purpose return to British foreign and imperial policy. Given this broad intention, it was fortuitous that South Africa should have been re-emerging as an issue in British politics at this moment. It was not only in matters of timing that the South African question provided an admirable opportunity for an attempt to educate the British public; its peculiarly intractable nature gave Chamberlain the chance to mount both a powerful and a sustained campaign.

II

British foreign policy during the last decade of the nineteenth century was governed by the intention to preserve British strength, power and prestige against the expansionist policies of other powers, and their attempts to undermine Britain's relatively isolated but commanding position. Southern Africa, supposedly an area where British influence was supreme or at least predominant, was, by 1895, becoming a focal point for European interest and British concern. Disquiet in the Foreign Office sprang from the weak position of Portugal, who, being desperately short of revenue, not only lacked the resources for developing her territories in Mozambique, but had great difficulty in preserving order among the native tribes nominally under her control. At the same time, her traditional policy of sympathy with British interests, and her wish to satisfy her own public opinion by showing a profit from her African territory, were found to be in growing conflict with each other. Britain was reluctant to see Mozambique developed by foreign concessionaires, for fear they might become channels for Great Power intervention and Transvaal intrigue. Moreover, she wished to prevent any decrease in the value of the rights of pre-emption over all Portuguese territory south of the Zambezi, reserved to her in the Anglo-Portuguese Convention of 1891. On the other hand, European powers – notably Germany and France – were strongly opposed to any Portuguese move which might promote British-sponsored development schemes. Not only would this increase British control over Portugal and the South African Republic, but it would greatly strengthen her hold over the whole of southern Africa and remove one more opportunity for bringing political pressure to bear on Great Britain herself. Faced as she was with these mutually exclusive attitudes on the part of those who might supply her with development loans, it is scarcely surprising that within Portugal those advocating the sale of her colonies became more vociferous, even inside the government itself.[9] In fact, foreign hostility and the strong anti-British bias of her own public opinion prevented such schemes from becoming a reality; but continued rumours of sales merely strengthened British beliefs that, despite official assertions to the contrary, Portugal was hardly able to stand on her own feet.[10] Portuguese governments, being denied such a definite solution to the problem of their African territories, took refuge in constant assurances to all powers that their sole wish was to preserve the *status quo*.

Such assurances however were of little worth in the face of attempts, in particular by Germany and the Transvaal, to build up their own economic and political strength and weaken Britain's position. During 1894, the apparent favour shown to German interests at the expense of British in the South African Republic had become a source of considerable complaint,[11] and these continued into 1895. Early in 1895, the mail packet steamer service between Portugal and South East Africa passed from English into German hands, with effects later described as being 'of the utmost prejudice to British interests in those colonies, both from a political and a commercial point of view'.[12] Later in the year the British Agent at Pretoria revealed the possibility that 'French and German investments will soon exceed English capital in the state', and it became clear that German trade, owing to the greater size and reliability of German shipping services, was increasing far more rapidly than English.[13] Various reciprocal shipping arrangements between Germany and the South African Republic came to light at the beginning of that year. These all assumed an increased importance following as they did the completion of the rail link between the Republic and Delagoa Bay in the autumn of 1894. The line was operated largely by the Netherlands Railway Company, who appeared to be making 'a somewhat successful effort ... to place British goods at a disadvantage compared with its more favoured rival, the German article'.[14] It was soon confirmed that the Transvaal Government, with French and German backing, was making attempts to get complete control of the railway through negotiations with the Governor of Mozambique, an official noted for his anglophobia.[15] Although these failed in the main purpose, the Railway Company acquired harbour rights at Lourenço Marques,[16] which became the basis for further trade and shipping agreements, news which appeared even more troublesome when it was learnt at the same time that a development grant on the Bay had been made to a German subject.[17] The growth of German economic interests was constantly stressed both in public, and in private conversations with the British Ambassador, as giving weight to German opposition to any progress in South Africa towards the commercial union which Britain was known to favour.[18] Such interests also provided a sound basis for growing political influence, Germany putting pressure on the weak Portuguese Government and encouraging the wishes of the Transvaal for independence from any British domination or control. A German naval presence at the opening of the Delagoa Bay railway was shortly followed by the upgrading of the German diplomatic representative at Pretoria. Then came German support, in notes sent to both Britain and Portugal, for the Republic's protest at British annexation of Zambaan's territory, lying between Swaziland and the sea, and Britain's declared protectorate over Amatongaland.[19]

Although often small in themselves, these events appeared as a concerted attempt to undermine British influence in the region. Lord Ripon had sensed the danger in September 1894, and submitted a memorandum to the Cabinet declaring that

> it is in my judgement essential that we should maintain the position that the Transvaal is within our 'sphere of influence' as regards other European countries and that we should retain in some shape or other definite *treaty* arrangements with the South African Republic, which would give full notice to foreign Governments that we would resist any attempt on their part to obtain political influence in any shape, direct or indirect, within the Transvaal territory.[20]

Although it was considered sufficient by the Cabinet simply to maintain the London Convention of 1884 and not to make fresh arrangements with the Transvaal, the gist of Ripon's advice was followed. Ambassadors in Portugal and Germany asserted British claims to the 'sphere of influence'. In both countries however, these claims clearly met with little practical consideration, and British official concern began to increase. Salisbury wished like his predecessor to maintain things as they were, but felt obliged in August 1895 to renew Kimberley's attempts to press Portugal for firm assurances as to the future of Delagoa Bay. No guarantee was forthcoming, but as the precarious nature of the Portuguese administration made it likely that its friendly attitude towards Great Britain would become the main point in Opposition moves to overthrow it, Salisbury accepted his Minister's suggestion that it was inadvisable to insist too strongly on British rights.[21] In October, the situation having deteriorated further, fresh enquiries were made at Lisbon, only to receive the answer that 'His Majesty the King of Portugal . . . is willing to give verbally the most positive and formal assurances to your Lordship that the Portuguese Government will not in any form whatever, either to the Transvaal or to Germany, and either previous to the Berne Award or after it, cede their rights over the Delagoa Bay Railway or territory'.[22] It was soon clear to an irritated Salisbury that these assurances were also worthless, and that with the erosion of the British economic position claims to a sphere of influence were becoming correspondingly less substantial.

Already in September 1895, Salisbury and Selborne had discussed the idea of purchasing the territory of Mozambique from Portugal, and of reducing European hostility by coming to some arrangement with Germany.[23] Attention focused on the Delagoa railway, and in the face of Portugal's behaviour a more positive policy seemed to be required.

> The measure of the value of the line to the Colonies is not so much what it would yield in their hands as the injury it would be capable of doing them if controlled by others. From an imperial point of view, it is absolutely necessary that we acquire the railway (and hereafter the Bay) at any cost. Here, again, the measure of its value to us is not only the use which we should make of the Bay, but of the effect on British interests of a German occupation of the territory which seems to be the necessary alternative.[24]

The conclusion to this Colonial Office memorandum, suggesting that Britain should stand up to German protests and somehow get Portugal to sell or lease the line to her, showed how feeling in Whitehall was hardening towards the end of the year. Salisbury shared in equal measure the sentiments being expressed in the Colonial Office.[25] It was clear to all concerned that the South African Republic, engaged for some time past in a tariff war with Cape Colony and Natal, was aiming to develop her foreign contacts and her route to the sea at Lourenço Marques in order to end her dependence on British-controlled channels of trade.

On 1 October 1895, the economic dispute in South Africa reached the point where the Transvaal closed the crossing places on the Vaal River which were used by the mounting volume of road traffic seeking to avoid the Republic's high rail freight charges. The Cape Government thereupon appealed for British intervention to settle the dispute. Chamberlain at this point was on holiday in Spain, and it was therefore Salisbury who initiated the forceful British response. At the time, Selborne, temporarily in charge of the Colonial Office, described how he

> went to Hatfield and found Lord Salisbury fully aware of all the circumstances of the case except the two recent telegrams from Robinson.[26] I explained to him our proposed line of action and asked for his authority to carry it out. . . . He asked me whether the Colonial Office considered the closing of the drifts to be an infringement of the convention. I replied that it was doubtful if it was an infringement of the letter, that on that point we were consulting the Law Officers, but that it was undoubtedly an infringement of the spirit of the Convention, and an act of extreme unfriendliness. He asked me 'does Rhodes ask for this support'? I replied 'Yes, the Cape Ministry ask for it officially and that is Rhodes.' He then said 'I entirely agree in

the line of action proposed. It is the right one. You have my authority to proceed, and I am convinced that Chamberlain will agree with me. The Transvaal government is unfriendly to us and it is a great mistake to run away from them. The Cape Government must be supported to the end in this matter.[27]

So it was that the British Government protested strongly to President Kruger over his closure of the Drifts, a protest which went far to secure their reopening a little over one month later. British pressure on the Portuguese was thus paralleled, as the opportunity arose, by similar pressure on the Boers, both courses designed to safeguard the imperial position and illustrating how British concern for her South African interests was mounting.

Salisbury's feeling that a firm stand had to be taken in South Africa to prevent the whittling away of Britain's supremacy was only strengthened in the remaining months of the year. Constant German interference made her the clear object of general displeasure alongside Portugal and the Transvaal. From Berlin, Lascelles' report on 30 December of Marschall's statement that Germany would view any changes in the Transvaal with great seriousness, called forth from Salisbury the observation that while Germany clearly intended to be disagreeable, she simply had no rights whatever in the matter.[28] These same pretensions even provoked Devonshire into one of his rare utterances on foreign policy. He confessed himself uneasy at the German attitude, and thought that the Kaiser was a young man to whom it might be best to speak 'pretty plainly'.[29] On the eve of the Jameson Raid therefore, a third strand was being woven into the pattern of British South African policy; it was to be made clear to those European powers, like Germany, who lacked actual territorial possessions in southern Africa that they had no business there. The future development of South Africa, whether of a political or an economic kind, was to take place under the auspices ultimately of the British Imperial Government.

It was not simply the local South African situation or a peripheral nationalist movement which worried the British. They felt that there existed throughout the late 1890s a distinct European challenge to their position in southern Africa as also on a world scale. The way in which Boer nationalism was intertwined with German and, to a lesser degree, French initiatives enhanced the vitality of both republican ambition and metropolitan expansion.

In proportion as it widened the prospects for a marriage between these forces, the combination of Portugal's aspirations with her basic political and economic weakness at home and in Mozambique further disquieted the British. British official sensitivity to the interconnected nature of these matters has not been sufficiently appreciated, but needs to be remembered throughout these years.

III

These were the questions which formed the substance of discussion on South Africa among Cabinet Ministers, and officials in both the Foreign and Colonial Offices, between whom much correspondence passed on the subject. To a lesser extent, these concerns – Boer and German pretensions, rival economic and political interests, and their relation to the general security of Britain's position – were also reflected in questions raised publicly by MPs who considered the Liberal Government insufficiently careful of imperial interests. Early in 1895, considerable resentment was expressed at Kruger's utterances in Pretoria on the occasion of the German Emperor's birthday celebrations,[30] and the fear was voiced that the Boers' presence in Swaziland would soon be followed by that of the French and Germans at St Lucia Bay.[31] Sydney Buxton, Liberal Under-Secretary for the Colonies, brushed these fears aside, although fully conscious of the Cabinet's own reservations on the subject, and took the opportunity to make it clear that the Liberals were in no way guilty of neglecting Britain's position. The territory between Swaziland and the sea had, he asserted, always been part of the British sphere of influence and would soon be 'more directly under British control'.[32] Similarly, in answer to another question, he acknowledged the ambiguous extent of British suzerainty over the Transvaal, but emphasised the Government's intention to uphold Article IV of the Convention which contained the essence of that suzerainty.[33] The House was apparently satisfied with these statements, and the issue was not again brought up against the Government. But the Government's own awareness that the situation remained unsettled was clear, for on two other occasions Buxton again stressed Britain's determination to retain control of the Republic's foreign relations, and to preserve the seaboard from foreign access. Finally a Blue Book was prepared on the annexation of Amatongaland, and presented to the House of Commons in June.[34]

Although it reflected a genuine Cabinet concern, this insistence on British claims also stemmed from Liberal attempts to divert their anti-Boer or humanitarian critics, who were attacking on two other fronts. The handing over of Swaziland to Boer administration had been portrayed by the Opposition as a betrayal of the Swazi nation, and they scornfully rejected the Government's trust in Boer promises of respect for native rights. No attempt was made to controvert such accusations beyond Buxton's defensive speeches, and these lost what little force they possessed when no other Liberal, except the notoriously pro-Boer Dr Clark, commented on the transfer except to criticise it. Despite promises, no papers were put before the House.[35] On this ground the Government felt too uncertain of their record, and attempted to retreat into silence, Buxton appealing to the public interest as necessitating the withholding of details.[36] The one Blue Book which had been produced at the very beginning of the session failed to prevent criticism of the Government, but beyond giving evasive answers to questions, the Colonial Office was not prepared to meet the clamour for information and evidence of a clear policy.[37]

Alternatively, the position of the Uitlanders, that large number of predominantly British immigrants who moved into the Transvaal in the years after the gold discoveries, was frequently raised. Although not considering itself directly interested, the Liberal Government had kept an eye on this large-scale immigration, for it soon became clear that it was a growing source of unrest in the domestic politics of the Transvaal and might therefore have repercussions beyond the Republic. The Boers were being forced to adjust rapidly to the presence in their midst of a largely alien, urban, industrial community, many members of which were, in Boer eyes if not their own, likely to be only temporary residents. Inefficiency and maladministration were only to be expected in such a situation, and the Boer Government became the butt of many complaints. Such expedients as the Boer practice of granting monopolies over essential goods and services – such as dynamite and the railways – were reasonable enough in view of the Government's rudimentary administrative machine, and its need for finance to meet the many other demands made upon it. Yet with little tolerance or respect existing between the two communities, such grants only too easily became sources for private enrichment at communal – often Uitlander – expense, and honest failings were often seen by hostile critics as evidence of inherent incapacity and corruption. Tension arising out of this situation was exacerbated by the moves of the Boer Government to protect itself and the rural Dutch community against domination by the new population, whose members, by virtue of their capital and labour, largely controlled the economic wealth of the Republic. The Uitlanders were progressively denied effective political rights, and many felt the rights of municipal government which they did possess to be inadequate. Political associations were formed to press for changes, culminating in the formation of the National Union in 1892. This body co-ordinated Uitlander protests, made contact with progressive Boer opponents of President Kruger, and in 1894 led the campaign against Boer attempts to commandeer British subjects for military duties. This dispute had led ultimately to appeals to Britain, and the High Commissioner, Sir Henry Loch, finally visited Pretoria to negotiate with the Boer Government for their exemption.[38]

It was not long after this that Sir Robert Meade had reported Knutsford as saying that 'the Tory party are very anti-Boer . . . not merely the small fry such as Ashmead-Bartlett, but Sir Michael Hicks-Beach & Balfour, the former having often reproached him with giving way to the Boers'.[39] The continued criticism in 1895 seems to bear out this judgment, certainly as regards the 'small fry'. There was among certain members of the Conservative party a lasting regret that the defeat of British troops at Majuba had never been avenged, and an intense dislike of the Liberals whose policy of withdrawal had prevented this. Such feelings showed themselves in continuous attempts to embarrass the Liberal Government over South African questions in the House. However, the attitude of the Colonial Secretary and his staff was naturally unsympathetic to the demands of men like Arnold Forster and Ashmead Bartlett about Transvaal affairs. Buxton admitted that the office had plenty of information, but asserted that, according to the Conventions, the Transvaal's internal affairs were none of Britain's business.[40] From inside the office, Meade wrote privately to his chief, reminding him 'that after all Kruger has some justification for dalliance with Germany. He is in a mortal funk of the Uitlanders whom Loch rather ostentatiously patronized. . . .'[41] Publicly, this kind of tolerance of the Transvaal continued, and the result was that, beyond providing what figures they had of the numbers of Uitlanders in the Transvaal, the Colonial Office refused information altogether. This greatly annoyed Arnold Forster, who finally reproached the Government with the fact that what 'was going on there was not fully made known to the House, and what was known did not come through the medium of the High Commissioner at all. Hon. Members learned through private sources many things connected with the Transvaal which were never communicated to the House, as they should have been.'[42]

With the accession to power of the Unionists, things changed. Although he had played no part in the recent attacks on the Liberal Government, Chamberlain now showed his intention to live up to his expressed aim to popularise the cause of Empire, one aspect of which policy naturally involved a ready response to currents of opinion in the House. The demands for information which the Liberals had refused to satisfy, the new Colonial Secretary tried in part to meet with the publication of two Blue Books during the second session of 1895. The Republic's objection to the annexation of Amatongaland, and the Government's firm reply were put before the Commons on 29 August, showing that the new Government intended to be firm with the Boers on this point. The impression was given that insistence on British rights would not be chiefly confined to utterances at Westminster, and that the Liberals' line of policy would be more strongly pursued.[43] This was followed by a batch of correspondence relating to the grievances of British Indian subjects in the Republic. This topic had been taken up in May 1895 by Arnold Forster and Ashmead Bartlett, along with Boer treatment of the African chieftain Magato and his tribe, and had been followed up in The Times. Buxton had in fact promised to present papers on the former subject, but these had not been published before the defeat of the Government; as far as the treatment of the natives was concerned, he had refused to make special enquiries on the ground that this was one of those strictly internal matters to be dealt with by the Transvaal's officials alone.[44] Chamberlain clearly did not share this attitude, for he announced in the Commons that the High Commissioner was making enquiries, and gave a sympathetic hearing to a Deputation on the matter.[45] Shortly afterwards, a Blue Book on the Indians was published, even though his staff were not at all sure of its value. Edward Fairfield, for example, minuted that the Indians 'are irrepressible and are pretty sure to do well, however legislation may hinder and handicap them'.[46] It was, however, less the intrinsic merits of the case than public opinion (and in these instances especially those aspects of it represented in the House of Commons) which was decisive. The unsatisfactory.replies of the Transvaal to requests for an enquiry into native affairs worried Meade, and Graham was troubled lest Ashmead Bartlett failed to receive an answer. Selborne's minute indicates where the decisive influence lay: 'This matter must largely depend on the exigencies of the House of Commons. Mr. Chamberlain will know best how far the House will expect the Govt to probe the matter.'[47]

Again, the difference from the Liberals was marked when the last despatch in Chamberlain's Blue Book on the Indians bore the same date as the day of presentation to the House of Commons, and doubtless impressed MPs so accustomed to departmental reluctance to divulge information. Earlier questions which the Liberals had promised, but failed, to take up were now being dealt with in a much more forceful way. In addition to this, Chamberlain's forthright approach to the treatment of both the Africans and the British Indian subjects in the Republic had other implications. By analogy, the problems of the Swazis which had troubled some Members earlier in the year could now be considered in safer hands. Secondly, these publications, on the eve of the Tswana chiefs' visit to London to request continued Imperial protection in preference to British South Africa Company administration, suggested that the Government would be unlikely to sell them down the river. Official utterances had already been stressing the importance of the welfare of the Africans in Bechuanaland in an attempt to calm the widespread support – led by the Wesleyan Foreign Missionary Society[48] – for their wish to remain under British control, or at least for safeguards against exploitation by the Company.

Clearly Chamberlain was demonstrating a certain sensitivity to expressions of opinion in the House of Commons, but there is more to his response than may be apparent at first sight. It has been suggested that Chamberlain was responding to voices from the floor of the House in a way calculated to give the impression that here was a Government and Minister determined, unlike the

Liberals, to protect those aspects of imperial interests that individuals apparently cared about. The implication was that all other aspects of imperial affairs might be considered equally safe in his hands; in other words, by acting vigorously in one or two matters which were evidently attracting public attention, Chamberlain was at the same time indirectly discouraging further scrutiny, leaving himself more free to deal with what he wished to emphasise as vitally important. It is necessary to stress that in his approach to the House of Commons, Chamberlain right from the start only responded to men like Ashmead Bartlett when they chose to raise matters which excited their concern. There is no evidence that he ever took the initiative in the sense of analysing carefully what interest groups existed in Parliament, who had or did not have imperial or specifically South African concerns, or follow up such an analysis by careful and individually tailored attempts to awaken fresh imperial sentiment or sustain those of long standing. Chamberlain's constant assumption was that ultimately his most effective way of swaying the House of Commons was through his influence over the electorate, and that arguments for empire therefore had to be equally suited to audiences inside and outside the House.

A similar attitude is in evidence in Chamberlain's responses to other issues when raised not at Westminster but in the press. Again, there is apparently no evidence that he ever took stock of the British newspaper or periodical world with a view to consistent and detailed attempts to influence its editors and the content of their publications. As was suggested in Chapter I, politicians had become increasingly sceptical of the value or even the possibility of such a course, and Chamberlain was no exception in this. A very few direct contacts were made and these are dealt with below,[49] but here it is sufficient to notice the Colonial Secretary and his staff taking up issues simply when they were raised by others, usually as they fitted in with those with which he was simultaneously concerned in the House of Commons. He could not really avoid responding to questions in his ministerial capacity; with the press, having much greater freedom, he selected those questions which reinforced his Parliamentary statements. Such was the case of the treatment of natives in the South African Republic by the Boers, the subject of serious allegations – again by Ashmead Bartlett – in the *Daily Chronicle*.[50] Fiddes, one of the younger members of the

Colonial Office staff, was very ready to accept these at face value, and when further press cuttings were sent by the Pretoria Uitlanders Association, he even suggested that they should be included in a Blue Book on the subject then in preparation. This was even before the High Commissioner had had time to investigate the charges, and in spite of the fact that the Uitlander allegations apparently rested on the evidence of the *Transvaal Advertiser*, whose editor other members of the Office agreed was 'almost demented' in his hatred of the Boers.[51] Fiddes's suggestions seem, however, to have met no particular rebuff, and the same eagerness was evident in Chamberlain's own response to the offer of information by the editor of the *Critic* on the same subject. Without checking this evidence, even though, as Chamberlain himself acknowledged, it was the first apparently authentic information received, he instructed Sir Hercules Robinson to press for a public enquiry at once.[52] Again the editor in question was known to adopt a generally provocative attitude towards the Boers, yet no precautions were taken. In contrast with other instances in which a much more critical attitude was taken especially of pro-Boer press reporting in and about South Africa, one is here faced with an example of Chamberlain's urge to publicity where, because many precedents inevitably gave critics of the Boers the benefit of the doubt, an issue was officially adopted once some evidence of public feeling manifested itself.

To some, Chamberlain's approach to the House of Commons and the press as just outlined may, despite his co-ordination of the issues dealt with, appear unsystematic and perhaps even strangely illogical in one who, if the preceding chapters are to be believed, was deeply concerned with 'public opinion'. This is not the case, however. His actions are only difficult to explain if one makes the double assumption that he should have been paying systematically detailed attention to both Parliament and press, because these represent 'public opinion' and therefore require encouragement or conversion. Chamberlain himself did not reason in this way. His tactical experiences as a politician had been primarily those of one leading forces of electoral weight, hammering at the gates of the establishment and attacking settled opinions from the outside, making himself a force to be reckoned with by Gladstone or Salisbury by commanding organisation and votes in the country. Chamberlain had no wish to wheel and deal in the corridors of

Westminster, and did not pay much heed to those who believed that politics consisted in whispering the right words in the correct ear at an opportune moment. He firmly believed that the behaviour and opinions of the electorate – which of course included MPs – was in the end of greater importance in securing one's desired goals than were MPs sitting alone as a formal body in the House. Similarly, Chamberlain did not believe that the only way to influence the content of newspapers and periodicals lay in having the ear of editors and leader-writers. What he saw as essential was a platform, and this of course he had as Cabinet Minister in the Commons. He knew that there many were certain to hear him, that they might also be influenced if they paid heed to the Blue Books which he was happy to publish in abundance. He knew too that parliamentary proceedings and publications were reported verbatim, or at least distilled and summarised, in the press, particularly those involving major political figures like himself. Even speeches made in his constituency were certain to be well publicised without him needing to lift a finger or risk alienating people by individual attempts at persuasion. In these circumstances, Chamberlain was convinced that endless lobbying was unnecessary; moreover, he was never one who liked to appear as a supplicant for favours.

His chief problem and concern was to explain and comment upon imperial policy for the benefit of an electorate alarmingly ignorant of such matters; obviously he had to do this in a way which would arouse lasting interest and carry conviction. 'Public opinion' for Chamberlain was for all practical purposes the opinion of the electorate; it was this which he set out to create or mould in certain ways in respect of imperial affairs. He watched the House as he watched the press, for indications of feeling in the country at large. He used the House directly – responding to its members and employing its machinery – and the press, more usually indirectly, to report the facts of his own case; through frequent utterances and by selecting carefully the facts which he revealed or emphasised, Chamberlain attempted to prompt and influence comment and discussion throughout the country. It was his intention that not only should MPs be influenced by his performances in the House of Commons, but that this effect should be reinforced by the opinion which he was seeking to nurture in the constituencies also being brought to bear on its representatives. Such a circular influence would, he felt, strengthen him personally in the conduct of his policy and the insistence on his own priorities, and slowly overcome the vagaries of the democracy which he and so many others criticised.

In many ways and particularly when set against later standards, this might be considered an unsophisticated approach to political campaigning. It is impossible to know now with any degree of accuracy who read Chamberlain's Blue Books; even the records of the Vote Office, which would have provided the historian with the names of those who at least received personal copies, it seems no longer exist. Nor is it possible to know who amongst MPs consulted such documents in the Library of the House of Commons. Similarly, the historian cannot know who read the reports in the press, or exactly who listened to the speeches even of Chamberlain himself, let alone the impact which was made upon listeners or readers. On the other hand, it is of some consolation to realise that there is very little evidence to suggest that Chamberlain felt any special concern about such matters. What evidence there is points to the conclusion that as long as the Colonial Secretary felt that he was using what channels of publicity existed to the limits that ministerial propriety allowed, and, from early in 1896, that he had an issue which could be used to project the importance of empire to the large audience he had in mind, then he was content on the whole to let such matters take their own course. Occasionally, as will be shown, a subordinate question might be allowed to drop out of sight; alternatively, if Chamberlain happened to notice isolated points which he felt might strike, say, a Roman Catholic or working-class voter, into his Blue Books they went! Yet these were infrequent occurrences. It was a sign of Chamberlain's self-confidence and reliance on his own political instincts that he trusted to the issues he selected to attract the audience he desired, and to be of sufficient force to penetrate downwards in society via the innumerable channels which existed of discussion, oratory, and gossip. Because these were the lessons which he had learned from his own past, and because too there was a physical limit to what any one man might do, these were tactics (with the same lack of attention to many of the details) which Chamberlain adopted in the later Tariff Reform campaign, and they are equally those which governed his handling of imperial affairs in the years 1895–9.

Having long before selected his cause, possessing after the

Conservative victory in the general election both a platform and the power to control the flow of information, comfortable in the knowledge that his views would be as widely and rapidly publicised as was then possible for a politician, Chamberlain was in these early months in office seeking particular issues which could be used as illustrations of his general argument. He responded to those brought to his door by MPs, public deputations, and the press. He himself took initiatives on questions of economic development; the publicly-announced policy of developing 'our estates', especially in the West Indies and in West Africa, and his attention to questions of trade, attracted much favourable comment.[53] But businessmen were only one of the groups amongst whom Chamberlain needed to popularise or promote discussion of the Empire. His handling of the Indian question and the Tswana chiefs in turn appealed to others, and certain of his actions had involved a direct response to vociferous groups in the House of Commons. Chamberlain knew that he had a record to live up to in connection with the protection of non-Europeans' interests, and was being reminded of this late in 1895.[54] These early activities were intended to emphasise the Empire's wider appeal, served to leaven the lump of a purely business Empire, and avoided the tedious technicalities of defence or strategy. If the Empire gained in appeal, this could hardly fail to rub off on the Colonial Secretary himself and so bolster his own political position.

Yet in his own mind, Chamberlain felt that he still lacked an issue which would appeal to all men regardless of their particular occupational or economic interests. He had learnt at the outset of his political career that single, or narrow and possibly short-lived, issues were not the best of vote-winners. For this reason he had progressively abandoned the politics of the National Education League for those of the Radical Programme. Similarly, in the 1890s he wished to bring home the breadth of the Empire's relevance and appeal. He shared the view that matters such as markets and their protection, defence, strategy, and great power rivalries were not likely under normal circumstances to interest the majority of the British people. Of course, there were small minorities interested in all these things right throughout the Empire, and as far as South Africa was concerned, the inveterate anti-Boer prejudice of a man like Ashmead Bartlett, the shipping interests of Sir Donald Currie with his Castle Line steamers, investors watching the fortunes of the gold industry, Cornish tin miners emigrating to try their luck, all these were testimony to a wide variety of public interest. Chamberlain was aware of their existence and that of their representatives whether inside or outside Parliament, but paid little systematic attention to them because he realised that few people would ever support the extension of imperial influence or control on behalf of any one of them, either in South Africa or elsewhere within the Empire. On the other hand, he saw the possibility that those people with such specific interests, interests hardly likely to wither and die altogether for lack of official support, might also be susceptible to other and wider appeals – appeals which in his political capacity he could readily exploit. Chamberlain therefore sought, as it were, the lowest common electoral denominator, striving to find for his imperial propaganda matters of an 'elevated', untechnical nature, questions involving 'principles'; in the absence of such questions, his inclination was to clothe less altruistic intentions with language in the humanitarian-cum-evangelical-cum-liberal mould. The exploitation of this kind of appeal would, he felt, alone remove the greatest obstacles in the way of a coherent, consistent, imperial policy.

The importance of Chamberlain's moves to give further breadth to the appeal of Empire can hardly be exaggerated. While he still disagreed with Gladstone's selection of causes, Chamberlain had had more than enough acquaintance with the concerns of provincial non-conformity and politics, had seen at first hand the outbursts of public feeling over Bulgaria, Gordon, and Uganda, and had imbibed sufficient of the liberal tradition, for him to appreciate the great power of the 'moral' appeal, the argument from high principle as a justification for action. Not simply the tactics but the subject matter of the Midlothian campaigns had provided Chamberlain with an object lesson. If he could somehow give his imperial policy and case for empire the stamp of righteousness, as well as make it an argument for economic success, then he felt he could win that wide public commitment to its preservation that was currently felt to be so often fickle or absent. He aimed to get away from the defensive tone which had characterised Liberal statements and policy. Instead, the identification of imperial effort and empire with liberal, humane, and, for many people, Christian principles, was likely in Chamberlain's view to bring more support to the cause of empire than anything else, however important other aspects of imperial activity might be to particular interest groups. Such a widely-based appeal, by winning over a large and steady majority of the electorate, could be a great help in counteracting the present unpredictability of the populace, whether its roots lay in the upper-class vacillation remarked upon by some observers or in working-class ignorance and apathy. It mattered not a whit to Chamberlain from what party, class, or interest group support came, as long as he could make himself a talking-point, carry conviction, and persuade people to vote in his favour whether it was in the division lobby or in the ballot box. Support on this scale would be forthcoming, he felt, if the right kind of issue could be found, one whose attractions transcended social and economic divisions. Chamberlain's constant attempt to create a large body of committed supporters, a body providing him with a political power base while allowing him as its leader a free hand, and one which was at the same time weighty enough to push other groups into line, was a characteristic of both his domestic and his imperial policy. He had tried this in his efforts to move the Tory party towards social reform, and he now aimed to win sufficient support for his imperial notions to hold both political parties to a consistent imperial policy. It was ever one of Chamberlain's views that colonial leaders could be cajoled and won round, and that the major political battles for empire had to be won at home.

IV

South African questions were merged from the very beginning with Chamberlain's attempts to bring the Empire into the centre of people's vision. It is noticeable that, while doing this, he made most of those topics which fell unreservedly into the lap of the Colonial Office. This reflected his awareness not only that these were early days and that it would therefore be wise as yet to avoid treading on other people's toes, but also that where Colonial Office matters overlapped with those of the Foreign Office, Salisbury as Prime Minister and Foreign Secretary was firmly in control. This was clear above all in the Drifts Crisis, even though the Colonial and Foreign Offices were here already on the same wavelength, but Salisbury's continuing concern and effective control were to be well demonstrated in the years to come.[55] Even before the end of 1895, this led to a situation where those questions troubling Salisbury and Chamberlain in the South African arena – essentially food for Cabinet thought ever since Ripon's Cabinet Memorandum of September 1894 – were becoming distinguished from those which Chamberlain was using as the basis of his imperial propaganda. In other words, circumstances were such that the basic problems of empire and the challenges to its existence as seen by imperial policy-makers were being dealt with quietly at one level, while popular support, the 'informed' public opinion considered so vital to continuity of policy and strength of national purpose, was being nurtured in relation to other questions. This was not the first time that there had developed a gap between the public language of imperial policy and the full range of policy-makers' intentions; under Chamberlain's direction, however, and in response to the changing conditions of British politics, the gap grew wider than it had ever been before.[56]

South Africa emerged as the principal focus of Chamberlain's imperial propaganda, and came eventually both to illustrate and in some ways to resolve this dichotomy between the language of imperial policy and the intentions of British policy-makers, largely as a result of the Jameson Raid. On 29 December 1895, Dr Jameson invaded the Transvaal from a base at Pitsani in that strip of the Bechuanaland Protectorate which had recently been transferred to the British South Africa Company by the British Government. While Jameson claimed initially to be responding to a specific appeal for help from the Uitlanders faced with the prospect of Boer violence, his object was in fact to spark off a revolution in Johannesburg, a revolution planned for some time past by the leaders of the Uitlander National Union in collaboration with certain mining houses, whose leaders were also out of sympathy with Kruger's Government. Of these, the most deeply involved was Cecil Rhodes, Prime Minister of Cape Colony and a man with extensive interests in both Transvaal gold-mining and the expansion of the British South Africa Company. Towards the end of December 1895, the Johannesburg uprising was apparently in danger of fading out, but Jameson's invasion, far from inspiring the revolutionaries to action as intended, proved a complete fiasco. Instead of overturning the Boer Government, the raiders were soundly defeated, and Dutch sympathy throughout South Africa rallied to Kruger.

In the period between the Unionists' accession to office and the Raid itself, there were extensive contacts between Chamberlain, certain Colonial Office officials, and representatives of the British South Africa Company, in connection with the transfer to the Company of territory in the Bechuanaland Protectorate for the ostensible purpose of building a railway to the north. In part already built, this railway had the dual advantage of linking the Cape with the Company's territories while at the same time bypassing the Transvaal. The evidence which has survived of these exchanges and related discussions shows that Chamberlain and his officials had considerable knowledge not only of what was brewing in Johannesburg, but of Rhodes' hand in the matter and of the plans which he had made to intervene in support of a rising against Kruger's Government. They knew too that these plans involved the placing of armed Company men on the border of the Republic within the strip of territory which they eventually handed over to the Company for its railway. Colonial Office knowledge, and the apparent fact that Chamberlain not only failed to try and stop Rhodes' proceedings but appeared to associate the Imperial Government in some measure with what finally ended as an outrageous attack on the Transvaal's independence, have been incorporated as the keystone in what one may conveniently if loosely call the 'Afrikaner' interpretation of the origins of the South African war of 1899.[57] This interpretation sees Chamberlain as the arch-villain of the piece, pursuing a vigorous anti-Boer policy from the time he reached office. At first this policy was secretive, with Chamberlain using Rhodes as the agent of Kruger's downfall and deliberately conniving in a wholly disreputable plot. After the Raid and the discrediting of the Cape Premier, this policy was brought into the open and pursued by Chamberlain aided and abetted in his turn by Milner. It was pursued regardless of the possibility of war, and taken to the point where at last the Republic had no alternative but to resort to violence if its inhabitants were to retain their sense of honour. It has been argued that it was the Colonial Secretary's intention throughout to destroy Boer independence, the crudity of his policy being illustrated from the start by his encouragement of Rhodes' designs in 1895 for Bechuanaland as a base from which to aid an Uitlander revolution.

This is a view produced by historians who, standing too close to the minutiae of events, have placed too great a weight of interpretation on too narrow a factual base. It is of course true that other scholars have, still more recently, focused their attention on the role of Milner and have attempted to explain the dynamic impact of British officials on the spot.[58] Although the inspiration for this shift in emphasis was no merely conventional flight by historians from a concern with the imperial metropolis, and the value of its results is unquestionable, it has also served to cloud one's vision of Chamberlain's role rather than to remove the need for a re-examination. When looked at in the whole context of British policy towards South Africa, British attempts to derive imperial advantage from the troubled situation on the Rand in 1895 can be seen to owe far more to the seriousness of developments in South Africa itself than to fresh ideas on the part of the British Government, or even to a new incumbent at the Colonial Office.[59] Chamberlain's own influence on South African affairs only really began to make itself felt after the Raid had taken place.

The Unionist Government was aware when it took office of conflicts taking place at three different levels in South Africa: the international with European rivals aiding and aided by the Transvaal, the local between the Transvaal and the British colonies, and that inside the Transvaal itself. The latter in particular was, as Chamberlain later recalled, 'the subject of constant conversation ... with every visitor from South Africa'.[60] At all three levels, imperial involvement sooner or later was inescapable, whether in terms of Britain's general claims to a 'sphere of influence', by direct appeal from a Colonial Government, or in respect of relations governed by the Convention of 1884 with the Transvaal, a Convention which in British eyes the Republic was now straining to the utmost. From the point of view of the Imperial Government, South Africa had been for most of the century an arena for constant indecision, failures, setbacks, and changes of policy. In the conditions of the 1890s, to a Britain increasingly unsure as to the security of her world position, the further surrender of responsibility or abandonment of long-held claims to supremacy were unthinkable; her position in South Africa at least had to be held even if it could not be turned to advantage. It is this essentially defensive frame of mind shared by British statesmen which needs to be fully appreciated; it governed their attitude to South African problems just as it did to domestic political trends. The Liberals had grown wary in 1894; and Chamberlain too, on one of the rare occasions between 1886 and 1895 when he publicly showed interest in South African affairs, exhibited signs of concern. He opposed the reappointment of Sir Hercules Robinson as High Commissioner to succeed Sir Henry Loch, as a man under the influence of Rhodes and therefore hardly likely to work for closer imperial links with South Africa.[61] It has been seen how this same defensiveness marked Conservative ministers' reactions to the Drifts Crisis; it also marked their response to the mounting German interference which was to culminate temporarily in the Kaiser's telegram congratulating Kruger on his defeat of Jameson's raiders.

Chamberlain's reaction to information about Uitlander discontent and to what he heard of Rhodes' schemes in the autumn of 1895 was of a piece with these attitudes. Within South Africa, Rhodes was simply far too powerful a man to be ignored or crossed by an Imperial Government aware of its weakness and conscious of the need for allies. Chamberlain did not like Rhodes, yet recognised that the only way to contain the effects of his schemes was to maintain an element of Imperial contact and control – sufficiently strong to give an hold over Rhodes should the impending revolution in Johannesburg prove successful, yet also fragile enough to enable Imperial innocence to be asserted should anything go awry. It was a difficult enough balance to strike, let alone to maintain, but any statesman in his position was bound to act so that, as he wrote to Salisbury on 26 December, 'If the rising is successful it ought to turn to our advantage'.[62] As Chamberlain rightly said, the British Government had done nothing to provoke trouble in the Transvaal; nor was it in any position to prevent or avoid the trouble which was brewing. At no point in Chamberlain's own exchanges or those of other officials with the Company's London representatives – Bourchier Hawksley its solicitor, Rhodes' own agent Dr Rutherfoord Harris, and Earl Grey, one of the Directors – does there seem to have been any suggestion that a refusal by him to interest himself in Rhodes' plans would cause those plans to be abandoned or the unrest in Johannesburg to cease. Such suggestions were in any case most unlikely, both for the reason that Rhodes himself was seeking to profit from the unrest that already existed, and because Rhodes' reckless abuse of power in pursuit of his own aims was already a well-established phenomenon.[63] Chamberlain had to face the possibility, if he refused to assist Rhodes, of a successful revolution in Johannesburg with which the Imperial Government had had no connection. Such an occurrence, bringing an alienated Rhodes and his allies to power in the Transvaal, would end Imperial influence in South Africa, leaving the British Government its by then irrelevant control of the Bechuanaland Protectorate and the scanty bargaining power arising from links with Natal. As the Prime Minister observed in a letter to Chamberlain on the eve of the Raid, 'It is evident that sooner or later that State [the Transvaal] must be mainly governed by Englishmen', and this raised the question of 'their relations to the British Crown or the Cape Colony'.[64] In the interest of strengthening those relations there was thus every reason for Chamberlain to go along with Rhodes as far as he felt he could legitimately or safely do so.

Underlying this desire to preserve imperial political influence were other highly practical arguments for keeping on speaking terms with the Cape Premier. Whatever Rhodes' views on the future of relations between South Africa and Britain and whatever the situation in Johannesburg, the case for economic development remained unaltered. No British statesman was unaware that the need for this development of the territories north and west of the Transvaal had been implicit in successive governments' recognition of the British South Africa Company, and that such development was the next step in the policy, pursued officially and unofficially since the late 1880s, of encircling the Republic and cutting it off from both the sea and external contacts not under British control. If the Imperial position was to be preserved in southern Africa and the economic strength of the Transvaal counterbalanced, the development of the Company's lands was vital. Even though the territory handed over to the British South Africa Company was eventually used as the jumping-off ground for Jameson's Raid, this in no way weakens those arguments which existed to support the provision of facilities by the Imperial Government to aid the construction of a railway to the north.

Concessions to Rhodes in the Bechuanaland Protectorate had been discussed for some time past, and, by the second half of 1895, offered the only immediate means of maintaining an Imperial foothold not only in the event of a successful rising and intervention in Johannesburg, but also of its postponement or failure. Lord Ripon had promised the Company imperial financial assistance with an extension of the railway to open up 'Charterland' as early as 1892. Later still, shortly before the Liberal Government's resignation in 1895, he strongly argued the case for transferring territory in the Protectorate to the Company as well. It was, he told his Cabinet colleagues, important that the British South Africa Company should be enabled to make money and survive, not least because the Imperial Government itself had 'a strong interest in maintaining the Chartered Company as a "going concern". In the event of the collapse of that company, public opinion would hardly tolerate the abandonment of the country. The Cape is not strong enough, nor would it be willing, to take it over – so that the Imperial Government would then be saddled with another, and for the time being, possibly a more expensive, Uganda.' Government support for the railway, in the shape of an imperial subsidy and the necessary land grants, offered the most effective means by which this might be assured, for without 'a railway, the difficulties of throwing mining machinery into Matabeleland are almost insuperable'.[65] Even while he opposed Robinson's appointment as High Commissioner, Chamberlain too had given his private assurance that he would not oppose Liberal moves to transfer the administration of part of the Protectorate to the Company in the interests of such a development.[66] Eighteen months later, he still believed that 'the development of Rhodesia can best be carried out by the intervention of a Chartered Company, and that Mr. Rhodes has peculiar qualifications for securing this development in the best way and at the earliest possible moment'.[67] In the autumn of 1895, therefore, influential Liberal opinion, Chamberlain's own penchant for railway building and economic expansion, the great problem of financing it from British Government sources, and the hostile attitude of the Boers to economic co-operation within South Africa, all combined to favour the presence of the British South Africa Company in the Bechuanaland Protectorate.

Rhodes, sensing his opportunity, approached Chamberlain immediately with a view to securing the administration of the Protectorate for his Company. Chamberlain, however, while immediately confirming his predecessor's approval of the annexation of the Crown Colony of Bechuanaland to Cape Colony, was less forthcoming in the question of the Protectorate. While Chamberlain wanted the development of the North, he was also determined not to weaken imperial control if he could possibly avoid it. Never one to shirk imperial responsibility, and less fearful than Liberal Ministers of a Chartered Company collapse, he was willing on the basis of his own business experience to drive a harder bargain, especially as he felt that the Company was doing less than it could to push the railway northwards. The story therefore of Chamberlain's involvement in the Bechuanaland Protectorate negotiations is far less that of direct preparations for an assault on the Transvaal, than of his attempts to extract imperial advantages from Rhodes' urgent desire to win control of the territory.

Despite the Cape Premier's pressure, Chamberlain consistently refused to part with the whole of the Protectorate. The Company's London representatives met the Colonial Secretary on three separate occasions in August, but, despite their revelation of Rhodes' Transvaal plans on the first of these occasions, failed to move Chamberlain. Rhodes therefore had to abandon his demands for the whole, and asked instead for a railway strip two miles wide and a block of land twenty miles square at Gaberones, to allow for the presence of employees, settlers, and the construction of a township.[68] Chamberlain's resources for obstruction and delay however were not exhausted, and as the Drifts Crisis came into prominence with Kruger's proclamation of 28 August threatening their closure on 1 October, the Colonial Secretary still seemed unsympathetic to Rhodes' ideas. The Colonial Office's reply, observing that the Company based its request on Lord Ripon's despatch dated 20 December 1892, pointed out that

> the promise therein set forth is made to the Bechuanaland Railway Company, and not to the Chartered Company, and [that] it does not contemplate such extensive land rights as specified in your letter, but merely land for carrying forward the line (at most two or three chains in width), besides sites for stations, sidings, workshops, yards, etc. Mr Chamberlain will at once telegraph to the High Commissioner, instructing him to use his best endeavours to obtain from the chiefs such land free of charge for the Railway Company, . . . [but] . . . As regards the larger land rights which your Company requires . . . the proper course for the Company to take is to direct its representatives . . . to approach the Native Chiefs along the line and at the terminus offering them 'reasonable inducements' to grant what is wanted.[69]

The same letter rejected the Company's request to be allowed its own police at Gaberones to protect the line and preserve order, on grounds of both legal and administrative difficulty and the fact that the question hardly seemed a pressing one.

This is not the response of a man, ardently desiring the downfall of Kruger's regime, who had seen in the outline of Rhodes' schemes the means by which it might be accomplished. It shows rather that Chamberlain's mind was fixed on driving the railway ahead, and that on the question of land grants and the Protectorate's future administration he felt no urgency or necessity for change. This same attitude had inspired his reaction a few days earlier to the news that Chiefs Khama, Sebele, and Bathoen had arrived in Cape Town en route for England to discuss the Protectorate's future. He explained that they could not be Government guests, and, it being the holiday season, that he couldn't undertake to be in London when they arrived; but he thought the visit might be useful, and certainly 'if they could postpone it till the end of November I would gladly see them'. However, it was the railway which lay uppermost in his mind, and, when later the same day, at his third meeting with Rhodes' agents, he learnt that the Company had decided to go ahead with the line at once, he again telegraphed the High Commissioner to see if he could not settle the matter of just enough land for the line with the Chiefs before their departure.[70] Other questions were still to remain for the future despite the fact that the Company desired a settlement by October.[71]

Both Rhodes and Chamberlain were, it seems, trying to outmanoeuvre each other, Rhodes making promises in order to get the territory which only the Imperial Government could give, Chamberlain doing his best to pin Rhodes down and strengthen the imperial position, feigning goodwill while trying to narrow Rhodes' freedom of action and hoping that delay might change the balance of advantage. Both for the time being needed the resources of the other and resented the element of dependence, yet each man persevered in the hope that he would come out on top in the end. It is difficult indeed to take at face value the expressions of mutual sympathy and understanding recorded in what survives of the exchanges between the Rhodesians and the Colonial Office. By the end of August, Chamberlain, now more fully aware of the difficulties of his position, was playing his cards very skilfully: relying on the fact of public concern at the prospect of Chartered Company control over the Protectorate and the Chiefs' impending visit, he was delaying progress towards a settlement in the interests of securing a better imperial bargain while conceding enough to avoid appearing unduly obstructive. However, the possibilities for manoeuvre were distinctly limited. There was, first of all, the question of the railway's route. Even if the general case for the railway to the north was overwhelming, the historian may well ask whether it had to follow the route actually negotiated, which gave Rhodes a base right on the Transvaal border from which to launch his incursion. Was there not an alternative for which Chamberlain might have pressed had he wished to keep Rhodes' men away from the Republic? The answer is almost certainly 'no'. Just as Rhodes had long been pushing Westminster to hand over the administration of the Protectorate to him, so the vision of a railway to Bulawayo was of some years' standing. Ripon's agreement of December 1892 has already been referred to, and Rhodes, in pressing his claims to the Protectorate again in 1894, argued that his policy of railway extension was based on the idea that the Protectorate 'should become a portion of the Chartered Territories. It was on account of this understanding that we undertook the extension of the railway from Kimberley to Vryburg and subsequently to Mafeking which is on the point of completion – and we are now arranging for the extension to Gaberones, with the ultimate object of reaching Palapye.'[72] North of Mafeking the line was inevitably forced to make a detour to the west to avoid the Transvaal; to take it still further westwards made no sense whatever, and would have entailed waste of time and needless extra expense both on construction and maintenance. An easterly route along the border, besides being more direct, traversed better-watered, more populous territory and took in the established administrative centre of Gaberones – all eminently sensible considerations for those naturally concerned with ease of construction, of supplies, and future settlement not least as an aid towards making the railway pay. It was of course these very attractions which had led Boer settlers to the region in years past, and now made the Tswana resent the Company's intrusion.

If from the European point of view the route of the railway was only open to diversion in matters of insignificant detail, Rhodes was also in a position to circumvent the delay arising from Chamberlain's separation of the issues of land for the line from those of land grants and administration in his 30 August despatch. Unsure whether or not the Drifts Crisis might precipitate trouble in Johannesburg, Rhodes was naturally anxious to secure his position

in advance of any such occurrence. In this he was supported by the
High Commissioner who, while as yet unacquainted with the plan
to capitalise on trouble in Johannesburg, nevertheless agreed with
Rhodes in finding Tswana resistance tiresome. 'I consider . . . that
Her Majesty's Government, have done so much for these Chiefs,
. . . [and] have the right to assume that in return for the protection
that has been accorded [since 1885], they can, with or without the
consent of the Chiefs, take such steps as may be necessary to foster
legitimate enterprise and the industrial development of a sparsely
tenanted wilderness.'[73] Not surprisingly, therefore, he strongly
backed Rhodes' decision to leave Khama, Sebele, and Bathoen for
the time being, and negotiate with other chiefs on the border both
for the transfer of administrative rights to the Company and for
land for the railway.[74]

Especially in view of his interpretation of Ripon's despatch,
Chamberlain could not now reverse his position and forbid such
negotiations. His past emphasis on the need to protect native
rights, and now Robinson's assurances that the chiefs in question,
Montshiwa and Ikaneng, were both competent and willing to make
an agreement, deprived Chamberlain of any real grounds for
rejecting the transfer, which was completed in mid-October.[75] It is
very doubtful whether Chamberlain could have avoided this
transfer to the Company, even though it was clear that Rhodes had
thereby acquired 'a "jumping-off place" even more conveniently
situated than Gaberones' in its relation to Johannesburg.[76] The
restoration of the link between railway and territorial
administration effectively give him both the right and a reason to
have his own armed police in the area concerned. Chamberlain
wanted the railway, and Rhodes had gone ahead and negotiated its
first section in a way which Chamberlain, with an eye on the public
at home, had approved in principle. If he were to obstruct Rhodes
further, he would run the serious risk of alienating him and possibly
of losing his railway. Moreover, Chamberlain had no reason which
could publicly be given for refusing to sanction the Company's
agreements with Montshiwa and Ikaneng without producing tur-
moil in South Africa detrimental to imperial interests. Finally,
Chamberlain must certainly have realised that there were other
reasons why he had to hand over territory for the railway before
any trouble occurred in Johannesburg. If Rhodes and the
Uitlanders were to fail in their attempt to bring down Kruger, then

to transfer territory and to get the railway going again at a later date might be extremely difficult. If, however, the scheme had already been officially sanctioned by the handing over of the railway strip, then, if either Rhodes or even the British South Africa Company should suffer, Chamberlain would still have grounds for urging that the Imperial Government should continue to promote the development of both the railway and the north.

If Chamberlain could now see nothing to be gained from engineering further delay, Rhodes was even more anxious for a settlement. Without the rest of the territorial strip, not only would his isolated possession in the southernmost corner of the Protectorate look slightly odd, but the presence of the required police force on the border would lack sufficient justification. Moreover, only if further territory and administrative responsibility were settled on the Company would a reduction in the numbers of the Bechuanaland Border Police and their recruitment into the Company to swell its own force be possible. Rhodes' position at least gave Chamberlain the chance to regain a certain initiative and to drive a hard bargain. The chiefs in London would come to an agreement only with the Colonial Secretary, and, with the Drifts Crisis still smouldering, Rhodes wanted a final settlement at a time compatible with his assessment of the situation in Johannesburg. Agreement was finally reached in the first week of November, and Chamberlain gained much for which he had contended from the very beginning because Rhodes gave way on several important points. He accepted the limited grant of land for the railway extension which he also undertook to begin at once; he gave up the Imperial subsidy of £200,000 towards its construction, and finally agreed to extensive native reserves still under imperial control and even within the railway strip.[77] Chamberlain for his part found a solution which pacified those both at home and in Bechuanaland who had feared the effects, after what had happened in Matabeleland, of Chartered Company administration on the non-European population; he secured the railway and future development of the territory at a considerable financial saving to the Imperial Government; and he left Rhodes with a major interest in continuing to court the favour of the imperial authorities.

Having proceeded this far with Rhodes on perfectly justifiable imperial grounds, it was certainly – given hindsight – unwise of

Chamberlain to go further and try, as he seems to have done, to influence through Rhodes the timing and outcome of any trouble in Johannesburg to suit imperial convenience. Nevertheless, his actions in this, while questionable in a way that the transfer of territory to the Company was not, are understandable when one recognises that he believed trouble certain to occur and had more reason to think that its organisers would succeed than that they would fail. Chamberlain, not surprisingly, was troubled at the weak position of the Imperial Government, at its inability to do more to influence the course of events. Suspicion of Uitlander intentions led him early in November, immediately before he transferred the border zone and the police to the Company, and again in mid-December, to require reassurances as to Rhodes' plan to hoist the British flag in the Republic after the rising.[78] The very strength of Rhodes' position, should the rising and his intervention be successful, also made it imperative that imperial authorities should be able to move in and give their whole attention to the crisis at once if it occurred. For this reason Chamberlain, one week before Christmas, gave indirect private encouragement to the plotters to get on with their scheming lest the Imperial Government's hands be full with further developments in the Venezuelan dispute that had suddenly blown up. Such preoccupations might make it difficult for Britain to appear as arbiter, and might open the way for intervention by foreign powers such as Germany.[79] In these circumstances, the risk Chamberlain took of overplaying his hand was small.

There were then sound political reasons for keeping on good terms with Rhodes, for cultivating him as a collaborator, if an untrustworthy one, on account of his own political and economic weight. There were good reasons, recognised by both parties and especially by Chamberlain, for pressing ahead with the economic development of the north – to which the railway was essential – and for settling further stages in this process in advance of any trouble in the Transvaal. There was the possibility of international complications which gave rise to Chamberlain's urge to see the British flag raised at once, and prompted him to try and influence the timing to some extent. These have been given insufficient weight in the analyses of Chamberlain's policy at this time. The main reason for this – and one which Chamberlain not unnaturally reckoned without – has been the existence and continued survival (albeit not in the original) of a series of telegrams passing between Rhodes and his associates in London in this period before the Raid. In them were described the behaviour and attitudes of the Colonial Office officials, and accounts were given of the progress of negotiations concerning Bechuanaland.

Although it is impossible here to consider these telegrams in detail, certain points need to be made, for, ever since their existence became known publicly in 1896, their interpretation has been considered central to an understanding of Chamberlain's attitude to South African affairs. Their existence has often proved an embarrassment to Chamberlain's apologists, not least his biographer Garvin, producing concealment and distortion in order to provide a defence of Chamberlain's activities. Critics hostile to Chamberlain have been aided both by the blunders of his defenders and by the exceedingly ambiguous language of the telegrams in portraying Chamberlain as totally unscrupulous and reckless in seeking the Transvaal's downfall. Indeed, it is sometimes difficult to avoid the feeling that not only has his involvement with Rhodes' plans been used to back up an hostile interpretation of his later conduct towards the Republic, but that the assumption that Chamberlain was largely responsible for provoking war in 1899 has influenced the construction put upon the telegrams, thus making the Colonial Secretary the historical victim of a vicious circle. Yet such a picture of Chamberlain's activities suffers no less from misrepresentation than that of his admirers has often done.

It has already been argued that there is a very strong case for a sympathetic understanding of Chamberlain's dilemma and behaviour in the last months of 1895. His handling of the Bechuanaland Protectorate question squares extremely well with traditional British policy, and with the new Colonial Secretary's awareness of the general conditions under which he had to operate his office. It also reflected to the full the defensive outlook with which British statesmen had come to approach South African questions by the mid-1890s. It is impossible, on the basis of evidence which shows only knowledge of Rhodes' plans and a wish to prevent the Imperial Government from being practically excluded from an effective role in South African affairs, to suggest that Chamberlain's course of action was culpably overhasty or embodied hostile motives and aggressive intentions. Certainly, when copies of the telegrams from the Company's files were shown to him in June 1896 by the British South Africa Company's solicitor in an attempt to force him to protect Rhodes and the Charter, Chamberlain recognised their superficially damning nature; it is true too that he toyed with the idea of resignation. However, it must be remembered that his first instinct was to publish them, alongside his own commentary. He only rejected this idea because 'on reflection I came to the conclusion that, although I might be able completely to satisfy the House of Commons and English public opinion, yet that the disclosure would be used by the enemies of England, both on the continent and in the Transvaal, and would seriously embarrass future action'.[80] In this he accepted the Prime Minister's view, for Salisbury, on seeing Chamberlain's memorandum setting out his defence, regretfully thought it impossible to publish – 'it touches on too many thorny questions of foreign and colonial politics. I am sorry for it – it sets out your policy in language that would be beyond cavil.'[81] His second thought, resignation, is also no confession of guilt, rather one example among many of Chamberlain's use of this tactic to clear difficulties from his path. Salisbury also refused to accept this alternative because it would have done nothing for the South African question except prompt people to believe in imperial involvement, and would have weakened the Conservative party at home.

Chamberlain's final decision, taken, it would seem, in June 1896, therefore involved partial suppression of the most seemingly incriminating telegrams and appearance at a public enquiry into the Raid to set the public record straight – an enquiry in the shape of a Select Committee of the House of Commons held eventually in the spring of 1897. Distortion and misrepresentation on both sides were the inevitable result of the course taken. For the Chartered Company after the Raid it became increasingly necessary to accentuate every shred of evidence suggesting Imperial complicity; for Chamberlain and his colleagues it meant that evidence which might in other circumstances have been openly allowed had to be neutralised lest it set critics on the path of information which had been suppressed; all parties sought red herrings aplenty.[82] It is extremely difficult, if not impossible, for any historian to know the extent to which these pressures resulted in conscious or unconscious distortion, or even at what point in time they began to make themselves felt. This raises further problems, for the bulk of the evidence associated with the telegrams – the glosses placed upon them and the additional revelations which they prompted in the documentary record – dates from after the failure of the Raid, and was therefore undoubtedly affected by just these pressures. Chamberlain's apologists, and what has for convenience been referred to as the Afrikaner school of historians, both failed to distinguish adequately between the circumstances before and at various points after the Raid; yet this is a distinction upon which it is necessary to insist for the simple reason that the nature of the evidence concerning the motives and involvement of the parties clearly varies according to the situation in which they found themselves. While Garvin's distortions are now generally acknowledged and allowed for, the more subtle bias of those who have corrected him has gone more or less unquestioned. The most recent detailed interpretations critical of Chamberlain's role rest not only, as suggested above, on a failure to appreciate sufficiently the framework of British attitudes and policy within which Chamberlain was working, but also upon a distinctly specious form of historical argument. Many of the misrepresentations by Chamberlain of his own position in 1896 and especially before the Committee of Enquiry the following year – misrepresentations inevitable given Chamberlain's choice of this third alternative – cannot be held necessarily to strengthen the case for censuring the Colonial Secretary *ab initio*.[83]

In the event, the course adopted after the Raid was an unfortunate one not just because it has created difficulties for later historians, but because it failed to quiet the suspicions of Chamberlain's critics. It was almost certainly responsible for creating more distrust of imperial policy in Dutch minds than Chamberlain's resignation would have done. Yet this failure cannot provide ground for damning Chamberlain any more than can the misrepresentations which perpetuated suspicion as to the exact nature of imperial involvement. It was rather a failure of planning, extremely difficult in the course of the Enquiry, and of simple human insight in miscalculating people's reactions, rather than a sign that a crime had been committed and had failed to pay. It was a failure that arose from Chamberlain's conviction of his own innocence in trying to resolve an extremely difficult situation, *not* from an attempt by him to cover up extensive culpability or special guilt.

It may be asked whether the Company's telegrams themselves,

or perhaps the internal correspondence of the Colonial Office – irrespective of constructions placed upon them after the Raid – are conclusive in suggesting that Chamberlain greatly exceeded anything which might reasonably be expected of a man in his position, and displayed unwarranted animus against the Transvaal. Again there are strong reasons for suggesting that they do not. A verdict of 'not proven' in this case does not rest simply on Chamberlain's own conviction that the telegrams falsified the nature and intent of his exchanges with the Chartered Company's representatives.[84] There are first, as mentioned above, the problems of interpretation such as that raised by comments on Fairfield's letter of 4 November 1895. Secondly, there is the testimony of those who had every reason to exaggerate Chamberlain's involvement. As good a definition as any of Chamberlain's position was provided by Earl Grey, committed as he was to the Rhodesian cause and responsible for having given unofficially to Chamberlain the outlines of Rhodes' plans. Writing to Hawksley in the aftermath of the Raid, he emphasised that it was extremely important to avoid

> letting Chamberlain's name come into the matter in such a way as to cause England and Europe to suppose that he had been a party to the 'job' to the degree that he will be believed to have been in it if our code ever gives up its secrets. If it does, everybody will believe that he was a much more inward conspirator than he really was, & England will in the eyes of the world be seriously discredited. As a matter of fact he has done nothing to be ashamed of. He was led to believe that the inevitable Revolution was about to take place & he very properly took precautions to ensure its success when it came about.[85]

This is a clear admission that the telegrams gravely misrepresented Chamberlain's relations or understandings with the plotters, and carries with it the implication that the Company's representatives had ulterior motives in framing them. Interpretations of the telegrams hostile to Chamberlain need therefore to be moderated in the light of the fact that the language used in them was inaccurate and exaggerated.

In addition, there is the inescapable difficulty arising from the unreliability of the surviving texts of the telegrams. It is abundantly clear from the recent discovery of different versions of some of the telegrams mentioning Chamberlain's dealings with Rhodes, that discrepancies were liable to arise in the course of enciphering and deciphering the original messages.[86] On occasion these discrepancies exaggerated the extent of Colonial Office knowledge, and obscured the nature of statements made to the British South Africa Company's agents. Although these discoveries hardly affect the *fact* of official knowledge, and the historian cannot assume that distortion or mistakes – as yet unknown – characterise the majority of the surviving telegrams, the evidence on which Chamberlain and his officials have often been attacked may be still less strong than it has occasionally been made to seem.

It is therefore clear that substantial reasons exist for suggesting that Chamberlain's role in the affairs of South Africa in the months before the Raid requires re-examination. It has been argued here that that role was much more cautious, less far-reaching in its actions and far less aggressive in intent, than has been suggested or assumed elsewhere. It is no longer disputed that some of the Colonial Office staff and Chamberlain knew far more than he – or his biographer, J. L. Garvin – was prepared to admit publicly. Yet there is still no convincing evidence for the suggestion that Chamberlain was deliberately striving to bring about the downfall of the Transvaal, through the promotion of internal revolution and armed interference from outside. With all British statesmen intent on preserving Britain's position, there is as yet no ground for assuming that Chamberlain could reasonably have acted otherwise. However, if his role in the months before the Raid was limited and South African issues played only a minor part in his general attempt to popularise the Empire, his attempt to recoup imperial losses after the Raid changed this situation out of all recognition.

V

To argue that British moves were other than defensive at this time is to misunderstand the perceptions, both of the South African situation itself and of the context within which it had to be solved, that were common to British statesmen. What was true in 1895 continued to be equally so after the new year had begun. Kruger's defeat of Jameson's raiders was applauded in a fulsome telegram to the President from the German Emperor. This occurred within a situation of increasing foreign success in areas of competition with

Britain, and hardening British attitudes. Chamberlain's reaction to the calculated insult of the Telegram was as swift and forceful as his denunciation of the Raid itself.

· I think that what is called an 'Act of Vigour' is required to soothe the wounded vanity of the nation.

It does not much matter which of our numerous foes we defy but we ought to defy someone.

I suggest a strongly worded despatch to Germany, to be published as soon as possible declaring that we will not tolerate any interference with the London Convention & will treat as an act of war any attempt to impair Art. IV to our disadvantage.

2ndly – an ostentatious order to commission some [?] ships of war & ... the immediate preparation of a force of troops for Capetown sufficient to make us masters of the situation in S. Africa.

3rd an appeal to our Colonies to complete their Naval & Military defences coupled with the offer to lend them all the money required. ... This would be most important politically. If we are the wealthiest nation in the world why should we not use our credit occasionally in an emergency like this?[87]

Even after more thought, both Salisbury and Goschen agreed with these suggestions, both by reason of the uncertainty of the Transvaal situation and the attitudes of the European powers who seemed uniformly hostile towards Britain.[88] A flying squadron was sent to Delagoa Bay. Diplomatic representations to Germany were only less forceful than they might have been because the Germans soon realised that they had overstepped the mark, and because Salisbury followed the Queen's advice to calm the situation when it became known that Germany had attempted to send troops to the Transvaal at the height of the trouble.[89]

At this time foreign criticism of Britain also gave rise to a debate on the nature of the control over Transvaal affairs which remained to Britain under the Conventions of 1881 and 1884. The German Government's view was that suzerainty had been abolished with the signing of the second Convention, leaving only the limitation in Article IV governing the ratification of agreements with foreign powers. On learning of this, Salisbury at once told Hatzfeldt 'that in our view, the preamble to the Treaty of 1881 by which the suzerainty was reserved had not been extinguished, and that the suzerainty consequently still existed'.[90] He also approved the notes for a speech by Balfour a week later – the first ministerial utterance after the Raid. It was an uncompromising statement.

A controversy has arisen between those who say that the Queen *is*, and those who say she is *not*, suzerain of the Transvaal. We need not dispute about words. The Transvaal is independent as regards *internal*, but not *external*, relations. Those are under our control. Our rights are not denied by any foreign Power, and we intend to maintain them.[91]

What is so significant here is that Salisbury, as far as one can see without prior consultation with Chamberlain,[92] felt that the Germans were attacking the 1884 London Convention, something which was moreover inseparable as far as he was concerned from the earlier Pretoria Convention. It was thus Salisbury's interpretation of the Conventions and his initiative early in 1896 which informed subsequent British policy on this central question in Anglo-Boer relations.

Whatever the various legal views on its abolition or continuance in 1884, the significance of suzerainty for Salisbury and, it would appear, for Balfour was wide and undoubted; Salisbury called it into play in response to what he saw as the cumulative attempts of the Republic and other powers to undermine Britain's position in South Africa. Exactly what Salisbury and Balfour were agreed upon, beyond a vague assertion of British rights and the intention to maintain them, is unclear. But this lack of clarity – despite the firmness of their statements – is itself revealing. Faced with the German contention that suzerainty did not exist, Salisbury, unlike Lord Derby in 1884, did not argue that the provisions of Article IV alone constituted the essence of that suzerainty. Instead he took a much more open position, asserting that suzerainty still existed because the preamble to the 1881 Convention had not been abolished. Salisbury's implication was clearly that suzerainty had some meaning beyond that specified in Article IV of the 1884 Convention; his vagueness lay in the fact that this further dimension was not defined. Balfour's statement too reflected an ambivalent attitude. At one moment he appeared to be dismissing the legal formulations of the Conventions out of hand; at the next he seemed to incline towards acceptance of Article IV as the embodiment of suzerainty. However, the conditions set out in Article IV, British control of the Transvaal's external relations, and the idea of suzerainty had still not been clearly defined or related one to the other. Both Salisbury and Balfour had left the way open for the extension of British pretensions.

By early 1896, finding itself under pressure and needing to define its rights to defend them, the British Government's awareness of a growing gap between the realities of its position and the claim to paramountcy or supremacy in South Africa became acute. Salisbury's response was intended, in the immediate circumstances, to assert the maximum legal sanction for British claims, and to preserve room for future diplomatic manoeuvre. He realised that his attempt to limit the pretensions of foreign powers and the Transvaal by dependence on an assertion of written conventional rights involved an element of retreat from an earlier, more confident *de facto* British position. This in turn led Salisbury to adopt a harder attitude towards the Transvaal than did Chamberlain throughout the rest of 1896.

For the future, however, it was Chamberlain's follow-up to his immediate repudiation of the Raid which was of particular significance. Confident of the probity of his policy before the Raid, and ignorant of the existence of the telegrams, Chamberlain had no fear for his own position when the Raid failed, and felt unhampered in considering its implications for Imperial policy. In an attempt to turn the disaster of the Raid to advantage, Chamberlain seized the opportunity to claim Imperial cognizance of the grievances of the Uitlanders. This was first done in a telegram to the High Commissioner on 4 January, in which he argued that the existence of such grievances, lying at the root of all unrest, clearly threatened the stability of South Africa; they were therefore something which could not be allowed to last, and he suggested certain directions which reform might take. Similar views were put forward again nine days later, and the evolution of the Government's position was completed in a despatch on 4 February, in which Chamberlain, following an earlier speech by Kruger, put forward his idea of a municipality for Johannesburg under Uitlander control.[93]

This is of the utmost importance, for there is no evidence for the pre-Raid period that anyone wished to take a stand on the question of Uitlander grievances in a dispute with the Transvaal, or that the Uitlanders were considered desirable or reliable imperial allies. However, in the situation created by the Raid and its failure, Chamberlain saw the importance of the grievances issue from several angles. Highlighted as they were by the Raid, grievances provided first and foremost a perfect example of the kind of question that he was in general looking for to publicise the purpose of Empire. They also offered the only apparent way of retaining the Imperial Government's grip on the immediate situation in South Africa, where an outcry against the Chartered Company, Rhodes and English interests was certain to develop. Far from grievances being adopted as an offensive move or as something which might divert attention from Imperial collusion with Rhodes, this was the most that could be done in a deteriorating situation. Grievances provided the only immediate means of self-defence for Britain in the face of Dutch reaction to the Raid, recognition of them going some way towards shifting responsibility for the present situation on to the shoulders of the Republic. However, it was also at this point that the defence of Britain's position in southern Africa was linked with the necessities of Chamberlain's education of the public in Imperial affairs; this was fortuitous, even though for the future of South Africa it was to produce grim results. By adopting the issue of grievances, Chamberlain saw the chance to create a new party in South Africa whose members might with profit look to the Imperial Government for support on issues at once close to their hearts and to their pockets. Grievances would provide him with an issue on which constant imperial intervention might be possible, thus reversing any impression that Britain was withdrawing from South Africa, and largely freeing the Imperial Government from having to rely on influencing individuals like Rhodes. Finally, in the defence of Englishmen's rights, he saw a cause which fitted ideally the requisites of his plan to find a peg on which to hang his campaign concerning the ideals of Empire. Seeing the rapidity with which he moved, it is quite possible that Chamberlain, with his thoughts running on questions of imperial publicity, took instinctively to 'grievances' even before he was able fully to analyse the effects of Rhodes' disgrace. Imperial consolidation, centralisation of initiative and control, strength through popular support and conviction in the Empire's value – thus Chamberlain's use of the grievances of the Uitlanders brought together the strands in his imperial thinking. It could not have been better if it had been planned. Yet it was a situation frought with danger, for while grievances and their remedy as propaganda required constant and simple reiteration, as a diplomatic problem involving the Boer Government the remedying of grievances demanded much more subtlety. The reasons for the triumph of the first approach to the detriment of the second, the extent to which consideration of public opinion affected the form of imperial policy, these constitute to a large extent the substance of what follows.

When Chamberlain sent his telegram on 4 January, in which he raised the issue of grievances for the first time, it seems that he believed in their reality and in the *bona fides* of the 'appeal' from Johannesburg to Jameson on behalf of their women and children. However, he was not firmly convinced of this view for long. Earlier Liberal refusal to intervene on behalf of the Uitlanders was not simply due to the fact that this was regarded as the Republic's own concern, but because, as Fairfield noted, 'We were then agreed that the agitation was fictitious to a great extent, and that all would be well if only things could be kept quiet.'[94] The Liberals had not bothered therefore to collect specific 'grievances' material, nor, it seems, had the Unionists, whereas for the native question which they had adopted, there was a definite 'atrocities bundle'.[95] Not only had material not been documented, but Chamberlain felt compelled to write to Robinson about the many mainly anonymous telegrams about grievances reaching public figures in London. 'I suspect that these telegrams may emanate from or may be instigated by a small number of persons for political purposes and with a view to prejudicing public opinion here.'[96] Immediately afterwards, on 1 February, Chamberlain even expressed to the press his disbelief in many of the allegations and complaints.[97] However, as Graham later remarked, 'it is difficult, in the face of accounts reiterated day after day, of what goes on in Johannesburg, not to believe that there is some foundation for their fears, and we should if possible avoid the imputation of sitting in armchairs thousands of miles away and not realising what is going on'.[98] Chamberlain clearly experienced the same difficulty in making up his mind, but his public behaviour was guaranteed to reinforce the idea that grievances were genuine.

Not only did official despatches endorse them – while avoiding details – but the structure of the Blue Book published on 11 February to precede the opening of Parliament emphasised them.[99] Opening with extracts from the Manifesto of the Johannesburg National Union, it closed with the 4 February despatch and an earlier despatch from Lord Ripon referring to the naturalisation and the franchise for the Uitlanders – thus giving the impression that not only had the grievances been a constant source of concern, but implying that the Boers, by their failure to give fair political treatment to the Uitlanders, had brought the Raid on their own heads. The enduring nature of such presentation can be seen from the fact that nearly four years later a writer in the *Fortnightly Review* made almost exactly these points.[100] At the same time, telegrams not only of the general kind in which Chamberlain professed to disbelieve, but which he later specifically implied were spurious, were included.[101] Others were deliberately left out in order to give more weight to grievances. From the material to be used, 'I have practically cut out all reference to Germany', wrote Chamberlain.[102] This is particularly significant, because it was the German interference which had roused most popular feeling. Sydney Buxton felt in February that Chamberlain had Germany 'on the brain', and Chamberlain himself certainly recognised the value of this focus when he advised Reginald Brett that, from Rhodes' point of view, evidence of a German–Dutch conspiracy 'would undoubtedly tend to divert the issue and share the blame'.[103] But he steered clear of this issue in public; despite the fact that, when writing to Balfour on 2 February, Chamberlain saw the 'alleged plot between the Germans and the Government of the Transvaal to oust British influence' as one object of any enquiry concerning the Raid, in the House of Commons shortly afterwards he avoided any mention of it.[104] Had Chamberlain really been unsure of himself in the aftermath of the Raid and fearful of 'discovery' as an accomplice of Rhodes, then he would have emphasised this most obvious of possible diversions. As it was, he tried to bring into prominence the very different issue of grievances.

Several additional reasons may be suggested for this slant to Chamberlain's publicity. Not only was the subject of German influence in South Africa very definitely the preserve of the Foreign Office, but foreign rivalries in South Africa could scarcely be the subject of any consistent or prolonged campaign by the Colonial Secretary. Salisbury had firm ideas about South African policy, and Cabinet control was effective. Moreover, it was important for Chamberlain that public feeling for the Empire should be placed on a firm base, not simply that of xenophobia. While anti-Boer feeling was incidentally encouraged by insistence on Uitlander grievances, the assumption of Britain's right and ability to secure redress was a much more positive conception, and its propagation

Chamberlain's root intention. The adoption of Uitlander grievances, free at this time from the later elaboration of which Milner was to make so much – that if they were left unattended, the loyalty of British South Africans and of those who looked to the Imperial Government would evaporate like dew from the Drakensberg – clearly parallels Chamberlain's earlier concern with the treatment of Africans and Indians. The defence of Englishmen's rights was an issue which would strike a sympathetic chord in the hearts of Britons at home; it was a matter of unquestionable principle, and so would be likely to secure their support for continued Imperial intervention in South Africa. From his personal point of view, all these issues had one other aspect in common. They could only be matters for the concern of the Colonial Office, matters for which Chamberlain carried personal responsibility. The successful handling of them could only secure his personal triumph, a triumph which would be recognised only if he ensured its publicity. Thus the adoption and publicity of Uitlander grievances became bound up with Chamberlain's dual intent: to awaken interest in the Empire by emphasising the aims for which it stood, and, through successful action, to strengthen his own party position. Because publicity was of over-riding concern to him, Chamberlain was happy to let the question of German rivalry in South Africa sink out of sight. Sometimes he had twinges of doubt or conscience about the line he was taking, stemming from his consciousness of the wilful distortions in the anti-Boer press, and of the Office's own lack of information. But the cry of 'grievances' was too good to be surrendered when so much was perhaps at stake. Consequently his statement to the press was half-hearted in its denial of allegations as was his action when he subsequently received the detailed reports he'd requested from the British Agent in the Republic.[105] On these latter he initially minuted 'Please consider whether these telegrams paraphrased & shortened might not be given to the Press. The statements about indignities to women etc. have never been officially contradicted & the Ashmead Bartletts accept them as gospel.'[106] But he eventually decided against any form of publication, which is scarcely surprising as he had himself given sanction to reports of 'unwarrantable indignities shown our women folk' by parading them in an earlier Blue Book.[107] Later reports on the state of Johannesburg, when they were eventually published, left the situation little clearer than before.[108]

There is certainly no doubt that Chamberlain's general motives for taking up the question of grievances were reinforced by the immediate pressures of the post-Raid period. His remark that the 'anti-Boer party here is very active, as you know', might have been made at any time in the first half of 1896.[109] Demands from Chartered Company sources pressed Chamberlain to demand reforms, while *The Times* argued that the High Commissioner's having encouraged the Uitlanders to surrender Johannesburg rather than support the Raiders placed the obligation to secure redress of grievances fairly on the Imperial Government. With Chamberlain learning that Rhodes intended to cite the state of Johannesburg and the Uitlanders in part justification of his plans, and on the assumption that he was apprehensive as to what might come to light of Colonial Office 'involvement', it has been argued that his endorsement of grievances was both an attempt at self-justification and a diversion of public interest.[110] However, these arguments are less than convincing. Chamberlain has too frequently been pictured in the aftermath of the Raid as a frightened man, trying desperately to cover up his tracks, seizing on grievances or the naval demonstration as red herrings, alternately blustering and conciliatory in an attempt either to secure a rapid diplomatic success, or at least to direct people's attention away from the Colonial Office to the Boers as those ultimately responsible for the whole unhappy situation. This explanation is, of course, a logical extension from the prior argument that Chamberlain deliberately aided and abetted Rhodes to an extent wholly incompatible with the obligations of a responsible minister. It has already been shown that this interpretation is at best questionable. Further arguments which assume it as a premise can therefore be no more firmly based, especially in view of the fact that an alternative explanation for Chamberlain's behaviour after the Raid is possible. That he should argue the force of grievances as a profitable line of policy fitted in perfectly with Chamberlan's earlier ideas, and his growing awareness of how carefully he was to be controlled within the Cabinet. Chamberlain endorsed the Uitlander grievances almost as soon as he repudiated the Raid, and some time before pressure was put on him by Rhodes and his cronies. Not until the visit of Hawksley to the Colonial Office on 4 February did Chamberlain learn even of the existence of the apparently incriminating telegrams.[111]

It would be a mistake to attribute pro-Uitlander or anti-Boer sentiments solely to the supporters of Rhodes and the Chartered Company simply because they were able to make a lot of noise. These sentiments had a far longer history, and Balfour's assertion that the conditions at Johannesburg were a disgrace which could not last reflected only the tip of the iceberg.[112] Commenting on the public feeling, Arnold Forster felt that

> On the one hand, there is the vast majority of the people of the United Kingdom, who love the Chartered Company very little, and the Boers not at all, but who do love their country and its traditions very much. And there is also that great section of the people of South Africa who would be loyal to the Empire if the Empire gave them a chance, and who are not longing for either a Dutch Republic or for a *regime* of Stock Exchange government tempered by filibustering.

Dislike of the Chartered Company, popular desire for an enquiry, and sympathy with the Boers over the matter of the Raid, went hand in hand with the fact that the 'vast majority of Englishmen have no particular love for the Boers, and are strongly of opinion that their behaviour towards Englishmen in the Transvaal has been, and is, unjust'.[113] It was to this majority above all that Chamberlain was directing his attentions in 1896 as in 1895. He intended that they too should know that the Government had not been indifferent to the situation of the British residents, that action was being taken on their behalf. At this time his continuity of purpose is further illustrated by the recirculation of papers about the British Indians in the Republic, to ensure that the Blue Book on their affairs should be up-to-date.[114] Thus the publication in the *London Gazette* on 7 February of the latest definition of the Government's position on grievances – the 4 February despatch – and the four Blue Books[115] which greeted the reassembly of Parliament were responses to a variety of needs. The most important of these, even in the wake of the Raid, was Chamberlain's wish to light on a course which would leave him a relatively free hand in the control of an imperial policy which could be used to catch the public's imagination.

IV

IN THE AFTERMATH OF THE JAMESON RAID

I

As far as the European powers were concerned, the tougher British attitude late in 1895, and her vigorous reaction to the Kruger Telegram had no marked effect on their behaviour. Penetration into the British sphere of influence increased and the attitude of Portugal towards Britain became less favourable still. Her success in temporarily pacifying the natives of Mozambique, her awareness of widespread anti-English feeling on the Continent, and delight at the discomfiture of Rhodes 'seem to have combined to create in their minds the general impression that no immediate necessity remains for courting the good offices of England, and that the study of her interests in colonial matters may now be safely subordinated to that of the wishes of other and rival nations whom it may be politic to humour'.[1] Although fully aware of the implications that German interference in the Transvaal might have for their own colony, the Portuguese showed no inclination to please England. Rather, the idea that it was her interest to stimulate foreign rivalry in the quest for concessions in Mozambique took on a more real form. The early months of 1896 saw a marked increase in attempts to obtain land grants from the Lisbon Government, and renewed efforts were made to purchase the Delagoa Bay Railway by interests with strong French connections. Of the Mozambique Company, the largest landowner in the colony, the Foreign Office learnt that the 'sympathy of the Portuguese directors is entirely in favour of France, and, though the capital is almost exclusively derived from England, the Company may be considered to be in French hands', while at the Colonial Office an eye was being kept on new financial ventures apparently backed by the French Government.[2] To a certain extent the French appeared the beneficiaries of Portuguese sympathies as a result of Anglo-German conflicts.

Other correspondence reached the Foreign Office pinpointing difficulties encountered by English investors faced with foreign rivals, and was confirmed by the British minister at Lisbon.

> It has been very difficult of late to get any Portuguese concessions handed over to Englishmen – because of the intimidation practised by the Transvaal and German Governments through their respective consular Agents ... it has been necessary to register companies abroad, and to interest foreigners in matters that would have been essentially English had it not been for the want of security which the Portuguese Government felt in granting direct on the Mozambique Coast and Delagoa Bay, ergo the Mozambique Company, the Zambezi Company, the French Distillers' Company, and others, which have had to be registered in Paris or to remain Portuguese Companies with simply agencies created in England with very limited powers.[3]

Moreover, the difficulties of obtaining concessions lay not only in gaining the initial consent of the Portuguese Government. By a Law of September 1894, all concessions had then to be presented to the Cortes for ratification – a process which gave scope for delay and interference, and kept up competition amongst speculators. Portugal faced a situation in which it was clear that her own people opposed any alienation of their rights in Africa, and that the rivalry of the Great Powers, evident in their continued representations, promised to make the ratification of concessions to non-Portuguese interests a source of trouble. Speculation, though dampened by the revival of native disturbances and government uncertainty, continued throughout 1896, and then revived markedly with the advent of a new ministry early in 1897.[4]

The news at about this time that the development of Mozambique would from now on only be put into the hands of bona-fide Portuguese companies,[5] afforded Britain little consolation. This move, while it attracted still more foreign capital into Portugal, appeared also to give a decided advantage to the French who, lacking any territorial ambition in that part of Africa had 'wisely directed their efforts to obtaining a financial and business hold on Portugal itself, in which they undoubtedly succeeded, and now find themselves in the position of imposing their own conditions upon the Government'.[6] Portugal might now be less likely to alienate her territory in a way which would infringe Britain's right of pre-emption, but her retention of a nominal sovereignty or directing interest hardly modified the effects of extensive economic development by those to whom concessions were granted. While those who provided the capital took possession of the substance, the Portuguese would retain the formal shadow and effectively remove all grounds for British protest. The staff of the Foreign Office tried to distinguish between 'speculative' and the more worrying 'political' concessions in which rival governments were interested. This did not however bring them peace of mind or allow them to be less watchful. They remained worried lest, in any case where foreign capital was involved, enterprises speculative in origin should subsequently assume greater 'political' significance. In the Commercial Department of the Foreign Office, Sir Clement Hill felt compelled to conclude his assessment of the situation on a rather doleful note.

> The air is full of rumours of concessions of all sorts in the Portuguese possessions south of the Zambezi and undoubtedly French, German, and Transvaal capital is largely interested in them, and seeking further acquisitions which may give their Governments ground for intervention in the future; but unless British capital will outbid its rivals, it is difficult to see what we can do so long as sovereign rights are not weakened.[7]

British officials' increasing concern with Portuguese behaviour closely paralleled their exasperation with the South African Republic. In both cases, legal documents were the bases for British claims, but in practice the provisions of both the Conventions and the Anglo-Portuguese treaty of 1891 were being twisted or circumvented to give other rivals an advantage. Despite the obvious weaknesses of Portugal and the Transvaal, both states continued to hold in their hands a number of cards which could be played at Britain's expense. In the case of Portugal, Britain's need to tread carefully was now even stronger than when Salisbury had held his fire in the second half of 1895. In 1896 and 1897, the Foreign Office was involved, under some domestic pressure, in prolonged negotiations with Lisbon on the subject of a new commercial agreement. One principal hope underlying these exchanges was that Britain might secure the concession of most-favoured-nation treatment in Portuguese colonies. Simultaneously, moves were in progress towards the delimitation of boundaries between the Portuguese and British territories in south-east Africa. With these additional cares, Britain was wary of anything which might turn the Portuguese still further against her. It was therefore with growing irritation that she watched others apparently benefiting either from her restraint or from her inability to intervene.

Faced with a barrage of information about concession schemes, discriminatory rail rates, and the growing volume of non-British trade, British officials began to define their attitudes more clearly. It was not simply the loss of potential commercial wealth to rivals which gave cause for concern. Always present, as Hill's memorandum showed, was the suspicion that economic gains might be sought in order to justify claims to political interest in southern Africa, or become the basis for future intervention. German and Boer activities provided ample precedents for such a conclusion. The wider aspects of this problem were summed up by Selborne in a long memorandum to the Foreign Office in March 1896,[8] and reiterated more succinctly the following October.[9] Looking forward to eventual English domination of the Transvaal through the natural process of immigration, Selborne foresaw as inevitable the creation of a United States of South Africa based on complementary regional political and economic interests. French and German intentions he argued were to destroy British dominance and encourage the formation of such a union outside the Empire, a union thus responsive to their influence and a grave source of weakness to Britain. In putting pressure on Portugal at Delagoa Bay, strengthening their economic position in Mozambique and the Transvaal, and encouraging the Republic to establish economic and diplomatic ties beyond its borders, European powers were undermining 'British influence and Empire'.

Selborne was seeking to rebut views Chamberlain had put to him shortly before. Chamberlain had thought long before that only a large immigration of English into the Transvaal could ever turn the position to Britain's advantage.[10] Yet by 1896, when just that immigration had taken place, the English seemed almost as much a threat to the Imperial Government's role as did the Dutch. 'May it not be,' he wrote, 'that a war with the Boers & their defeat would be the signal for that United States of S. Africa which would be the worst possible result for us? As long as the Transvaal threatens the Cape & Natal they will remain loyal however they may bluster.'[11] Several months before Salisbury had responded to Selborne's original memorandum in similar vein. There might, he thought, be consolation in that if 'there is a permanent strain between the S.A. Republic & the Cape Colony, there is no danger of their combining in the immediate future to set themselves up as the United States of South Africa' outside the Empire.[12] Both Salisbury and Chamberlain were primarily concerned to make the most of the here and now, rather than adopt the long perspective of Selborne. With Britain's position threatened on all sides, even the slight temporary advantage to the Imperial Government of conflicts inside South Africa was to be welcomed. Intervention at every conceivable opportunity could alone retrieve the reality of paramountcy in South Africa. However, in the long term both men accepted Selborne's main thesis and its corollary, that to forestall the creation of such a state and thereby maintain paramountcy, the Transvaal would have to be eased into a form of confederation by the Imperial Government.

II

Throughout 1896 and 1897 the most effective way of achieving this was held to be possession by Britain of Delagoa Bay. This would surround the Transvaal, and control of either the port at Lourenço Marques or the railway would enable the economic balance to be redressed in favour of Britain and the Cape. What was more, such a foothold at the Bay would provide the Imperial Government with a powerful bargaining counter in the aftermath of South African confederation. However, with little immediate hope of achieving this and continental powers apparently proof against direct British approaches, the Foreign and Colonial Offices between them evolved a different line of attack. Following the stand taken on suzerainty in January, the Foreign Office set out to insist on the strict observation of Article IV of the London Convention, informing Portugal that no further steps were to be taken in the ratification of her extradition treaty with the Transvaal.[13] Although this procedure had not been overlooked by the British Government in 1894 and 1895, its attitude was much more systematic and determined from this time onwards.[14] Thus the British Government began a policy of limiting the pretensions both of foreign powers and of the Republic by falling back on the assertion of its written conventional rights. Following Cabinet discussion in April, based on correspondence in which Kruger pressed for modification of Article IV and the substitution of a new *treaty*, this policy was developed to the full.[15] In consultation with the Foreign Office, the Colonial Office requested the Law Officers for their interpretation of Article IV in order to co-ordinate the position of both departments. Both were in complete agreement that the widest possible interpretation favouring Britain's intervention should be obtained, Chamberlain's minutes at this time closely paralleling Salisbury's earlier statements.[16] This renewed firmness was however an attempt to cover up a British retreat; whereas suzerainty was the legal and conventional expression of Britain's originally *de facto* position of paramount power, the Conventions themselves were now becoming the basis of the British position – a development comparable with British attempts to obtain written assurances from the Portuguese in 1895.

British determination to be uncompromising was only strengthened by information gathered as a result of the settled policy from March onwards of recording all German immigration into the Republic;[17] a watch was also kept on German arms exports, believed to be the source of the Transvaal's rapidly increasing armaments. It was soon learnt that Salisbury's approach to the Portuguese had been successful, the Government agreeing to abide by Article IV of the Convention.[18] The Transvaal's extradition treaty with Holland was similarly taken up in July, and an explanation demanded as to the Republic's failure to submit it to Britain.[19] Following Chamberlain's advice on this occasion, the Foreign Office, having got its way, was inclined to ignore the Boer comments. When however Chamberlain went on to suggest that that no objection should be made over the Transvaal's failure to submit its accession to the Geneva Convention for British approval, Salisbury strongly disagreed. The Transvaal was still refusing to submit its treaty with Portugal, and as far as international agreements were concerned, 'Circumstances might ... arise in which Her Majesty might become party to a treaty to which it might be contrary to Imperial interests that the South African Republic should accede; and for this reason, as well as because of their possible accession to a convention to which Her Majesty is not a party, it appears expedient that great care should be exercised to prevent the present case from serving as a precedent'.[20]

This suggests two conclusions. Chamberlain was not only wholly in step with the Cabinet, but Salisbury appears to have determined the general line of policy, and also to have intervened on questions of practical detail, being prepared to overrule Chamberlain's efforts at moderation. At the same time, the international aspects of the South African question remained of the first import to the British Government. In the Colonial Office the memorandum entitled 'Case against the South African Republic', compiled by Fiddes in July, dealt almost exclusively with the international aspects of the Transvaal's transgressions, and their continual abuse of territorial arrangements in South Africa.[21] This was a view confirmed by the Consul at Lourenço Marques, who summed up Transvaal policy as 'one of quiet acquisition aimed at undermining Great Britain's right of pre-emption should Portugal decide to sell, so that both possession and sentiment may be urged in the ear of the International Powers should ever the approach of the transfer of the Delagoa waters and port ever come to be one of the burning questions of the day'.[22] The policy which had won Swaziland for the Boers was being, it seemed, slowly applied to Mozambique.

Towards the end of the year the Colonial Defence Committee came to the conclusion that the hitherto normal garrison in Cape Town was now insufficient to defend the coaling station and the Simonstown base. When, in November, Chamberlain took up this recommendation and made proposals for troop increases, his prime diplomatic justification was that such a move would show the Imperial Government's determination to observe the *status quo* and ensure observance of the Convention.[23] There was even speculation as to whether the Boers' arming and Kruger's remarks about Rhodesia might not foreshadow a new trek.[24] Although the Cabinet decided for the moment not to go ahead with these suggestions, this implied no change in the nature of their concern about South Africa.

III

As the policy of exploiting Article IV was quietly developed during 1896, Chamberlain continued his activity on other fronts. His definition of the British Government's position on grievances was completed, as we have seen, in his despatch to Kruger on 4 February. Only three days later, while Kruger had still received only a telegraphic summary of the despatch, Chamberlain had the complete text published in the *London Gazette*. It was widely felt that this public detailing of grievances together with suggestions for a remedy left little room for future manoeuvre, and Kruger himself understandably resented the breach of diplomatic etiquette involved in this unorthodox procedure. Such reactions, while justifiable, give scant recognition to the difficulties of Chamberlain's position and the limited range of options open to him. In certain respects the 4 February despatch marked no new departure for, as Chamberlain pointed out in Parliament, reports had already been published in the press in which he had emphasised grievances as the fundamental problem.[25] In so far as Chamberlain took the opportunity to suggest that a separate municipality might provide an answer, the scope for discussion was in fact widened, for, in inviting Kruger to negotiate, Chamberlain – in line with Cabinet thinking – had definitely excluded questions relating to Article IV such as suzerainty. So much for the nature of the despatch; but the question remains as to why, even so, did Chamberlain publish contrary to accepted conventions? To seek an answer in terms of the impending Parliamentary debate, or of pressure from Rhodes as the spectre backstairs, is less than convincing.[26] For some time the Colonial Office had thought of publishing a Blue Book for Parliamentary purposes in which the despatch eventually dated 4 February would form a 'fitting close',[27] and a second isolated publication only four days earlier was therefore unnecessary. Moreover, whatever Hawksley and Rhodes may have said when they visited the Colonial Office on 4 and 6 February, Chamberlain had his own very good reason for publishing the despatch just then.

Even though at this time he was sceptical of some reports from Johannesburg, Chamberlain felt that there were many real grievances and, for the reasons already set out, it was vital that the British public should realise this. However, to make sure of this was no easy task. For many people, sympathy with Jameson was allied with disgust at the Uitlanders' refusal to help him; many others were more concerned with the Chartered Company, either to defend it or to demand withdrawal of its Charter and to deny the reality of grievances as a justification for the Raid. Even after the appearance of both the Despatch and the Blue Books, Buxton was surprised at how much more even the House of Commons seemed to care for the Chartered Company than for the 'far more important' question of the Uitlanders.[28] In these circumstances, the

news that Chamberlain received on 4 February from Robinson[29] –
that the 'save our women and children' invitation to Jameson,
published in *The Times*, was never sent from Johannesburg at all –
was grave. It was certain to become widely known before long,
could only confirm belief in a Chartered Company plot, and would
further undermine confidence in reports of Uitlander grievances.
Full public endorsement of grievances might go some way to
prevent this, and in effect play down the whole question of German
involvement of which Chamberlain was acutely conscious at this
time.[30] Thus publication of the 4 February despatch was important
in Chamberlain's view for its effect on the public at large, and it also
served – not that advertisement was needed – to draw attention to
the Blue Book in which it appeared a few days later. Although
official endorsement of grievances inevitably aided Rhodes, it is
not at all clear that pressure from Company sources was a factor in
Chamberlain's decision to publish, and even less can it be shown
that Chamberlain was attempting to protect Rhodes and himself by
confusing the British public with a fine red herring.

The success of Chamberlain's moves was plain when the
Commons came to debate the recent events; speakers generally
praised the Colonial Secretary's actions, acknowledged the reality
of grievances, and demanded an enquiry into the Chartered
Company's administration. Labouchere recognised Chamberlain's
clear understanding of the problems, and 'was glad to see that,
while the Colonial Secretary was prepared to do his best to remedy
whatever grievances these people had, he had not allowed these
grievances to be dragged as a red herring across his path, not to be
diverted by them from standing to the views he had expressed in
regard to the recent raid'.[31] Buxton talked of the 'moral right' of the
Government 'to intervene in regard to the Uitlander question . . .
on a friendly basis', and gave his support to their policy.[32] Balfour
endorsed the idea of a municipality for the Rand, and saw
justification in that 'the action of my right hon. Friend in doing his
best to introduce what is called the Imperial factor into this
controversy is not only approved by the English subjects in the
Transvaal, but by the English and Dutch population in other parts of
South Africa'.[33] This turn of debate was encouraged by reticence on
other matters. For Harcourt, Salisbury's statement that the
Transvaal had appealed to foreign powers for help was 'the most
material matter in this whole controversy', but his demands for

evidence were rebuffed by Balfour. Similarly Curzon declined to give information about Portugal's refusal to allow German troops to pass through Delagoa Bay to the Transvaal.[34]

This debate reflected very much the shape of things to come. It established the already clear division between the line which the Foreign Office and Cabinet adopted in their discussions on South Africa, and the question of grievances which Chamberlain was making his own. The former was obviously not to be the focal point of discussion on South Africa amongst MPs, even though it was only in mid-1899 that grievances came to the centre of Government policy. Here too, however, Balfour had provided a pointer to the future by his admission that grievances had brought the Imperial factor back into the picture. Such had been the impact of Chamberlain's general handling of the Raid crisis, that MPs began to look to him alone for a forceful policy. Gibson Bowles criticised what he thought had been Cabinet interference with the construction of the 4 February despatch, and J. M. Maclean expressed his conviction that Chamberlain would prevent the Transvaal being 'made a nursery that could be used by continental powers to destroy our interests in Africa'.[35] Chamberlain's campaign at both the general and the personal level was beginning to have its effect.

IV

Chamberlain was aware that the naval demonstration in January had met little response from the powers in South Africa, and was of course acquainted with the line of attack being worked out in conjunction with the Foreign Office. In these circumstances, and supported by a favourable atmosphere in Parliament, Chamberlain felt able to be equally tough in his direct dealings with Kruger. It is this which explains his increasingly belligerent attitude in March and April as he tried to get Kruger to Britain for negotiations. His first attempt to regain the initiative at the diplomatic level had of course been his taking up of grievances immediately after the Raid. This failed, owing to Robinson's refusal to raise this question with the Boers at that moment, and so Chamberlain tried again, sending an invitation to Kruger to visit London.[36] This second phase of his post-Raid policy was destined however to meet no greater success,

owing this time to Kruger's insistence that no official discussion of
Uitlander grievances was possible, and his desire that the London
Convention be replaced by a treaty. Robinson too remained
convinced, and had a considerable weight of South African
opinion to support him, that matters should be left to cool down of
their own accord.[37] Chamberlain was exasperated with what he felt
were the delaying and obstructive tactics of the Boers, and the
constant refusal of his High Commissioner to press Kruger to
negotiate. His own political position, South Africa, and the Empire,
all he felt demanded continued activity and a solution as quickly as
possible; otherwise the situation, from a British point of view,
would deteriorate beyond recall.

This combined sense of urgency and frustration led Chamberlain
late in March 1896 to talk of war with the Transvaal. Talk of war
however did not imply that actual war was conceived either as the
next or even a likely step.[38] Rumours circulated to the effect that
Chamberlain was thinking of an ultimatum, but at no point did the
Colonial Secretary himself use such a term. Despite his annoyance
with Robinson, he constantly asserted that he did not believe that
there would be war, and thought 'at the present time we have no
reason – either of right or interest – which would justify the
enterprise'. But, he added, 'Kruger will not be wise if he dismisses
the possibility . . . – or assumes that if it came the result will be
favourable to him.'[39] This particular comment was provoked by
what Chamberlain thought was Fairfield's erroneous comparison
of 1896 with the situation in 1881, rather than by Chamberlain's own
contemplation of war. At the same time, historical parallels, as far as
South Africa was concerned, were never far below the surface in
the minds of British politicians, and particularly so with
Chamberlain who as a member of the Liberal Cabinet of 1880–5 had
had a special responsibility for South African questions.

With memories of 1880, of the Warren expedition, and the Drifts
crisis, Chamberlain – along with many other people – was
convinced that the Boers would only move in his direction under
pressure; if even the illusion of pressure could be created, then
Kruger might come to meet him. Reasoning thus, Chamberlain
showed that there was yet another role for 'public opinion' to play
in defence of imperial interests. Writing to Robinson in March, he
referred to his attempts to keep an angry public opinion in check,
the intention being to suggest to Kruger that by immediate

negotiations he would achieve better terms than if Chamberlain were later forced to bow to public expectations; 'complications . . . will certainly result if an early attempt is not made to come to an agreement with Her Majesty's Government'.[40] So sensitive to public criticism himself, Chamberlain often tended to assume that other statesmen were similarly affected. The Colonial Secretary's moves to increase the South African garrison at this time were intended to strengthen the same impression, but he never thought of war as a reality which might stem from any action of his own. Chamberlain had faith in such an approach because he was very conscious of the difference between his own position, and that of those who, for whatever motive, advocated forceful intervention in the Republic's internal affairs. He explained himself to Fairfield:

> I quite understand the little game [of the war party]. But I do not mean to carry out a policy for the benefit of these gentry and I entirely agree that we have no *casus belli* at present. . . . I do not think it wise however to explain this to [sic] the housetops & I do not mind the noisy exultations of the Jingo party, since it does not commit me & *may* put some pressure on the people in the Transvaal who are afraid of war.[41]

Unfortunately, this view of the well-meaning role of the British Government or, more particularly, of Chamberlain, was not held anywhere in South Africa, despite Chamberlain's public discouragement of those pressing him to intervene.[42] The Transvaal Government, distrusting Britain of old and now hoping for foreign support, feeling itself both aggrieved yet wholly in the right and in a strong moral position, resolutely refused to acknowledge any British claims to intervene or advise. Episodes like the publication of the 4 February despatch had, however mistakenly, only strengthened the impression in Dutch minds that the Imperial Government was involved with the Jameson fiasco, Rhodes, and the Chartered Company. This distrust was also shared by British officials on the spot, and this lack of sympathy between Downing Street and Cape Town only made it more difficult for Chamberlain to understand how his actions were regarded in South Africa. Robinson, it was thought at home, did not keep the Colonial Office in touch with South African feelings.[43] Moreover, to those in South Africa, the suggestion that the British Government could not keep a section of its public in check was hardly convincing in the light of Chamberlain's own earlier attempt to give a lead on grievances.

Thus although his original proposals had made some impression at Pretoria, Chamberlain's subsequent tactics were insufficient to make Kruger unsure of his ground, with the result that the idea of an immediate conference was abandoned in April.[44]

Chamberlain undoubtedly learnt from this second failure to bring grievances to the fore, but it was a lesson in tactics alone and resulted in no change of aim. He reasserted in his speeches his intention to do all in his power to obtain redress of grievances.[45] But he was never again to rely on the noisy state of a sector of British public opinion. Instead, pressure would be maintained by Chamberlain's taking a clear public stand to an even greater degree, pushing for reform and attempting to lead public opinion in the same way. Government policy was to continue, using 'every legitimate means, especially . . . the pressure of public opinion in South Africa'. While thus again defending his action early in February, Chamberlain now went still further and openly committed himself to a policy of continued publication. 'Much', he said, 'must depend – and this is the real crux of the situation – upon the drift of Dutch public opinion in the Cape Colony, in the Transvaal, and in the Orange Free State, with regard to the position of the Uitlanders.'[46] All governments, not just Chamberlain's own, had problems with their own public opinion, which Chamberlain felt could be influenced from outside as well as led from within. What was more, the two-way importance of sentiment and understanding in the imperial relationship – especially if this was to become a closer one – meant that Chamberlain's propaganda had a dual role. First and foremost, it was the home audience with whom he was concerned, but colonial opinion needed to be cultivated as well if imperial consolidation was ultimately to be the order of the day as Chamberlain hoped. The Uitlander question was of some import in a purely South African context, but its handling was governed by its adaptation as a peg on which to hang a campaign for Empire.

In view of the fact that many of those matters which had deflected public attention away from grievances were now losing their attraction, Chamberlain's reaffirmation is scarcely surprising. Outside the Foreign and Colonial Offices, the awareness of foreign interference was subsiding by the middle of 1896; the trials of Jameson and the Johannesburg reformers would be finished before long; and concern with the Chartered Company was likely to ease, pending the Parliamentary Enquiry, which already promised to be long delayed. In its widest sense the 'public opinion' to be educated included everyone not wholly behind Chamberlain. His general object was to make any opposition to the political consolidation and economic development of the Empire as small and as silent as possible. The extent of this public with which he was concerned, and the degree of unanimity he desired to achieve are unparalleled in the activities of earlier statesmen. With regard to South Africa, it was his intention to show that the imperial presence was necessary to the preservation of civilised government, that in South Africa the values on which the Empire rested were at stake. Chamberlain was doubtless aware that others were thinking on the same lines as he was, for on 1 May the formation of the (later Imperial) South African Association was announced. Perhaps this in itself was illustrative of the success which Chamberlain's approach and policy had so far achieved, if one may go by its billing in The Times, for the Colonial Secretary seems to have had no links at any stage with the Association's origins or development.

> Objects: to uphold British supremacy and to promote the interests of British subjects in South Africa, with full recognition of colonial self-government. Methods: The work of the association will consist in placing before the country the fullest information upon the political, commercial, and other questions which affect the various peoples and communities in South Africa. This work will be performed by the publication and distribution of pamphlets and leaflets, and by organizing public meetings. These meetings will be addressed by speakers either personally acquainted with South African affairs, or who have made them the subject of their special study. The operations of the Association will be strictly confined within the limits laid down, so that, whilst incidentally giving its support to the policy set forth in Mr Chamberlain's despatches and speeches, its main work will be educational work throughout the country.[47]

With headquarters in Westminster, the association included the usual quota of titled personages and a large number – nineteen – of back-bench MPs on its organising committe, and in the first year of its life appears to have held 130 meetings or lectures all over the country. Its audiences were put at some 50,000 people, and 150,000 pieces of literature were distributed.[48]

V

In these circumstances, the first fruits of Chamberlain's tactical change were apparent even before the Commons Debate of May 1896. On 30 April, immediately upon Kruger's reception of the Government's withdrawal of their invitation to a conference, a Blue Book was presented to the House.[49] This contained not only the exchanges on the subject of Kruger's visit, but also a long section on the surrender of Johannesburg in January and the trial of the reformers, terminating with the news that a penalty other than death was being considered for the ringleaders. Again the latest telegram in it was dated 30 April, the day of presentation in the Commons, in order to convey the impression of frankness and spontaneity. Although in its final form the Blue Book was not available from the printers until 8 May, the day of the debate, it illustrates the importance which Chamberlain attached to the timing of his publicity. Moreover, appearing as it did before the final result of the reformers' trial was known,[50] it served to revive the acrimonious public debate on those subjects, with the widespread resentment of what was felt to have been Boer sharp practice over the surrender and maltreatment of the prisoners. That the two sets of correspondence were put together implied that Boer obstruction also lay behind the failure of Kruger to visit Britain, and Chamberlain was setting precedent after precedent in his publication of official correspondence, not only on negotiations which had failed but also on questions still very much under consideration.

With the exception of Chamberlain's own speech, the May debate itself contained little of particular importance. References to foreign intrigues still appeared, almost no mention was made of the failure of the conference moves, and the Chartered Company was variously attacked or defended. Over grievances, opinion was divided as to their reality and, even if real, as to whether they were matters for the consideration of the British Government.[51] Clearly, if a campaign attached to grievances was to be successful in the ways Chamberlain wished, there was much to be done. In his despatches on the grievances question, he had pointed to the treatment of the Uitlanders as the source of unrest throughout South Africa, and therefore as something with which Britain as paramount power was concerned. Now, responding to the tone of the debate, he suggested that British concern with grievances might also put an end to foreign interference. In 'a crisis like the present, when our authority in South Africa has been shaken by our own subjects, and when it is universally believed in South Africa itself that our authority is being undermined from outside – (Hear, hear!) – I say, under those circumstances we are bound to pay some attention to the views of that section of the population who, at all events, are well wishers to the British rule'.[52] Reform in the Transvaal was clearly portrayed as the fundamental problem, and to earlier arguments was now added the idea that intervention would secure loyalty; publicity had led to yet another twist in the British case. To his declaration of intent to work with public opinion, and this attempt to turn discussion towards the desired object, Chamberlain added a third point. He roundly condemned those who talked of ultimatums and war, thus publicly stating views the essence of which he had earlier expressed to Fairfield.[53] The war-party had now outlived even its earlier limited usefulness. In other words, the principles by which Chamberlain was guided in his handling of the South African issue had remained constant. They were, first, the importance, indeed the necessity, of public opinion as an element in diplomacy – for which purpose guidance by selective publication or careful speech-making was necessary. Secondly, there was the constant emphasis on the redress of Uitlander grievances, considered important as a policy issue, as a fit subject for a diplomatic method involving public opinion, and once of personal benefit to Chamberlain in that he would control it. Finally, the question of foreign intrigues had to be played down, although of the utmost concern, because it was unsuitable in these foregoing respects.

In declaring his intentions to the Commons regarding opinion and publication, Chamberlain was on relatively safe ground, and had met very little criticism. Publication of the 4 February despatch had attracted some sarcasm from Rosebery, and Lord Stanmore recalled some of Lord Salisbury's 'very weighty words with regard to the increased danger and risk which, in these days of rapid communication and universal publication, attends ill-considered and intemperate speeches with regard to foreign affairs'.[54] Privately, Ripon, while unsure of the effect of this particular publication on Kruger, thought it might be all right from a Parliamentary point of view.[55] Publicly at least, only Harcourt seemed annoyed. 'Half the mischief in the world is done by these documents – whether Dispatches or leading articles – which are written for home consumption.'[56] On this occasion Balfour leapt – as fast as one so languid was able – to the Colonial Secretary's defence, drawing attention to the widespread approval of the publication; he felt that in the interests of consistency one could hardly say to the press, 'We are now going to put you on starvation allowance as to what the Government policy is.'[57] The press itself was inclined to agree. The *Quarterly Review*, commenting on the fears 'that a consistent foreign policy is now impossible in England', approved the recent signs of popular interest and enthusiasm.

> There is every reason to believe that they [the British people] will adopt and vigorously prosecute a foreign policy which is made clear and intelligible to them; but the statesmen who formulate it must be perfectly frank with their countrymen, and resist the temptation, for the sake of a momentary advantage in Parliament, to have recourse to quibble, chicanery and intrigue.[58]

Elsewhere the cry was that 'Education in the large citizenship of the Empire must be made to reach all classes and conditions of men', while Westminster ought to show itself as 'a centre of Imperial knowledge'.[59]

With time, the attitude towards what Chamberlain called his attempt 'to diplomatise on new methods'[60] became one of general acquiescence. Certainly no one appeared to disagree with George Wyndham's general defence of the practice. 'Public despatches', he argued, 'were not printed for private circulation only. . . . They should be put before the people of this country that they might be seized of existing facts in South Africa, so that when the Government of the day announced their policy the people of this country might be in a position to pronounce upon it.'[61] It was a fair statement of Chamberlain's intentions, and in fact Chamberlain's style of diplomacy came under fire only late in 1899, as the Opposition cast around to find the causes of the war. Although some of Chamberlain's speeches in the summer of 1899 provoked criticism, the Liberals were constantly willing to accept the publication of material by the Colonial Office, their position out of power denying them many official sources of information. Even when in disagreement with Chamberlain's policy, opponents tended to see his open diplomacy as a saving grace. Munro Ferguson, for example, in April 1897 criticised Chamberlain's handling of the crisis, but thought it 'some consolation to know that Mr Chamberlain was the author of his own diplomacy. It was an open diplomacy in which murder must out.'[62]

VI

In 1896 however, diplomacy using the grievances issue was subject to difficulties which did not hamper the pressing home of failures under Article IV. Individual grievances had in the past been less systematically watched, and, despite Chamberlain's intention to publicise them, he was faced for the time being with an embarrassing lack of detailed information. This had to be remedied before a really coherent policy of publication could be evolved to support direct Colonial Office pressure on the Boers. In the meantime however, there were still ways of counteracting the effects of this deficiency. Particular exchanges of despatches might be released to the press. Towards the end of May, for example, when the acting High Commissioner telegraphed information as to the shocking accommodation of the reform prisoners, Chamberlain wanted it published immediately. 'Publicity may shame the Boers into decency – in any case it will tend to provoke indignation at the Cape & elsewhere.'[63] After all, Robinson had recently told Chamberlain that public opinion was an influence to which Kruger was 'not insensible'.[64] More for the benefit of the home public was the Blue Book published towards the end of July,[65] dealing with the commandeering of British subjects by the Boers for military service. This developed a point Chamberlain had tried to make in an earlier publication, that the grievances of Uitlanders had a long pre-Raid history, and illustrated even more clearly the petty or uncooperative attitudes of the Boers which had been so marked in the previous Blue Book. Furthermore, even if one felt that most grievances did not warrant imperial intervention, the commandeering question was likely to be seen as an exception to the general rule.[66]

The construction of this Blue Book showed how careful the Colonial Office was to give the appearance of being open, while avoiding any topics which might weaken their case for grievances. Following the usual practice regarding the business of former administrations, Fairfield wrote to ask Ripon if he had any objection to the full publication of Loch's description of the troubles at Johannesburg two years previously. He continued

> In these days of preternatural suspicion we dare not publish an extract as Labby [H. Labouchere, MP], who was the man who moved for the paper, would say that the omitted part contained filibustering matter. I don't think that the Transvaal can well object to the tone of the despatch so far as it relates to the grievances, and the rest is complimentary to them.[67]

Thus this Blue Book was to give the same impression as had Chamberlain in April, when 'although the Government do not think that the present is the most convenient time, they will be perfectly ready to put down the Colonial Vote for discussion at an early date'.[68] The Colonial Secretary's willingness sprang from his conviction that a debate or carefully constructed Blue Book could effectively focus argument and discussion on certain issues. So when Ripon replied to Fairfield assenting to the publication of Loch's despatch, but expressing doubt about his own reply to it, if that was also to be published, he found that the Under-Secretary had the matter in hand.

> Your reply to Loch . . . goes not only into the question of Suzerainty, but refers to the very awkward fact that the Cape Govt refused to amend their Commandeering Law as to . . . tally with what we were asking the Transvaal to do. We have cut out all reference to this. Therefore at most only an extract from our letter could be published.[69]

Eventually nothing of this reply appeared. However, as Fairfield noted, this would not leave a careful reader wondering as to the British Government's reaction to Loch's success in negotiating a settlement, for 'you will notice that in the proof of the small Parliamentary Paper, a telegram no. 17 p. 13 is to be published in which you congratulate Loch on his success'.[70] The final touch was the inclusion of a long report of a Uitlander National Union meeting to discuss grievances, after the commandeering negotiations had ended. This set out a long list of particular grievances, and a defence of the character and serious intentions of the Uitlanders which included (of special importance in Chamberlain's eyes in 1896) a disclaimer of any association between Rhodesian finance and their agitation.[71]

The fact that his own case for Uitlander grievances concided so with the Chartered Company and Rhodesian appeal to grievances as a justification for the Raid was one of Chamberlain's biggest problems. It was also a dilemma which Chamberlain must have known full well could only be at all resolved once the British Parliamentary Enquiry into the Raid had been held. In the meantime, the issues would be chewed over by various protagonists. Knowing that he had hardly enough material to carry through a clearly differentiated line of his own, Chamberlain let his policy of publication fall into temporary abeyance after the end of the Parliamentary session on 14 August. He had toyed momentarily with the idea of publishing by itself evidence of Boer discrimination against British trade, thus incidentally showing how the grievances issue was capable of extension, but for the time being decided against it.[72] Of course, Chamberlain, like any other Cabinet Minister, did not give his whole time and attention to South Africa or any other single issue. However, knowing that there were writers in the country prepared to follow lines close to his own without prompting,[73] aware that his propaganda campaign was well off the ground, and knowing that bodies like the South African Association were at work,[74] Chamberlain was able to turn to other things with a quiet mind.

VII

It is convenient at this point, having shown the extent of Chamberlain's concern with publicity, to consider further Chamberlain's attitude to the press, and the connection which he saw between the various aspects of his attempts to form a definite public opinion. During the Liberal administration of 1892–5, the natural exclusiveness and reticence of most nineteenth-century civil servants was reinforced by Ripon's and Buxton's attempts to keep the Colonial Office as quiet as possible, both for their own benefit and for that of the party as a whole. Official preference for peace and quiet here coincided with political expediency, since even at its best Liberal colonial policy was liable to excite Tory critics. Chamberlain's arrival brought changes, not least those necessitated by his policy of actively promoting links between the colonies and Great Britain which contributed much to the vast increase in the volume of work in the late 1890s.[75] That such changes could be satisfactorily brought about in bad physical conditions while Chamberlain maintained his popularity with the Office staff – as one of his private secretaries states was the case – says much for his capabilities.[76]

On questions of publicity, Chamberlain's attitude coincided to a certain extent with those held by his staff. By nature he was sceptical of the intentions of the press, and, although ready to use it if any clear advantage was to be gained and if he controlled exactly what was to be published, most approaches from journalistic sources, hostile or sympathetic, met with rebuff. Early in 1896, when offered an introduction to the London Correspondent [sic] of Die Volksstem, Chamberlain minuted 'I am in mortal terror of Correspts of Papers who report interviews with statesmen & accordingly declined with thanks.'[77] This was not just a temporary attitude, for the next year, in answer to the request for an interview from an Austrian paper, he replied, 'Certainly not. It is my invariable rule to decline all interviews for publication.'[78] Organisations received much the same treatment as individuals. Reluctance characterised Chamberlain's response to the founding of the Foreign Press Association; even though both the Foreign and Colonial Offices sent representatives to its foundation dinner, this seems to have constituted little more than lip-service to the Association's professed aim to create better understanding of British foreign policy, rather than a positive gesture of goodwill.[79] More significant was the proposal by Reuter for much closer links between itself and the Colonial Office: in return for a £500 subsidy each year, its services throughout the Empire would be improved. The response to this was governed by the Office's distrust of Reuter in South Africa. Selborne thought that, generally speaking, it was a proposal 'not lightly to be rejected', but 'Caution is, however, necessary. We know that no Reuter's telegram emanates from the S.A.R. until it has been approved by the State Secretary's Office. Should we subsidize an agency so dependent & so much the tool of those we have to contend with?' Edward Wingfield was not keen, and Chamberlain finally decided

> I do not like this proposal. The only way in which I think we could enter into special relations with Reuter would be if we wanted fuller Reports of Speeches or Documents sent to the colonies or elsewhere, than they would forward in the customary course of their business.
> But this must be a matter for special arrangement at the time. For

the present I think we must civilly decline their offer.[80]

Clearly all initiatives in publicity were to come from the Colonial Office or from Chamberlain personally, the general assumption being that attack was the best means of defence, a philosophy peculiarly Chamberlain's own in respect of publication. One of the reasons for such an attitude was that the press was traditionally looked upon as a source of information supplementing official reports, and in this capacity, particularly with respect to South Africa, it had been found wanting. The reports of Reuter's Agency in South Africa were distrusted even early in 1895, and criticism of their connection with the Boers was a frequent characteristic of Office minutes thereafter.[81] Even when they were not factually wrong, they were thought to be no less misleading. 'The plain truth is that the SAR Government through Reuters agency pursues a policy of encouraging the belief that the Govt. intend to give reforms . . .',[82] was the view expressed early in 1897, and echoed by the rest of the staff.[83] Similar criticisms were made of the *Daily Telegraph* correspondent in Pretoria who, it later appeared, was the same person as Reuter's agent.[84]

There are examples of equal scepticism about the value of reports from anti-Boer sources, but these were made almost without exception by Edward Fairfield who retired from the headship of the South African department towards the end of 1896. Early in that year he wrote, 'As to what Sir H[ercules] R[obinson] knows of public opinion here, I have heard that what the Press agencies are cabling out is practically the Anti-Boer side of English opinion', and it was clear that he had little respect for what he called 'the "Reptile" Evening Press, in the pay of the Kaffir Circus'.[85] In 1899 however, Lambert thought fit to comment 'It is quite clear . . . that the news agencies are being worked by SAR for all they are worth (Reuters have not yet taken up the *Daily Mail* challenge I think).'[86] For him all the bias lay with the other side, despite the fact that there is much evidence to suggest that the influence of anti-Boer forces over the press had by then greatly increased.[87] Fairfield's scepticism was the product of long experience, many contacts and much personal knowledge of British involvements in South Africa; his retirement was as a result a great loss to the Colonial Office. Both he and Sir Robert Meade, who retired at about the same time, were representatives of an older generation of civil servant; experience had taught them something of the inwardness of things South African, making them more ready to wait upon events. None of their younger brethren ever criticised Chamberlain in the same way, or showed much willingness to question the value of sources of information, journalistic or otherwise, if critical of the Boers.[88] The particular significance of this tendency among the younger members of the Office, together with their appreciation of a strong and vigorous Minister, lies in the fact that it reinforced Chamberlain's own disposition to advertise his own policy.[89] Generally, it meant that Chamberlain pursued his own South African policy, and was influenced only in comparatively minor ways by the views of his staff.

Whether or not they were critical of the press as a source of information, the Colonial Office staff were not infrequently forced to conclude that even the English press at home was better informed than they were on events in South Africa. When cuttings from the *Morning Post* and the *Cape Times* concerning Boer defences arrived in April 1896, they caused a stir. Fiddes was prompted to observe 'It is so difficult to get information from S. Africa that I think before telegraphing again we had better see what we can do here',[90] and Selborne approached the paper in question to see if he could glean more on the matter. Similarly, newspaper reports were often fuller than telegrams from officials. In certain exceptional cases *The Times'* reports, notably of Jameson's trial and the proceedings of the South African Committee of Enquiry, were kept in lieu of an official report, and *The Times'* account of the Reform Committee trial enabled Fairfield to construct a day-by-day record for future reference. Later on, the same paper helped the Office to understand the workings of the controversial Immigration Law.[91]

However, this passage of information was a two-way process, and as might be expected, the Colonial Office was very careful about what it released. Occasionally, the Office made statements which it considered were purely in the public interest, a practice which Chamberlain seems to have adopted instinctively. Following a letter in the *St James Gazette* in 1895 about the claims of the Chartered Company in Bechuanaland, he minuted 'The pretensions of the Kanya Co. are unfounded. ... It is desirable if possible to counteract the efforts of Company Promoters to get support (whether English or Foreign) for rotten concessions.' As these two companies were engaged in a legal dispute, the Colonial Office was unable to intervene, but, added Fairfield, 'I think an active policy of contradicting positive lies would always be useful. We have smashed up two or three bad swindles in this way in past years.'[92]

Another practice which Chamberlain and his staff adopted, albeit under some pressure, was the publication of telegrams at times of emergency. For some weeks after the Jameson Raid, a sequence of the official telegrams passing between England and South Africa was issued, in order to show what the Government was doing to ease the tense situation. At the same time, lists of those engaged in the Raid and the names of the dead and wounded were systematically published, but even so the Colonial Office found itself swamped with enquiries. In the absence of expressions of opinion on the exact reasoning which lay behind this spate of publication at such a hectic time, it seems likely that the intention was to fend off inquisitive reporters and to calm the public temper. Yet even in this way the Office was not wholly successful, since the lists of the Transvaal's prisoners were given only to *The Times* and not to the Press Associaton for general distribution. Similarly with the announcement of the mobilisation of the flying squadron on 8 January, an oversight which led to Salisbury's receipt of a strong protest from the owner of the *Morning Post*.[93] Calming the public temper was certainly the object early in February 1896 when Robinson's reports on improvements in the treatment of the Raid prisoners were immediately given to the press; a later telegram was similarly withheld, because, in Fairfield's opinion, the 'matter has dropped out of public notice'.[94]

Such a practice was infrequent, but occurred on two later occasions, during the sittings of the South African Committee in 1897, and shortly before the outbreak of war. Then, the motive was significantly different, and represented a definite extension of the limits within which publication in the press was thought justified. At moments of tension and great difficulty it was occasionally felt necessary to see that the British point of view reached a wide audience; yet orthodox methods like Blue Books or speeches, or wholly unofficial contacts with individual journalists, were not always adequate. Then releases to the press were the only possibility. This putting over of one's own side of the case was often aided by requests for advice from papers sympathetic to the Government.

March 1896 found Chamberlain answering questions from the editor of the *Daily Telegraph*, regarding the Government's attitude on matters for discussion should Kruger visit England, and on Jameson's surrender.[95] Similarly in August 1899, the editor of the *Standard* asked for guidance concerning the Smuts franchise proposals, the substance of which were still publicly unknown. In addition to his secretary's confidential statement, Chamberlain suggested

> I think we might hold the following language to any members of the Press to whom we are in the habit of speaking confidentially.
>
> 'That the ways of the Boer are peculiar & that as we have been taken in before . . . we are unable to say whether the latest proposals offer a satisfactory basis of settlement. But there is no doubt that they are a substantial advance on previous proposals & it appears to me that the Boers are dying *by inches* & that we may fairly hope to get them down gradually to our terms. But it must not be supposed that all danger is past yet.'[96]

This was certainly sent to S. H. Jeyes, and to Flora Shaw of *The Times*. The growth of these habitual contacts between certain newspapers and the Colonial Office, carefully limited though they were, is a distinct feature of the period 1895–9. At a time when the Foreign Office was becoming still more doubtful of the value of any such contacts,[97] the Colonial Office was exploiting them for the first time. The nature of Miss Shaw's connections with the Office, particularly during the pre-Raid period, has long been a subject of discussion. These are of less importance in themselves than for the fact that they continued when Frederick Graham was head of the South African department, despite interruption by her expedition to the Klondyke in 1898. There is no doubt that the Office staff here felt themselves on sure ground. Material on maladministration in the Republic was provided for the Office's use, and her articles were open to its influence.[98] On one occasion in 1899, after Milner had forwarded a report of a speech by State Secretary Reitz which the Office thought inflammatory, Graham suggested that Miss Shaw should take up both the speech and the book on which it was based. Chamberlain agreed, as did Selborne with the comment 'Yes. Surely the *Times* will use it.'[99] At the same time officials took care to see that such links were in no way allowed to deteriorate, apparently communicating, at least with *The Times*, in person rather than via the Press Association.[100] Cultivation of the paper's support in Whitehall was infinitely more subtle than that of the South African parallel between Milner and Monypenny, but none the less real.

Although the evidence is thus very fragmentary, it seems to lead to the conclusion that the Colonial Office, under Chamberlain's prompting, showed in its handling of publicity in the newspaper press an increasingly attentive attitude towards public opinion. Chamberlain's broad intention to keep people informed resulted in a strong tendency to try and ensure, as circumstances in South Africa altered, that the public were given the 'right' view of the situation. Nevertheless, he always recognised that such a goal could never be pursued through the use of the press alone. While anxious to inform people, Chamberlain also recognised that the more frequently papers became vehicles for disseminating official views, the less adequately they reflected or influenced the public viewpoint. The Colonial office kept a close eye on the press; the historian hears none of those slightly ostentatious confessions that one 'never read the papers', at this time one of the common hallmarks of members of the ruling classes. Moreover, while journalists and editors cultivated their official contacts, they were anxious to maintain their independence of officialdom. A distinct pride was taken in this independence which so differentiated English journalism from much of continental practice. The result was, as suggested above, that direct contacts between the Colonial Office and the press were essentially sporadic. Again it must be stressed that this does not mean that Chamberlain's consideration of public opinion at large was inconsistent even if it was often careless of detail or ill-defined. Recognising the value of approval and support freely given, Chamberlain devoted himself above all to the open explanation of his policy in the House of Commons, a practice which served two objects. His speeches and Blue Books were designed for the Commons both with the intention of making South African policy quite clear as part of his energetic handling of Imperial affairs, and for the purpose of consolidating in his favour the party support which he felt he needed. The essence of these Parliamentary proceedings and publications was then distilled for the benefit of the public at large by the press, a function of which the importance was clear especially in 1899, when Blue Books were published during the Parliamentary recess. Thus publicity and the press played an important and consistent role in Chamberlain's treatment of South African questions. In the normal course of events, he relied upon the press to provide the general background of South African news, and from time to time to convey the Colonial Secretary's personal statements, given in the Commons or in other public speeches, to their wider audience. Direct approaches to the press of the kind outlined above were moves designed to meet more immediate situations which the less flexible methods of Parliamentary speaking or publishing were ill-suited to manage.

V

FROM THE CRISIS OF APRIL 1897 TO GRAAFF REINET

I

It was an unavoidable result of Chamberlain's attempt to marry diplomacy with publicity that certain issues would become progressively simplified, and that others would be abandoned altogether if their further elaboration seemed likely to cause embarrassment. That the treatment of Indians and Africans in the Transvaal was subject to considerations of this kind became clear towards the end of 1896. These had figured prominently in Chamberlain's early indictments of Boer behaviour, and consequently he was alarmed at the constant attempts of the Natal Government to pass legislation involving overt discrimination against Indians on the ground of their colour. As he explained to Governor Hutchinson, it 'is very difficult to argue with President Kruger about the grievances of the Uitlanders while we treat our visitors with so little confidence'.[1] It was but a different version of the conflict with the Cape Government over its Commandeering Law during the earlier dispute with the Boers. There was, however, again little that the British Government felt able to do in the face of Natal's determination, except insist on racially neutral forms of legislation, which the Colony might then administer in a discriminatory fashion.[2] At the same time, Fairfield concluded that it would be useless to espouse the cause of the Africans in the Transvaal without simultaneously attacking the policy of the Chartered Company. Yet if the Colonial Office were to do this, especially while the Matabele War was in full swing, 'we should offend the most rabid anti-Boer in the country as much as the Boers themselves'.[3] It would also have been unwise from an imperial point of view to give the British public yet another stick with which to beat the Chartered Company while it still suffered from hostility arising out of the Raid. The Colonial Office grew more and more aware of the risk of uniting South African opinion against the Imperial Government on the native question, and when early in

1897 they realised the further danger of destroying confidence in the Government's impartiality at home, the case for abandoning the non-white populations, at least in public debate, became overwhelming. Although in May Chamberlain said that the Government was watching non-white affairs closely, this was his last positive reference to the matter until after the outbreak of war in October 1899.

Office minutes throw some light on reasons for the prolonged silence. Considering the Africans in both Rhodesia and the Transvaal, Graham drew the following conclusion.

> The wrong doing of the Company and its officials in Matabeleland is no justification for (often worse) wrong-doing in the S.A.R. . . . But I fear the game is not worth the candle. The S.A.R. Govt take very good care not to openly infringe the very vague provision of Article XIX of the London Convention and we shall never get decent treatment for the natives of the S.A.R. without at least a threat of force. And the native question is unfortunately one on which we could not count on support in So. Africa. The Dutch we should have against us, and even the British would be indifferent. Unless some very flagrant case again arises . . . I think we had better leave the matter alone.[4]

Evidence being given to the South African Committee which was then in session did not help matters, and Selborne expressed his fear 'that the revelation of what has been going on in Rhodesia will be bad possibly very bad. Therefore certainly we can make no representation at present.'[5] No imperialist wished to have exposed the hollowness of favourite myths, and the British public, still in process of being 'educated', would be unlikely to dismiss maltreatment of Africans as 'merely the surf that marks the edge of the advancing waves of civilization'.[6] Chamberlain agreed with his staff, and advised Milner – by then the new High Commissioner at Cape Town – that nothing was to be gained by taking up the native question again just then.[7]

Nothing could have been more complete than Chamberlain's change of front on these issues. In February 1897, Fairfield had warned against the effects of his using the Indian issue as a *casus belli*,[8] and by May the staff were anxious not to raise the matter at all with the Boers. Later that year, Chamberlain even undertook to 'moderate and guide' British public opinion on the native question, about which 'it is so often ill-informed'.[9] Following this, Graham even wanted to prevent the publication of an ISAA pamphlet on the subject, lest pressure be put on the Government to intervene on behalf of the Africans. In the event, Chamberlain agreed with Wingfield's more confident feelings, that 'it will do no harm to expose the views of the S.A.R. Govt. and H.M.Gt. is strong enough to resist any pressure . . . to take up the cause of the natives without a legal pretext'. As Selborne lamented, 'we are really hopelessly handicapped in the protection of the Transvaal blacks by what has gone on in Rhodesia and the Cape Colony'.[10] Thereafter, the prospect of Members of Parliament even raising questions of African well-being caused concern inside the Colonial Office, and Wingfield thanked his lucky stars that at least 'the champions of the Indians are not very formidable in the House of Commons'.[11] The native question was only officially resurrected after war broke out in 1899. Then the Office staff debated whether or not to publish correspondence on Boer native administration,[12] and Chamberlain claimed in the House of Commons that although native grievances had not been mentioned in Blue Books or in debate, they were very real. Although an assertion with much truth in it, in this case it was deservedly squashed by the Irish Nationalist, John Dillon, as 'a reason which was thought of at the last minute, in order to bring within the war party large sections of philanthropic but ignorant people in this country who know nothing at all about it'.[13]

The Indians fared a little better at the Colonial Office, hardly on account of support from the Government of India but rather because they had greater propaganda value. Chamberlain felt able to take up the case of the 'respectable Indian', 'as a means between S. African opinion & the claims of H.M's Indian subjects, championed by the India Office, for complete equality'. Championing the cause of such fortunate souls might 'show up the S.A.R. government once more as lacking in courtesy and intent on evading its obligations and therefore incapable of being trusted or negotiated with by anybody under the sun'.[14] As far as most Indians in South Africa were concerned, the Imperial Government had well and truly sold the pass, in more ways than one, and was now interested simply in the contribution of the Indian question to the total effect of the grievances campaign.

II

As the interests of the non-white populations were allowed to fade from sight, so it was more important for Chamberlain to document in detail white grievances. During the autumn and winter of 1896–7, the Republic passed laws dealing with Alien Immigration, Aliens' Expulsion, and the Press. On all these, Chamberlain chose to take issue with the Boers on the grounds that they constituted, by either nature or application, breaches of the London Convention. It has often been suggested that in the Colonial Office everything the Boers did was suspected of hiding an anti-British motive, but this highly critical attitude and stringent interpretation of the Convention sprang from a defensive frame of mind common throughout British governing circles and beyond. The behaviour of the Transvaal and European rivals generated a conviction that Britain's standing in southern Africa was being undermined, and determination to rescue Britain's position of supremacy affected the approach of all officials to little things as to great. When Meade sent to the Foreign Office a text of the Immigration Law with the Law Officers' opinion that a violation of the Convention had occurred, Bertie automatically assumed that the 'law as passed will no doubt be applied in a manner discriminating against intending British immigrants'. 'Would it not be sufficient for our purposes', he went on, 'if we could get the law reduced to whatever proportions are intended for application here against the admittance of destitute aliens?' Salisbury did not dissent from Bertie's initial point, and further thought that objections to the Immigration Law could not affect immigration legislation of Britain's own in any way. He argued that 'a Convention between a suzerain and a dependent Power is not *eiusdem generis* with a Treaty between two independent Powers. Therefore any signification we assign to its provisions cannot affect the interpretation to which we would submit in construing a treaty of the latter class.'[15] The Foreign Office dealt with the matter at once, and as Salisbury clearly agreed with Chamberlain that the Law Officers' misgivings were unwarranted, the official reply instructed the Colonial Office to proceed with the protest; the advantages would outweigh any problems with Britain's own Aliens Bill. Protest was considered both reasonable and best suited to Britain's interests.[16]

Nothing happened at this time which might have softened the British Government's attitude to the Transvaal. Against the background of continued uncertainty as to Portuguese intentions and further German interference,[17] it was learnt that the Boers were pressing the Portuguese to ignore Article IV by submitting the extradition treaty to ratification by the Cortes.[18] Shortly afterwards, news arrived from Britain's new Agent at Pretoria, Conyngham Greene, of the Boer Executive Council's policy resolution:

> To elicit all they could from England and to temporize and then to decide how to answer her 'requests'. They saw no reason for altering their policy but resolved to continue on the same lines, since they were strong enough to do this; and, in the meantime, instructions should be given to Beelaerts [Transvaal diplomatic representative in Europe] to sound friendly Powers in Europe, and in case the South African Republic should be obliged to resist her [Britain's] 'preposterous' demands to gather what attitude they would take.[19]

MacDonell had already reported strong rumours of fresh concessions in Mozambique to agents working on behalf of Germany and the Transvaal, and Greene confirmed that German plans were afoot to develop the Eiffe-Katembe concession near Lourenço Marques as a German naval station, and base for Transvaal steamships manned by German seamen. Germany had moreover advised the Republic to continue protesting over Amatongaland, and when the news of the Republic's discussions with the Orange Free State on the question of a defensive alliance was received, it was noted that one of the conditions embodied therein was the occupation of Lourenço Marques in case of need.[20]

Quite apart from the fact that the South African question could not be at the front of Chamberlain's mind twenty-four hours a day, exchanges in progress with the Republic and the change of British Agent in Pretoria made further progress in defining the British Government's attitude towards the question of grievances rather difficult at this time. But Chamberlain let no possible chance escape. At the opening of the new Parliamentary session, although no place was found in the Queen's Speech for South African affairs, Chamberlain, in moving for the re-appointment of the Committee of Enquiry into the Raid, commented on the continued lack of reforms in the Transvaal and stressed the need for the Select Committee to investigate the reality of grievances in connection with the Raid's origins.[21] This insistence reflected not only his own belief that the wider the scope of the Enquiry, the less mischief it might do,[22] but also embodied an assumption voiced by a number of MPs who criticised the setting up of any enquiry when clearly

Uitlander grievances lay at the root of things.[23] In this way Chamberlain combined response to a section in the House and the country with a suggestion that would further his own ends. Chamberlain had known for some six months that the telegrams in the Chartered Company's possession would be a liability from both the Government's and his own point of view if they came to light publicly, even if he was confident in his own mind that he could explain them. He also wished to avoid any possibility of the Select Committee's proceedings recreating the conditions of January and February 1896, when discussion had tended to focus on the Chartered Company and the personalities involved. If grievances were lost sight of, much of Chamberlain's work in the past year would have to be redone.

III

During the lull in events at the turn of the year, some in the Colonial Office chafed at the sense of inaction. Selborne, nursing grandiose visions and ever impetuous, hoped that 'it is known in S. Africa, that it has been leaked out in fact, that we are upholding our rights' in the matter of the Aliens legislation.[24] But Chamberlain's own public assertion that 'up to the present time, the response of President Kruger and of the Transvaal Government has, to say the least of it, been inadequate'[25] involved no personal venting of hostility. He knew well the Cabinet's attitude to the Aliens legislation, and Ministers' determination that the Convention breaches should be brought to an end. When the Boer reply to Chamberlain's representations on the Immigration Law arrived on 15 February, rejecting all suggestions that their recent legislation breached the Convention, it provoked even greater firmness all round. A resolute reply was necessary, and in order to reinforce the impact on public opinion, Chamberlain now conceived the idea of sending two despatches, one dealing with the Immigration Law again, the other setting out the range of Boer attempts to evade their obligations.[26] This was duly done, and the two despatches were presented to Kruger on 15 April.

The extent of the Cabinet's concern at Boer obduracy is illustrated in its decision, shortly before 13 March, to send a force of ships to Delagoa Bay in support of the despatches. As Chamberlain wrote to Green, 'I am unwilling, as at present advised to send out reinforcements of troops, because such might have a provocative effect. . . . Accordingly the Government have decided as an alternative . . . to arrange for a considerable force of ships . . . to rendezvous . . . at Delagoa Bay. . . .'[27] Although he appears to have supported it, there is no evidence that Chamberlain actually proposed this naval demonstration, and he clearly opposed the sending of troops which seems to have been suggested, in this adhering to his attitude as expressed the previous December.[28] Evidently, however, others in the Cabinet were not prepared to sit still, and decided on a move at once less provocative than the movement of troops and yet designed to kill two birds with one stone: Transvaal intransigence and foreign pretensions. For the benefit of Britain's European rivals, it was intended to repeat the message implied in the despatch of the flying squadron of January 1896. A message was sent for Green to deliver to Kruger when presenting the other despatches; this stated that

> Her Majesty's Government had been considering how it might be possible to demonstrate their determination to maintain their rights in their integrity to the Transvaal Government. They had accordingly decided that a considerable force of ships, larger than any they had ever before had in these waters, should rendezvous at Durban and then at Delagoa Bay, thereby indicating their intention to all the world of preserving the status quo in that place.[29]

Salisbury and Goschen had toyed with the idea of such a demonstration late in 1896. On that occasion it had been dropped, although early in the new year the Prime Minister had persuaded the Admiralty not only to station a warship at Delagoa Bay, but also 'that whenever there is a German Ship of War there, the British force should always be superior to the German'. Now the Cabinet decided to put the earlier idea into practice.[30] In the event, both the French and German governments saw British moves in the same light as the flying squadron of the previous year, as indeed did *The Times*.[31] But the Transvaal, it was argued, being acquainted with the true inwardness of things, would relate the demonstration both to its foreign intrigues and to the despatches received at the same time.

Foreseeing something of the Cabinet's determination when faced with the Boer reply, Chamberlain intended that it should be backed by public understanding and approval. 'The time is coming when further papers should be presented to Parlt.', he reminded his subordinates shortly after the reply had arrived. Selborne stressed that 'One object should be that it [their next despatch] shall, when published, carry with it public opinion at home and in South Africa'.[32] Any failure now to stand firm would be fatal. 'Great Britain would be considered by Germany & France, by the Dutch S. African republics, and by our own colonies, to have abdicated from her position of paramount power. Public opinion, certainly in the Unionist party, at home would take the same view and the Government would suffer severely in the public estimation', was his view a little later.[33] In these years, it was a notable characteristic of Selborne to be *plus royaliste que le roi*. Without the cares attaching to official responsibility which Chamberlain himself shouldered, Selborne was always there to keep his chief up to the mark, whether or not Chamberlain himself showed any signs of relaxing the line he had taken from the beginning.

On this occasion, however, Chamberlain's own actions bear comparison at almost every point with those in the corresponding period of 1896. Again there were rumours that he was contemplating an ultimatum, and again neither Chamberlain nor his staff considered such a possibility. As he explained to Greene, his policy was 'to maintain the peace until time and the increase of the British population gradually bring about a solution'.[34] Now, as in the previous year, he felt that there was no case sufficient 'to justify extreme measures.' The one aspect which did differ was the role of public opinion. In 1896 he had depended on giving the impression that the Government might have to follow a bellicose public opinion if Kruger were not forthcoming with reforms; moreover, he had felt able to take the initiative with the publication of his 4 February despatch. This time, however, Chamberlain recognised the problem posed for him by the quieter mood of the public, and his inability to give a lead in advance. 'I desire to publish as early as I possibly can but I suppose that it would be impossible to do so, after our last experience, until this despatch has been delivd.', he wrote.[35] It was far from his intention to annoy Kruger a second time with a breach of diplomatic good manners.

This situation reinforced his desire not to provoke the Boers, and so he reluctantly supported the naval demonstration. However, further reflection brought with it doubt as to the effects of the demonstration. Officials inside and outside the Colonial Office stressed the risk of loss to British prestige should the move fail, and Chamberlain, never really sure that Kruger would draw the right conclusion,[36] eventually overcame his scruples against sending troops. Other Cabinet members appeared to be having similar doubts, for when Chamberlain called a meeting to discuss the question, Balfour, Goschen, and – surprisingly – Hicks Beach agreed that a force 'should be sent chiefly for political reasons'. No one quite knew how the Boers would react. 'None of us believe the Boers would take the offensive, . . . [but] none of us can deny that it is possible.'[37] As Selborne had suggested to Chamberlain there was always the possibility that legitimate British complaints under the Convention, together with growing internal criticism, might drive the advisers of the Boer Government to suggest war as a way out of their embarrassments.[38] Pressure on Kruger therefore had to be such that he would have all illusions destroyed, and back down without considering force, as it was felt from past experience the Boers might do.

In other words, the Cabinet and Chamberlain, far from wishing to force a war, were more fearful of the Boers provoking one, and piled on the pressure in order to remove all possibility of an armed conflict. Chamberlain now felt that increasing the troops now – in line with the Defence Committee's recommendation the previous November – would also reassure loyalist opinion in South Africa, which had just made itself strongly felt by protests against what it considered disparaging comment given as evidence to the South Africa Select Committee.[39] The only person who appeared to disagree was Lord Lansdowne, but for reasons which in no way weaken the argument. Content to wait and see what would be achieved by the naval demonstration, he wrote 'I confess I should have thought it better to leave matters alone, & to send an ultimatum followed by an overwhelming force when the moment for putting our foot down had arrived.'[40] Later, when discussing the actual tactics of reinforcement, Lansdowne favoured sending the troops to Natal rather than more distant stations. 'The occupation of Laing's Nek would be a very provocative demarche and might precipitate a collision. I confess however that I do not see how we are to intimidate Kruger without provoking him, & I would prefer to risk the provocation rather than adopt trivial and meaningless measures elsewhere.'[41] Balfour, while in agreement at the meeting, later expressed the view that it was 'a nice point whether the sending out of 3000 or 4000 men will prove a sedative or a stimulant'. But he was prepared to admit that Chamberlain's methods might be the best, and like Lansdowne did not for one moment question the necessity of dealing with South Africa in some way; resolute government might serve for the Boers as well as the Irish.[42] Certainly this episode showed the whole Cabinet convinced of the value of firmness in South Africa, and of the opinion that a stop had to be put to the behaviour of the Transvaal.

IV

Chamberlain, however, was still unhappy, and as further illustration of his belief in the important role of public opinion, went back upon his earlier decision to wait until the despatches had reached Pretoria before publishing. On 12 April, three days before Kruger received them, the latest correspondence was presented to the House of Commons. This timing reflected a notable compromise. In presenting the papers just before the House (and therefore the Select Committee on South Africa) adjourned for a fortnight, Chamberlain gave notice of these despatches while Members were still at Westminster. The final release of the Blue Book did not occur until 24 April, to allow for the delivery of the despatches and their final printing.[43] Nevertheless, it still appeared within the recess period which ensured it the maximum attention in the political columns of the press, and avoided the possibility of immediate criticism or awkward questions from MPs. At the same time, it appeared soon enough to make its impact in advance of Boer reaction. Two months earlier, Chamberlain had said in the Commons that he would lay this correspondence when it was 'terminated', and on 2 March, while exphasising that it was still incomplete, stated that it would be laid when the time arrived for doing so.[44] While the Government might consider the correspondence 'terminated' by their demand that the Immigration Law be repealed, the whole affair was in no way yet finished; and in no sense was there any earlier statement committing Chamberlain to publish when he did. The final advertisement of the British Government's stand came in public speeches. Chamberlain took the first possible occasion, which happened to be the farewell dinner to the new High Commissioner for South Africa, Sir Alfred Milner, and so made a speech widely considered rather out of place, even if it indicated where his priorities lay.[45] On 11 May news arrived that the Boers had given way on the legislation in dispute.

The conclusions drawn from this outcome of the confrontation over the Aliens legislation was that the only language the Boers understood was a determined, uncompromising one. It also confirmed the widely held belief that given sufficient evidence of British determination to use force if the need arose, the Boers would undoubtedly retreat. No longer would the Transvaal be trusted with that inch which might enable it to take the proverbial mile. This crisis, like that of 1896, also showed the dangers inherent in Chamberlain's approach to negotiation. Anxious to carry the public with him, he was unable to countenance much of the delay or inactivity which under normal circumstances gave time for reflection, for the appearance of the unexpected alternative. Publication and definition of the stand taken at the earliest opportunity inevitably made him appear far more precipitate and intemperate than he was, and more so than would have been the case with a more discreet mode of approach. Of course, publication of Boer despatches might have its uses in keeping the Boers to their word, in preventing any of the backsliding for which they were thought notorious. In practice, however, it was with the British stand that Chamberlain was almost exclusively concerned in these first years of the conflict. Boer hostility to the English was assumed by almost all British officials, and in questions affecting the Uitlanders the Boers had already been judged and found wanting; new thought and judgements were not required. It was scarcely easier to pin them down on this question than on many others where they were acting with less than due regard for British interests, but this was the issue with which, Chamberlain had decided, Imperial activity in southern Africa was to be identified for the instruction of the public. In many ways it was the striving for, rather than the achievement of, the goal, from which Chamberlain felt the real benefits to the imperial cause were derived, in the education in the aims of Empire which it provided for many people. In 1897, the point had not been reached when propaganda was in danger of losing its effectiveness for lack of results. Indeed, the Boer retreat could be construed as a partial victory for imperial determination; certainly its effect was in the long run to spur

Chamberlain, and his colleagues both in the Colonial Office and the Cabinet, on to greater efforts. In the meantime, Boer mistrust grew and Republican attitudes hardened still further.

On other occasions in 1897, Chamberlain, feeling it less important to choose his moment, appeared as willing as possible to supply demands in the House for information,[46] and published when he could. Hearing that despatches relating to the Drifts Crisis had been asked for at the Cape, Chamberlain suggested getting 'a friendly questioner to ask me for the same papers here & lay on the Table immediately'. A question was duly asked by a Liberal Unionist a few days later, and the papers published on 4 May to coincide with the Debate in the Cape Parliament.[47] These, by illustrating the Boer attitude on a question well prior to the Raid and unconnected with grievances, and coinciding with the Republic's repeal of the Immigration Law, again only emphasised the widespread impression that the Boers were naturally recalcitrant and would give way under pressure. This Blue Book was devoted to the one subject, but this was not Chamberlain's invariable practice. That which had appeared three weeks before, as well as setting out the British Government's arguments concerning the breaches of the Convention, contained material on the operation of the Immigration and Press Laws, monopolies in the Republic, and the incivility of Boer officials. Although this correspondence was presented chronologically with no attempt at special emphasis, *The Times* for example drew attention to the instances of Uitlander disabilities, and even the *Manchester Guardian's* critical report of what it considered 'a record of petty disputes' served to keep the issues to the fore.[48]

Throughout this period, the Select Committee on South Africa – of which Chamberlain was a member – was enquiring into the Jameson Raid, and to an extent this too was turned to the Colonial Secretary's purpose of elaborating on the nature and reality of Uitlander grievances. One opportunity arose when W. P. Schreiner remarked in evidence on the absence of pro-imperial sentiment and loyalty among the British in South Africa. This was vehemently repudiated by telegrams from every part of the country, all of which were passed to the Chairman of the Committee and selected ones given to the press. In response to Fiddes who was pressing for the release of one from the South African League, Graham reminded him that the 'telegram from the Mayor of Port Elizabeth was the only one hitherto given to the Press. But it contained the views of a public meeting of the inhabitants, and expressed confidence in H.M. Govt. It was therefore a special case.' He further thought that some of the telegrams would get into the papers anyway. Chamberlain added 'I agree. We cannot give any kind of official sanction to telegrams of this kind. (A Town meeting with the Mayor in the Chair is a different thing) But I should be glad if they got into the Papers unofficially for what they are worth.'[49] Every little helped, and in fact Chamberlain's hopes were fulfilled. A report of the South African League's protest was printed in The Times, whose own correspondent also cabled that there would be a series of protest meetings. Where further press reports duplicated telegrams being received at the Colonial Office, the staff were content to let them suffice; others akin to that from Port Elizabeth they sent for publication.[50] The idea was to ensure that the British public was not misled by Schreiner's picture, and to show that instead many South Africans supported the British Government – an important consideration when the naval demonstration at Delagoa Bay was being prepared.

Schreiner's comments on Uitlander grievances also provoked strong protest, this time from the Uitlander Education Council on the Rand, which Chamberlain thought of special importance. However, he agreed with Just's observation that it would not accord with earlier practice to give it to the press. It would, thought Chamberlain, be possible instead to arrange a question in Parliament, but this would depend on the effect of future witnesses before the Select Committee.[51] As no question was later raised, Chamberlain was apparently satisfied with the discussion at least of this particular point. That he was so owed much to his own questions to one of the Reformers, Lionel Phillips, which extracted the maximum of information about the effect of the Boer Government's restrictions.[52] Indeed Chamberlain could be well satisfied with the whole grievances issue as discussed by the Committee. The idea of a German conspiracy was effectively dismissed, and grievances, having been the other main plank in Rhodes' attempt to justify the plans of 1895, therefore had much time devoted to them. The final report of the Committee, while refusing to allow that they in any way excused Rhodes' or Jameson's actions, endorsed the point that Chamberlain had been trying to establish: that the complaints of the Uitlanders were a real cause of great discontent, and local agitation over a period of years before the Raid had failed to achieve any improvement. Chamberlain had done what he could with his own questioning of witnesses to bring about such a result, and the Committee's conclusion was as much as he could reasonably have hoped for.[53]

V

While Chamberlain remained anxious about public understanding of South Africa's significance, events in other quarters were taking another turn. Despite the hard line taken by the Cabinet in March and April, their discussions then marked the beginnings of a change which was to affect the attitudes of the majority towards South African policy well into the summer of 1899. Salisbury, conscious of the continuing hostility of the European powers, began to question the wisdom of forceful action in southern Africa, especially when, after fifteen months, British pressure seemed to have achieved very little. In the midst of the Cabinet exchanges on the troop increases, he learnt of the hostile French reaction to the naval manoeuvres at the Bay.[54] This made it clear to him that a forward policy in South Africa, far from advancing or at least protecting the British position, might jeopardise it there and elsewhere. Writing to Chamberlain, Salisbury, while accepting his views on the bad image of British policy in the eyes of the colonial loyalists, urged upon him that a Transvaal war 'will have a reaction on European politics which may be very pernicious'.[55] More specifically he told Lansdowne that

we should become intensely unpopular in Holland if we took any action against them [the Transvaal] of which complaint could fairly be made. But just at this time I dread great unpopularity in the Netherlands. In the next year or two the young Queen of Holland will probably be married. If she marries anyone under the Emperor William's influence, the Germans will get out of the Dutch some form of *Kriegs Verein* which may enable them to man their fleet with Dutch sailors. His great ambition is to have a fleet, but until he gets a maritime population he cannot have a fleet. Some control over Holland is very necessary to him.

I am much struck by Monson's account ... of the very strong feeling that would be aroused against us in France if we took action against the Transvaal. Any adventurous policy in that direction would turn a vast amount of European opinion against us.[56]

Moreover, it seemed that British action had revived ideas of a Franco-German rapprochement to put pressure on Britain in Egypt, and Hatzfeldt in conversation with Sanderson strongly defended the Boer position.[57] Two days after this talk with Hatzfeldt, came yet more bad news; not only were the Boers continuing negotiation with the French for a line of steamers, but the French and German consuls had both advised the South African Republic not to yield to British demands over breaches of the Convention.[58] At this point Chamberlain suggested to Salisbury that he try to resolve matters by direct representations to the German Government, saying that, although Britain intended to maintain her rights, she had no designs on the Transvaal's independence; similarly to the French, to them adding that Britain's policy would in fact benefit their commercial interests. This was clearly a compromise solution, and shows how the British Government was being slowly pushed into a state of indecision. Salisbury partially adopted the idea, advising Monson that if he was approached by the French he should feel at liberty to use the Colonial Office argument, though not otherwise.[59]

The naval demonstration also adversely affected relations with Portugal. Following the initiative of London financiers in January, the British Government, still intent on bolstering up Portugal, had tried to win over the Portuguese Government by supporting fresh proposals for a loan.[60] Although contacts made slow progress, by mid-March more confidence in a positive outcome existed than had done for a long time,[61] despite reports of growing French influence in the country. However, Portuguese suspicion of Britain was revived by the naval presence,[62] and, despite Chamberlain's cordial interviews with the Ambassador, Soveral, they eventually concluded that French offers of a loan were more attractive.[63]

The British Government's position was an extremely difficult one. The Portuguese were still weak and vacillating. Whereas in late 1895 this had been one of the circumstances prompting Salisbury to adopt an uncompromising line in southern Africa, in the hope that Portugal would thereby realise that her interests would be best protected by association with Britain, by mid-1897 he was in no mood to court the Portuguese. Irritated by their reaction to the naval demonstration and by the failure of all attempts to make them stand firm, he ceased to worry about Portuguese feelings; 'I think we injure our nerves by unnecessary solicitude on this point', he remarked.[64] But he still felt sufficiently concerned to protest to Lisbon about the growing pressure inside the country for the sale of her colonies.[65] On the other hand, despite retreat over the Aliens legislation, on other questions of concern to the Foreign Office the Boers remained as unrepentant as ever. The Republic's shareholding in the Mozambique Company was increased, and Dr Leyds, after smooth utterances in England, visited Lisbon to negotiate the further extension of the Eiffe-Katembe concession, for which his Government and German capitalists were prepared to provide considerable capital.[66] Kruger's own speech to a secret meeting of the Volksraad showed how additional support for Leyds' activities was expected from an alliance with the Orange Free State. By negotiating European treaties through their neighbour, 'We shall then settle our affairs, internal and foreign, without British intervention; in fact under the present Convention, we shall have what is unquestionably our right, and with the concurrence of the European nations, a voice in securing proper administration in Delagoa Bay, our own port.'[67] Salisbury's unease at the European reaction to British moves in the spring reflected his belief that good relations between the European powers were of prime importance; the possibility therefore arose that in certain circumstances a compromise on South African questions might be reached in the interests of these good relations. For the moment however, as his instructions to Monson showed, the Foreign Secretary was still confident enough in Britain's strength to wait for an approach from France or even Germany. While he was now prepared to forgo 'any adventurous policy', his earlier staunch defence of British claims he felt precluded direct advances to other powers in the manner suggested by Chamberlain.

VI

A change of pace was also necessitated at this time by the final retirement of Sir Hercules Robinson, now Lord Rosmead, and the appointment of his successor. Naturally Milner had to be given time to settle in and make himself fully acquainted with the world at Cape Town. Moreover, such was Milner's prestige and so great the welcome from all sides which met his appointment, that any sudden moves from the Colonial Office at this moment would have been felt tactless in the extreme. Doubtless Chamberlain had an eye to the popularity of Milner's appointment when he decided on it, but it was left for Selborne to voice what so many felt. 'There I verily believe we have the best man in the British Empire for the toughest job in the British Empire', he wrote.[68] No one gave a thought to the possibility that Milner's training and experience might have been wholly unsuited for equipping him to deal with the Boers, not to mention the self-governing colonists. A man with his views on democracy as practised at Westminster was scarcely one to dissent from the general assumption of colonial inferiority in this respect. Instead, the innate versatility of the British ruling classes was taken for granted, especially in one both intellectually distinguished and Balliol-bred. With the Colonial Service itself apparently short of such men who might fill the post, Milner was an obvious choice it seemed. There was therefore all the more reason for deferring to Milner's own expressed wish to settle the problems which faced him quietly, and without undue interference from Downing Street.[69] In playing cricket, even radicals did not queer other people's pitches.

Not long after his arrival at the Cape, Milner declared that the essence of South African politics lay in 'certain personalities', and by October suggested that the key to the situation lay in the local politics of the Cape. He felt at this stage that time and patient, private discussion would improve the outlook.[70] Whatever the historian's difficulty in explaining the rapidity with which Milner's opinions later changed, there is no reason to doubt these early expressions of his views; it is after all hardly surprising if Milner, administrator by training, for long felt that much could be solved by quiet patient work or discussion behind the scenes, especially while the Transvaal's internal difficulties looked like bringing reformers to the fore. To this end, Milner was, if anything, anxious to play down questions affecting South Africa as far as those at home were concerned; that his own silence helped was clear. 'As you say, the papers tell you mighty little, which is a good thing, for my first prayer, when I came out, was that S. Africa might cease to be the subject of continual, mostly mischievous comment in the English press. Whatever has to be put right here . . . can best be put right "on the quiet" ', he explained to a friend.[71] Circumstances at home suggested that Milner would get his way. In April, Selborne felt that 'the public attention is so fixed on the Eastern Question that we are able to deal with S. African affairs in a much less disturbed atmosphere at home than would otherwise be the case';[72] later on, the Jubilee celebrations, while stimulating both jingo enthusiasms and good will towards the colonies, did little to increase the public's real knowledge.[73] With some good luck, Milner could feel that he might depend on a favourable mixture of enthusiasm and ignorance to support him from afar without questioning his actions too closely.

Chamberlain, however, was less than happy. The very diversions which momentarily seemed to favour Milner were the things against which he had been fighting solidly for two years. While sentiment was vital, even those aroused by the Jubilee were worthless to him if lacking the ballast of solid understanding. His speeches, it is true, gave little sense of this. Pleading for the avoidance of fresh irritations in South African affairs, he referred to the recent action of the Volksraad over the Aliens legislation; given 'the evident desire President Kruger has exhibited to meet us in the most open manner I think I am justified in concluding that we shall reach a thoroughly satisfactory result'.[74] Yet this reflected his interpretation of events there rather than his feelings about opinion at home. The South African question, apart from its own intrinsic importance, was the most striking to hand from an educational point of view and could not be left to slumber. A West African frontier dispute with France was not the stuff of Empire, even if it was the way empires were built, and much else was too mundane, matters of routine which could awaken little enthusiasm. So, somewhat ironically in view of his speech a few days before, Chamberlain mooted the idea to his staff of composing a long despatch for publication, 'setting forward more in sorrow than in anger and in moderate terms all our grievances agst the Govt. of the S.A.R. & expressing regret at their unfriendly attitude'. Again Kruger was to be reminded of his failure to fulfil promises of reform and to consider the franchise, education, a Rand municipality, and the dynamite and railway monopolies. Chamberlain also proposed bringing up the Aliens legislation again, together with the Press Law, and the question of the dispute between Government and Judiciary which he had hitherto avoided.[75] Not only was the public memory short and reminders therefore necessary but novelty too was essential if boredom was not to set in. Thus did the necessities of a policy based on publicity strengthen the impression that the Imperial Government would never be satisfied, would never let sleeping dogs lie, and so weaken simultaneously the chances of successful negotiation.

Chamberlain was afraid that with the end of the Select Committee proceedings the whole question would fade for those outside the Colonial Office. Some falling away or diversion of interest was evident in an article by a friend of his in the *Edinburgh Review* in July.[76] Public judgement it thought was in danger of being overwhelmed with masses of detail, and was absorbed with the personal questions raised by the Committee of Enquiry. But its own effort to draw out the strands was hardly comforting. Although it was admitted that 'Boer prejudices and retrograde instincts . . . made their government . . . at least very slow to deal with a situation which had rapidly developed', 'it is no longer possible to deny that the Uitlander grievances have been very coloured in order to afford justification or excuse for aggression'.[77] While this remark was not applied to Chamberlain, it hardly showed confidence in the existence of grievances. Furthermore, the article suggested, it was unreasonable even in the best of circumstances to expect rapid concessions on matters such as those complained of. As far as the wider aspects of the British South African position were concerned, it was nonsense to talk of paramountcy in a situation where Portugal, Germany and the Orange Free State had equal standing with Britain. The only grain of reassurance for Chamberlain was the approval given to his two despatches of 6 March as attempts to uphold imperial rights.[78]

Graham's reply to Chamberlain's suggestion showed that he appreciated his chief's motives; but he thought it would be difficult to say anything in addition to that already printed and published without making it exceedingly long. This was naturally something to be avoided in most publications of Chamberlain's kind. Graham continued 'I venture to doubt whether it would excite public attention in this country. The Press have apparently decided that it would not.' He agreed with Chamberlain's diagnosis of opinion, but, given their dependence on the press, thought there was little which could be done. Furthermore, there was little to be gained by irritating the Dutch, or by doing something which 'would be regarded as a disclosure of weak policy'. Wingfield agreed, and Chamberlain, accepting their views, decided that the wisest course would be to wait for Milner to bring up the question again.[79]

On one issue alone did he feel able to take a stand late in 1897, that of suzerainty. This had been brought to the fore by the Republic's suggestion in their reply to the 6 March despatches that disputes over the interpretation of the Convention should go to arbitration. Given the aim of British policy to limit any third party intervention in South Africa, as well as the assertions early in 1896 that suzerainty still existed, it is not surprising that Chamberlain came out against such a proposal.[80] But other motives were also present to his mind. The publication of important South African despatches was now a matter of course, and it was unavoidable that if this Boer note of 7 May was published, that the British answer which it required should appear with it. Failure to answer the request for arbitration would only confuse home opinion in view of past declarations that the Imperial Government intended to maintain its conventional rights: and in South Africa where, according to Milner, such arbitration would be widely unpopular, such an omission would be construed as weak policy. In public exchanges it was always important to deny one's opponent the opportunity of having the last word. The final draft of the despatch was welcomed by both Milner and Selborne as a fine statement of the British position which should certainly be published one day.[81]

It is clear that consideration for their wider public, quite apart from their interpretations of Boer behaviour, encouraged in those concerned with South Africa an intransigence scarcely compatible with the give-and-take of more traditional diplomacy. This followed from the need to present complicated issues in black and white. Chamberlain had seen fit even to ask himself the question 'What is the exact distinction between supremacy, suzerainty & paramountcy? . . .', only ten months before.[82] Now he still admitted that the issues with which the 'suzerainty' despatch dealt were not burning ones, and were 'more theoretical than practical'; but he thought it best to clarify the position. A minute by Fiddes, when breaches of the Swaziland Convention were being discussed in June, is relevant here.

> Public opinion would hardly appreciate our rather fine distinction between the Swaziland & the London Conventions, & if we promise a 'full consideration' to the proposal for arbitration in respect of the former, we familiarize the public mind with the idea of arbitration in respect of our treaty engagements with the Transvaal & make it more

difficult to resist similar proposals in the case of the London Convention.[83]

Chamberlain took the point,[84] illustrating how clear uncompromising statements were necessary to aid public comprehension – some would say 'mystification' – and to lessen the risks of unwelcome courses being pressed upon the Government. Attack was the best means of defence, particularly when that defence would have to be a public one.

VII

In the autumn of 1897, further publicity, much as Chamberlain might regret it, waited upon Milner who was then sending back news of the growing economic troubles facing the Republic, troubles aggravated by the widespread rinderpest epidemic. Moreover, the proceedings of the Transvaal's own Industrial Commission and the growth of divisions within the Boer establishment, raised further hopes of reform without the need for much imperial pressure. Milner delayed delivery of Chamberlain's despatch critical of the dynamite monopoly, as it seemed that the growing weight of disapproval of Kruger's Government inside South Africa might complete the process which eighteen months of British intervention had begun. Milner also believed that increasing criticism and unpopularity might persuade Kruger and the Transvaal Government to be more amenable. Kruger's lack of external support he was convinced had made for success in April, but whether the Republic's formally more liberal attitude would continue was not clear.[85] The future and the prospect of reform all depended on the cumulative economic troubles breaking the local Boer and his Government before they destroyed Uitlander morale. In June Milner had been extremely sanguine.

> I think we can afford to wait, that time fights on our side, & that all our disasters of recent days have been due to precipitation. The difficulty is that the oppressed majority in the Transvaal cannot be expected to, & certainly do not take quite so philosophic a view of the situation. The great question is whether their material condition can be so far ameliorated, & sufficient hope given them of an improvement in their position, to keep them from doing anything foolish until either 1) the Reform party in the Transvaal gains the upper hand or 2) the

stick-in-the-muds do something so outrageous as to compel Great Britain to interfere & finally settle the business.
My belief is that the way out is on line No. 1.[86]

For the moment any move by the Imperial Government would be ill-advised, and at the beginning of December Milner was still urging wariness lest any step reunite Boer factions in the face of an apparent threat to the Republic's independence.[87] However, as he came to see things, he thought, more clearly, so he grew in the conviction that it was necessary to arrest the decay of loyalty to Britain and, if possible, to win Dutch sympathy at least outside the Transvaal. The acting High Commissioner had pinpointed a major aspect of the problem for Milner on his arrival.

A speaker in the House of Assembly said recently that the Transvaal had come to occupy the position in men's eyes of a leading state in South Africa. This is true. . . . Not the general feeling from the question of race alone, but the being in the right, the aggrieved, the originally small and despised but now successful State, wealth, vigour in administration, however mistaken, and, last, but not least the personality of Kruger have all served to invest the Transvaal with a glamour misleading men's minds and causing them to lose the sense of proportion. For in reality the position of the Transvaal is false, hollow, and insecure. . . . The idea that such a State could lead and dictate is a bubble which would collapse when pricked.[88]

Milner rapidly came to agree, to believe that the bubble should be pricked, and that South African opinion needed watching. The result was that solving things 'on the quiet' came almost from the beginning to include the pursuance of certain policies likely to encourage popular support. Foreign arbitration on matters in dispute between Britain and the Transvaal he rejected above all on the grounds that it would be unpopular with both Dutch and English, rather than for the legal reasons arising out of the Convention. The 'exclusion of foreign interference, is always a safe card to play, as far as local feeling is concerned', he told Chamberlain.[89] An even more sensitive point, as already mentioned was the native question, on which any intemperate or ill-informed discussion in England, Milner feared, would do infinite harm.[90] Listening to local opinion also had another practical aspect, in that it could be used to support Milner's own views in despatches home, especially while he was new at his post.

Milner's concern for the state of opinion at home also had its positive side. A state of ignorance in Britain could have its uses, but far more Milner feared that this could lead to misguidance. The Boer executive was apparently congratulating itself on Leyd's reports from London of much support being gained for the Republic in Parliament and other influential circles.[91] For this reason Milner was anxious that the little won by the Transvaal's climbdown over the Aliens legislation should not be exaggerated; he had been concerned too that Sir Gordon Sprigg should attend the Jubilee, lest only the Dutch viewpoint should reach England in the person of the Cape's Chief Justice, Sir Henry de Villiers.[92]

Towards the end of the year his ideas began to alter significantly. Even while optimistic as to the outcome of the Industrial Commission, he was conscious of the continued and growing unfriendliness of the Republic on such issues as the Swaziland boundary and the Portuguese extradition treaty.[93] Events early in 1898 – the re-election of President Kruger, the renewed attack on the independence of the High Court, delay over the Report of the Industrial Commission, and renewed efforts to secure European diplomatic representation – all combined to suggest to Milner that his earlier policy had been largely unsuccessful.[94] His feeling grew that a final showdown with the Transvaal was certain. He had already begun to toy with the possibility of writing despatches home designed for future publication at a time of crisis,[95] and early in the new year abandoned altogether any idea of public justifications simply for isolated actions. He still disliked what he now referred to as 'this useless protesting', but began to stress its necessity for the compilation of a comprehensive indictment of Kruger's government. With a view to unveiling it at 'the great day of reckoning', he wrote, 'I want to have a pyramidal grievance by then, slab upon slab, each beautifully polished, slowly erected during preceding [moves].'[96]

For a while Milner kept his thoughts close, and Chamberlain sat in London unaware of the direction in which they were moving. While awaiting news from the High Commissioner, he was, Grey thought, fully occupied with West rather than South African affairs. Grey also gave as reason for Chamberlain's inaction his wish 'not . . . to give the opposition any material which will enable them to harrass him on South African questions'.[97] Nevertheless, Chamberlain had no thought of giving up those publications intended to keep things quietly simmering in the public mind and now almost second nature to him. Already he had insisted on sending the 'suzerainty' despatch at a time when both he and Milner were agreed on keeping imperial intervention to a minimum. Now, not being one to let the opening of parliament slip by without trying to catch attention, the Colonial Secretary seized the opportunity to publish a new Blue Book containing that despatch as its *pièce de résistance*.[98] Perhaps Milner resented Chamberlain's pushing the suzerainty despatch through; perhaps he interpreted its publication as a fresh initiative by the government. Certainly in his new frame of mind, he was irritated and depressed by Chamberlain's further statement to the Commons, when questioned, that 'Her Majesty's Government will continue to abstain from interference in the internal affairs of the Republic as long as the terms of the Convention of 1884 are strictly observed'.[99]

Milner's fear was that his earlier policy of lying low and being as conciliatory as possible, which Chamberlain now seemed at once both to support and to discard, not only achieved nothing in Pretoria but increased the disillusionment of British subjects everywhere by hiding from them the fact that the Imperial Government had their interests at heart. This disenchantment he thought could only be further enhanced by statements like Chamberlain's at Westminster, and could alone explain the noticeable lack of indignation at what Milner regarded as an outrage, the Boer government's dismissal early in February of its Chief Justice, Kotze.[100] Following on the heels of Kruger's re-election, this incident was the last straw for Milner, an attack on basic principles of justice which he felt simply could not be allowed to pass without forceful protest. Feeling that Chamberlain misunderstood the real need for temporary collaborators with the Imperial Government, and thinking them apathetic or disheartened Milner therefore sought to encourage these good souls to show themselves.

Even before he learnt of Chamberlain's parliamentary statement implying that Kotze's dismissal was not a matter for the Imperial Government, he began to work for 'a strong expression of local opinion' in favour of the Chief Justice.[101] His first move was to make the most of a visit to Cape Town early in February by J. P. Fitzpatrick, secretary of the Uitlander Reform Committee before the Raid. Although barred from political activity for his part in the plotting,

Fitzpatrick was still working behind the scenes for reform, and, given the gloomy prospects, wished to gauge the attitude of the imperial authorities. On visiting the High Commissioner's residence at Newlands, he was invited to call again, and Milner urged him to organise public protest in support of Kotze. Appreciating the difficulties of Fitzpatrick's position and warning him to be very careful in his activities, Milner nevertheless promised that 'if you keep within the reasonable limits, I will stand by you and I will make that promise good *at any cost!*' Not only did Milner reassure the Uitlander leader of the Imperial Government's support, but expressed his view that 'There is only one possible settlement – war! It has got to come.'[102]

Milner also told Greene of the public demonstration he had in mind

> I think some Boers might be got to join in it. If that is too much to hope, surely the Uitlander community, irrespective of race, ought to be able to get up a *monster address* to him. . . . I believe *that* would be taken up by public opinion both in the Colony & in Europe, and very likely not in England only but in France and Germany as well. Some spark is wanted to light the bonfire. But one of our stale old protests under the Convention is not that spark. It would be incomparably less effective than demonstrations of feeling on the part of the people, whose interests are directly affected.[103]

In reply, Greene, who had established close contact with Fitzpatrick, described how the Uitlander had clearly been reassured and was singing Milner's praises; 'I feel sure your interviews with Fitzpatrick will bear good fruit, and re-establish confidence in Johannesburg', he concluded.[104]

These contacts with the Uitlanders were the essential preliminaries to the speech which Milner delivered on 3 March 1898 at Graaff Reinet, in the heart of the Dutch-inhabited areas of the Cape. Usually thought of as his first important public pronouncement on the South African situation, this speech was as much the end of a phase in Milner's career as a beginning. Already he had passed from trying quietly to win support by moderation to encouraging local agitation; now, he sought as one of the aims of the speech to give that agitation a lead. The speech at Graaff Reinet assumes significance rather as the public climax of the first phase of Milner's abandonment of any impartiality traditionally associated with the position of High Commissioner. Although prompted by the presentation of an Address by the local branch of the Afrikaner Bond, Milner's peroration was both in timing and tone premeditated.[105] It was intended, as he had previously suggested to the Governor of Natal, to bring about a necessary 'separation of the sheep from the goats in this sub-continent', of those who actively disapproved of the Transvaal regime from those who accepted or admired it.[106] The core of the speech consisted in the argument that Dutch loyalty could best be shown not by the presentation of Addresses, but by attempts to encourage reforms in the Transvaal, and in arguing thus Milner did his best to make the speech contentious. When eventually he forwarded the text of it to Chamberlain, he explained that it has been intended to effect a periodic cheering-up of the loyal British and to divide the Bondsmen in the Cape.[107] This certainly made sense, for not only did the speech coincide with the re-emergence of Rhodes as a prominent figure in Cape politics, but Milner also claimed to have thereby purposely forced the resignation of the one Bond member of the Cape Ministry.[108] In terms of Cape politics, the speech was rallying call to the Progressive forces, who faced the prospect of a general election before long.

Whether at this point one emphasises Milner's reported words to Fitzpatrick about war, or relies instead on Fitzpatrick's much later recollections where Milner is seen as working for peace,[109] there can be no doubt that Milner now aimed at a confrontation with the Boers. He meant to make them face the fact that, as he put it to Chamberlain, there had to be 'reform in the Transvaal or war'.[110] The Graaff Reinet speech was intended to prepare the ground for that struggle. It is impossible to say what he felt were the odds on such a confrontation in the spring of 1898 producing war rather than a negotiated settlement. However, if the Boers were to do what Milner felt increasingly unlikely and embark on comprehensive reforms, then an awakened public opinion was required to ensure their completion just as it would be if war were to result. In Milner's own thinking there was a nice distinction to be drawn between bringing matters to a head and actually provoking the struggle oneself; it was the behaviour of the Boers, not the British, which would make war inevitable, and Milner thought now only of preparing his side to meet this situation.

This of course gave the Graaff Reinet speech yet another dimension, in its relation to opinion in Britain. Milner hoped that it would coincide with or shortly precede the demonstration by the Uitlanders on behalf of Kotze, and that the combination of events would make people at home sit up and take notice. At this time he was far more worried than he had previously been by what was happening in England. Those who ought to have known better were almost his worst enemies. Not only was there Chamberlain's dismal utterance about the limits to British concern, but 'What nonsense Stanley is talking about S. Africa now he has got home! It makes my head ache to read it.'[111] Earlier he had welcomed temporary diversion of the British public's attention, but here was the active misguidance he had feared. In these circumstances therefore he tried to force Chamberlain's hand. It was not simply that he disagreed with Chamberlain's tactics; even more, he did not understand the significance of Chamberlain's handling of the South African question so far. It seemed to him rather a cat and mouse situation in which the cat, like most political animals, was afraid to pounce. Yet impatient and autocratic though the High Commissioner might be, for him as previously for Chamberlain it was the public handling of the question which now began to assume extraordinary importance. For Milner it was soon to be that element in the situation on which all hope of a settlement favourable to the Imperial Government would hang.

Milner felt that such a local outburst of feeling as he hoped would occur over Kotze's dismissal would be in itself sufficient justification for action by the British Government, but in order to reinforce its effect he now wrote his first official despatch specifically designed for publication, setting out all the points at issue with the Boers whether or not they fell strictly within the Convention.[112] It implied a rejection of the limited stand on the Convention being taken by the British Government, and in a covering letter Milner explained that, looking at the Transvaal question 'from a purely South African point of view', he would be inclined to work up to a crisis. His further comment, that the final decision must rest with Chamberlain since any really firm policy depended on 'the Imperial outlook as a whole', was a pure formality and in the circumstances, empty of meaning. Milner was actively striving to create a crisis at a time when the international horizon was not very bright, and so, despite his formally correct remark, must have decided to ignore this fact and adopt the 'purely South African point of view'.

The extent of Milner's irresponsibility is as breathtaking as his planning was clever. Dating these despatches 23 February, he sent them to London by sea in the full knowledge that the normal passage from Cape Town took almost three weeks, and that they would therefore arrive only in mid-March, after his Graaff Reinet speech and the commencement of Uitlander protest. Relying on his contacts in Johannesburg to set their ball rolling, he took great pains to see that his own speech should make the maximum possible impact both in South Africa and at home. He prepared copies for special distribution to the press, and in the afternoon before its delivery dictated a summary to *The Times*'s correspondent, to ensure its publication in London the next morning.[113] His idea was that news of the speech and the Uitlander demonstration should appear at almost the same time, each gaining force from this coincidence and from their apparent independence of each other. Hoping to provoke a sympathetic reaction in England, Milner tried to create a situation in which Chamberlain – still ignorant of the 23 February despatches and having been given no warning that Milner intended delivering a major speech – would be faced with disturbance in South Africa and a British public once again interested and demanding action. In such circumstances, the 23 February despatches – arriving at the Colonial Office on 14 March – were designed to provide exactly the arguments for intervention just when they were needed and might have most effect. Milner hoped that Chamberlain, being taken by surprise, would have little choice but to adopt the hard-line policy he desired.

In an attempt to make doubly sure of success, Milner tried to reinforce the impact of his despatches on the very day after their arrival in London, by sending a violent telegram regarding Kotze and the High Court. 'This, it may be said, is an internal matter with which we have under the Convention no right to interfere. My view is that even if there were no Convention the immense British interests in the Transvaal and our responsibility for South Africa generally would justify our intervention to prevent acts of flagrant injustice and tyranny.'[114] Faced with events beyond its control, the Colonial Office was thus presented with weighty exhortations to action and the arguments by which intervention was to be supported.

VIII

Milner's schemes none the less fell very flat. Inside South Africa, despite his feeling that initial reactions to his speech had been satisfactory,[115] no movement in favour of Kotze or anything else ever got very far. The failure in England was as result even more complete, for, arrangements notwithstanding, The Times printed nothing. As the most vocal supporter of a firm policy towards the Transvaal, it judged the speech to be of extreme importance and so preferred to wait until the full text arrived by sea. Information and editorial comment were long delayed, and from a public point of view the speech was effectively removed from its context.[116] Comment in other British newspapers was diffused over the next week or so, and, in view of Milner's intentions, the speech was generally misinterpreted by attempts to see it as wholly conciliatory.

The Colonial Office, believing its own policy and Milner's the same on all important points, and unaccustomed to vigorous unannounced moves by its High Commissioner, was taken aback. Selborne had a certain instinctive sympathy with Milner's intentions, and on his 23 February despatch minuted 'What I regret is that all these things are not known throughout South Africa and Great Britain. Everything that can be published should be published and before it becomes stale.' But even here there was no real understanding of Milner's more immediate aims. In the circumstances, Chamberlain's rejoinder was not without a certain exquisite irony. 'But this is Confidential & Sir A. Milner does not wish publication which would only stir up Jingo feeling here at a time when we want to keep things quiet.'[117] It was not at all Chamberlain's idea to be bounced into action by agitation, however it was inspired. His own approach was designed to create a strong undercurrent of public conviction, in tune with his own ideas, which would avoid such temporary upheavals. Imperial and foreign policy was not to follow this kind of outburst, but should be able to rely on extensive popular support whenever it was required. When Selborne appeared to misunderstand this, Chamberlain gently get him right. On yet another of Milner's despatches about the High Court, the Under-Secretary had minuted 'I do wish our public here and in South Africa could be kept informed of all these things.' Chamberlain's reply was quite explicit: 'I think all that is here has been satisfactorily reported in this country. But there is no objection to letting the Press know the facts if they desire the information. As we can do nothing until some outrage on justice directly affecting British subjects or infringing the Conventions has been committed I do not see that agitation on this side would be useful.'[118] A gentle undercurrent of information diffused in the general interests of imperial policy was not to be allowed to get out of hand thereby threatening the handling of the specific issue at the heart of Chamberlain's propaganda.

In the meantime, Chamberlain responded to Milner with an extremely stiff-toned despatch, rehearsing all the reasons for non-intervention, and asserting that 'the principal object of H.M. Government in S. Africa at present is peace. Nothing but a most flagrant offence would justify the use of force.'[119] There was little to be gained from crying 'Grievances' at the Boers yet again. This was especially so considering that the dynamite monopoly or anything else associated with the Industrial Commission would be popularly considered a limited 'capitalist' grievance, and perhaps revive speculation about the Raid. Furthermore, however alien to British traditions the dismissal of the Chief Justice might seem, there was no evidence to suggest that the Uitlanders' situation had worsened as a result. Most important of all, yet apparently ignored by the High Commissioner, the British Government's view of the international outlook made deeper direct involvement in the South African arena undesirable. In this latter respect, at least, Milner did take Chamberlain's reprimand to heart, as letters to his friends that summer and his later behaviour were to show.

VI

THE ANGLO-GERMAN CONVENTION OF 1898 AND OTHER DIVERSIONS

I

As 1897 ended, the international outlook for Britain was gloomy. Events in the Far East and deteriorating relations with the French preoccupied Salisbury and his colleagues, and Portugal discovered just how the balance of opinion was tilting away from her after her recent antics, when Soveral's approaches to the Foreign Office in December met with a very cool response.[1] British statesmen had drunk sufficiently from the bitter South African cup in the early summer of that year. However, the little required to bring it once more to overflowing was soon provided in the shape of renewed fears of French advances. The Mozambique Company renewed its proposals for development loans, and with Leyds' assistance attempted to promote a new telegraph cable scheme. Reports reached the Colonial Office that two rival French groups were interested in the scheme, the Banque de l'Afrique du Sud, and the Banque de Paris et Johannesburg, the latter supposedly favoured by the French Foreign Office.[2] Changes in the law requiring ratification of concessions by the Cortes, giving the government of the day greater powers of decision, were followed by Government moves to raise loans for development on the security of customs receipts in Mozambique.[3] German interests too were apparently making progress, for the confirmation of the Eiffe-Katembe concession involved provisions for harbour developments; this was something about which the Colonial Office had been worried for some time, and fears increased lest Britain's pre-emptive rights should be further undermined.[4] British officials in a defensive frame of mind, bombarded with endless rumours and tit-bits of information, inevitably tended to be suspicious, to over-rationalise and impose a false coherence on these apparent inroads into the British sphere. While schemes often had insignificant results and official fears turned out to be exaggerated, they still seemed real at the time, and so tipped the balance of British sympathy again in

Portugal's favour.

The occasion for the next Portuguese approach was the presence in London of the Governor of Mozambique, whom Soveral brought to meet Chamberlain and Balfour. Bertie's financial schemes of March 1897 were revived, and Britain's preference for arrangements which directly involved the railway and the port of Lourenço Marques made plain. These provided by far the best security for any loan, and would have enabled Britain to control directly any further penetration by Germany or France, quite apart from tightening her grip on the Boers.[5] Again the talks were adjourned after a temporary loan was raised elsewhere by the National Bank of Portugal. Yet when Soveral again came to Chamberlain, the latter was still prepared to listen because at last the Portuguese Government had decided to include the port and railway in any arrangement arrived at with Britain.[6]

To this latest move, Salisbury was unsympathetic, feeling himself unable to 'see what we are to get in this division – beyond the honour of defending Portugal'.[7] On the other hand, he was equally unenthusiastic for any agreements with the other powers in South Africa, especially considering French and German behaviour in the previous year. Salisbury was faced with the necessity of working either through Portugal or the powers in order to put real pressure on the Transvaal and so safeguard British supremacy. Yet by the early summer of 1898, neither forceful nor vaguely conciliatory policies – adopted since May 1897 – had improved relations with Europe or brought the Transvaal to heel. It seemed that everyone, except possibly Portugal, could only benefit from the collapse of the British position in South Africa, and for this reason any successful British action was certain to create offence. Chamberlain for his part favoured, now as always, an arrangement with Portugal, and was backed up in this by Milner, for the Portuguese syndicate created to finance the Berne Award had failed and the Republic was trying to fill the gap.[8] Balfour also shared this view, but both he and Chamberlain had simultaneously come to favour the idea of an arrangement with Germany as a solution to many of Britain's problems, particularly in the Far East. Here was the makings of a dilemma. For a solution wholly satisfactory to Britain in South Africa, Germany had to be completely excluded as a political influence there; if such a solution were to be achieved by a firm stand on behalf of Portugal, then undoubtedly any accommodation of interests in China would be more remote. Without such a firm stand, an unhappy compromise was almost certain to result.

Similar difficulties were present on the broader international front. The German Government was interested in the South African question for two reasons. The prospect of influence and of material gain, especially at her rivals' expense, was at least as attractive there as in other parts of the world. At the same time, the South African question – since preservation of Britain's position there was one close to British statesmen's hearts, and the Germans rightly felt that they were working from a position of strength – might be used as a lever to edge Britain into the European alliance which Germany was seeking. Salisbury and his colleagues wished, first, to remove points of tension between Britain and Germany throughout the world as a means of promoting European peace and British security. They also wished to prevent Germany strengthening herself anywhere at Britain's expense. Yet they failed in their various ways to recognise how much concession was necessary on this second point to allow them to achieve their wider aim. Some like Salisbury had their doubts as to the wisdom of conceding the alliance, and preferred if possible to seek peace by settling problems individually. Others, especially Chamberlain, while more sympathetic to the idea of an alliance with Germany in certain parts of the world, turned out to be unhappy about conceding the detailed demands Germany wished to make as the condition of such an alliance. In the case of South Africa, where Britain felt there was very little she could afford to give away and wished if anything to recover her position, both approaches to it, either as a single problem or as a part of a wider scheme, were therefore likely to run into difficulties. All British ministers were inclined to think that while there remained other unsolved problems and therefore possible sources of agreement or compromise, one could stand more firmly in South Africa where considerable British interests were at stake. Yet if the Cabinet was agreed that opportunities existed for promoting general peace and security without necessarily giving away much ground in southern Africa, Germany appreciated Britain's weakness there, and for that reason pressed her hard on that spot.

These strains within the Cabinet in the summer of 1898 aggravated a situation originally arising from tactical indecision, where neither forceful nor more conciliatory policies had stabilised the South African situation. Salisbury's diplomacy illustrated the dilemma. When Hatzfeldt informed the Foreign Secretary that Germany expected her interests to be considered in any agreement resulting from the current talks with Portugal, Salisbury's response was very different from his defiant attitude late in 1895, despite the audacity of the German demands. After telling the German Ambassador that any financial dealings between Britain and Portugal were a purely private concern, and explaining that 'our motive for action was to maintain the status quo in respect of the Portuguese possessions and to prolong the life of Portugal', he added that should Britain fail in her negotiations, then Anglo-German discussions would be desirable.[9] For some time Salisbury had been not unsympathetic to the idea of a general arrangement with the Germans, while simultaneously believing that Germany would try to obtain terms amounting to little more than blackmail. Wearied by the Portuguese and suspicious of the Germans, Salisbury wished neither to make a choice between two evils nor to abandon all his hopes for a settlement. His statement to Hatzfeldt suggested to the ambassador that he wanted an agreement of some kind. Earlier still, he had admitted that 'With respect to a general alliance with Germany . . . there might be much to be said for it so long as it dealt with general European interests . . .'.[10] It was clear to Hatzfeldt that, while it might be circumscribed, the principle of an agreement was not ruled out, and that it was up to Germany to make the most of her opportunities. South Africa provided just that situation in which Germany could apply pressure to Britain. Although Salisbury's answer to Hatzfeldt in June was not intended to hold out the specific prospect of an agreement, nothing could have given Germany greater encouragement to try and wreck the negotiations with Portugal. The result was that German protests at Lisbon, Portuguese awareness of Salisbury's lack of sympathy, and the knowledge that he had not turned down the German advances, all combined to bring the talks to complete deadlock.[11] Salisbury then expressed to Chamberlain his irritation at the Portuguese attitude, ignoring the fact that his own behaviour had contributed much to it. If Portugal was dissatisfied with the British guarantees, then, he thought, the negotiations might as well stop. Britain would look after herself, Portugal would then have to get her loan from France or Germany, and would only have herself to blame if

Germany eventually seized a base in Africa as she had at Kiaowchow.[12] Chamberlain himself also indicated, one might say inevitably, an ambivalent and similarly unhelpful attitude in conversation with Soveral, being convinced that the 'German Government had established a regular state of funk in the minds of this imbecile government'.[13]

II

The annoyance, lack of ideas, and wishful thinking exhibited here were, of course, unlikely to result in successful diplomacy. But they were a symptom of the situation in which Britain found herself in South Africa, rather than a primary cause of the failure of the Anglo-Portuguese negotiations. However, it was Salisbury who had entered into talks with Hatzfeldt, effectively unsettled the Portuguese, and adopted the principle of an agreement with Germany to the extent that he was later able to deny any opposition on his part to such an arrangement.[14] From this position the way rapidly became plain once the Portuguese had withdrawn from the scene. Salisbury's suspicions as to the probable German demands were no weaker than before, but an arrangement with Germany now held out the only hope of stabilising the situation in southern Africa. Salisbury had often demonstrated his belief in the need to preserve British supremacy in South Africa. He was hardly sanguine as to the result of negotiations with Germany, justifiably as things turned out; but in order to maintain Britain's position as far as was possible, he accepted that there was no alternative but to go ahead and get what he could wherever in the world it might be.

It was the German view that the 'control of Delagoa Bay and the Railway would practically give the sovereignty of the whole of South Africa to Great Britain', and that this was something that no German Government could accept without compensation. For this reason, the Salisbury–Hatzfeldt conversations soon centred on the question of territorial compensation for Germany, should Portuguese default on a loan bring about British control of the bay and railway.[15] Further Cabinet discussion on 19 July persuaded Chamberlain that, although the possibility of future agreement with Germany remained, her position on South Africa was intolerable. Thus he approached a position which Salisbury had already foreseen and accepted.

> In other words, Count Hatzfeldt asked . . . as the price for German assent to an agreement with Portugal which Gt. Britain & Portugal were free to make without consulting any other Power, not only that Gt. Britain should introduce Germany into the bargain on equal or more than equal terms, but also that Gt. Britain, without any compensation whatever, should surrender two important positions in her undisputed possession.
>
> The arrangement with Portugal, if it had been made would have brought no accession of territory to Gt. Britain. On the contrary it was intended to maintain the status quo and to prevent [?protect] the territorial rights of Portugal & the only advantage which would have been secured by Gt. Britain was the *certainty* that these rights would not in any case be alienated to any other power. To suppose that Gt. Britain would give up important and valuable positions . . . to secure the support of Germany to such an arrangement as this is so preposterous that it leads inevitably to the conclusion that the proposal was only made in order to bring all negotiations to a close.[16]

To Salisbury he stressed the absurdity of the Germans' raising for consideration Samoa, Tonga, Timor and Walfisch Bay. 'Unless they are able to modify the opinion they have formed of the value of their neutrality we must look elsewhere for allies.'[17]

The question was 'where?' Chamberlain had no alternative plan to offer. Any new approach to Portugal was out of the question, as was one to France. To break off negotiations with Germany would make Britain's holding her own at Delagoa Bay more difficult than before, and destroy all chance of any favourable settlement in the Far East. On the other hand, if an agreement with Germany might be humiliating, at least it offered the hope of agreements to come in other parts of the world and a remote possibility of future gain in South Africa. Chamberlain however, convinced of the reality of Britain's pre-emptive rights in Mozambique under the 1891 Anglo-Portuguese treaty, was consequently very unwilling to guarantee Germany territory in return for her allowing Britain to exercise what was, in his eyes, already Britain's right. In fact, unless Hatzfeldt acknowledged that the advantage was all on the German side, and would in return extend the scope of the settlement to include China, then, Chamberlain concluded, it was not worth continuing the talks.[18] Initially expecting more than either Salisbury or even Balfour, Chamberlain was correspondingly more disappointed at the meagre results of the negotiations. He objected to their course for two reasons: first, because Germany refused altogether to include the wider ground in the Far East that he wanted, and then (feeling that an agreement with Germany in the South African context alone could not improve Britain's position there one whit) because he saw no point in giving Germany something for nothing.

However, there was no fundamental difference of view in this divergence from the thinking of Salisbury and Balfour. Chamberlain only pursued his objections so far, and in the end it was he who gave way before the arguments of the Foreign Secretary and his deputy. Balfour took the view that the pre-emption right, however sound from a legal point of view, was practically worthless. He assumed that Portugal would borrow continuously, borrow eventually on a joint Anglo-German offer, and finally default, rather than take the step of selling her colonies. Both he and Salisbury were prepared to submit to this self-denying ordinance in order that, while England and Germany agreed only to act together on a loan to Portugal, before the latter's default on that loan 'no control of any part of South Africa including Delagoa Bay, should be assumed by either of the lending Powers'.[19] Such a course was for them better than certain alternative evils. Balfour recognised that in the unlikely event of Portugal deciding to sell, Britain might face the armed resistance of both Germany and France if she tried to take up her pre-emptive rights. In addition, he felt that if England pressed for an agreement

> which rendered it possible for England to get what England wants while Germany did not get what Germany wants ... then ... Probably, they would break off negotiations and wait for a time when England, being in difficulties elsewhere, would become more malleable with regard to South Africa: or they might try and do what they are always threatening, namely coming to some agreement with France about Portuguese finances.[20]

This reflected an analysis of Britain's situation in southern Africa even more gloomy than that favoured by Chamberlain himself. The Colonial Secretary still thought the business highly unsatisfactory, but allowed himself to be brought round to Balfour's view. He finally agreed that there might be some value in paying 'blackmail' to Germany, but he undoubtedly remained distrustful, and could not even console himself with the thought that the convention might lead to further amicable settlements. With the Far East excluded this time, Chamberlain was convinced that the Germans, being not the slightest bit grateful for British sacrifices, would be equally unreasonable on all as yet unsolved questions.[21]

'I have signed the Anglo-German Convention – for good or ill', wrote Balfour to his uncle.[22] His lack of enthusiasm fairly reflected the nature of the Convention. By June 1898, it had appeared to the Cabinet that they were failing in their aim to preserve the *status quo* and Portuguese integrity, and subsequent moves represented an attempt to avert the increased foreign control which all members of the Foreign Office dreaded, in a situation where England's influence was no longer the deciding factor. Salisbury's response to Hatzfeldt's approaches and the eventual agreement were but the latest in a series of moves by Britain to maintain her influence in South Africa, a position with which control over Delagoa Bay, either directly or through Portugal, was associated. In the end, limited concessions were made to Germany and agreed by Salisbury, Balfour and Chamberlain in the interest of easing South African tensions slightly, and, as far as was felt possible *in South African circumstances*, in the interests of world-wide rapprochement with Germany. There was no more that Britain felt able to offer Germany in South Africa, and since those concessions alone did not wholly satisfy the Germans, little progress was therefore made on the international front, just as Chamberlain had feared. In this latest stage, as in previous ones, the basic guidance was Salisbury's in so far as Britain had any freedom of movement, although on this occasion the final details of the agreement were left in Balfour's hands during August. That Britain had been forced to come to terms with other powers as a result of their success and the increasing militancy of the Transvaal, indicates, in the South African context as in the global one, not a new policy but a defensive move, a change in methods resulting from an attempt to achieve the same objects from a position of retreat.[23] The final agreement with Germany was essentially a holding operation in which Salisbury realised he was playing rather desperately for time. Balfour tried to argue in the Cabinet that it would lead to less German involvement in Transvaal affairs, and might therefore result in a modification of Boer policy towards Britain. But this was at best a faint hope. In fact Germany had pushed Britain into the Convention and only stood to gain from it. If the full provisions of the Convention and its Secret Note were called into play, it would mean a considerable revival of German economic and political interest in the region, and therefore, not surprisingly, the question of existing concessions and economic rivalries which had so worried Britain was nowhere mentioned. The implications of this fact were to become clear to Cabinet and Foreign Office before the year was out.

III

When Chamberlain put Milner firmly in his place in March 1898, there were many reasons other than those mentioned in his despatch of 16 March which led him to be so insistent on attending only to clear breaches of the Convention. First there was his own developing interest in the world-wide details of foreign policy. From November 1897, when the Kaiser occupied Kiaowchow and the Far East had become the focal point of European attention, Chamberlain's horizon, if not his perceptions, widened; he found less time for the South and West African affairs to which he had given so much labour in the previous two years. Hand in hand with his thoughts on the Far East went his increasing involvement in trying, as already indicated, to turn the possibility of an Anglo-German alliance into reality, an idea he was to toy with off and on for the best part of four years. It was this joint concern which led him to give way to Balfour's arguments in respect of the Portuguese territories; had it clearly been only the dubious benefits to the British position in South Africa at stake, Chamberlain would doubtless have refused 'blackmail'. In March 1898, therefore, the last thing he wanted was a disturbance in South Africa which might either upset negotiations with the Portuguese in just the same way as in 1897, or disturb the atmosphere on the eye of his proposal of an alliance to Hatzfeldt. South Africa ranked high among Chamberlain's priorities, but it was certainly not always at the top of the list; practically speaking this would have been impossible, and in Chamberlain's calculations the South African question, while possessing its own intrinsic importance, was above all significant for its use as a tool in pursuit of greater goals. Apart from Chamberlain's own preoccupations, 1898 was in any case a vintage year for foreign 'events' – the Spanish–American War, Kitchener's march and victory at Omdurman, followed in its turn by the Fashoda Crisis. It was no strengthening of Britain's position in South

Africa which led to official silence in public on matters South African; as has been seen, that position was if anything weaker than before. But problems elsewhere were more serious still, events more spectacular, so that the attention of politicians and the public was fully occupied. This being the case, there was nothing to be gained by attempting to revive interest in South Africa. Of course, Chamberlain's own interest never lapsed, for he was in effect dealing with South Africa's place within the wider framework of foreign policy during the negotiations with Germany. These negotiations themselves probably brought home afresh to him the hollowness of Britain's 'supremacy'. Yet for the moment, with public attention unavoidably preoccupied elsewhere, Chamberlain rested on his oars. His behaviour is thus explicable once more within the framework of his concern with imperial publicity. Not only had he made his point many times as to the nature of imperial concern with the Transvaal that he wished the British to bear in mind, but in the crisis atmosphere of 1898 people could be left to draw for themselves the conclusion that an empire devoted to noble purposes needed constant support amidst so many threats to its well-being. For the meanwhile the Transvaal, beset with its own troubles, could be left, as the Colonial Office put it, 'to stew in its own juice'; Milner, in the position of under-chef, was given the task of watching it.

An additional consideration arose from Chamberlain's uncertainty as to the nature and strength of loyalist sentiment in South Africa, while still being faced constantly with the problem of deciding on what scale the Imperial Government should intervene. Colonial self-government had to be respected, and no Uitlander wished automatically to exchange Dutch overlord for Downing Street. Too much concern might be equally as fatal to British influence as too little. The spectre of an Uitlander Republic and a United States of South Africa had been raised at the time of the Raid, and was still something to be avoided at all costs. Chamberlain's idea of a Johannesburg municipality, of 'Home Rule for the Rand', was one response to this whole problem; he thereby balanced the needs of his imperial propaganda and the possibility of success in the Transvaal against the dangers inherent in winning too much for the Uitlanders. The decision to follow up only distinct breaches of the Convention – while largely a necessity arising out of Kruger's refusal to touch other subjects in 1896 – also reflects the same mind at work. Not only was this wise for the purpose of negotiating with the Boers in full view of the British public, but it was also prudent when, as far as Chamberlain could see, there was still little evidence of desire on the part of the British in South Africa for Imperial intervention. By early 1898, the generally sympathetic attitude of the Imperial Government towards grievances had been amply advertised. At the same time, its concern was to limit the scale of interference, a policy indirectly sustained by the belief that the continual influx of British immigrants would eventually tip the scales permanently in Britain's favour. If more intervention would be welcome, then there were various ways in which that desire could be made known to the Imperial Government.

From the point of view of home opinion, Chamberlain's behaviour at this time had other arguments in its favour. It would have been fatal to his plans if the idea had grown that he was acting as a propagandist on behalf of the Uitlanders. Such personal motives as did exist in Chamberlain's wish to follow an independent line would have been highly exaggerated, when already the strength of Liberal hostility to him was always very marked. For this reason the Colonial Secretary was constrained to keep his publicity within bounds at the best of times. It has already been suggested that to some extent Chamberlain felt the press were also doing his work for him in the early months of 1898, as well as they could be expected to.[24] The contribution of the press was also supplemented by the work of the ISAA. A letter to the Colonial Office four months earlier had described the success of its recent campaign.

> The public meetings which have been held during the past five weeks ... in Lancashire, Yorkshire, Durham, Northumberland and Scotland ... have been large – the nine Scottish audiences, for example, totalling 6,600 – and they have been 'open', Radicals and Conservatives attending in about equal proportions. Yet though everything necessary to back up the resolution appended hereto was said without any sort of reserve, no dissent was in any single instance expressed, and wherever the resolution was put it was carried unanimously.
>
> That on South African politics the Radical rank and file is out of sympathy with its leaders and its Press-organs is, in the light of the platform experience of the South African Association, an unquestionable fact. Any measure tending to Anglicize the Transvaal would be applauded by Radical and Conservative alike.[25]

Activity continued into 1898 both in London and the North,[26] and the Annual report for 1897–8 showed an overall increase in activity. Some 140 gatherings, 200,000 pamphlets, and an increasing demand for its handbook for speakers were all noted, as well as an increasingly favourable notice in the provincial press and growing demands for lectures 'especially from the Radical Associations in the Metropolis'.[27]

In the House of Commons too the South African question was rarely allowed to drop entirely. Those MPs connected with the ISAA made little mark, because in keeping with their manifesto they limited their Parliamentary activity. Thus matters found themselves in other hands. Although Arnold-Forster abandoned his frequent questioning once the Unionists took office, something of an anti-Boer campaign waged by Sir Ellis Ashmead Bartlett kept issues before the House. Although a figure open to mockery, Ashmead Bartlett was also a force to be reckoned with. His own publications had sold well,[28] and the knowledge of detail exhibited in his many questions was undeniable. If this failed to catch people's attention much was to be gained by the simple force of repetition, and even his arch-critic, H. W. Lucy, saw him as the real representative and exponent of Conservative uneasiness about the treatment of the Uitlanders.[29] In May 1896, Chamberlain, while rejecting his bellicose suggestions, held him up as the supporter of a consistent policy towards the Transvaal, and in 1899 Michael Davitt deplored the war as marking the adoption of Ashmead Bartlett's policy. The Colonial Office was well aware of his importance and, while on occasions it felt compelled to ask him to avoid certain matters such as the native question,[30] was otherwise content to let him have his head.

IV

Nevertheless, inside the Colonial Office things kept ticking over. With Chamberlain holding to the policy of protest at breaches of the Convention, grievances did not feature much in the correspondence between Britain and the Republic. Lambert however was busy compiling Part II of the Case against the Transvaal, which illustrated just how closely grievances and Transvaal misgovernment were being watched.[31] In the summer, as press coverage of South Africa gave way to other enthusiasms, the idea of getting a series of articles on Transvaal corruption published in a newspaper was discussed.[32] However, as the negotiations with Portugal and Germany got under way, and the prospect of isolating the Transvaal brightened slightly, attention focused on public opinion outside Britain. In the aftermath of economic depression, Dr Leyds was travelling in Europe attempting to negotiate a £2½ million loan to set the economy back on its feet. The Colonial Office therefore welcomed signs of growing French and German dissatisfaction with conditions in the Transvaal as making his task more difficult. On receiving from the Foreign Office a cutting from the *Journal des Débats* critical of the Republic, Lambert remarked that it was a 'good article. You will remember that similar articles have appeared in the *Kölnische Zeitung*. All this stands in the way of a Transvaal loan. The publication of a few English official papers ... would do still more.'[33] Chamberlain and Selborne had already had similar thoughts, and so the office began preparing their Vice-Consul's report on the Republic's finances for publication.[34] At the same time, the Orange Free State's denunciation of her commercial treaty with Portugal prompted Chamberlain to ask

Would it be worth while to give this information to the Press. If the O.F.S. are playing into the hands of S.A.R. to their own detriment it might be worth while to let the Burghers know what is going on. I do not think the majority of the O.F.S. are at all inclined, as the President may be, to sacrifice O.F.S. interests to President Kruger & Dr Leyds.[35]

Milner was asked to consider putting it in South African papers. At all costs the image of the Transvaal was to be shown constantly in its worst light, in the hope that Britain might reap some benefit.

The Anglo-German Convention itself, despite speculation and requests for information in Parliament, was kept secret, which meant that once again the real nature and effects of Cabinet concern about Britain's international and South African positions was kept well out of the public eye. Although this was, in Milner's words, due rather to 'the thick veil of secrecy maintained by the F.O.' than to Chamberlain's own efforts, the effects for the latter's imperial policy were equally important. It accorded with his own moves in 1896 to minimise the publicity given to foreign involvement in South Africa, and thus helped preserve the particular focus on South African affairs which Chamberlain had established.

It was at this point, however, that the Colonial Office staff began to realise that their insistence on taking up only breaches of the Convention was a limitation rather than a help. An important factor in bringing them to this conclusion was the conflict between this policy and their desire to continue publishing material about conditions in the Republic. If the Convention was abused, then such breaches might form the central feature in a Blue Book and provide the opportunity to publish additional material, as had been done in 1897. In 1898, the only significant feature in the Anglo-Boer exchanges was the Republic's rejection of the case put forward in Chamberlain's 'suzerainty' despatch. While this was clearly relevant to the Convention, both the Foreign and the Colonial Office knew that their case could be challenged and so, having asserted their own position, were unwilling to invite powerful public counter-arguments. Correspondence on the dynamite monopoly was again discussed for publication, but, as before, fear of being tarred with the 'capitalist' brush, or intervening when the British community themselves did not desire it, were powerful reasons for holding back.[36] There was unanimity on the kind of issue to which the British public would be sympathetic; none could beat the scandals of other people's misgovernment and support for the underdog. The Boers' lack of civilisation and the rights of Uitlanders tore at John Bull's heart-strings. His feelings of moral superiority, the idea of the Empire's civilising mission, the old Palmerstonian plank of defending British subjects everywhere were all brought into play by cultivating an awareness of the failings of others. Yet the lack of a particular occasion justifying publication now created a serious problem as to what might be published without appearing needlessly partisan or provocative. Debate inside the Colonial Office finally drove Selborne to declare 'On this question of publication we need a policy. I suggest that the S of S be asked to discuss this with the H.C. when he comes over & give us a direction.'[37] Chamberlain agreed that this was the best that could be done, and so they awaited Milner's arrival home on leave.

It was already very clear what Milner's answer would be. In his letter to Chamberlain in February preparing the way for Graaff Reinet, he had condemned the Conventions as 'miserable' things; believing that 'the points which arise under [them] are very apt to be thin and technical . . . some trumpery thing which nobody cares about, and which would excite absolutely no sympathy either in S.

Africa or elsewhere'.[38] Milner was in favour of starting from the general grounds of grievances, of the intolerable treatment of British subjects, from which Chamberlain himself had set out when he proposed his municipality for the Rand after the Raid, but from which too he had been forced to retreat.

Milner however was already well beyond being troubled by legal niceties or accusations of partisanship. With war in prospect and the Empire at stake, few holds could be barred. Writing home, Milner elaborated his views on the general situation. One month after the March fiasco, he remarked that yet another Transvaal crisis had been passed without a row, and, illustrating both how his views had hardened and a fair capacity for self-deception, explained that 'If it had not been for all our troubles elsewhere, *I should not have striven, as I did, for a peaceful issue*. The Boer Govt. is too great a curse to all S. Africa to be allowed to exist, if we were not too busy to afford the considerable war, wh[ich] alone can pull it down.'[39] No longer were personalities the key to South Africa's problems, and if a flicker of optimism had existed in February it had certainly vanished now. He later professed belief in reform, but he did so in ways which enabled him to prepare for a war. To Selborne he explained how 'Two wholly antagonistic systems – a mediaeval race oligarchy, and a modern industrial state, recognizing no difference of status between various white races – cannot permanently live side by side in what is after all *one country*. The race oligarchy has got to go and I see no signs of it removing itself.' He had abandoned any hope of substantial Dutch support and saw the campaign moving on to a wider front. In the same letter, he stressed the need for the support of the British in such a conflict, and added

> whether we shall have the whole of British S. Africa enthusiastically on our side, depends, as it seems to me, on our previous policy being a sufficiently broad one, and on letting everybody understand that, whatever the immediate occasion of our quarrel, our real cause is not a phrase, or a technicality, but the establishment of a good system of government – pure justice and equal citizenship – in the Transvaal.[40]

Milner was in effect expanding on Greene's description of the feeling in Johannesburg, which was 'that if Chamberlain means nothing more than academic wrangling, he had better drop that, as it does no good'.[41] The High Commissioner still felt sure that his lack of success, and South Africa's failure to respond, during

February and March, were due largely to lack of faith in the British Government's intention to do anything for them. In fact yet another reason for the Colonial Office's failure to react positively in March was the conviction that opinion at home would not have supported intervention at that moment. Selborne, now understanding rather more of Milner's thinking, put the 'domestic' point of view to his colleague. He was sure

> no greater calamity could befall the British Empire and South Africa than that once again one political party in the United Kingdom should reverse the action taken by the other in respect of the Transvaal. Above and before and beyond all other considerations we must carry with us the force of an almost unanimous public opinion at home in our dealings with the Transvaal, and no such force or anything like it would be at our backs now in support of the general case against the SAR as it stands at present. 'Previousness' followed by 'reaction' has blighted our South African policy for years and years, and we are still under the shadow of the reaction which followed on that accursed raid.

Selborne was confining his remarks to the Transvaal, but, of course, it was Chamberlain's object in educating public opinion to avoid any reversal of policy by political rivals on any imperial question. The Under-Secretary ended his letter with the observation that if the war Milner foresaw was inevitable, then, above all, 'It must command the practically unanimous consent of the British in South Africa, ... and the action must be endorsed by the practically unanimous assent of public opinion at home.'[42] While this last remark made sound practical sense, it also revealed a significant difference between Chamberlain's thinking and that of Selborne, who was clearly beginning to move towards the views of the High Commissioner. Selborne looked at an aroused public opinion as something necessary to sustain Britain in a war with the Transvaal. Chamberlain, on the other hand, intended that his general education of the public in imperial matters and South African details should produce sufficient public interest and support that, given the evidence of British determination, any challenger would quake and war be rendered totally unnecessary. In Chamberlain's view, wars only arose when people felt that they had a chance of winning; if, however, British power were wielded by politicians who could be seen to possess popular backing, few of Britain's enemies would dare to draw such an optimistic conclusion.

Nothing illustrates better than this correspondence how the twin problems of democratic party politics and the ignorance of the electorate were basic to the reasoning of the Colonial Office under Chamberlain. While many others appreciated those problems, at the Colonial Office their solution guided the forms of policy. While propaganda – concentrated largely, for reasons already explained, on the South African situation – was bringing the Empire slowly forward in the public mind, public opinion in Britain was still felt to be unreliable when it came to any particular issue. This exchange between Milner and Selborne raised a question which was to become crucial to South African policy. Selborne, the politician, talked in terms of creating a consistent and reliable public opinion which would withstand the swing of the party electoral pendulum, and so secure the Empire's future. This was the goal defined long ago by Chamberlain in his talk with Balfour in 1886; it involved the creation of a state of public opinion which would persist and free the hands of the statesmen to deal not simply with a single crisis, but with the conduct of policy over a long period of time. Chamberlain, capable as he was of determination and single-mindedness, was still a politician, and so subject to pressures of all sorts from people and issues demanding his attention. It was in this capacity that the actual struggle in South Africa and the propaganda derived from it were important for him, the process of heading for this particular goal possessing quite as much importance as the actual achieving of it. If in the course of the diplomacy people came to understand, as they thought, 'what South African policy was about', not only would British supremacy be asserted, but the settlement would be secure from domestic political challenge and destruction. As with South Africa, so, Chamberlain hoped, with the Empire as a whole; this was the beginning and end of his thinking, and something in relation to which South Africa, while of growing importance, always remained subordinate.

It was then the campaign itself, one which for the moment used South African issues and did not involve any intention of war, which was to win people's hearts, create trust and confidence, and then leave ministers to their own devices. This was essentially a politician's goal, of importance in a situation where the eventual outcome was uncertain and where the routes to a satisfactory ending were thought to be several. In the narrowly South African context, it was particularly relevant to policy-makers like

Chamberlain, out to avoid a war, but also determined to make the Transvaal eventually toe the line which marked out the field of British supremacy. Milner, by contrast, now believed war virtually inevitable, and was also contemptuous of popular feelings and 'vacillating' politicians; for him there was no question of a reliable public opinion. As Graaff Reinet had indicated, he was now beginning to see that its cultivation might temporarily be necessary; his letters to Selborne too show him beginning to talk of the need for a propaganda campaign of the kind that Chamberlain had already mounted. Yet for Milner, this was to screw up South African opinion to face the prospect of war and could afterwards be dropped; public opinion had for him none of the long term importance which was Chamberlain's prime concern. Milner always hoped to keep such politicking to a minimum, even if he was realist enough to appreciate the importance of public opinion at times to politicians at home, especially such as the Colonial Secretary.

Milner's letters to Miss Synge and Selborne show that his belief in the inevitability of war was linked to certain prior assumptions. First, if British supremacy and influence were to survive, it was *necessary* for 'the race oligarchy . . . to go'; secondly, only war 'can pull it down' for it showed 'no signs of removing itself'. War's inevitability in fact only arose from Milner's further decision that in these circumstances he should not strive any longer for a peaceful conclusion. Naturally, the High Commissioner was far too astute to suggest that he was preparing the ground for victory in a war, for this was clearly not the intention of the Colonial Office or the British government. While offering his views simply as expressions of opinion, Milner gave the impression of continuing nevertheless to follow the Colonial Office's lead. In fact, he set out to take advantage of Chamberlain's concern with public opinion as the now necessary support for a successful and sustained imperial policy, and of the Colonial Secretary's presentation of imperial policy to the public as something concerned above all with the promotion of 'civilisation' and 'good government'. At the time of Graaff Reinet, he had failed to do this successfully, but he soon showed in his handling of the franchise question how he had learnt from his mistake.

Milner had himself often spoken as though he considered the large-scale enfranchisement of the Uitlanders a solution to the whole problem of securing British supremacy; Uitlander domination of the Transvaal government and the transformation of that country as a result could be seen as a prelude to incorporation of the Transvaal into that confederation of states which was Milner's ultimate aim. However, this clearly squared ill with his private sentiments as expressed early in 1898, after the re-establishment of the conservative forces in Transvaal politics with Kruger's re-election. Where was the importance of the franchise for Uitlanders if war 'had to come'? When the Republic finally did give way on the grant of a franchise in the summer of 1899 Milner was still never satisfied, and pushed constantly for further concessions until the Boers dug in their heels and refused anything more. To understand why Milner behaved thus, it is necessary to offset his statements about enfranchisement against other of his considerations. Initially, arguments based on the nature and behaviour of the Republican regime had led him to suggest the need for war; this in itself implied less than wholehearted belief in the value of simply insisting on the franchise for the Uitlanders. It was reinforced by reservations which he developed explicitly as the practical implications of the franchise policy became clearer. As time went on, Milner increasingly feared Dutch powers of organisation and survival, and foresaw their exploitation of the political system to circumvent any mechanistic solution giving a vote to the Uitlanders. This was a strong theme in his criticisms of Boer concessions sent to the Colonial Office in 1899, and rapidly became a conviction not of momentary despair but one normally at the front of his mind. There was also the question of speed. To Milner the imperial consolidationist all haste was necessary if the disintegrating forces inside and outside the Empire were to be checked, and he did not trust the representative assemblies of South Africa to compose their differences either efficiently or with any speed. This reflected not simply his reservations about colonial or Transvaal politicians, but his irrepressible scepticism about popular feelings and loyalties in general. The Uitlanders were a poor crowd on the whole, and who was to say that once satisfied in the matter of political rights they would not turn their backs on the imperial government, or even the other South African colonies? It was difficult even in 1898 to sustain Uitlander 'loyalty', and Milner was not convinced that it would last. Fears of this kind were not confined to the High Commissioner, as the memoranda circulating inside the Foreign and Colonial Offices in 1896 had shown.

Confronted with these uncertainties, war – which conventional wisdom privately assumed would be short and victorious if ever it happened – had certain obvious attractions for Milner. It promised a rapid solution and a clean slate in the Transvaal; victory would deliver the Republic into the hands of the Imperial Government, not those of the Uitlanders, and the future of southern Africa would be framed in London rather than by local politicians in either Cape Town or Pretoria. Imperial supremacy was hardly likely to be better demonstrated or more securely established, if, like Milner, one was inclined to minimise the political problems which any war might produce. As he told Fitzpatrick, 'the job . . . is very easily done and I think nothing of the bogies and difficulties of settling South Africa afterwards'.[43] As a result therefore, Milner, despite his own abhorrence of politics, found himself developing tactics based on ideas about the nature of public opinion and using the franchise issue as his rallying cry. Believing that it was necessary to force things to a crisis, he set out to carry public opinion with him at the same time. Trusting partly in the responsiveness of politicians to popular feelings, Milner intended that the British government should be brought to act decisively as soon as public opinion showed signs of outrage and readiness to support an armed struggle, for one could not trust to it in the future. Milner's thinking on the wider aspects of imperial affairs in South Africa ceased early in the summer of 1898. From then onwards the history of British policy in South Africa is the tale of how Milner's methods, with their emphasis on the short-term exploitation of public feelings in a move to turn the weaknesses of politicians to imperial advantage, combined with Chamberlain's already established concern for the long-term safeguarding of the empire through an 'educated' public opinion, to secure the High Commissioner's object of a solution by war.[44]

V

For a number of reasons Milner was allowed a very free hand in Cape Town in 1898 even after the failure of his spring offensive. Not only was Chamberlain occupied with other affairs, but the extraordinary confidence placed in him by men of all political complexions continued to put him in an enormously strong position. From that vantage point he exploited the freedom which being the 'man on the spot' thousands of miles from Whitehall inevitably gave him. Remembering the failure of the Uitlanders to back Kotze when he had hoped for such a gesture, Milner became more and more absorbed by the problem of stirring up public support. He was aware of a slightly vicious circle. The Colonial Office, while carefully nurturing opinion at home, was not disposed to anticipate a desire by South Africans for further imperial intervention in the Transvaal before such a feeling was widely expressed. On the other hand, as far as the High Commissioner could see, the Uitlanders looked first for some sign of determination from the British government, being unwilling to make a fruitless appeal for help. At the same time as his friend Gell was commenting on the difficulties of understanding the significance of Cape politics, Milner gloomily observed that people in England, even Chamberlain himself, just didn't know the truth about South Africa.[45] Nevertheless, he continued to believe that the support would be forthcoming from all quarters when it was finally required. As he told Goschen, 'Just at present, I feel S. Africa must "take a back seat" & my whole efforts are devoted to keeping it in the background.'[46] While he followed this line and attention was generally directed elsewhere, he could hardly hope for increased public comprehension and was content to accept that 'the B[ritish] P[ublic] cannot attend to more than two things at once, and they now have the Spanish–American War and Khartoum, and it is folly to expect them to take an interest in anything else'.[47] He told Greene that he did not in 'the least mind public attention being directed elsewhere during the slow operations of the siege. We can easily make noise enough to attract it when the time has come to storm'.[48]

Making enough noises at the right time depended, however, on various groups of people doing what was required of them. As far as the Uitlanders in the Transvaal were concerned, Milner had few fears as long as the 'siege' was not too prolonged. Contacts with their leaders were kept up, although after his false move in March, Milner felt compelled to have Fitzpatrick warned 'not to force the pace'.[49] In order to complement their activities, he was also cultivating his contacts with pressmen in South Africa, especially Edmund Garrett, the Editor of the *Cape Times*. Towards the end of

1897, Milner had made two lengthy trips north and south through Cape Colony. Recording his impressions for Selborne, he observed that

> the country people generally are well affected, – the English absolutely so, the Dutch quite disposed to be so if they were let · alone. A great effort is being made to work up the Afrikander feeling in view of the elections next year. As the Dutch farmers are very ignorant, and only read the papers which systematically mislead them, it is difficult to remove false impressions. The Governor can do something when he is on the spot, but, of course, in an enormous country with a scattered population it is difficult to get around.[50]

In such circumstances, Garrett, as the editor of the only daily morning paper in Cape Town, a paper which also had the largest circulation of any in the whole of South Africa, could well be a valuable ally. Thus it is not surprising to find that, especially in a situation where personal friendship and similarity of views already existed, professional co-operation between the two men blossomed rapidly. Garrett quickly came to have considerable inside knowledge of the High Commissioner's policy.[51]

Milner also kept an eye on the press at home, knowing its importance but often doubting its reliability. He had thought its recent handling of Chinese affairs irresponsible, and especially after Graaff Reinet was sceptical as to its appreciation of South African questions. By September he was warning one of his friends 'Don't believe anything you read. The papers are all in the hands of one or other of the contending factions and no unbiassed opinions anywhere.'[52] He could take a little comfort from George Wyndham's explanation, that 'a great part of the comparative sobriety in the comments of the Home Press is due to the fact that both sides trust you from Harmsworth of the Daily Mail in the extreme right, to Massingham of the Chronicle in the extreme left',[53] but by the time he received this reassurance he was about to leave the Cape for a spell in London. There he intended to explain, above all to the Colonial Office, the true inwardness of things. Since March he had done his best to prepare the ground there as well. Not only had he welcomed visitors at Government House who would spread the gospel when they returned home, but he had constantly sent back despatches indicating that British opinion and loyalty in the Transvaal were in danger of collapse in the face of economic depression and inaction by the British Government.

Greene, also taking his leave and arriving in England some time before the High Commissioner, gave the same story, explaining the causes of the Uitlanders' relative silence by stressing the abject attitude of the capitalists; the working man, thus deprived of his natural leaders, was too cowed by repression to contemplate agitation.[54] The Colonial Office was persisting in its concern with 'breaches' of the Convention, and before he departed for England Milner only grew more fearful that 'the C.O. [was] losing sight of the essentials of S. African policy over the technicalities of these wretched Treaties'.[55] Plain speaking was needed, rather than obsession with matters like suzerainty – 'of etymological rather than of political interest' – and a recognition that the 'right' interpretation of the relevant Conventional clauses was merely the matter of a particular moment.[56] In person he felt he could make up for the deficiencies of despatch writing; the inescapable fact of distance worked both ways. So, desperate for a rest and needing the services of a good optician, Milner took ship and reached London on 18 November.

VII

MILNER IN ENGLAND, THE GREAT DEAL, AND THE UITLANDER PETITION

I

Shortly before Milner boarded ship at Cape Town, an appeal to Britain as suzerain power in the Republic arrived at the Colonial Office. The request for aid came from an American speculator, Brown, whose right to certain mining claims had been contested by the Republican Government. It had been Chief Justice Kotze's judgement in favour of Brown which had provoked the conflict between High Court and Government in 1897, and now the plaintiff was seeking British aid in the face of the refusal by the Republic's courts to hear his further appeal against the Government under Kotze's judgement.[1] Lambert, fresh from revising his case against the Tranvaal, observed that although

> to publish a Parly paper showing that we had represented Mr. Brown's case and – inevitably – been rebuffed, would impress public opinion here with the unsatisfactory state of the Courts in SAR & therefore make easier any action to which their vagaries may force us later the grievance would be a difficult one to present. It would neither be a breach of the Convention nor an outrage on suzerainty – if such a thing exists. We have waited too long to protest against the remodelling of the Court on its merits and we have not yet conclusive evidence of untrustworthiness in the case of B[ritish] subjects.

This was a pity in view of his opinion that this was the strongest evidence of arbitrary behaviour by the Courts which had come the way of the Colonial Office. Eventually it was decided to tell Brown that he would have to appeal through his own government. Then, thought Selborne, 'probably after a diplomatic wrangle we should end in the usual impasse, but it might be an instructive object lesson on the present value of the High Court to the British public when printed in a Blue Book'.[2] In short, publication while difficult at the moment would be possible and most likely effective after 'a diplomatic wrangle'. The year 1898 had been singularly lacking in such opportunities, and the Colonial Office staff were anxious for a change. Public opinion, apart from its wider significance, was still seen as something which would be important in putting pressure on Kruger to put his house in order. Chamberlain was also beginning to realise that under certain circumstances the education or guidance of public opinion was not so easy. Success depended on having both an attractive focus for interest and the excuse for publication.

These attitudes taken together had dangerous implications. Should the Boers openly defy the Convention or countenance an outrage at which Britain might protest, this would indicate their increased defiance in the face of British pretensions. Yet at the same time, it was increasingly Chamberlain's view that British opinion might only become firm if such defiance were in evidence. This raised the question as to who would then give way first, to which the answer for the Imperial Government was provided by recent experience – that the Boers would always back down under pressure as they had done in 1895 and 1897. Greene had put it very succinctly after the latter crisis. 'The Boers are accustomed to deal forcibly with those whom they know to be weaker than themselves, and this is the line of treatment which they can best understand.'[3] Such was the conventional wisdom; but there was always an element of uncertainty in this situation and Chamberlain was not anxious to become involved in a war. Ideally therefore there existed one alternative, some event which could be used to sanction renewed official British pressure, which could also provide the opportunity for enlightening the public at home and abroad about conditions within the Republic, and at which the Boer Government had not connived. In such circumstances, the Boers, being caught unprepared and therefore initially undisposed to resist, might retreat on a scale unknown after the Raid or the crisis of Spring 1897. Of these three criteria, the decisive one was the suitability for publicity, for that was the one most difficult to satisfy. It was also the case that, after a relatively barren period, those in the Colonial Office anxious to publish a growing pile of, to them, outrageous details, were ever more likely to seize on a particular event of relative insignificance or even to be deliberately provocative in order to release this backlog of grievances. Publicity created its own necessities, but in constantly bowing before them, a train of events might be set in motion which could not be controlled.

II

The pressures on those controlling the 'grievances' side of the attack on the Boer position mounted all the more as the failure to solve the international challenge to Britain's position in southern Africa became increasingly evident. The Anglo-German agreement in its South African context was barely even a path between the devil and the deep sea, and left Britain in a situation which appeared to be certainly no better and perhaps even worse than before. It was not long after the completion of the Convention that those with their sights fixed on that corner of the globe began to realise the extent of its defects. In November, Bertie noted that the agreement really precluded Britain from further opposition to the development of already existing concessions in which German interests were involved, notably the Eiffe-Katembe concession on Delagoa Bay itself, which it was still feared would be developed in the interests of the Transvaal.[4] The Foreign and Colonial Offices concluded that there was no ground now for any objection to its exploitation. However, in order to safeguard the British position as far as possible, an exact definition and delimitation of the German rights and territory should be obtained from Lisbon.[5] It was evident that no one trusted the Germans despite the recent agreement, and the fear persisted that some form of political control would follow economic development. At the Colonial Office, Lambert summed up the prevailing feeling; it is, he wrote, 'pretty safe to say that the question never will be settled till the place is actually English, and whatever the agreement may contain we are bound to watch it very closely'.[6] The only way of neutralising foreign concessions at all effectively was to press for the ratification and development of those claimed by English subjects. Accordingly the British Government adopted the cause of the English Lingham concession in November 1898.[7] These moves show just how far it was felt the English position in South Africa was being undermined. Under the pressure of events, the Imperial Government was now effectively promoting the exploitation and development of Mozambique which previously it had done everything to resist. The ultimate confession of weakness came with Salisbury's later negotations and agreement with the Portuguese in October 1899.

Given the opportunity, the Foreign Office officials indicated that they would adopt any scheme which would give them an advantage over their rivals. But in order to get the Lingham concession under way, Salisbury was compelled to accept Portuguese assurances that they would retain ultimate control over the Katembe grant; the exact delimitation which he had earlier insisted upon was not forthcoming.[8] This he did reluctantly, trusting neither Portuguese nor Germans; recognising the necessity of the situation, he had to content himself with renewing instructions to the Consul at Lourenço Marques to watch every move at the port.[9] This being the state of affairs, a Bill then brought before the Portuguese Cortes which, in MacDonell's opinion, would if passed 'inevitably open the door to unrestricted foreign speculation', only encouraged British uneasiness.[10] Lambert's expressed view that it was becoming ever more important to get hold of the Bay was widely shared.[11]

The fact that the negotiations of mid-1898 had in no way solved Britain's problems was constantly re-emphasised. Not only did the danger of extensive foreign developments appear to loom large, but Portugal, scared off by Anglo-German collaboration, turned to the French as possibly less demanding creditors. Despite British and German official expressions of displeasure, a loan had been arranged by the end of September 1898, and the British Minister was forced to conclude that for the time being 'the subservience of the Portuguese Government to France appears to be complete'.[12] Not only was French influence obviously gaining ground, but a further expansion of share capital in Portugal led by April 1899 to a notable Belgian interest in the Mozambique Company. This was particularly noted because the Belgians involved had Congo connections and experience, and the South African Republic was at this time in contact with Belgian financiers willing to advance money to Portugal.[13]

This ability of the Transvaal to appear somewhere in the background of almost every financial or concessionary scheme concocted for south-eastern Africa had been only increased by Dr Leyds' resignation as State Secretary of the Transvaal, and his appointment as 'envoy extraordinary and minister plenipotentiary in Europe', following Blokland's death. Concern at the news was widespread. From The Hague it was reported that Leyds had been named Minister at various European capitals, while at Paris Monson expressed his view that any loss of face on the part of British diplomats should be avoided, as well as anything 'giving away our position on the general question of suzerainty'.[14] The Foreign Office, while rejecting Chamberlain's habitual suggestion of direct representation to the foreign governments involved, had no doubts on the fundamental fact that British suzerainty conferred on Leyds an inferior diplomatic status.

> In these circumstances, if Her Majesty's Government were to make an objection to the reception of Dr. Leyds in any special diplomatic capacity, it would inevitably raise a question with one or more of the foreign Governments, to which representations had been made, as to the international position of the South African Republic. This might place Her Majesty's Government in a very embarrassing position, for some of those Governments would be glad of an opportunity to argue with Her Majesty's Government the claims advanced by President Kruger, and an offer might be made to refer to arbitration the question of diplomatic representation. The result of such a reference which it would be difficult to refuse, might be an award actually calling in question the Queen's suzerainty over the Republic.[15]

In the end, the Foreign Office continued to insist on the suzerainty it had vehemently asserted early in 1896. Word was sent out, however, that 'the British Representative should avoid placing himself in the contingency of having to raise the question of precedence',[16] and British diplomats played hide-and-seek in order to prevent their own species of diplomatic protocol being called in question. Salisbury would have preferred to avoid such foolishness, but realised that little was to be achieved by despatches sent to the Boer Government. Nine months later it was still felt in the Foreign Office that the 'place at which to settle the question is Pretoria', but again, even as circumstances changed, 'the present time is not a propitious moment for putting on the necessary pressure there'. British ambassadors and their wives continued to plead illness or prior engagements, and informal ways were found of intimating the official view to foreign governments which successfully avoided any open challenge.[17] Legal forms were to be preserved even though British statesmen were ever conscious that the substance of their South African claims was still in danger of erosion throughout 1899. After four years of unsuccessful diplomacy, the incentive to turn to other wholly different lines of attack on the Transvaal was very great. Much as Salisbury and the Foreign Office disliked the kind of issues which grievances afforded, increasingly the Colonial Office line of attack seemed to be the only one left with any promise of controlling the Transvaal.

III

So it was that Milner descended on London at a time when the Foreign Office and Colonial Office officials were in a state of indecision. He intended, as he told Fiddes (now the Imperial Secretary at Cape Town), to interview 'all the leading politicians and pressmen . . . and to stamp on rose-coloured illusions about S. Africa'.[18] It was therefore inevitable that Milner found his two months at home provided little relaxation, and he had to trust simply that the change of scene and the sea voyage would reinvigorate him. His time was spent writing hundreds of letters, and in trying to see almost anyone of importance who might in turn influence either opinion or policy towards South Africa. Few people can have escaped his attention as his diary shows.[19] Pressmen of all persuasions were seen, and with those of them who were personal friends – E. T. Cook, Spencer Wilkinson, and Flora Shaw, for example – Milner often had long and detailed discussions. It was through his influence in this professional quarter that Milner was able to arrange an appointment of considerable significance for his own attempts to influence loyalist opinion in South Africa.

At least since July Milner had known that Rhodes and his Johannesburg allies, as the directors of the Argus Printing and Publishing Company, were searching for a first-class journalist to edit their chief paper, the Johannesburg *Star*, and lead their campaign against the Boer Government.[20] The kind of man they had in mind was another Edmund Garrett.

> He must have faith in the English speaking race and be able and willing to render substantial aid to Sir Alfred Milner in forwarding the Imperial Policy in South Africa. He must be a man who would, by instinct as it were, be on the side of America in the campaign to free Cuba. His mission would be to educate, guide and unite the men who read English on the Rand and who are for the most part today an incoherent and factious crowd. He would have to do in

Johannesburg what Garrett is doing at the Cape, and more. He would have to do much of what Sir Alfred Milner is doing there.[21]

Milner, with his attitude to the Progressive Party at the Cape, his encouragement of Uitlander leaders, and Graaff Reinet behind him, was clearly a man who held the 'right' views. He also had the necessary contacts at home. A copy of this letter was sent to him through the British officials in Johannesburg, and his advice sought about candidates for the post.[22] By the time Milner arrived in London, however, although the search had spread far and wide, nobody both willing and suitable had been found able to accept the job.

Those engaged in the search took up at this point the idea of associating the *Star* with *The Times* in London, thinking that the editor of the one might also act as Johannesburg correspondent for the other. Julius Wernher wrote to Phillip Gell, full of enthusiasm. 'Your plan strikes me as excellent if it could be carried out. . . . Mr Walter is a peculiar man to deal with & it would require high influence to make him willing. Sir Alfred could be of great help and the arrangement ought to suit the *Times* as it would help them much in the future to guide them in the present where there is no policy in the country regarding South Africa.'[23] It was decided at first to seek a suitable editor who might then be suggested to *The Times*, but again no success was to be had. Milner, who had had a 'long talk' with Wernher on 16 December, wrote to Gell at the New Year with the opinion that his idea for an editor was 'exactly right'.[24] Still, however, there was no editor. On 9 January, Milner again had a meeting with Wernher; almost certainly, the decision was taken on this occasion to approach *The Times* directly, to see whether they would supply someone whom they could allow to be under the direction of Milner and the House of Eckstein, rather than answerable solely to Printing House Square. The next day, therefore, Milner saw his long-standing acquaintance G. E. Buckle, the Editor of *The Times*. Afterwards, he had some doubts as to the success of the interview, but everything went ahead just as he had wished. The organisers of *The Times* agreed amongst themselves, and on 17 January William Flavelle Monypenny visited the High Commissioner. Obviously both of these old Balliol men approved of the arrangement and of each other, for the following day Milner saw Gell and asked him to make sure that Monypenny was acceptable to Wernher and Beit. A final lunch with Buckle on the

19th was sufficient to confirm the appointment.[25] Its significance was to be illustrated after Milner had returned to the Cape.

Much of Milner's time was also spent, naturally enough, at the Colonial Office. Although a large part of this was devoted to routine business, the rest Milner occupied in talking over problems with the permanent staff, particularly Just, Lucas and Graham. Lucas had long been a close friend, and it was upon these men that Milner relied for steadying Chamberlain, should political pressures make him waver. The fears he harboured as to the apparently niggling attitude of the Colonial Office, illustrated in the previous nine months, were only confirmed by his first interviews with the Colonial Secretary. 'About the Transvaal he was not satisfactory', he bluntly recorded in his diary.[26] Milner now realised that Chamberlain's attitude over Graaff Reinet was not merely a flash in the pan, and he began to suspect that for a problem of great imperial importance, one in which it was essential to arouse British interest as well as restore South African confidence, even Chamberlain's vision was too narrow. This only encouraged him to increase his attempts to draw attention away from such 'abstractions' as the suzerainty question.[27]

In attempting to assess the impact of Milner's visit both on the High Commissioner himself as well as on the Colonial Office staff, the historian is faced with certain problems; it is, for example, difficult to know just what passed between Milner and the members of the South African department, for no record seems to have survived of those long winter conversations. Very probably one was never made. Milner's own feeling was that while perhaps little obvious change in attitudes had taken place, everyone had listened to him with more understanding than he had expected.[28] He was certainly much clearer in his own mind as to what his own tactics should be once he arrived back at the Cape. Having stated his views time and time again on the whole subject of South Africa,

it is no use trying to force them upon others at this stage. If I can advance matters by my own actions, as I still hope I may be able to do, I believe that I shall have support when the time comes. And if I can't get things 'forrarder' locally, I should not get support whatever I said. I quite realise that public opinion here is dormant on the subject, though it would take, I believe, but little to wake it up in a fashion that would astonish us all. My great fear is lest the waking up should come suddenly, perhaps irrationally, over some 'incident', which may turn out more or less hollow, instead of gradually in support of a policy, carrying conviction to all but the absolutely biassed.[29]

His diagnosis of the South African problem remained exactly what it had been almost a year before, but his attitude to the active implementation of a policy to cope with it was very different. He was now convinced of the necessity to move events on in South Africa itself, whereas before November 1898 he had tried to get the Colonial Office to take a firm line even in advance of this. As regards the 'awakening' of the British public, before his visit Milner had hoped that it could be rapidly roused over some particular incident, at which point the full iniquity of the Boer Government would be revealed by the publication of the official British 'case', that 'pyramidal grievance' which between them the High Commissioner and the Colonial Office had long been fashioning. But from January 1899 onwards, Milner emphasised the importance of a gradual awakening, thinking that the British public, and perhaps even official, opinion would only stand firm at the right moment if the ground were well prepared beforehand. His conviction that such support would be forthcoming, so long as he played his cards correctly, was as great as ever.

In confessing himself now more of a gradualist in his approach, Milner had moved a little nearer to Chamberlain's own position. The Colonial Secretary, from long experience, appreciated the value of sustained activity, and the strength of ideas developed over a period of time. However, when all circumstances are taken into account this was to prove far less important than the extent to which Chamberlain was moving to meet his High Commissioner. Those doubts about present tactics which had already assailed the Colonial Office were only strengthened by Milner's powers of persuasion after his arrival in person. This was evident in Chamberlain's reaction to renewed unrest on the Rand. On the night of 18 December, a drunken brawl had ended with the shooting of an Uitlander, Edgar, by a Boer policeman. This incident was immediately taken up by the South African League throughout South Africa; by convening meetings and drawing up petitions, they did their best to involve the local British officials at Johannesburg.

General Butler, acting High Commissioner in Milner's absence, did his best to cool the situation down, and refused to take cognisance of the dispute by receiving any petition to the Imperial Government. With Milner present in person however, there was little chance that Butler's strong criticism of the League and the press for grossly exaggerating the episode would be given much chance of a fair hearing. His assertion that imperial and British interests could 'best be advanced by the steadily applied forces of peace and progress', and his plea for the avoidance of a 'surgical operation' in South Africa fell on rather unsympathetic ears.[30] Selborne lampooned the unfortunate General, proudly recording his burst of inspiration for Milner's amusement.

> My name is High Commissioner Butler;
> The world has ne'er seen a ruler subtler.
> I had not landed at Cape Town a day,
> When I saw that Milner had gone astray;
> Fiddes and Nicholson, Clarke and Fraser
> To serve Rhodes somehow will tell any blazer.
> In the Transvaal the Briton *is* the blight,
> For the Boer is sweetness and Kruger light.[31]

There is no doubt, however, that Butler's strictures on the League and its associates contained much truth, and Milner knew as much certainly after, if not before, he returned to Cape Town. His own private secretary reported that the unrest was being encouraged by Garrett and Edmund Powell, Editor of the *Cape Argus*, who were 'trying to start a feeling of sympathy in the Colony – to reopen the Uitlander question'. Even Fiddes admitted that Garrett's carefully implied association of the movement of imperial troops with his reporting of the Edgar affair was 'really . . . rather scandalous'.[32] Yet Milner never for an instant allowed his conviction that the whole episode was a genuine outrage to be in doubt. Of the Colonial Office staff, only Wingfield felt that Butler might have a case; most of them leaned towards Milner's view, and Chamberlain at once felt that it might be a case for strong action by the Imperial Government. He showed how his views were slowly changing under Milner's influence when he remarked that 'The Edgar affair may be very important & may give us the right of remonstrance & action – outside the Convention – which we have not hitherto had'.[33] Here was the beginning of the Colonial Office's final abandonment of the Conventions, its taking a stand on the broader issues of what Greene, echoing a traditional language, had called 'the ordinary rights of British subjects the world over'.[34] A combination of frustration with the Transvaal and irritation with the failure of the Conventions to provide sufficient support for the kind of issue he wished to use was beginning to push Chamberlain and his colleagues in the High Commissioner's direction.

IV

It was not simply the presence of Sir Alfred and his spirited disbelief which undermined Butler's influence. Other reports from the staff in South Africa before and after the Edgar affair consistently emphasised the reliability of the South African League and the ordinary Uitlander. The previous November Greene had reported the views of certain of their leaders in a manner which confirmed for Lambert that they 'represent the democratic English opinion so to say – the opinion of the small people as opposed to the capitalists . . . they are probably the soundest element from the Imperial point of view in S.A.R.'[35] Butler himself forwarded a memorandum from Fraser which further confirmed the League members' respectability, their importance in forming mass opinion, and their non-capitalist leanings; and Milner after his return to the Cape did all he could in his despatches to stress their soundness and importance from the imperial point of view. This was a line of argument to which Chamberlain was very susceptible. Given his lack of success during 1898 in bringing about any changes in the Republic's attitudes, he was better able to appreciate Milner's arguments that unless something was done very soon, the loyalty which existed in South Africa would evaporate. Moreover, the loyalty of the ordinary man in the street was something he found far more convincing than talk of such sentiment among the capitalists upon the Rand. Not only had the Raid soured him, along with many other people, in that respect, but imperial sentiment was the very thing that Chamberlain, convinced of its existence, was trying to awaken by the education of the man in the street at home. Finally, Chamberlain had always been ready to take steps which might increase the pressure of public opinion on Kruger, both at home and in South Africa.

Events at this point, however, forced Chamberlain to take up a waiting position. Anxious as he was to take advantage of the new unrest, and conscious that his adoption of the Edgar case would both reassure the Uitlanders and dovetail neatly with his handling of grievances to date, delay was necessary while the situation on the Rand remained so unstable. When Milner left England the agitation seemed to be continuing, and the policeman Jones, said to have murdered Edgar, had yet to be tried. Later events only seemed to confirm Chamberlain's feelings that here was an important issue. A large Uitlander meeting was disrupted, it was said, by the Boers; some of their leaders were arrested, the rights of meeting and assembly were further restricted, and Jones was eventually acquitted to the accompaniment of some less than tactful judicial comments, which only inflamed feelings further. Equally important in delaying any action by Chamberlain were the remarks of the acting High Commissioner. In view of Milner's rejection of Butler's interpretation, the Colonial Office had no option but to wait until Milner himself had checked the situation; given their added sympathy with Milner, it was necessary to wait until Milner had returned in order that Butler's reports might be balanced by Milner's for purposes of publication.

These considerations led Chamberlain to depart from his normal practice of marking the opening of the new Parliamentary session with something on South Africa. No papers were laid when MPs returned on 7 February, and no mention was made in either House during that month. Both Parliament and the Press seemed to be with Chamberlain in awaiting the outcome of events. Details were reported constantly in the daily papers, but the periodicals tended to withhold their views. Questions in Parliament only revived after news of Jones' acquittal, but although Chamberlain at once took the opening and asked Milner for a report 'suitable for publication', he was able to tell the House no more than that it was still unclear whether or not Government action was called for.[36] He was in no position to take a real initiative for again events were overtaking the Colonial Office; for the second time in a few weeks Chamberlain and his colleagues at home were relegated to the role of anxious spectators. The difference this time lay with Milner, whose hand was all the stronger for his being once more the man on the spot.

Given the fundamental insecurity of Britain's position, the British Government felt obliged to cultivate allies wherever they might be found. It was of course this which had made it necessary for Chamberlain to maintain contacts with the capitalists before the

Raid. Whatever regime might be in power, the mineowners were certain to wield considerable influence, and for that reason their collaboration with the Imperial Government was desirable. However, their willingness to collaborate with the Imperial Government depended very largely on the latter's ability to serve their ultimate purpose, a secure prosperity and increasing profits. The fiasco of the Raid followed by Britain's continuing inability to win any real concessions from the Boers, led many to wonder whether their aims might not best be furthered by coming to terms with the Boer Government on all matters in dispute, rather than looking to the imperial authorities.

At the end of 1898, Chamberlain had been disturbed by the news of the Republic's intention to prolong the dynamite monopoly with the financial burdens which this imposed upon mining companies, for this seemed to make the possibility of a Boer–capitalist compromise a very real one. Fraser reported that the Transvaal Chamber of Mines would make no direct appeal to Britain for not only did the Boers regard such a move as treason, but many of the magnates themselves had little faith that the Imperial Government would protect them. Anxious himself to avoid giving public support to the Rand capitalists' cause, yet welcoming publicity as such and wishing to retain the support of this powerful element in the Uitlander community, Chamberlain adopted Frederick Graham's suggested solution. An official despatch of protest was sent,[37] together with the verbal proviso 'that if the Government will deal satisfactorily with the matter, it will never see the light & no one will know anything about it; but that if something is not done quickly we shall be forced by the complaints of manufacturers in this country to publish the despatch'.[38] Milner approved of this and of Chamberlain's further suggestion to the Chamber of Mines via Fraser, that they should themselves make a strong public protest. The Chamber was also told confidentially that Britain was taking up its cause.[39]

In February, the Republic, aware of the divisions within the mining community and sensing the predicament of the Imperial Government now that the Chamber was offering £600,000 to buy out the dynamite monopoly, approached the heads of the largest mining firms with terms for a settlement of the whole Uitlander question. The offer held out the possibility of settling the Republic's dispute with the Chamber of Mines on the extent of mining activity underground, offered to set up new machinery for the consideration of financial policy, and proposed that the Volksraad should consider the enfranchisement of the Uitlanders after a period of five years. In return it was suggested that the capitalists dissociate themselves from the South African League, put an end to their press agitation against the Republic, aid the Boers in settling disputes with Britain over the treatment of Coloureds and Indians, and, finally, help the Republic obtain a loan in Europe.[40]

These new developments were thus known to Chamberlain when he spoke in the House of Commons on 7 March, and inevitably meant that he was again compelled to wait upon events. Not only were the Boers' intentions unclear, but it would have to be seen how far the firms approached represented or would guard the general interests of the Uitlanders.[41] Commenting further on the details of the Boer offer, Chamberlain showed how different still were his own views from those of his officials in South Africa. 'With respect to political reforms, I should advise those approached to press before anything else for the grant of a genuine municipality for the Rand', he wrote. This would solve all the problems of the Uitlanders, and he consequently dismissed any question of pressing Kruger on the franchise suggestions in the Boer offer. To raise the franchise and ignore the earlier suggestions for the Rand was an irrelevance. The full franchise, he thought, was not really of much importance, particularly if delayed or awarded selectively, and to emphasise it would be needlessly provocative. Chamberlain was still wedded to his belief that grievances and their redress were the central issues. Convinced 'that the British public is . . . more likely to be stirred by concrete cases of oppression than by the general injustice of non-representation of the Uitlanders in the Legislature', he could see no point in changing the long-established focus of discussion.[42] Thus, when approached by the London representatives of Consolidated Gold Fields and by Wernher Beit anxious to know government intentions, Chamberlain insisted that 'our policy was to get a Municipality', and added that he 'did not expect to succeed at present'.[43] To give this still more point, he made municipal reform a major theme in his Commons speech on 20 March.[44] By so doing he hoped to strengthen the capitalists in negotiating, as he hoped they would, for a muncipality; to give more open evidence of support for the

Uitlander cause, which he had intimated recently only to the magnates; and to re-emphasise what he thought would be a popular remedy in English eyes.

Milner, however, thought Chamberlain's stand disastrous. The preoccupation with municipal government showed how far Chamberlain was from understanding either the points at issue between the capitalists and the Kruger government or the temper of Uitlander politicians. Milner had always been aware of the importance many Uitlanders attached to the franchise, and even in his less aggressive days had written to Chamberlain that, although it might wait, 'there will be no ultimate peace without extension of the Franchise'.[45] In August 1897, he had suggested that the maintenance of British supremacy in South Africa might well depend upon the English party in the Transvaal getting the franchise.[46] When conveying the news of the Republic's 'Great Deal' offer, Milner had welcomed the franchise proposals, suggesting that it was now necessary above all to link a redistribution of seats with enfranchisement, and favouring an immediate start rather than in five years' time as offered by the Republic. Here was his chance to rally the Uitlanders and to force the issue. Subsequently disappointed with Chamberlain's reply, he confined himself for the moment to humouring the Colonial Secretary. A muncipality might be 'better worth having' than the franchise, but it would be infinitely harder to get, he said, and added 'It is evident that no improvement in the attitude of the Transvaal Government to Her Majesty's Government, but rather the reverse is portended by the advances to the Uitlanders'.[47]

V

In order to back up his own despatches and in line with his words to Selborne in January, Milner turned his attention more directly to what was happening on the Rand. There, amidst continuing unrest which in itself gave so much point to the Republic's advances to the capitalists, the South African League was quietly organising a monster petition to the Queen. Because of Milner's and Greene's absence from South Africa early in the year, and the secrecy which the League had adopted to guard against the further arrest of its leaders, British officials, it seems, had been little involved in the actual origin of the second petition. Indeed, it seemed to take them by surprise; Monypenny who arrived in Johannesburg on 26 February later reported that the Petition 'was to everybody – to Milner, to Greene, and to myself, a bolt from the blue but we all had to recognize that it created a situation which must make or mar us'.[48] Surprisingly sudden though it might be, here at last was the powerful public expression of Uitlander opinion for which Milner had long been looking, and which he was determined to exploit to the full. This entailed the skilful drawing together of the petition movement and the Great Deal negotiations.

Greene quickly picked up the threads after his return to Pretoria, and discussed with the leaders of the League just how the Petition should be presented and made public. On the one hand, it was important to avoid any breaches of etiquette by the League or any accusations of undiplomatic behaviour by British officials of the sort which had occurred at the time of the Edgar affair. On the other, it was very necessary to achieve by timely publicity the maximum impact on both the Boer Government and public opinion.[49] The first of these goals was not difficult to achieve; the League was as anxious as Milner that there should be no mistakes this time and its leaders agreed to accept the procedure approved by the High Commissioner.[50] Absolute secrecy was insisted on, with only the barest formal exchange of notes between Greene and the League when the Petition was handed over for despatch to Milner.[51] The announcement of the Petition was also controlled by Milner and Greene, and involved questions of both method and timing. It was here that Monypenny joined in the action.

The new editor had consulted the High Commissioner in Cape Town before journeying north,[52] and once in Johannesburg was in constant contact with the British Agent from whom he learnt most of the details about the situation on the Rand. This process took some time, and Monypenny only took over practical direction of the *Star* on 15 March after thorough preparation. A few days before, Greene told Milner how

> *Monypenny.* Came to see me today and we had a long chat: he
> ·seems sound on all points except the S.A. League, on which he
> appeared uncertain. When, however, I had explained to him that
> they agreed to limit their agitation to constitutional means, in
> support of the Reforms of which all parties recognize the necessity,
> and bound themselves to be guided by me, as in the past, he was

quite reassured, and said, while he might not support them publicly in his paper, as a political Body for fear of spoiling the game, he wd. take care that their objects and efforts were supported. This is, after all, what we want.[53]

Monypenny's own letters bear witness to the remarkable success of this priming. After five days in the editorial chair, his mind was clear that the Boers 'are very Oriental, treacherous and cunning in a small way, but with no backbone and no real cleverness. You can always treat them by straightness and firmness and I am very sanguine now that within a few years we can have our own way.'[54]

With the leaders of the League and Monypenny following the straight and narrow, there remained the question of timing the announcement of the Petition. It was felt vital that this should occur soon after the delivery to the Transvaal Government of the reply of the mining houses to the Government's proposals. This it was thought would avoid giving the Boers the pretext for backing out of the negotiations before the reply was received, and at the same time impress them with the solidarity of the Uitlander community. Again Greene's role was crucial, this time through his constant contact with Fitzpatrick who kept him informed of all progress in the capitalist negotiations. By Tuesday 21 March all was settled, and Greene cabled the final timetable to Milner. The reply of the mining houses was expected by the end of the week, and so Greene arranged to receive the Petition on Friday in time for it to reach Milner the following Monday. On that same afternoon, the *Star* was to announce receipt of a Petition by the High Commissioner, and would comment on a summary of its contents. 'M[onypenny] will also warn Editor of '*Times*' by a private & secret cable beforehand that an important message for Monday's issue is to follow. Above arrangement enables the *Times* to be first in the field in publishing the news, which would not be possible if it waited till Tuesday. . . .'[55]

The timing was as crucial here as it had been in Milner's plans at Graaff Reinet. When the probable duration of the capitalists' deliberations as to the terms of their answer was still uncertain, and it looked for a moment as if the Petition might also have to be delayed if they were still to coincide, Greene felt 'it would be better to hold it over till after Easter, as during Easter the Telegraph office here will be closed to the public, and the result would be, as in the Edgar case, that Reuter wd. educate the B[ritish] P[ublic], & we should have no chance of communicating with the outside world.'[56] A scoop for *The Times* and the *Star*, the favourable announcement of the Petition in both Britain and South Africa on the same day, and 'something . . . done to counteract the "Reuter" telegram, which is sure to put the [Boer] Govt. complexion on the incident & deceive the British Public'[57] was not all Milner hoped to achieve. The Petition itself was concerned simply with the grievances of the Uitlanders, and made no direct mention of the franchise; it did however illustrate the hollowness of those moves towards municipal self-government which the Boers had already countenanced. It therefore showed Chamberlain, who had been kept in the dark as to its very existence, not only the strength of feeling which existed, but also that the idea of a municipality was a feeble one. Publication was important too not only from the general educative point of view but also, Milner felt, to bypass the lack of Colonial Office publicity. Chamberlain and his officials still felt it impossible to publish, not because events were now moving too fast but because little could be gained by it while there was no possibility of other action at least until the Petition arrived in London. It was thought better to wait, even with respect to the material on the Edgar affair, and then to present it 'as a significant & striking illustration of the state of things described in the petition of the 21000 now on its way'.[58] Although reasonable enough, the Colonial Office's reticence coming on top of Chamberlain's municipal addiction irritated Milner, who throughout March continued vainly to push for the adoption of the franchise question. Not only did the Uitlanders want it, but 'Political reform goes to the root of individual grievances, and moreover it may become, if it is not today, a stirring battle cry, exciting sympathy throughout the Empire, and even in some foreign countries'. While Chamberlain, hardly impervious to the appeal of 'a stirring battle cry', wished to avoid changing the focus in England, Milner tried to create the impression that commitment to an Uitlander franchise was so deeply rooted in South Africa 'that it would be disconcerting and weakening now to attempt to change the platform'.[59]

Although this claim was hardly justified when the High Commissioner penned this despatch, despite Monypenny's ardent advocacy in the *Star* and *The Times*, it was more so by the time it reached Chamberlain some two and a half weeks later, for by then the British officials in South Africa had brought about the

publication of the Great Deal negotiations. The mining houses'
reply to the Boer offer was finally presented to the State Secretary
of the Transvaal on 28 March, a day later than planned owing to last-
minute difficulties in persuading all the negotiators to sign. This
gave rise to some discrepancy between the first reports of the
Petition, *The Times* hailing it as planned on 27 March as 'a moderate
and weighty statement' while the *Star* altered its course and only
published a statement to the effect that the Uitlanders were about
to present a Petition to the Queen. From Milner's point of view,
however, it was important as the latest example of the considerable
divisions amongst the mining houses on the attitude which they
should adopt towards the bulk of the Uitlander community. It was
only with the greatest difficulty that Fitzpatrick, using as a weapon
the fact of the Petition's existence, managed to secure a grudging
unanimity and a firm stand on the question of the franchise in the
reply to the Boers. In raising the quesiton of the franchise, first in
their initial approach to the capitalists and then in Kruger's own
speeches during March, the Boers had played into Milner's hands.
They had thus implied the absurdity of Chamberlain's ideas about a
municipality, and unwittingly reinforced this aspect of the Petition.
This was capped by the capitalists' reply, where the franchise was
acknowledged by the industrial leaders themselves as 'a vital point
upon which a permanent and favourable settlement must hang',
and further endorsed with a memorandum on the subject by a
number of prominent Uitlanders led by Fitzpatrick.[60]

Milner, Greene, and Fitzpatrick had thus managed to achieve a
unanimous commitment to franchise reform at the same time as
the petition movement bore its fruit. They were in no doubt that
here there lay the route to a solution to the Transvaal problem.
Throughout discussions on the Great Deal, however, the
Republican Government had insisted on total secrecy. Milner was
acutely conscious that this left open the possibility of the Boers
abandoning the whole offer – hence his insistence on the Petition
being kept quiet until the last possible moment, to avoid provoking
just such a move; in the same circumstances, he was afraid that the
fragile unity of the mining houses might collapse at any time. If
either of these things happened, then the petitioners would be
isolated, the Uitlander community clearly split, and Milner's plans
for securing imperial intervention in ruins. Unable to go himself to
Johannesburg to stiffen the Uitlander ranks, he sent Fiddes instead,

only reluctantly allowing the Imperial Secretary's wish to stay in Cape Town until his son returned to England.[61] Although this visit was planned early in March, it was not until Fiddes had arrived in Johannesburg and the Petition had arrived in Cape Town that Milner informed Chamberlain he had sent the Imperial Secretary to find out the state of feeling there; he had sent him, he said, for it seemed that a 'fresh reform movement of some kind is evidently in contemplation'.[62] Such studied vagueness at this moment ill became Milner, but his pretence at ignorance went a long way to reinforce the impression of Uitlander spontaneity which he was trying to create in order to convince Chamberlain and the British public that grievances were so acute, and that no mere Convention should be allowed to stand in the way of intervention. Fiddes meanwhile was doing his utmost to impress on the Uitlander leaders, especially Fitzpatrick, that they must continue working away if they wanted the Petition to have any effect.

Despite the High Commissioner's reservations concerning Chamberlain's ideas, Fiddes reported how he and Greene had told Fitzpatrick that Chamberlain was wholly sympathetic to their cause, and was 'only waiting for a sufficiently strong & precise appeal from the Uit[lande]rs to enable him to overcome resistance in the Cabinet & in England'.[63] It was clear however that the Johannesburgers found such assertions unconvincing. Fiddes went into more details about the mining houses' representatives' continuing unhappiness over their reply to the Boers, and suggested that further steps were essential. His letter deserves quoting at length. It is, he wrote,

of vital importance that these negotiations shd. somehow or other become public property at a very early date; because (1) they show the capitalists in line with the signatories of the petition (2) they refute the idea, sedulously fostered by the Govt. & half believed by even those friendly to the cause, that the capitalists have been approaching the Govt. with plans for selling the Uitr. community for their own advantage. F[itzpatrick] agreed to the desirability of publication in principle, but felt grave difficulties. – If the Govt. promptly broke off negotiations on receipt of the reply, I understood that the difficulties wd. partly if not entirely disappear. But he considered that the Govt. would keep them going – or at any rate make no sign – for a time; &, this being so, to make them public meanwhile wd. not only expose someone to a charge of bad faith, but be contrary to what he knew to be the express wishes of his partners. He therefore hoped to gain the end in another way. . . . *If* this fails F. says some other means must be found, but he wishes to avoid the responsibility of finding them if he can. . . . He evidently wd like *us* to get it done. . . . F. has been working under such difficulties & dangers to himself that it is wonderful that he shd. have accomplished so much. He is in it heart & soul, & absolutely on *our* side, but the time has come when he feels he has done his share. Smuts (St[ate] Att[orne]y) has already told him that he is morally certain that he is at the bottom of everything; that he has not been able to get proof as yet, but when he does he will 'put it into him for all he is worth'.

Speaking of Mr. C[hamberlain]'s allusion to the absence of any sufficiently strong appeal from the Uitrs. as a reason for noninterference, F. said with the greatest earnestness: 'Mr. C. can push this line too far. He has now got an appeal from 22,000. If this isn't enough, he will never get another. We (the capitalists) can make our peace easily enough with the Govt., & we shall do it if this last effort isn't enough for Mr. C. . . .' I can't represent to you too strongly the earnestness with wh. he said this, and I stake any reputation I have on his genuineness. If you can't move Mr. C. on this, the game is up. Greene will be hopelessly discredited both publicly & privately, & you may as well put up the shutters of the Agency & save the treasury a waste of money. Of course the thing has come more suddenly than we expected; but it *has* come & we must either 'go into it baldheaded' or drop the whole business – probably for ever. Personally I have not much hope – none at all except in you. If you were up here yourself I am sure you would feel that this is the turning point in the business so far as you are concerned, and a fortiori so far as any other possible H[igh] C[ommissione]r is concerned: & if we don't convince you it must be our fault in the representation of facts.

F. leaves for C. Town on Wednesday & will see you personally; but we think it important that you shd. know his position before seeing him.

In these circumstances, publication of the Great Deal negotiations was crucial to Milner. Only this could prevent the capitalists and Boers from turning back in their tracks, and go some way towards keeping loyalists up to the mark. Publication of the commitment of both the capitalists and the Uitlander leaders to the franchise and the details embodied in the Memorandum attached to the reply, would ensure that both the situation in the Transvaal and the solution were brought into the open simultaneously. The mining leaders would be much less likely to abandon a position thus publicly announced; the admissions implicit in the Boer offer would stand even if, as in fact happened, the Republic broke off negotiations; an opening would be created for imperial intervention, and the apparent generosity of the capitalists would be established for the benefit of all onlookers, particularly those at home in England. Milner had two long meetings with Fitzpatrick when the latter reached Cape Town, on 31 March and, after receiving Fiddes's letter, 3 April. He pressed Fitzpatrick hard to get the correspondence into the open, and his powers of persuasion seem to have decided the issue for Fitzpatrick immediately contrived to get the details of the Reply published.[64] When it appeared a few days later in the Cape *Times* and the *Star*, Greene wrote exultantly to the High Commissioner that the 'publication of the substance of the Reply of the Industry in the "*Times*", and of the full text in the "*Star*" last night, is a splendid stroke and strengthens our position enormously'.[65]

VI

With things now moving in South Africa, Milner's attention was already turning once more back to London. He felt that the British Government was very slow to move, and that opinion there had to be woken up. Looking ahead to the possibility of Fitzpatrick's publication, Milner felt that if the Uitlanders stuck to the line taken up in the Great Deal negotiations, this would make 'the issue clear both here and in England and ought certainly to direct attention to and excite interest in the question again'. It was too soon for a real showdown, 'to break the crockery' by provoking the final, probably bellicose, confrontation, for people 'generally would not understand why'.[66] Given a little time and energy things could now be changed. It was in this vein that the High Commissioner wrote to Greene on the day of his second talk with Fitzpatrick.

> Public opinion has been quite averted from S. Africa and is only gradually regaining interest in that subject. Considerable progress has been made in this direction lately, but after all it is only a beginning, . . . what the Uitlanders have to do is keep pegging away . . . if any considerable section have the capacity to stick to their guns then I believe they will win almost universal support in Great Britain. Remember that the Uitlander programme, as represented by the franchise memorandum, is only just formulated and not yet even published. Time must be allowed to get it generally known and appreciated.[67]

Milner's intention now as in 1898 was to force Chamberlain's hand, again trying to present him with a situation in which he would have no option but to intervene. Although plans had gone awry in 1898, Chamberlain laid himself open to this kind of embarrassment by virtue of his constant public utterances, and had only himself to blame if people took advantage of the opportunity. After their experience the previous year, there was some apprehension in Government House circles of the Colonial Secretary's wrath at having the Petition 'sprung on him',[68] but, with his schemes this time falling perfectly into place, that was something the High Commissioner was prepared to ignore.

Knowing Chamberlain's emphasis on public opinion, Milner now saw his way plainly. The Uitlander rank and file had to endorse the solution of franchise reform, revealed to them by the Great Deal publication, as the follow-up to their Petition, thus confirming the recently established impression of Uitlander solidarity. Agitation on this front had then to be sustained until British official and public opinion could be brought into line. Now as always Milner's links with the press were important. Fiddes, while in Johannesburg, went to see Monypenny and Pakeman, the editor of a new Uitlander paper the *Transvaal Leader*. Afterwards he was glad he had done so, 'for both needed guidance badly, especially Pakeman. But I succeeded in convincing both, and now, unless they go back on me they will strike the right note if necessary.'[69] Milner's intention was that these papers should help him 'to get the Uitlanders – as they cannot have mass meetings – to express in any way they can . . . their approval of the scheme of reforms *outlined in the memorandum*. . . . It would, so to speak, *canonize* that scheme as the Uitlanders recognized programme, their Petition of Right – at present it is merely the opinion of a few individuals. . . .'[70]

The extent of Milner's backstage management was not at all understood in London, and officials in South Africa did their best to foster this ignorance. After these recent events, it was a somewhat twisted logic which inspired Fiddes's letter to Selborne on his arrival back in Cape Town. 'This last [Uitlander] movement has come somewhat unexpectedly, but we didn't make it & we have got to reckon with it. It hasn't been engineered in any way by any of us – indeed our influence has been in the direction of moderation.'[71] Nor was the true nature of their contacts with the press revealed. Milner was desperate to avoid any 'of the newspapermen letting drop a hint that I had touched them up', for this he knew would

destroy Chamberlain's confidence in him.[72] Instead he wrote to
Chamberlain condemning 'the great English newspapers [which]
no longer have correspondents of any position in South Africa, the
men who supply the meagre private telegrams which they
occasionally receive being, with perhaps one exception, mere
newsgatherers of an inferior type'.[73] This prompted Lambert to
regret that 'the London papers . . . are so poorly served in S. Africa.
Could we not hint to the *Times* that it would be well to have a good
special correspondent there?' Graham in reply referred to the fact
that 'Miss Shaw, some time ago, led me to understand that they did
not think it worth while to have a first class man'.[74] When
subsequently Monypenny was attacked by an irate Boer, and
Milner thereupon sent a panicky telegram urging immediate
intervention should the *Star* be suppressed, again no one seemed
to appreciate its significance.[75] Yet the *Star* was the lynch-pin in
Milner's elaborate structure, for the policy set out in its columns
had to be followed by all the other Argus Company newspapers in
South Africa. Not only did these enjoy a wide circulation locally,
but it was from their editors acting as foreign correspondents that
almost all English newspapers received their South African
information.

Official publicity was the other string to his bow, and he now
tried again to get the Colonial Office to publish without carefully
choosing their moment. He wrote to Selborne, the most
sympathetic of the Office staff, stressing this particular point.

> What I wish particularly is that all this mass of material, which we are
> pouring into you, may not go wholly unutilized for the instruction of
> the public, even if it produces no impression at all – on the action of
> the Govt. Then one's time will not have been wholly wasted in the
> long run. Will you not publish a Blue Book and see that Edgar
> shootings and Jones trials, amphitheatre meetings, *Lombaard*
> incidents, etc. etc. etc. get rubbed into the public mind. I wish to
> goodness some of my vitriol could get in too. But I am afraid to put
> too much vitriol into public despatches lest they should never see
> the light of day.[76]

Chamberlain himself was never one to appreciate enforced
inactivity, and his speech in the House of Commons on 20 March,
aimed at strengthening the capitalists' hand, showed him trying to
keep a hand on the wheel. With the franchise question aired and
the arrival of the Petition, it was clearly time again to be up and

doing. Milner's continued emphasis on the danger of Uitlander despair at imperial impotence was seen as 'strong confirmation of Mr Chamberlain's views in favour of speaking plainly even at the risk of this country refusing to follow up words by deeds'.[77] All Chamberlain's hopes for a personal success and for the future of imperial interests rested on Britain's being associated with any settlement of the Transvaal question. For that reason South African opinion could not be allowed to falter or get too far ahead. Unaware of the extent to which Milner was pushing things on, the Colonial Office staff saw their only remedy in stepping up their education of the British people. 'We have first got to educate public opinion in this country and at the same time if possible to give a word of encouragement to the party of progress in So. Africa', intoned Graham, and his colleagues' response was inevitable. 'A Blue Book must be got out without delay.'[78]

Milner's plea to Selborne fell then on receptive ears. Chamberlain showed which way the wind was blowing when he made a short but very firm statement about the reinforcement of the Cape garrison. This was well received in South Africa, bringing, as Greene told Milner, 'the Cosmopolitan waverers down on our side of the fence who only await [the] slightest sign of firm policy on the part of H.M.'s Government'.[79] As far as a Blue Book was concerned, the members of the Colonial Office had been looking forward to it and formulating their ideas for some time. It was still considered important to emphasise the reality and grossness of grievances, but now in the shadow of the Petition and of renewed agitation the bona fides of the petitioners had to be established. Chamberlain had stressed in 1896 that those engaged in the Raid were a minority whose number did not justify withholding reforms from all other Uitlanders. This still had to be proved for the public's benefit, and Greene's report of an interview with Johannesburg working-men was therefore welcomed. 'This goes a considerable way towards supplying the blank which Mr. Chamberlain wants filled up', remarked Just.[80] This emphasises the width of the audience Chamberlain hoped would eventually be reached by his publications. The reality of grievances meant not only their occurrence, but their effect on men of all classes, working-men as well as the professional people in the South African League. Such examples Chamberlain hoped would attract wide sympathy, of importance not only in the South African context but also for the future role of the Imperial Government.

However, signs of that same uncertainty about grievances which had existed at the time of the Raid still appeared. When a letter from an ex-member of the South African League arrived, arguing that the Uitlander working class couldn't care less about the dispute, Graham in a rare moment of enlightenment suspected 'that he is right as regards a great many of the working men, who only want to be left alone – as do a great many of the Boer farmers. It is eminently a politicians dispute.'[81] Nevertheless, the show had to go on, for too much national pride and too many personal reputations had been committed for there to be any thought of drawing back. Besides, others were at once ready to assert the alternative view, for, as Wingfield noted in his rejoinder to Graham's minute, 'He may be right as to many of the working men but a larger number of working men as well of other classes can scarcely fail to feel the pressure of misgovernment by a Dutch oligarchy.'[82]

The climax of the Blue Book was to be Chamberlain's answer to the Petition, of vital importance since for the first time the Imperial Government was taking up grievances at the request of a large body of Uitlanders. It was generally felt that a clear statement of Milner's views was required, but there was some indecision as to whether these should be sought before or after the composition of Chamberlain's despatch. Graham's view, backed by Wingfield and Selborne, was that Milner's despatch 'should bear a genuine date and be printed, as received, after Mr Chamberlain's. It may then be pointed to as a complete confirmation of the views already taken by H.M.G. and a justification of even stronger measures than they have proposed.' Chamberlain himself was less sure. He felt that the appearance of calm and impartiality was essential, for the benefit of both the Dutch and British public and especially for his numerous critics.

> What I fear is the charge that I have rushed off a despatch without waiting to know the views of Sir A Milner. Of course I do know them from secret despatches but I can't say this & I think it will be considered too 'pushful' if my despatch *seems* to be altogether independent of Sir A M's views.[83]

The Colonial Secretary's view was accepted, and so Milner's views were sought before settling Chamberlain's reply to the Petition, the official request to the High Commissioner being so phrased as to make the extent of previous consultation and Colonial Office knowledge seem minimal. Thus at a time when imperial control was required to be stronger than ever, the demands of Chamberlain's publicity campaign and his own political situation resulted in delay and led the Colonial Secretary to put his trust in the man on the spot whose reputation at home still stood so high.

Along with the official request for Milner's views went a much fuller secret cable explaining that, as Chamberlain was considering a lengthy despatch for submission to the Cabinet which would serve as a reply to the Petition, together with a Blue Book to be published as soon as this despatch should reach South Africa, a full and frank statement of Milner's views was needed. 'General object aimed at is to inform public opinion as to true state of affairs.'[84] Milner delightedly sat down for four days, and composed not only his famous telegram fully endorsing all the complaints of the petitioners and comparing their position to that of Spartan 'helots', but also a plan and detailed list of despatches for the intended Parliamentary Paper.

> I hope that Blue-book will not be confined to recent events but embrace history of past two years fully, dealing with treatment of High Court & of Report of Mining Commission, Aliens Expulsion & Press Laws, Dynamite juggle, Hess Case, War Tax, Cape Boys & ill-treatment of natives. . . . As regards my own position I should welcome the greatest publicity. The unpopularity wh. I am bound to incur with a certain party here is of small account compared with the supreme importance of making ~~the British~~ [deleted in Milner's draft] public realize the true state of affairs.[85]

The High Commissioner felt correctly that events were moving in his favour. The necessities of publicity were now creating their own demands on Chamberlain as he endeavoured to keep British and South African opinion in step for the good of the Empire. The Colonial Secretary's own political position led to more weight still being given to Milner's opinions. Inside the Colonial Office itself Selborne was pushing his chief as hard as he could in Milner's direction.

> My first care has been to avoid a despatch, that wasn't going to be followed up, and on the face of it ought to followed up or cry shame on us. Our chief on the other hand was first & foremost for educating the public at home & considering their deficiencies of knowledge I am all for this so long as my point is not contravened. I think I have

got over the difficulty by getting him to address the despatch as a reply to the petitioners and not as a remonstrance to the S.A.R. Govt, a point of form of real importance. Granted that you are not prepared to follow up your remonstrance for certain if necessary, it is futile to pitch your abuse strongly, whereas you can speak your mind more freely to a third party. I am not afraid that we shall pin ourselves to the Convention – quite the contrary, I am drafting for the wider ground. . . . Of course I can't swear that our chief will approve it, but we have talked it round & over & all about & I have tussled with him a good deal more than usual. . . .[86]

No wonder Milner felt able to come out into the open as the champion of the Uitlander cause. His letters betray his optimism, and illustrated the importance of the state of public opinion as governing the stand he was prepared to take. The Cape Dutch he thought were advising the Republic to give way, agitation continued on the Rand, English public opinion was beginning to be impressed with the seriousness of the situation, and the answer to the Petition boded well. The High Commissioner foresaw little difficulty with the Cabinet and was sufficiently sanguine to count on the support of Liberals at home.[87]

Thus confident, Milner tried again to create the situation he had angled for at the time of the Great Deal negotiations. On 8 May, he telegraphed Chamberlain suggesting that the Republic should be invited to a conference, such an invitation to be added to the impending indictment of the Republic in the reply to the Petition.[88] Since this reply was of necessity a public document, again the substance of negotiations was to be brought out into the open. By doing this Milner hoped 'to force the S.A.R. Government into some definite position – yes or no – about the franchise'. Continued agitation by the Uitlanders to this end, this time with the power of the British Government behind them, 'would keep up English interest and *rub the real issue well into the public mind*'.[89] Milner, never a politician and hating the compromises of democracy, was trying to use publicity to force through the clear solution which he feared secret discussions between Boer and Briton would never provide. Publicity was to be used to tie the hands of politicians on both sides, to limit their capacity for sidestepping issues and for delaying the inevitable.

VIII
THE BLOEMFONTEIN CONFERENCE

I

As conflict with the Boer Government over Uitlander grievances and possible remedies grew in the early months of 1899, Chamberlain's course and the views of his colleagues, both in the Colonial Office and in the Cabinet, came to be shaped by Milner's insistence that British Government inaction was undermining South African loyalty to the Empire. If this loyalty were not retained by action to protect the interests and rights of Britons there when they appeared to be threatened, then the imperial hold on South Africa would soon weaken and the formation of that United States of South Africa would take only a short time. In other words, refusal to support British subjects effectively when they needed and asked for such support, would undermine British paramountcy quite as effectively as would refusal to act against foreign attempts to control Mozambique, or Boer moves towards Delagoa Bay. It has already been seen how Salisbury, Balfour and other Ministers were aware of the challenge to the British position posed by Portuguese weakness, Boer ambition, and jealous European rivals. It is clear that on occasion they were prepared to act forcefully in defence of that position, sometimes more forcefully than Chamberlain himself had wanted. It is certain too that they were concerned at the various threats to paramountcy throughout the period 1895–9, and that after mid-1897, they were increasingly aware that their's was a losing battle. The Anglo-German Convention of 1898 is evidence that almost anything might be countenanced which promised to halt the process of slow disintegration.

Such attitudes among Ministers inevitably influenced their approach to the evidence of grievances and arguments for supporting the Uitlanders which Chamberlain had all along presented, either publicly or at Cabinet meetings. So it was that at this point the fundamental agreement within Salisbury's Cabinet came into play. The Foreign Office and service ministries were fully aware of the South African situation from their respective standpoints. They knew, as did the Colonial Office, that the Boers were still building up their defences and armaments, and continued active on the Continent, and that the *status quo* in Portugal and Mozambique remained unstable. That Chamberlain should present other evidence of a threat to British paramountcy was, in view of the known attitudes of the Boers, no surprise. In 1897, Lord Salisbury had had no hesitation in accepting the reasoning behind Chamberlain's proposal for troop reinforcements, namely 'the bad effect which is being produced on South African opinion, and may be produced in the future by the inaction of the British Government in the face of Kruger's enormous preparations',[1] even though at that point in time he had reservations about the remedy proposed. To explain his readiness to accept Chamberlain's view, there is no need to invoke either carelessness or senility on Salisbury's part; nor is the Prime Minister's willingness to defer to majority opinion and an acquaintance with details closer than his own in itself sufficient explanation. The fact is that Milner's evidence and Chamberlain's arguments about things South African derived their strength from their being for the whole Cabinet, and in so many ways simply the reverse of a coin which they felt they already knew. With an awareness that British supremacy was threatened was coupled the assumption – usually unspoken – that it should be defended. It seemed that now in South Africa, where all other ways of containing the Boers had failed, even the loyalty of British subjects (professions of which imperialists have always wanted to believe) was being tested to the utmost, as the Petition to the Queen showed. For this reason, the Cabinet, when it came early in May 1899 to discuss South Africa and the answer to the petitioners, was confronted with a case which it was half-ready to believe even before it was presented. Ministers were disinclined to do other than accept Chamberlain's growing insistence that 'If we ignore altogether the prayer of the petitioners, it is certain that British influence in South Africa will be severely shaken'.[2] Moreover, in the aftermath of Fashoda, it was generally felt that Britain could with greater confidence and less risk take a stern line with the Boers. Since other alternatives had disappeared, it was not surprising that Chamberlain's offer of the case for remedying grievances was taken up. That there was such a case for the Boers to answer on the grievance issue, that it could be seriously adopted by the Cabinet, and that a positive response was required to the Petition, was due above all to Chamberlain's public development of it. That it arose now in the form that it possessed was the result of Milner's work behind the scenes on the Rand.

Balfour knew more than most of his colleagues, yet he showed no disposition to question Chamberlain's assertion that action was required. While appreciating the Boer argument in his curious philosophical way, he was in no doubt that the British case was justified. 'All these grievances are serious, and they are doubly serious because they are inflicted by a minority upon a majority.'[3] Nor was this a position peculiar to Balfour; Chamberlain's note included with his revised draft of the Answer for the second round of discussions on 9 May indicates that other comments from the Cabinet had been equally restricted.

> The general effect of the changes is to lessen the emphasis put on financial grievances and to lay more stress on the personal disabilities of the Uitlanders and the inequality of their treatment as compared with the Boers. I have endeavoured to show that this is inconsistent with the spirit of the Convention.

With the spirit of the Convention at stake, no criticism was levelled at the assertion of British paramountcy, which in turn meant that the British Government 'cannot permanently ignore the exceptional and arbitrary treatment to which their fellow countrymen and others are exposed, and the absolute indifference of the Government of the Republic to the friendly representations which have been made to them on the subject.'[4]

The problem as Balfour saw it sprang from the fact that the Boers would almost certainly resist any practical reforms, as they had done in the past. If continual insistence met equal resistance in the normal course of events, then force as a remedy had inevitably to be considered. It had been used before in South Africa; but could the use of overwhelming force be justified *now*, to obtain a municipality or the franchise, and in defence of such concepts as the 'spirit' of the Convention and British paramountcy? In his own mind, Balfour perhaps required a more specific moral principle upon which to base a decision to use force; certainly he wanted one with which to confront critics at home and abroad. His reluctance to countenance the use of force to obtain British demands reflected not simply a general aversion to war, but also the remains of that general retreat from adventurous policies in South Africa adopted since May 1897. At the same time, he apparently did not exclude force as a solution to the present difficulties in the South African situation. Although suggesting that it would be a good tactical move first to pay the indemnity for the Jameson Raid, he wrote 'we are obviously on much safer ground when we are dealing with outrages to individuals. Whenever such occur, it seems to me that we should be justified in insisting upon ample reparation, and, if reparation was denied, then proceeding to exact it by force.' Believing that a majority of the Republic's population was English, he wondered whether this 'state of things, without parallel in history, may be perhaps a sufficient ground for exceptional measures'.[5] Balfour's surveys of arguments in no way ruled out war. His letter to Chamberlain continued

> If we are to insist at the point of the bayonet upon anything, I still feel that the most plausible demand would be for a measure of municipal reform sufficiently comprehensive to give our countrymen ... reasonable security for liberty and property, ... the right to serve on juries ..., and the right to levy an Education Rate for schools in which English should be taught.[6]

Balfour is the only member of the Cabinet whose expressed opinions at this time have survived. Given his fertility of resource as a politician and his capacity for producing arguments to suit any contingency, it is difficult to assess his true feelings. It cannot however be denied that he concerned himself with justifying further British intervention; the need for this he did not question. In so doing he furnished his colleagues with arguments for a policy which clearly involved the risk of precipitating a war for a series of municipal reforms which had been the basis of Chamberlain's recommendations to Kruger since 1896. Perhaps Balfour's arguments convinced other members of the Cabinet as much as those of Chamberlain; more probably they simply embodied what was the majority feeling when confronted with Milner's 'helot' telegram of 4 May. There is no reason to think that there was other than general agreement that the Boers' behaviour towards the Uitlanders ultimately threatened the British position in South Africa. Lord James confirmed as much when he defined the basic aims of Cabinet policy as '(1) to protect the British flag in South Africa, so as to secure its predominance, and (2) to avoid war'.[7] Lord Salisbury simply informed the Queen that the final despatch had been unanimously approved by the Cabinet.

It was in this way therefore that the preservation of British supremacy in South Africa, of prestige and paramountcy, became finally caught up with the question of grievances and their remedy. Grievances had been first taken up by Chamberlain; the equation of their remedy with British supremacy had subsequently been confirmed as a result of Milner's efforts; and in its decision to take a firm line with the Republic in answer to the Petition, the Cabinet endorsed a policy designed to maintain that supremacy at all costs short, as they thought, of a war. The result was that grievances, both in terms of demonstrating their reality and of remedying them, now had so much capital – of various kinds – invested in them, and carried with them the necessity of publicity to such a degree, that real diplomatic negotiations on these questions were in fact becoming almost impossible. As Salisbury showed in his letter to the Queen, the existence of serious grievances was officially considered an indisputable fact; 'it would be difficult to acquiesce by our inaction in the grievous wrongs that are being inflicted on Your Majesty's subjects . . .'. Later still, he felt that 'we cannot abandon them [the Uitlanders] without grave injustice – nor without endangering Your Majesty's authority in the whole of South Africa'.[8] Salisbury and Chamberlain, seeing a real problem, long felt that remedies were negotiable. Meaningful diplomacy, however, presupposes the acknowledgement of the problem by both sides. Most Boers never really accepted the existence of grievances except as something blown up by the Uitlanders to an absurd degree; even those who recognised that the Boer state had its share of anomalies and problems, did not acknowledge Britain's right to intervene. The Cabinet struggled to put its demands in moderate form, but having done so, felt itself ill-rewarded. Salisbury again put the point to the Queen: 'we are most earnestly anxious to avoid any rupture with the Boers if it is possible. But they do not assist us to do so. Our last despatch was very carefully considered by the Cabinet, and by general admission, was very moderate in its demands, and very considerate in its language. But it was rejected by the Boers without ceremony.'[9] The British Government failed to appreciate that, whatever its language, even its raising of grievances was in Boer eyes immoderate. How much more so was this the case with Milner's handling of the exchanges in the summer of 1899. It would be foolish to see Boer concessions as the product of negotiation. They were nothing more than grudging surrenders, held back as long as possible in the face of apparently uncompromising demands. Yet the longer the Boers delayed, the more the British Government felt that it had to appear inflexible; so the scope for genuine exchanges decreased, especially as the constant publicity felt necessary by Chamberlain and Milner led to simplificaiton of the issues involved. Chamberlain's past now began to catch up with him rapidly, and the policy of publicity came to be revealed as one which, instead of freeing Ministers as he had intended, committed them more and more narrowly in just the way that Milner, believer in the 'inevitable' war, had intended.

II

At this moment, however, Milner himself began to feel that his earlier optimism had been misplaced. While the British Government was considering its reply, negotiations inside South Africa resulted in the President of the Orange Free State's proposal for a conference at Bloemfontein between Milner and Kruger; discussion between the two should deal, it was suggested, with the situation created by the Uitlander petition. Milner, giving as his reason the fact that the British Government had not yet declared its views either on the Petition or on the general situation in the Transvaal, found it 'very hard . . . to see what good an interview at this moment could effect'.[10] For him, in other words, the public assertion was vital, and he betrayed his belief in the futility and inappropriateness of negotiation by referring to the proposed conference as an 'interview'. 'It is a very clever move and has already produced one effect, viz. that of mollifying the British Press a bit and relaxing for the moment, unfortunately as I think, the screw upon the enemy.'[11] As the inquisitorial metaphor suggests, Milner was concerned with tactics first and foremost before he ever raised with Chamberlain the actual issues to be discussed with Kruger. 'The issue turns entirely . . . on our keeping up the impression, which we have certainly given, of serious determination. . . . I hope that in England people can be prevented from running away with the idea that we have finished with the crisis.'[12] For the moment, however, there was little he could do but trust that movements of opinion already started would continue. Chamberlain was far more sympathetic to the idea of a conference. Such a meeting was in line with both his own expressed wish to avoid any ultimatum, and with Milner's suggestion for a similar meeting which he had included in the Government's own reply to the Petition. It is true that he regretted the delay now necessary before this despatch could be sent, and the loss of a chance to publish the 'grievances' Blue Book; he realised that once again the Imperial Government had been deprived of the initiative by events inside South Africa. British public opinion expected every form of diplomatic approach to be exhausted; it would see Kruger's presence at the Conference as indicating a conciliatory frame of mind, and, in the absence of a clear picture of the grave situation which had resulted in the Conference, would be less inclined to support pressure by the Imperial Government.[13] Nevertheless he still welcomed the possibilities of a settlement afforded by the meeting. Chamberlain was not a warmonger, realising that war would very likely undo the work of imperial propaganda on which he was engaged; in trying to create and mould a public opinion one of his main objects was to enable statesmen to avoid armed struggle, even if the support created might sustain British efforts for a time in any war which did occur. It was a long time before Chamberlain admitted that war in South Africa was inevitable, and he retained to the end a trace of hope that a Boer surrender would come without it in the face of a British show of armed strength. For this reason he suggested that Schreiner, the Prime Minister of Cape Colony, should be present at Bloemfontein as representative of a large sector of Dutch and colonial opinion. He also tried again to widen the scope for negotiation. While prepared now to accept Milner's insistence on the solution of an Uitlander franchise, and not wishing to fetter his initiative Chamberlain reminded him that he 'should not, however, lose sight of possible alternative in shape of full municipal rights for populous mining district and Johannesburg'.[14] This he still believed was something which commended itself to the British public, who were unlikely to see any point in pressing for a franchise to make British subjects into foreign citizens. Other potentially provocative issues were also avoided; Chamberlain refused to raise the question of suzerainty again at this time, despite the arrival a fortnight before the Conference of the Boer claim to be a 'sovereign international state', a claim as irritating as it was inadmissible.[15] Chamberlain could after all afford to hold his fire for a while, for he did not see in the proposal for a conference the extreme cunning and deviousness detected by Milner. He certainly trusted the Boers no more than he had ever done, but if they were on the run then it was enough to be firm rather than needlessly bellicose, especially given the construction which the British public placed on the Conference. A genuine settlement at Bloemfontein would still have brought all that Chamberlain wanted – a dramatic climax, brought about by imperial intervention in a righteous cause, marking the successful outcome of a course the Colonial Secretary himself had set in motion soon after arriving in office.

Milner, however, refused to have Schreiner present at the Conference and ignored the municipality. Although Chamberlain may be criticised for not taking a more decided line with his High Commissioner at such a point, there were reasons for this. While they might have hoped against hope, nobody in the Colonial Office really expected much to come of the Conference, not least because it had in no way been associated with a firm stand by the British Government on the matters raised in the Petition. Graham had been watching both the London and the provincial press, and felt sure that while 'the abnormal conditions in the S.A.R. have attracted a great deal of attention ... lately, & generally speaking sympathy is expressed for the Uitlanders', 'so far as we can judge, ... there is still a good deal of misapprehension as to the circumstances, and as to the aims of H.M.G.' In these circumstances

> the utmost we can do is to make it quite clear that the unreasonable conditions are imposed by Krüger, not by us, & put ourselves right with public opinion in S. Africa, ... and in this country, especially that section of it which is under the impression that Mr. Chamberlain at all events is not anxious for a peaceful solution. Speaking generally the best way to attain this object seems to be to leave Sir Alfred a free hand.[16]

The Colonial Office, as they had concluded a month before when considering their reply to the Petition, felt that moves by the man on the spot would command more support than if Chamberlain were held responsible. That such a decision could be made reflects strongly on the problems which Chamberlain's belief in the importance of carrying public support had created. This, combined with the weakness of Chamberlain's own popularity, led him to abandon control of the Anglo-Boer exchanges at a most critical moment.

Chamberlain and his staff were not alone in their thinking. A certain dislike and distrust of Chamberlain within the Conservative party rank and file appeared to be reviving in 1899, after having lain dormant for a while.[17] Yet at the same time belief in the importance of having the people at one's back was widespread, having been greatly strengthened by experience of the Fashoda crisis. The *Quarterly Review*, for example, commented on the hatred of being beaten which

> is deeply rooted in the British working man. . . . Like other instincts it is spontaneous, and its operaton is by no means necessarily accompanied by thought. . . . It is often accompanied by – and, if 'men of light and leading' exercise their legitimate influence, it may be more and more constantly associated with – the desire that the power of Great Britain and of the British Empire should be exercised not merely in furtherance of the material interests of the nation, but for the advancement of civilization, and freedom among mankind at large.[18]

Such support and resolution brought peace and diplomatic success if a lead was given. These had always been Chamberlain's convictions, and now others were reiterating them.[19] Inevitably the man of 'light and leading' on this occasion had to be the High Commissioner. Chamberlain knew already the extent to which events and the pressure of opinion in South Africa had necessitated changes of plan. Milner however was in South Africa, in closer touch with public opinion there, and presumably able to carry out any necessary tactical decisions. The goodwill with which he had departed for Cape Town still existed, and he would not lack guidelines, for the Government's attitude as summed up in the Reply to the Petition was to reach him before the Conference began. With publication having played such a great part and therefore continuing to be necessary, Milner's personal credibility in Britain was a great asset. At the same time, the Colonial Office did not see that Milner had blotted his copybook as far as the Dutch in South Africa were concerned, whereas Chamberlain's own unpopularity was only too well realised. Thus Chamberlain withdrew from any initiative in deciding the course of the Bloemfontein Conference. He contented himself with publishing the correspondence on the dynamite monopoly, an illustration of the Transvaal's intransigence which would be useful in guiding the public attitude, especially as the excuse for it was provided by a publication of the Boers' own.[20] Chamberlain, in an attempt to give the world some inkling of the British Government's feelings, authorised Milner to publish an 'interim' reply to the Petition.

Milner's own supporters both in South Africa and England were also working hard. Monypenny reported that he was doing his best to keep the pot boiling so that the League could organise meetings, and was relieved that in Greene's absence he had coped satisfactorily with the announcement of the Conference.[21] Milner's colleagues in Johannesburg were also, on the High Commissioner's instructons, trying to get influential signatures on yet another Petition, trying to mould the Uitlanders' programme in order to involve the British Government, and promoting the cause of an Uitlander Parliament to take shape after the ban on the Reform Committee's political activity expired on 31 May;[22] this latter scheme had as its immediate object the association of the Uitlanders with the forthcoming Conference at Bloemfontein. It was however one thing to order and quite another to accomplish. The British officials found their task difficult, and apparently met with very little spontaneous support. Evans' attempt to find men 'who know what they are about' as Walrond had instructed him, was somewhat barren.

> I have been at the people here in regard to forming a Committee such as you have proposed but no one seems to put much energy into the matter. It seems to me that it is of the greatest importance that such a Committee should be in existence at the moment the conference is going on, as it is on the cards that H[is] E[xcellency] might from time to time require information which could only be given to him by a representative body. I shall keep pegging away at them to form such a committee.[23]

At home too bodies like the ISAA were working steadily on Milner's behalf, and all was ready for a great pro-Milner demonstration. Wyndham wrote to tell him that

> The view which I inculcate & which will be & is being inculcated by all sections of the press including the *Chronicle* is this: – 'Milner, Milner, Milner. Things change too fast & S. Africa is too far for us to judge. But we sent out our best man who made Egypt & left for S. Africa with a chorous of God speeds from all parties. He is on the spot & we must, *Chronicle* & all, support him.' That, also, is Chamberlain's

line. The Cabinet, so far as I can judge, are going somberly [sic] to
work on the same tack. . . . I can say without hesitation that opinion
here is incredibly better than it was 5 or 6 weeks ago & that it
improves daily & hourly. Frivolous delays by Kruger will not be stood
provided, of course, that he is not rushed too fast for the limitations
of his mind & the minds of his entourage.[24]

It was encouraging too, and Milner must surely have chuckled,
when Just wrote to warn the High Commissioner that the
capitalists, notably Beit and George Farrar, were successfully
influencing the Liberal press in favour of the Uitlanders, and
expressed his concern about such allies.[25] Phillip Gell, as one might
expect, showed better acquaintance with his friend's mind, when
he asked if he was satisfied with the tone of the home press. 'Let me
know if you want any hint given to them, for I can say things
informally wh. it might not be wise for you to write – . . . I can get at
any London paper & the *Manchester Guardian*.' Milner was the
focus of attention, and his role was to give a lead. 'I am sure that the
general feeling here among the City people & the Papers is the
desire to back you & strengthen your hands – if only they know
what to be at.'[26]

Public opinion clearly had to know when to follow and when to
lead. The controversy was being raised to the level of generalities,
since distance and complexity rendered the details
incomprehensible to any save the man on the spot. Britain was
being asked to abandon the discussion and checks upon her
representatives which were a vital part of her democratic tradition.
It is here that the serious flaw in Milner's approach becomes clear.
In some respects Milner and Chamberlain were undoubtedly
following the same path. Unanimous support for their respective
policies was what they strove to create. In Britain this necessitated
bridging the gap between those with and those without access to
detailed knowledge of South Africa; in Parliament, that between a
Government and an Opposition party whose task it was to ask
questions and to present alternatives. In terms of ideas they were
faced with divisions for or against a consolidationist approach to
Empire, and also with those who believed that the ends of any
policy in South Africa did not necessarily justify drastic means, in
this case a possible war. They complicated their task still further by
attempting to make many people think about Empire and imperial
questions who did not normally incline to do so. In the first place,

Chamberlain had long felt, quite apart from South Africa, that the future of the Empire and Britain's place in the world rested to a very large extent on the creation of an informed public opinion. Subsequently, this had come to be seen as necessary to the success of British policy in South Africa, similar conclusions being reached whether one saw, like Milner, a need to whip up public opinion to sustain Britain in the war which was coming, or whether, like Chamberlain, one saw in the creation of national awareness and agreement a way of isolating and browbeating opponents, enabling politicians to achieve a settlement of particular problems without a struggle. However, Milner's lack of either patience or flexibility, and his determination to see the question through, exposed further difficulties inherent in the policy of publicity. Reluctant to acknowledge, or perhaps not fully aware of, the diversity of views which confronted imperial policy-makers, Milner, now careless of partisanship, was attempting by means of a single general 'case' to win as many adherents to his cause as possible. Unanimity being crucial if the outcome was to be war, generality and one-sidedness had for Milner the advantages that criticism became difficult through lack of information, and simplicity appealed to a wider audience, who might, in a democratic society check those of their representatives who chose to voice their doubts. Once in motion, however, such a course demanded constant publicity, and mistakes could be disastrous because it was difficult to disguise them. Moreover, for Milner's policy to stand any chance of success, personal trust in him was essential. In these circumstances, the Bloemfontein Conference, held at the beginning of June, and Milner's role in it turned out to be of immense significance.[27]

The Conference opened in the capital of the Orange Free State on 31 May, but not in the easy informal way originally if unrealistically hoped for by the Free State and Cape politicians responsible for the idea. Milner had refused not only Schreiner's presence, but also that of Hofmeyr, leader of the Cape Afrikaners, and he further insisted that President Steyn should not be allowed to act as mediator between himself and Kruger. Seeing little point in the Conference, Milner did his best to eliminate anyone likely to introduce moderation or compromise into the discussion; as his own right hand man he took the Imperial Secretary, G. V. Fiddes, scarcely one to restrain the High Commissioner. Reducing the

Conference in advance to a series of straight exchanges between Kruger and himself was also necessary to Milner because the proceedings were to be published. Milner felt he might trump the Conference card by using the talks as a platform for the display of his position, so that the world outside would see the Conference in relation to the other British Government publications yet to appear.

Opinion in Britain seemed to be with him; Gell described how the

> dynamite despatches have been exceedingly useful in educating public opinion, and the Boer reply to C[hamberlain] has hardened people's hearts. . . . Everybody is inclined to take for granted that you are sure to be in the right, and to give you a free hand and expect that the Government will feel bound to back you up. People's attention is alert & your public backing is – to the best of my perception – very strong.[28]

If he handled the Conference correctly, Milner felt that the cause of the trouble in the Republic, Uitlander grievances, and its solution, the immediate grant of a liberal franchise, would be understood by all. Publication of the proceedings would also help prevent Boer deception later on. Clarity or, indeed, simplification at the Conference followed by rapid decisive action would alone sustain public interest, that interest necessary in Milner's eyes to bolster up the British Government in putting continuous pressure on Kruger, necessary in both Britain and South Africa to persuade Kruger that concessions were expected of him, and essential, finally, if war were to follow a Boer refusal.

Kruger approached the Conference determined to prevent any infringement of the Republic's independence, and for that reason unsympathetic to any course which might be interpreted as surrendering to terms dictated by Milner. On the other hand, he was prepared to bargain on equal terms, trading the franchise for such concessions from Britain as payment of the indemnity for the Raid, or neutral arbitration in disputes between them. He brought with him advisers representing a wide cross-section of Boer opinion, and consulted with the Free State leaders, who were in turn in touch with politicians in Cape Colony. However, Kruger's slightly more flexible approach was of little use when up against the fact that questions of publicity made Milner determined to confine discussion to the franchise, and were to lead directly to his rapid abandonment of the meeting. After exploratory talks on the first day, Milner put forward a scheme involving immediate enfranchisement for all Uitlanders who had lived on the Rand for five years, and the creation of several new constituencies on the Rand designed to give the Uitlanders at least nine members out of a First Volksraad total of thirty-five. In reply, Kruger eventually offered progressive enfranchisement of the Uitlanders after naturalisation and commencing in two years' time, together with five seats in the Volksraad and the right to vote in presidential elections; he also offered to omit any specific renunciation of former allegiances from the oath to be taken by aliens on becoming naturalised, an existing requirement which many Uitlanders apparently found offensive. There were various other detailed provisions, with some of which Milner disagreed. These, however, were unimportant, for the High Commissioner proceeded to reject Kruger's plan in principle, on the grounds that it required most Uitlanders to become naturalised well in advance of receiving political rights, and it would not secure immediately a large number of Uitlander voters.

Able to get nothing more from Kruger largely because of his own unwillingness to raise other matters before the franchise question was publicly settled, Milner cut the Conference short on 5 June, and returned to Cape Town. The Government House team were pleased with its termination; 'we didn't expect to score over this Conference: it was a cunning move of the other side; our one desire was to get through it with as little damage as possible: & I don't think we left much of our wool among the brambles', was how Fiddes summed it up afterwards.[29] It was also for reason of publicity that Milner went on to minimise even the concessions which Kruger had actually offered. Telegraphing to Chamberlain immediately after the Conference about the proposed delivery of the reply to his own 'helots' despatch and its publication in England, he said

> I recognize necessity publish despatch as powerful summing-up of grievances for information of public. But I suggest following alterations . . . [on the subject of Uitlanders voting for the President, and the oath of allegiance]. The words which I wish to omit were perfectly correct when written and are correct but their publication now would call pointed attention to concessions just offered by President S.A.R. which however inadequate look big on these two

points.[30]

III

The fact that Chamberlain accepted the proposed alterations is an illustration of the spot in which Milner had landed him. Chamberlain was very angry both at Milner's limiting discussion almost entirely to the franchise, and at his breaking off the Conference so soon.[31] In this way the High Commissioner had greatly decreased the chances of obtaining concessions from Kruger and, failing that, of showing up the Boers' obstinacy. Kruger might in the eyes of the Government House staff have Kaffir blood in him, but they were not prepared on that account to allow him a 'Kaffir bargain'. Yet if Milner had to some extent betrayed the trust placed in him, there could still be no question of repudiation or reprimand unless the British Government were prepared to abandon their pretensions in South Africa altogether. If Milner resigned, South Africa would be lost for certain, but this was inconceivable, given the Cape's traditional place in imperial thinking and the new power which was South Africa's with the development of the gold-mining industry. If Britain in Egypt appeared to be threatened by an approach towards the headwaters of the Nile, how much more was the attitude of the Transvaal a threat to the Imperial position. In the middle of May, George Wyndham had given it as certain that although 'Salisbury may have views about the [Hague] Peace Conference, [and] Beach may have misgivings about his miserable Budget . . . the Cabinet as a whole will back you solid'.[32] The results of the Bloemfontein Conference if anything stiffened their resolve to see things through.

As for the Colonial Secretary, he saw that Milner's behaviour at Bloemfontein threatened his whole purpose in giving him a free hand. This made the publication of the Blue Book on grievances doubly important: it had now not only to justify the British Government's position in taking up the Petition, but had to restore any ground lost by Milner's stand at the Conference. It was published on 14 June, as soon as possible after the delivery of Chamberlain's despatch of 10 May which conveyed the Reply to the Petition. Special arrangements had been made for its printing; well before the end of May, the Stationery Office had been requested to authorise overtime working, and on 10 June an official Colonial Office request was made that, contrary to normal procedure, printing should go ahead several days before formal presentation to the House of Commons.[33] Material had of course been in process of collection for some months, and the problems of arrangement were debated throughout May.[34] Its purpose was varied – to support the complaints in the Petition from official sources to show their weight and consistency, to illustrate the genuine nature of the movement on the Rand and the totally unhelpful attitude of the Boer Government. There were a multitude of difficulties in trying to present all this in a form at once convincing and readable, not to mention the complications arising out of General Butler's refusal to allow the editing of his despatches sent during Milner's absence in London. On the whole these were overcome. Sir Edward Hamilton, for example, had stressed the absurdity of any stand taken on the franchise leading to war; although after reading the Blue Book he still thought that to demand municipal reform would be better than to insist on the franchise, he felt obliged to confess that Milner 'certainly makes out a much stronger case than most people like myself expected – the ill treatment of the foreigners at Johannesburg appears to be decidedly gross'.[35]

Publication of the grievances Blue Book, of the British Government's commitment to obtaining redress, and Milner's identification of redress with securing an Uitlander franchise, undoubtedly brought home to people the seriousness of the situation. What it was unable to do was preserve Milner's own image in all quarters. Seen in the light of his behaviour at Bloemfontein, the 'helots' despatch was widely interpreted as a first-class example of hotheadedness. Educated opinion, especially amongst Liberals, began to turn against him. A friendly editor, summing up this shift of attitude for Milner, commented 'In the absence of any strong lead, the cat is jumping, I think, very much against extremities.'[36] The corollary to this was Gell's letter of the same date, reflecting the views of one who, even more than Milner, looked to 'the people'.

> This last week has from the English point of view been the climax of your reputation. . . . After the Conference, there was a little inclination here & there to say that 'you broke off too abruptly' – that 'you might have pushed K. further' etc. . . . But your telegraphic

despatch & Chamberlain's letter wh. came out on Wednesday have knocked the bottom out of all such criticism ... just now, your position is stronger than it has ever been. The *Man in the Street* has awoke to you & believes in you. You know as well as I do, that your reputation hitherto has been limited to the Official Classes & the Press. Now you have been on all the 'Contents Bills' in England for three weeks. ... So that *now* everybody has been interested in your despatch; a month ago, it would have been passed over.[37]

Publicity had apparently brought with it the wider interest which Milner had sought to arouse, but the very methods and language which had made this possible had begun to destroy the support which had been his at the top. Events had shown that the methods Milner had chosen were incapable of maintaining the support he desired. His apparent temperament and his propaganda still had an appeal, but no longer carried universal conviction.

From the point of view of the Cabinet, the appearance of the grievances Blue Book was, with its inclusion of the Reply to the Petition, no more than the publication of details about which the Government had firmly made up its mind more than one month before. It was realised however that, while retreat in South Africa was impossible, people outside the Government, lacking that same education which the Cabinet had received over the previous four years, were now quite suddenly confronted with the possibility that force might be used in South Africa. Salisbury told the Queen that it 'was recognised by all members of the Cabinet that any actual break with the Transvaal would not be cordially supported here, and would cleave the Colonial community at Cape Town into two hostile camps. For these reasons war would be very much to be deprecated.' But firmness had to be maintained, and a week later the 'opinion prevailed that the Boers were less resolute than they had been, and that some moderate concessions might be expected. But it was better to take the steps necessary to put our forces into a state of full efficiency in South Africa by sending transport and munitions of war.'[38] Balfour summed up the position now arrived at by Ministers.

... it seems clear (1) that the attitude taken up by the Transvaal Government is in itself unreasonable; (2) that it is producing a feeling of unrest throughout South Africa, which is not only throwing upon this country a heavy financial burden, but it is imperilling that amalgamation of the Dutch and English element on which the future of the country depends, (3) that the illiberal laws which exclude the

Uitlanders have been passed contrary to declarations made by the Boers in 1881, and (4) that friendly argument unaccompanied by other pressure, has never yet extracted anything, however reasonable, from the President or his Government.[39]

That being so, the Prime Minister had concluded that 'the Govt. must go on, & apply steady & increasing pressure to Kruger, but there is no need to hurry, & that anything approaching an ultimatum should be delayed as long as possible.'[40] Further consideration of the question and the course of the Bloemfontein Conference had convinced the Cabinet that the Boers needed coercing – as in 1897 – and their apparently uncompromising attitude had prompted Balfour to abandon the idea that he had expressed early in May that the Boer position was understandable. If the British Government showed determination it was likely to win over wholehearted support at home, keep up Uitlander spirits in South Africa, and so once again force Kruger to yield without war. Selborne imparted the general feeling to his friend.

The idea of war with the S.A.R. is very distasteful to most people. Consequently the Cabinet have undoubtedly had to modify the pace that they contemplated moving at immediately after the Bloemfontein Conference. There is no idea of retreating from the intervention which was commenced by your action at Bloemfontein and our reply to the petition, but we cannot force the pace.[41]

Chamberlain was wholly in agreement with his colleagues. The letters quoted above show that the general belief in the possibility of securing British paramountcy by means other than the use of force had received a rude shock; hence the beginnings of military preparations. It is also clear that the reason why war was not as yet considered a practical method by the Cabinet lay above all in the uncertain state of public opinion in England. For this reason the Government was still happy to accept concessions, and hoped that the quiet military preparations would encourage the Boers to grant these in some form. It was this which explains Chamberlain's sharp despatch in reply to the High Commissioner's pressing for decisive action. Milner had demanded 'some intimation that Her Majesty's Government realise the necessity of putting an end to the present state of things, and that if adequate franchise is unattainable, remedy must be sought by other means. This will give franchise a last chance, and pave the way to other action, if franchise fails.'[42] Even before the Conference, Chamberlain had been a little alarmed at Milner's growing impetuosity,[43] and now he flung the High Commissioner's own words back at him.

> You have said yourself that we could not go to war about franchise and that ultimatum would be premature. Delay in these circumstances affords time for reflection and further concession. [What did Milner mean when he talked of 'other means'?] . . . There would be no meaning in a demonstration in the shape of large reinforcements unless it were to support an ultimatum, and public opinion seems to be with you in thinking that the time has not yet come for this. . . . To provoke a Parliamentary division by premature action and thus show Kruger that the country is divided would be mischievous and tend to confirm his obstinacy. At the same time we do intend to bring to a state of efficiency forces already in Africa, . . . arrangements which may help to convince Kruger that we are in earnest though not very important.[44]

Behind the scenes therefore Chamberlain looked for any sign of concession by the Boers which might lead to a negotiated settlement. He tried using Alfred Rothschild as an intermediary,[45] and several times reminded Milner that he should examine any apparent concession. If the outcome of negotiations which had begun between Kruger and Hofmeyr 'afford any basis for settlement so much the better', and if not, then Chamberlain made it clear that while he would continue pressing for the franchise he also intended to reopen the question of municipal rights, the demand to Kruger most satisfying to public opinion at home; only then would an ultimatum be considered.[46] Publicly as always Chamberlain followed a more uncompromising line, partly a result of simplification for the public's sake, partly to confirm for the benefit of the Transvaal Britain's determination. It was clear that a lead had to be constantly given to the public if Britain's position was to be preserved, and only if it was preserved would Chamberlain's own position be secure; this was especially so now, for the more Milner forfeited confidence, the more directly did all onus fall on Chamberlain's shoulders. The problem of knowing when to lead and where to follow public opinion had always existed for Chamberlain. Not wholly confident of his political security, and subject, like any politician in a prominent office, to a host of conflicting pressures, he had a strong practical need to compromise while being by instinct rather intolerant and unyielding. Ever since he had come to power he had pursued the issue of grievances, in itself something of a middle way. Now in

June 1899, with the evidence before it together with Milner's lead on the franchise, he felt the British public was faltering. His own recent attempts to give Milner the chance to rally support had not been very successful. This reasoning finally overcame any indecision, and Chamberlain composed a speech on the situation for delivery at Highbury on 26 June. His determination was subsequently reinforced by Selborne who, while setting out the general case for a determined stand, employed arguments and flattery well designed to exploit the Colonial Secretary's particular weaknesses in an attempt to move him towards Milner. The moment was just right, he wrote, if Chamberlain wanted to thwart the scheming of his Liberal opponents. 'It seems to me just the occasion for that instinct of yours, which has so well served you hitherto, to assert itself, rising to meet a difficulty in the face, to give the lead to your friends, to take your fellow countrymen into your confidence.'[47]

The speech was a great success, less for its novelty than for its timing and its mode of delivery. It contained nothing beyond that which Balfour had told Fowler and the Cabinet had decided at their meetings. Chamberlain rehearsed again the themes of all his previous publications on the South African situation, and, while emphasising that the Government in no way desired war, also let there be no mistake about Britain's determination to have a satisfactory settlement. In the Cabinet Lansdowne and Ritchie both thought the speech an excellent one,[48] while some measure of its effect outside can be gauged from another of Selborne's letters, which strongly reinforced Chamberlain's own diagnosis of the situation.

> I met Bartley, M.P. today. As you know he is a [one word illegible] and not fond of L[iberal] U[nionist]s. He came up to me and said 'look here, you know that I am not alone on the Tory benches in not loving this Government too dearly, but if you will only have the pluck to see this Transvaal business through and stick as an absolute minimum to Milner's proposals, . . . we will stick to you through thick and thin.[49]

From this speech onwards it was their diagnosis of the state of British opinion which determined all the actions of Chamberlain and the Government. Milner, realising that he was somewhat out of favour, acknowledged that it was 'certainly unfortunate that the same man should within a week have to appear as the calm, &, as far as possible conciliatory diplomatist, & the firebrand exciting his country to a policy of action'.[50] While this showed him sensitive to official coolness, he clearly did not understand where he had gone wrong. He continued to cry 'wolf' and to blow hot from Cape Town in what he saw as attempts to strengthen Chamberlain's hand, and to get the Government to commit itself to a definite position in advance of the impending Boer announcements on a further franchise scheme. Again he wanted that public commitment in order to make bargaining and negotiation impossible. Constantly he reiterated the by now well-worn arguments about the unity of South African loyalist opinion, and the danger that British inaction might demoralise her supporters. In all this, however, he was unsuccessful, for the Cabinet did not share his view that there was no incompatibility between his apparent roles of 'conciliatory diplomatist' and 'firebrand'. His despatches were still published in the Blue Books – there was no feasible alternative – but they impressed the Colonial Secretary, who now found Milner 'overstrained' and 'really rather trying', less and less. Chamberlain knew full well that he and his colleagues were prepared to follow, more or less, the policy advocated by Milner; but they differed considerably on timing, and still were not convinced that war was necessary however much British officials on the spot might urge it. British public opinion demanded that all diplomatic possibilities should be exhausted before more forceful steps were taken. Although therefore Government utterances were designed to prevent an Uitlander loss of confidence, as much as to lead home opinion, the latter was their prime concern. Ministers on the whole shared Salisbury's belief that Britain was the only power to which South Africans could appeal if in real difficulties, and could therefore be made to await Britain's pleasure.

IV

Now that the Cabinet's line was firmly settled, the three aspects of Chamberlain's policy of publication began to play their roles simultaneously and in very clear relation to each other, as they had done during the crisis of April 1897. From the time of his Highbury speech on 26 June, Chamberlain saw his task as the final consolidation of British public opinion behind the Government in order to push the Boers into a steady retreat. The Highbury speech was but the first of three, all very similar and made at monthly intervals, which consistently stressed the general features of the situation and the Government's determination to achieve a satisfactory settlement. All three were carefully timed and constructed. The first Birmingham speech, allowing some days to pass for the digestion of the Blue Book on grievances, set out the Imperial Government's position in relation to the case for grievances therein displayed. The Boer response to this stand, and to the friendly persuasions of politicians from both Natal and the Cape, was made plain in two successive proposals for franchise reform on 7 and 18 July. The latest of these offered a seven-year retrospective franchise, together with a number of changes in the procedures for voting and registration and six Uitlander seats, rather than the five-year residence qualification and more extensive redistribution of seats for which Milner and some of the Uitlanders were contending.

Chamberlain himself was delighted and told both Milner and a *Times* reporter that he saw in them an end to the crisis.

> If Kruger has really given seven year retrospective franchise and five seats . . . I congratulate you on a great victory. . . . No one would dream of fighting over two years in a qualification period. We ought to accept this as a basis for settlement and make the most of it. Krüger [sic], we should assume, has conceded in principle what we asked for, viz. immediate substantial representation.[51]

However, distrust of the Boers was not to be dispelled overnight, and some of the Cabinet were clearly less sanguine than their Colonial Secretary. Salisbury wrote to congratulate Chamberlain on having at last persuaded Kruger that the British Government was in earnest, and urged him to keep up the pressure. This he suggested should be done by the movement of troops on the northern side of the Transvaal, where interference by the Cape or Natal Parliaments would be avoided, and where there was room for the bulk of the South African garrison.[52] Chamberlain thought Salisbury's suggestion, if feasible from the military point of view, an admirable move. While the danger of losing present advances by future restrictive conditions remained, one had to be careful until an actual settlement had been recorded.[53]

In Cape Town, however, Milner was aghast at the British reaction to the Boer offer. Although this came closer to his Bloemfontein demands, it still did not meet them in detail, and in so far as he felt the Imperial Government should state its own terms and not bargain, he still felt the difference wide enough to warrant rejection. Although the Boers had conceded something, and might therefore still offer more, perhaps going even beyond the High Commissioner's Bloemfontein terms, Milner himself was beginning to question the whole principle of a constitutional adjustment. The fundamental weakness of this approach was made plain by the Transvaal Volksraad itself which, despite Kruger's resistance, passed a resolution calling for a further redistribution and creation of seats in the following year, a creation 'clearly intended to swamp those that might by then have been granted to the gold-fields'.[54] If this were to happen, the Uitlanders would never carry real political weight in the Transvaal, and whatever Kruger might offer there could clearly be no guarantee that it would not be neutralised. Only one option lay open to Milner if the effective control over the Republic which he aimed at was to be achieved rapidly – war. From mid-July therefore, Milner finally abandoned any lingering traces of hope for a peaceful settlement and worked without reservation for war, no longer because its prospect might just be sufficient to extort a vote for the Uitlander, but because no likely scheme could be foolproof.

Chamberlain, while similarly anxious to establish an imperial future for the whole of South Africa, still stuck to his earlier approach and remained calm. He was evidently prepared to accept a franchise on the July basis, and even still favoured the idea of a municipality for the Rand. Not trusting the Uitlanders, he was less concerned than Milner that Kruger's scheme would not immediately deliver the Republic into their lap. Moreover, since his handling of the South African question had throughout been dictated by the need to use it for its contribution to his education of the British public, he had no wish to jeopardise that education entirely, or to lose a personal short-term triumph, by dropping the franchise idea and heading for the battlefield. It was therefore in the interests of a franchise settlement that Chamberlain now felt it necessary to remind the British public just what one was up against in dealing with Kruger and his Republic. Papers on the Bloemfontein Conference were immediately presented, although scarcely a tactful move from the Boers' point of view; these were followed a few days later by correspondence on the reforms themselves, printers' overtime again being requested so that the printed copies might be delivered as soon as possible.[55] In this way the details of the franchise demanded were re-emphasised, and the very latest correspondence made available; the second of the two Blue Books contained much material on Uitlander opinion, including their criticisms of the latest scheme, in addition to the official exchanges.

While these were at the printer's, the Cabinet turned its attention to a discussion of Chamberlain's draft despatch in response to the new Boer proposals. When these had been made, the Cabinet had decided on another conference between Milner and the President, this time of a more formal kind with the evident intention of avoiding a repeat of the Bloemfontein fiasco. Milner, considering the Boer proposals still inadequate and sensing perhaps the attempt to keep him in check, proposed in return an enquiry by a mixed British and Boer commission into the possible operation of the reforms. Chamberlain combined these ideas, suggesting a joint commission to consider the practical application of the Franchise Law which would be followed by the conference to settle outstanding details and any matters still in dispute. Salisbury wholeheartedly approved of the draft, as did Walter Long, who added 'I sincerely hope we shall not relax our preparations one jot until all is signed, sealed and delivered. I do not trust Kruger and in any case the chance for making up for lost time is too good to be lost.'[56] Chaplin and Arbuthnot were in full agreement with Chamberlain. Of the others whose opinions have survived, Ritchie and Balfour both felt that some of the references to past events might be needlessly irritating in view of the despatch being a provisional acceptance of Kruger's proposals.[57]

Balfour's comments were again extensive, but his initial reservation was deprived of its force when he added

> I have some doubts myself as to the advantage of comprehending in one document all the subjects dealt with in the Draft Despatch. It is at all events worth considering whether the Despatch might not be cut into two parts – the first part of which should deal briefly and exclusively with the present phase of the suffrage question, while the second dealt with the recent history of our negotiations with the Transvaal, the breaches of the Convention, and schemes for future arbitration. This however is a question of form, on which I feel in no way disposed to press my opinion.

In other words, Balfour did not question the wisdom or the truth of

Chamberlain's comments on Boer bad faith; he would simply have preferred to see them in a second despatch. His continued distrust of the Boers was evident in his further comment, doubting the wisdom of proposing a second conference between Milner and Kruger. Intervention was justified, and the chances of its success should not be jeopardised by risking Kruger's rejection of this suggestion, with the harm this would do Britain's image. That Chamberlain continued to insist on this being included suggests that in some ways he was still more prepared than was Balfour to meet the Boers with an open mind. He also believed that such a combination of Conference and Inquiry would, as Just put it, 'strike the public eye & imagination & imply a climb down on President Krüger's [sic] part from his attitude of 'noli me tangere' on internal affairs'.[58]

With this settled, the recent Blue Books – as had been the case in June – provided the background to Chamberlain's second major speech of the summer, this time in the Commons Debate on South Africa on 28 July. This, like its predecessor, was designed to show Kruger that there must be no trifling, and was intended to still rumours of divisions within the Cabinet. As on earlier occasions, Chamberlain looked to distillation of the Blue Books and the reports of his speech in the press to reach the wide public on whom he had his eye. On this occasion the speeches of his colleagues were equally important. Balfour made his position clear with a very decisive speech on the eve of the debate. Salisbury's was particularly awaited, for then, as indeed subsequently, South African policy was attributed by many to Chamberlain alone; 'popular fancy, more especially on the Opposition side, clothed him in white robes of peace, placing in his hand an olive branch', was how Henry Lucy described it.[59] In the event, Salisbury left his wife desperately ill at Walmer and journeyed to London to make it clear that the members of his Cabinet were wholly in agreement with one another. Many felt his speech was even stronger than the Colonial Secretary's.[60] Quoting a phrase of Selborne's, that having put her hand to the plough Britain would not turn back, Salisbury agreed that the recent advances by the Boers were useful, especially if they were genuinely carried out. Yet he was clearly not convinced either of the sufficiency or of the good faith of the present franchise proposals; hence his veiled threat.

> If it ever happens that the validity of these Conventions is impeached I believe they belong from that time entirely to history. . . . If this country has to make exertions in order to secure the most elementary justice for British subjects, I am quite sure we will not reinstate a state of things which will bring back the old difficulties.[61]

The Prime Minister had also approved the draft of Selborne's speech, telling him not to alter a word of it, after expressing his own view that 'of course the real point to be made good to South Africa is that we not the Dutch are Boss'.[62]

V

For Milner, meanwhile, July was an unhappy month, and he realised that problems at home were still much greater than he had anticipated. Letters arrived which told him of the effects of the Bloemfontein Conference and the grievances Blue Book on English opinion. 'Discouraging telegrams from home', 'some disagreeable private letters', and again 'rather discouraging private letters' are the entries in his diary.[63] 'Things seem to have been going badly in England during the last few days and the Rand is making further concessions at a very alarming rate', he wrote on 18 July, and five days later concluded 'British opinion is going to be befooled, and that is the long and short of it.'[64] The one thing Milner wanted above all was that the British Government should define its own position on the franchise instead of waiting to see what the Boers might offer, in order to prevent divisions of opinion in England and 'loyal' South Africa from growing. Yet Salisbury and Chamberlain both resented any attempt to rush them, and Selborne had already tried to explain to his friend just why.

> We have between us moved public opinion, almost universally, forward to the position of accepting the eventual responsibility of seeing a remedy applied, and this is a great step forward; but we have not convinced them yet either that you can't believe a word Kruger says, or that he has never yielded and never will yield till he feels the muzzle of the pistol on his forehead, or that the surest way to avoid wai is to prepare openly for war.[65]

Selborne felt that this conviction would come, but by mid-July only George Wyndham among Milner's correspondents thought that British opinion felt the need to 'vindicate our supremacy & that you must guide us as to How and When'.[66]

Most reports simply confirmed Milner's worst fears about the failures, as he saw them, of a democratic system, and began to undermine his confidence in popular judgement. Sir Edward Grey thought that 'the state of public opinion in this country is so strongly against going to war, that it is not possible for the Government to go to that length upon the present issue respecting the franchise. Before the Blue Book was published public opinion was in a state of suspense & could I thought be guided by the Govt. Now that the case is before the country the current of opinion has set decidedly against war ... war in the absence of further provocation is not practicable.'[67] Grey also suggested that a municipality for the Rand might be more popular at home than the franchise. E. T. Cook and Phillip Gell brought out other aspects of the situation. It seemed to Cook that personal rivalries did much to prevent the Government taking a firm stand, and that many people held aloof out of their hatred for Chamberlain. 'With any other Colonial Sec[retary], I think the country would have rallied much more strongly to you. As it was, nearly all Liberals are furious with you, and a good lot of Tories also are really ag[ain]st any strong policy.'[68] Gell confirmed all this and continued

> Any overt act of *Boer* hostility, & the country would catch fire. A fresh murder would start the people. . . . Again if England would intercept warlike stores consigned to the Transvaal – (paying for them) – I believe $\frac{7}{8}$ of the country would be delighted. . . . Pending any such opportunity, I assume that details as to the Franchise will not be the subject of further Diplomatic discussion. People here are getting off the main line on to that.[69]

British opinion in such a state could not possibly give that impetus to its political leaders for which Milner had hoped. Moreover, British supremacy wrapped up in the cause of the franchise as a means to good government was not proving the rallying cry which Milner thought it would be. Now indeed it seemed to be creating a diversion, for obsession with the practical details destroyed its use as a slogan. Added to this, the complexities of the various franchise proposals were difficult to follow, and so clouded the basic issues still further. Even Cook had indicated his bewilderment to Milner, and his letter showed that the absence of a Government statement early in July only encouraged the rumours of Cabinet division. For Milner this was indeed a vicious circle, and the whole problem of British opinion was thrown into relief for him by the belief that

> Loyal British S. Africa has risen from its long degradation and stands behind me with an enthusiasm which has not been known since before Majuba. It is a great thing to be *the leader of a people*. . . . I have absolutely rallied all our forces on the spot. Of course there are some English against me. But these . . . had irrevocably 'ratted' long before. And on the other hand I have brought into the field scores. . . .[70]

He felt he was doing his best to sustain this enthusiasm, despite reports of jumpiness and sheer fright in Johannesburg, by publishing a summary of Chamberlain's Highbury speech when it arrived, but felt that only still more forthright utterances by the British Government would really prevent a total collapse. He fell back on appeals to Britain's self-respect. 'There is a diminishing interest in the difference between the schemes respectively put forward. . . . What men really want to know is whether Great Britain is going to prove herself in fact what she has so often claimed in name, the "Paramount Power" in S. Africa.'[71] But he had little confidence in this kind of rhetoric, and his views about the British public began to change. If the British Government retreated from a strong policy and he had to resign, he would take it as it came. 'I shall simply deplore the blindness of the British public. But, after all, how can they know? Who could understand the deep duplicity and utter insincerity of the Afrikander, unless he had experienced it?'[72] Even though he was still ready to find an excuse, Milner now saw that a failure of the Government would not be a failure simply of parliamentary leadership, but a national failure, a sore blow for one who styled himself a 'British race patriot', and never called his own motives in question.

This awareness of weakness at home prompted Milner to step up his efforts to get at the British press. Garrett was in England, convalescing for his tuberculosis, but at the same time doing his utmost to influence those Liberals who had swung away from Milner after Bloemfontein. He urged J. A. Spender, editor of the *Westminster Gazette* to 'Talk to Dodd [of the South African League]. He's genuine, & he knows, & he'll make you *feel*, & then the W.G. will drop "conciliating" till this job's through (without actual fighting, but for God's sake don't say so or we're done)'.[73] Spender's reply simply indicated where Milner had made his mistake.

> Before the policy of demanding the franchise was a fortnight old he burnt his boats by sending that despatch. . . . The despatch was intelligible & right if it meant war immediately. . . . Since war was impossible for three months, I simply don't understand it. It invited agitation, divided opinion, gave time for counter-preparations . . . But . . . The Imperial Govmt has had no policy since the raid, for good or ill, it has just begun to try the franchise remedy . . . &, if it sticks to it, must get more.[74]

Thus Milner's 'helots' despatch was for many people what his Graaff Reinet speech had been for Chamberlain. Although Garrett needed little prompting, Milner wrote to his friend, whose presence at Cape Town he sorely missed, saying that British insistence on a written embodiment of the franchise terms was vital. This he thought could be made a matter of principle, and therefore better to fight on than the details of any measure. The letter ended 'Keep *"Daily News"* alive and realise that, in so doing, you contribute most valuable help even if otherwise temporarily inactive'.[75] In similar vein, he wrote several times to Gell after mid-June pleading that he should 'lose no opportunity of getting the liberal Press to appreciate his point of view'; sympathetic visitors to Government House also found themselves being pressed to write to influential people at home, using Milner's factual information.[76]

All his activity was geared to provoking a popular demonstration or a public lead by the Government which would achieve much the same thing. After Chamberlain's telegram outlining for him the effect of the first July proposals of the Boers on home opinion, Milner cast around for additional issues and told Chamberlain that the subject of the Republic's large artillery orders 'greatly needs ventilating. . . . Action directed to prevent the establishment of military power overshadowing South Africa would surely be approved by public opinion'.[77] No doubt it would, just like the second 'murder' which Gell had suggested; but in themselves these were not issues of the kind Chamberlain looked for. He had omitted the paragraph on the Transvaal's military strength when publishing the 'helots' despatch, and included the Edgar case less for its own sake than for the outburst of feeling it caused and as an example therefore of grievances stretching far wider. Positive sentiments and rational persuasion were Chamberlain's objects, yet Milner's telegram just referred to reflected the way in which the

High Commissioner was attempting to move the terms of the controversy on to yet another plane for the benefit of the public. British supremacy had always been his aim in South Africa, but the controversy with the Republic had not been couched specifically in these terms. In British Government circles it had been taken for granted, even if the degree to which such supremacy was seen as threatened by the Boers had once given rise to differences of opinion. The public aspects of the dispute had, however, always concentrated on details, albeit details with a common denominator. Chamberlain's awareness of the need to be convincing had meant that the equation of Uitlander grievances with a threat to British supremacy had yet to be clearly and consistently made. Milner had regretted Chamberlain's earlier omission from his 'helots' despatch, and now hoped that by bringing out the military aspect of the Boer activities, he would finally encourage people to see it for themselves.[78]

The need for such a move was even clearer after Milner had recovered from the shock of Chamberlain's announcement in *The Times* that the crisis was over, given the recent franchise proposals. The High Commissioner felt that all might just be redeemed by the forthcoming Parliamentary debate, and again illustrated his belief that public commitment would prevent retreat. To Chamberlain on the eve of the debate he wired 'I hope debate may bring out wider aspects of question which have been lost sight of in long wrangle over details of Franchise Bill. It is practical assertion of British Supremacy in forcing S.A.R. to move in direction of equal rights and genuine self-government which is the real issue.'[79] Despite his assertion of its connection with the virtues of good government, Milner's 'supremacy' was not without its racial undertones. He had earlier mentioned to Selborne how he felt that the 'meetings in Australia in support of Uitlanders' complaints are important facts. This objection of ours to the *permanent inferiority* of men of British race is a strong point to fight on.'[80] Now he noted in his diary that the debate in Parliament would be the 'turning point', one way or the other, on the question of the British Government's commitment to supremacy in South Africa.

VI

Gloomy though Milner might be, he still over-estimated the extent to which he and the Government were out of step in their attitude to the Transvaal. Late in June and in July, having asserted their control over the speed at which events moved ahead, Salisbury and Chamberlain had no wish to appear in conflict with their High Commissioner. To the Prime Minister in particular, speed was of the essence of the problem. His commitment to upholding 'the power and authority of the British Empire . . . the position of Great Britain in South Africa'[81] was no less than it had ever been, but if he could achieve his aim by moving slowly and showing determination without provoking a war, then he would do so. Thus the Cabinet decided on defining its position only in the debate at the end of July and not before. In another important respect, they spoke on lines which Milner could only approve. Supremacy in South Africa was now clearly expounded as the fundamental aim of British policy. Chamberlain took particular care to associate the defence of Uitlander interests with British supremacy. He and his staff shared Milner's fear that perhaps the franchise issue was now something of a hindrance to popular understanding of what was at stake; Chamberlain himself had even at the start not been at all happy with Milner's bringing the franchise to the front. However, now that the Boers themselves had suggested extensive franchise reforms, and thereby implicitly admitted the justice of pressure for such an end, Chamberlain and his colleagues could clearly equate refusal to grant satisfactory concessions with a threat to British supremacy in South Africa. It was to rub this point home that, as soon as the Boers received his latest despatch, Chamberlain chose this moment to present further correspondence with the Republic on the suzerainty question, in which the Boers had laid claim to the status of a sovereign independent state.[82]

IX

THE PRELUDE TO WAR

I

Early in July, a lull had followed Chamberlain's speech at Highbury before the Boers made known their proposals for reform. Now, after the Debates in Parliament a similar pattern was repeated. This time however, the delay was rather longer. As August wore on and no reply was forthcoming to the suggestion for a Joint Commission of Enquiry, Chamberlain proposed that Milner appoint his own commission and that the Government should then press for immediate compliance with its recommendations. Failing this, he suggested that an ultimatum should then be sent, supported by a large British force of troops.[1] Salisbury was reluctant to begin the immediate manoeuvres which this would have involved, partly because he shrank from the prospect of 'the scandal which will certainly be created by the condition of our military preparations'. He was also facing opposition from Hicks Beach who was alarmed at the possible expenditure now that the Government had decided to reinforce Natal with two thousand men, and was considering moving – in accordance with Salisbury's earlier wishes – troops close to the frontier of the Transvaal. He therefore felt that 'the wiser plan is not to incur any serious expenditure until it is quite clear that we are going to war' despite the extra delay this would cause.[2] Lansdowne's military advisers however were convinced that the Boers were dithering, requiring only the extra persuasion of British troops,[3] and other Cabinet Ministers were also less sympathetic to the Chancellor's worries. Balfour and Goschen, after seeing Milner's telegram of 16 August saying that the Boer reply had arrived but was unfavourable, both felt that 'progress should be made at once with the purchase of mules etc without waiting for the Cabinet. Every day becomes important & I feel now that Beach must realize this as much as the rest of us. Balfour spoke of writing to him last night.'[4] If a letter went from Balfour it seems not to have survived, but Goschen continued with his naval planning and wrote to the Chancellor five days later about the cost of transports. By then, however, he was able to add that he hoped they would not be necessary,[5] for news of the so-called 'Smuts proposals' had arrived.

These latest proposals were spelt out by the Attorney-General of the Republic in conversation with Conyngham Greene, and were sent home in the form of a memorandum together with Greene's account of the actual conversations.[6] They appeared to concede all that Milner had asked in connection with redistribution and the franchise at Bloemfontein, and so the Boers confirmed yet again the view that they would give way under pressure. Chamberlain was very excited, feeling that these new franchise conditions constituted a complete surrender and 'ample justification for the course we have taken'. Two days later, he wrote 'I really am sanguine that the crisis is over'.[7] He reprimanded Milner, who was angry with Greene and still wished to concentrate on the Joint Commission which these new proposals were intended to replace, and informed him that the Boers should be encouraged to put their suggestions on record – thus repeating his reaction to their offers in July. To Lansdowne the Colonial Secretary wrote to say that while the pressure should not yet be relaxed, he saw no occasion now for reinforcements,[8] a sign of his real conviction.

Sadly, his jubilation turned out to be premature. Hearing of the Smuts proposals, the Republic's representative in London wrote home to the State Secretary:

> With regard to the Suzerainty Question it is the earnest hope of our friends that our Government did not touch upon this point, for that would just give Chamberlain the opportunity he is hoping for and by means of which he will get the mass of the public more powerfully on his side than by means of the franchise ... in case we demand the withdrawal of the Suzerainty assertion our enemies will make it appear that we wish to escape from our obligations springing from the Convention, and wish to come to a secret understanding with Foreign Powers.[9]

This was however exactly what the Republic had done. In making its proposals, it asked for certain guarantees.

> The Government of the South African Republic ... will assume that Her Majesty's Government will agree that a precedent shall not be formed by their intervention for similar action in the future, and that no future interference in the internal affairs of the Republic will

take place contrary to the Convention. Further that Her Majesty's
Government will not insist further upon the assertion of suzerainty,
the controversy on this subject being tacitly allowed to drop. Lastly
. . . arbitration, from which the foreign element is excluded, to be
conceded.

Even in his first moments of excitement, Chamberlain had realised
that this was a problem, but he clearly hoped to devise a form of
words which might either satisfy both sides or be a subject for
further negotiation and definition. His telegram telling Milner to
get the proposals in writing from the Republic gave his opinion that
if the Uitlanders did achieve the immediate and substantial
representation embodied in the offer, then these assumptions
could be admitted. On the question of suzerainty he referred the
Republic to an earlier despatch, and declared that Britain had no
intention to pursue the matter at the present time; as far as
intervention was concerned he hoped that 'fulfilment of the
promises made, and the just treatment of the Uitlanders in future
will render any future intervention on their behalf unnecessary'.[10]
Arbitration, as he later showed, he was prepared to accept in
principle. On 21 August, however, the State Secretary made it clear
that the Republic did not merely ask for assurances on these
matters, but made the concessions it offered expressly conditional
upon such guarantees being given. Milner interpreted this as a
stiffening of the Republic's attitude, and although Chamberlain
made no change in his earlier suggestions now being embodied in
the draft of an answering despatch, he was undoubtedly irritated at
the prospect of protracted bargaining.

From the first, other Ministers were less enthusiastic than
Chamberlain. Foremost among those who welcomed the signs of
further concessions were Beach and Goschen, but they seem to
have been so for reasons other than any feeling that the proposals
were adequate. The Chancellor, thinking Chamberlain's reply to
Milner an excellent one, then seized the opportunity to renew his
attack upon War Office expenditure, seeing in the proposals a
chance to save his budget.[11] Goschen too criticised the War Office,
though for rather different reasons; he felt that if one looked 'not
only at what is fair and generally expedient, but specially at the War
O. plans [which he thought 'sickening' in their inefficiency and
unbelievable slowness] & other endless delays it would be madness
in my judgement rashly to reject any fresh concessions'.[12] Salisbury,

anxious to keep the peace within his Cabinet, patiently explained to Sir Michael that in fact the War Office was less culpable than it might appear; the real reason for the delays and the need to use home troops was that 'the Indian troops are so riddled with venereal & other complaints that they are comparatively unfit for service'. Moreover, troops would have to be sent in any case, for even if there were a settlement now, Boer bitterness would necessitate strengthening the Natal frontier. Not that the Prime Minister was at all sanguine at this moment. 'At present I understand the Boer's offer in effect to be – the Bloemfontein demands; *but* a renunciation of the Suzerainty in exchange. This does not seem a possible solution.'[13]

Of the other Ministers who looked carefully into the Boer offer, Balfour seemed to think that any peaceful settlement would inevitably be incomplete, and for that very reason unwelcome.[14] It was however Lansdowne who, on this occasion, was clearest as to what had to be the Cabinet's conclusion in the light of their past claims, private and public. For the moment he felt Kruger would back down, and was therefore averse to sending reinforcements which might precipitate unnecessary hostilities. But of the proposals themselves he wrote

> It is hard to say whether they are made to us in good faith. The concessions may prove to be illusory, but in appearance they are a very great advance both upon the Bloemfontein proposals and the subsequently revised scheme. They seem to merit benevolent examination.
>
> But the conditions as to suzerainty and future non-intervention are obviously inadmissible, and, if literally persisted in, will render a peaceful solution, to my mind, impossible.[15]

There is little to suggest that Chamberlain's reaction to the Smuts offer was out of line with that of his colleagues, and it is difficult to see how, in the light of its previous actions, the Cabinet could have gone further to meet the Boers. At last, in the face of British insistence, the Boers were retreating, and on questions which they had hitherto maintained were beyond the purview of the British Government, except for 'friendly representations'. Renewed firmness was bringing signs of success, inevitably encouraging when British policy, despite a fundamental commitment to defend the imperial position, had long met nothing but setbacks. With the question of European rivalries still unsolved, success in direct confrontation with the Transvaal could only strengthen the overall British position. Considerations of this kind were sufficient to predispose the Cabinet to support a forceful policy, to weaken the few criticisms which Ministers did have of tactical suggestions coming from Chamberlain, and at least in the past had encouraged them at times to advocate action more vigorously than Chamberlain himself.

When Boer resistance appeared to be reviving – in Reitz's qualification of the Smuts proposals, and the subsequent Boer refusal to stand by other concessions which Smuts appeared to have mentioned to Greene in conversation, but not to have included in the formal proposals – it is not at all surprising that Chamberlain felt this no time for magnanimity. Once again he fell back on publicity as a means of strengthening his stand. When the news of the proposals arrived, the Colonial Office staff had set about the immediate preparation of a Blue Book containing more correspondence on the franchise. Again they arranged for overtime, and for printing to begin 'notwithstanding that they [the Stationery Office] had not received notice of presentation'; the papers were in fact presented on 24 August and were delivered to the Commons late the following afternoon.[16] The Blue Book illustrated how negotiations were dragging on, gave further evidence of Uitlander opinions, and included evidence of support for the Government's policy throughout South Africa and in other parts of the Empire.

It was designed to set the scene for another speech by Chamberlain, delivered at Highbury to his Liberal Unionist constituents on 26 August. He reaffirmed the Government's stand in no uncertain terms. Kruger might dribble out reforms 'like water from a squeezed sponge', but meanwhile British patience was running out. War was a possibility which ultimately only action by Kruger might avoid, but 'if the rupture which we have done everything in our power to avoid should be forced upon us – I am confident we shall have the support of the vast majority of the people of the United Kingdom, and . . . of the people of the British Empire'.[17] Having said this, Chamberlain sent his reply to the Smuts proposals. Unlike the other two outstanding statements of the British position (those of 10 May in answer to the Petition, and 27 July in response to the earlier franchise offer), this despatch of 28 August was not discussed by the Cabinet, owing to the difficulties of consultation in the summer recess. However, it was based very largely on Chamberlain's telegram to Milner, mentioned above, with which Ministers were already acquainted. Only Hicks Beach, when he saw it shortly afterwards, was disturbed by certain phrases in which it differed from the earlier despatch and which, he felt, made it less conciliatory particularly on the issue of suzerainty.[18] Nevertheless, anxious as he was to avoid repeating the mistakes of a much earlier phase in Conservative South African policy, even he did not object to Chamberlain's assertion that Britain simply could not commit herself absolutely to non-intervention in the future, which was the real sticking-point for the Republic's Government. Five days later, on 2 September, the Boers replied to his despatch by withdrawing entirely the Smuts proposals, and reverting to the earlier British suggestion of a joint enquiry plus a seven years' franchise offer; as a result all meaningful negotiations finished.

II

The significance of public opinion in the calculations of Chamberlain, Milner, and the British Government was however in no way diminished. It will be remembered that one of the prime purposes of the Parliamentary debate at the end of July had been to bring out the wider aspects of the South African question which were felt to be in danger of being submerged by details about votes for the Uitlanders. Even before the debate, Goschen detected the beginnings of an increased determination in Britain, and told Milner that although a war would not be popular, people were prepared to accept it as inevitable.[19] After the debate, this judgement was endorsed by other of his correspondents, and even the ISAA decided to relax in its organisation of mass meetings.[20] H. S. Wilkinson, one of those journalist friends with whom Milner had spent much time on his visit to England, welcomed the change of emphasis, and thought that 'British supremacy' provided a *casus belli* 'which can never be got out of the difference between your Bloemfontein proposals & the offers which Kruger & the Africander [sic] leaders make to confuse opinion in England without righting the Uitlanders' wrongs'.[21]

Reassuring though this might be, attempts to educate and focus public opinion had still to continue. For Chamberlain in particular continuity, in so far as it was possible, had always been desirable in promoting popular understanding of the true significance of Empire. How much more so was it necessary in July 1899 when popular support had become above all an immediate tactical necessity, to indicate to both British and Dutch in South Africa the determination of Government and people in England and their ability to act if needed. For both the Colonial Secretary and the High Commissioner, nothing which might achieve this (and in so doing contribute to Chamberlain's long-term aims), and thereby increase pressure on the Boers could be left untried. Fears in the Colonial Office that franchise and supremacy might lead people to forget other grievances led to several suggestions for publication in the press of information showing the Boers in a bad light, such as the great increase in their armaments.[22] Eventually these ideas were more or less abandoned; apart from the unsuitability of some of these issues, in a situation where discussion focused almost entirely on supremacy and the franchise, it was felt that such individual reports would achieve little. Moreover, the Colonial Office had far more confidence in the impact made by its own Blue Books; something printed in this way 'would give at least as much publicity as giving to any one paper, & is a more permanent record'.[23] So, towards the end of August, the idea of having two kinds of Blue Book was accepted, one with correspondence about reforms, the other an 'omnibus' grievances issue. Thus basic problem and remedy were to be separated, and the real priorities of the Imperial Government re-emphasised; the franchise was of secondary importance, a means to the greater end of civilised government, with which Chamberlain had all along been trying to equate British intervention and supremacy. The result was that the Blue Books published in September and October concentrated almost entirely on political reforms.[24] In the end it was simply the volume of work and the outbreak of war which prevented a fresh publication on the lines of the June Blue Book containing the Petition.[25]

In South Africa, Milner never really recovered from his fright in July that everything he had striven for would collapse utterly in a failure of public comprehension. While it was true, as he told a friend, that 'there will always be, when I return to my books in Duke Street, the recollection of the time when I had done all the man on the spot could do to recover the position',[26] he had no wish to live on memories or to anticipate Mr Prufrock in contemplating coffeespoons while following the social round. He wanted a lasting success, and began in mid-August to be alarmed lest South African morale collapse. Anxious to do something, he wrote to St Loe Strachey, encouraging the editor in his course, and had further long consultations with Garrett – now back in his chair – and Monypenny.[27] In the short period that Garrett was away from South Africa, Milner had also approached Leo Maxse, editor of the strongly imperialist *National Review*, with an invitation to take over the editorship of the *Cape Times*.[28]

Nevertheless both men were, by the end of August 1899, far more sure that public opinion everywhere was on the right lines at last. Their activities were now dictated above all by the need to keep it there, and they were no longer tormented by the uncertainty as to whether public feeling would ever respond, or understanding ever dawn. In his speech of 26 August, Chamberlain had expressed his confidence in popular support, and, having despatched his reply to the Boers, he wrote to Milner voicing his conviction that, all things considered, great progress had been made.

> It is a great thing to say that the majority of the people have, as I believe, recognized that there is a greater issue than the franchise or the grievances of the Uitlanders at stake, and that our supremacy in S. Africa and our existence as a great power in the world are involved in the result of our present controversy. Three months ago we could not – that is to say we should not have been allowed to – go to war on this issue – now – although still most unwillingly and with a large minority still against us – we shall be sufficiently supported.[29]

Faced with such claims and remembering Chamberlain's reliance on instinct rather than detailed analysis, one is inevitably led to wonder how Chamberlain could be so sure of his success. It is certainly the case that in order to rally the widest possible support to the cause of Empire, the Colonial Secretary had been attracted to the idea of identifying imperial action with the positive remedying of abuses. South Africa, brought into prominence largely as a result of the Raid, provided a focal point for this process of identification. Increasingly thereafter, the maintenance of the British position and interests in South Africa became equated with the existence there of those positive benefits, peace, stability, and good government. That there was a reality of a different kind behind imperial policy was shown by Cabinet and Foreign Office in their discussions of strategy and *real politik*. This however remained hidden from the wider public gaze – largely because of Foreign Office preconceptions, but also because Chamberlain did all he could to hide it and to direct attention elsewhere. There can be no doubt that in focusing attention on grievances, Chamberlain – aided by the efforts of Milner, and the failure of the Boers to take the wind out of his sails after the Raid – was wholly successful. In July 1899, Campbell-Bannerman had referred to the franchise question as one upon which 'for some time past, by general agreement apparently, the controversy ... has been concentrated', while in October Redmond still felt able to assert that the Transvaal had never tried to evade British control of its foreign relations.[30] The strength of this current of discussion was so strong, that attempts by the *Manchester Guardian* to obstruct it, by raising, for example, Chamberlain's change of tactics over the native question, failed altogether.[31]

To achieve this focus, Chamberlain disclosed official diplomacy to an unprecedented degree. The South African question was discussed and analysed endlessly in print and on platforms throughout the country. It was thought among many educated people that if the country could not be roused to appreciate its importance, then it was incapable of understanding anything. After all, it was said, democracy is a form of government, not a creed of life, and as such could be altered; if the British system was to remain unchanged the people now had to prove themselves. As a result, South Africa and subsequently the war became in the eyes of many a testing point for the efficacy of democracy. This kind of reasoning can be found in many different quarters whether academic, military, or parliamentary.[32] Perhaps the most coherent presentation of these ideas came in a series of articles in the *Morning Post* in July 1899. Written by H. S. Wilkinson, defence expert and admirer of Milner, they were published together at the end of that month entitled *British Policy in South Africa*, and united all the arguments about Democracy with analyses of the failures to date of South African policy.[33]

However, while Chamberlain might be aware of his success in these two respects, his belief that a majority approved of and would support his policy of pressure, even to the point where a war became inevitable, still leaves part of the question unanswered. The importance Chamberlain attached to guiding or giving a lead to the public reflects his assumption that many popular attitudes could be determined from above. If one made sufficient noise, put out enough propaganda, and controlled both discussion and much information, the lines thus set and the information imparted would percolate downwards through a host of different verbal and written channels. The longer it could be sustained the deeper it would penetrate and the more effective it would be. Generally speaking however, the efficacy of actions based on these assumptions had to remain the subjects of a pious hope. Chamberlain and his officials were aware of the limitations imposed on their own attempts to publicise their case. Blue Books initially reached a select audience, their own press contacts could only play a limited part in their schemes, and speech-making might lose its effect with over-use. Similarly, ways open to them of assessing opinion could only be extremely partial and rudimentary. Newspapers reflected opinion, but just whose it was difficult to say. Gossip in Westminster and Whitehall reflected divided views, and helped sometimes only a little to know the feelings of the electorate upon which Chamberlain had his eye. It was Chamberlain's belief in the necessity for awakening a wide popular interest in a positive idea of Empire, and the vast area of uncertainty as to whether such could be or had been achieved, that gave both persistence and importance to his campaign and his handling of publication. For a long time, he was forced to trust his own instincts, listening to those views available to him and extrapolating his judgement as to what was required for the country at large. Occasionally he received signs – information from the ISAA for example – that he was on the right track. Then, from June 1899 onwards, as the crisis developed, evidence of a wide popular reaction to his policy became available to him. This came above all in the form of resolutions passed at meetings of all kinds up and down the country, large numbers of which appeared in the press or were sent directly to the Colonial Office,[34] and reflected part of a much wider interest in the question, many other meetings being held at which the resolutions were only verbal or where speeches alone were made.

The initial impetus to the flow of speeches and resolutions seems to have been provided by the ISAA, which organised a series of meetings, beginning in April 1899, as a response to the Uitlander Petition and urging the Government to take up the petitioners' case. With the failure of the Bloemfontein Conference, a second series was started, passing a resolution of much wider scope, which requested the taking of 'all steps to establish the principal of entire political equality for all white men from the Cape to the Zambezi, and for the maintenance of British supremacy throughout South Africa'. Their activities, as in 1897 and 1898, focused on London and on large towns outside the south-east of England, especially those in Lancashire, Yorkshire, and the North-East.[35] The work of the Association was supplemented by considerable propaganda put out by bodies more directly connected with South Africa, such as the mining houses and the South African League.[36] Many of the resolutions arriving at the Colonial Office in the early summer, June and July, seem to show the influence of the Association. Coming mostly from areas where its speakers had been active, many of them voiced strong support for the Government in very similar terms.

Selborne's view at the end of July that the provinces and *hoi polloi* had been much more favourable to Milner's views than either London or the 'governing classes', if not based on, was at least confirmed by those resolutions surviving from this period.[37] As awareness of the possibility of war spread, the practice of sending resolutions to the Colonial Office grew. By mid-September there were very few parts of the British Isles which had not responded in this way. So too, as the prospect of war grew, the tone of the resolutions altered. The Government was increasingly asked to do all possible to avoid a collision by continuing negotiations, and Selborne's forecast was borne out. 'Public opinion insists on our using great patience and endeavouring to avert war. It will acquiesce in war if it is convinced that without war we cannot secure practical (as distinct from pedantic) compliance with your Bloemfontein demands.'[38] He was writing in July, but as the numbers of resolutions increased, it was not the mounting expressions of regret at the probability of war and the urging of all possible negotiations which really distinguished them. After all, in this they only paralleled the earlier reactions of the Cabinet.

Coming as they did from almost every part of the country, they represented a wide cross-section of interests. Some fifteen per cent of them were from apparently unsponsored public meetings, the rest from a host of political associations, working-men's clubs, and church gatherings, the latter mostly Nonconformist. The extent of their agreement is remarkable, and showed the accuracy with which Selborne or Chamberlain could speak of 'public opinion'. Although few went as far as the Blaby Working Man's Association, feeling, in their support of the Government, that 'the question of the future supremacy in South Africa is one that affects most deeply the well-being of the working classes in this country', at the other extreme barely a handful of socialist or Irish organisations condemned the Government's policy outright.[39] In July, the *Manchester Guardian* had lamented that 'To this day one finds innocent people who imagine that the Colonial Office is not interfering in the internal affairs of the Transvaal at all, but simply exercising such ordinary rights of protection over our subjects living there as we should exercise if they were living in any other State', and found it hard to accept that other people were impressed by the ideas of suzerainty, supremacy or paramountcy.[40] To its greater horror it found that such people were alive and kicking still more vigorously well down the social scale early in October, when it sent a correspondent into the East End of London.[41] The nature of the resolutions bears a more consistent witness to the success of Chamberlain's strategy, and the Colonial Secretary and his officials regarded them as sufficient evidence of extensive popular backing. The great majority, while preferring peaceful means of redress, accepted the case for grievances, and wholeheartedly endorsed the policy of obtaining justice and equal rights for British subjects in the Transvaal. British supremacy – which increasingly crept into the phrasing of the resolutions – was identified with the maintenance of those rights.

III

That such consistency was both achieved and sustained in the six weeks after Chamberlain's claim to have the majority of his countrymen with him, owed not a little to the Colonial Secretary's watchfulness, and to further twists in the presentation of British policy as the Cabinet debated an ultimatum to the Boers. This was no easy task, for, even as he wrote so confidently to Milner of the extent of their support, Chamberlain felt constrained to admit (and Headlam, in printing his letter, to omit) the fact that 'the technical *casus belli* is a very weak one'.[42] Not that Chamberlain himself suffered any twinges of conscience over this deficiency, for the

form in which he had cast his diplomacy had all along been
intended for the benefit of the public to provide its own
justification by being based on universally admired, liberal
principles. The weakness of the *casus belli* in the legal sense now
merely illustrated for him the weakness of the Conventions, and he
referred to the issues at stake as 'a holy cause'. What he felt had
been Boer insincerity in the matter of the Smuts proposals had
caused the iron to enter his soul, and he was now convinced that
war preparations had to be made. If the Boers retreated in the
meantime – which to the last he felt was just a possibility – all well
and good; but if they did not, then war and the worst would be
theirs.

Having progressively developed the South African question in
public as a matter of principle – the misgovernment of British
subjects being intolerable, especially in an area for which the
Imperial Government had a special responsibility – neither
Chamberlain nor the British Government could give way without
losing all credibility both at home and abroad. Privately, of course,
the Cabinet believed that British supremacy there was essential to
imperial strength and security, but its members felt too that this was
now incapable of being defended without substantial public
backing. Hence the crucial importance of the fact that the British
public now, as far as Chamberlain and the Cabinet could see,
supported the equation of British supremacy with good
government in South Africa. The importance of politicians' –
especially Chamberlain's – ideas about the relation between
foreign policy and public opinion, and the effect of public opinion
on imperial policy becomes plain at this point. If Chamberlain had
not come to the Colonial Office with his intention of educating the
public; if he had not incorporated the South African question into
this campaign and given it the form of 'grievances' which required
redress; had Milner not appreciated the key role of a vociferous
public opinion, and exploited both it and the possibilities of
publication to bring British statesmen closer to his way of
proceeding; then the Cabinet could not have felt that in the
question of grievances lay the only chance of asserting British
supremacy in South Africa, for the ground would have been in no
way prepared, and there would have been no likelihood of the
extensive popular support either to force the Boers into retreat or
to uphold Britain in a conflict with them. Without the added

dimension of publicity, with a less radical Colonial Secretary or High Commissioner, the South African problem would have remained a source of quiet Cabinet concern and been subject to prolonged and detailed, if fruitless, negotations with the Boer Government.

However, just as Bloemfontein and the 'helots' telegram had started the collapse of liberal opinion, so again, the shift to emphasise British supremacy created a similar danger. With the emergence of supremacy as a public issue, the debate about South Africa was finally detached from those technicalities over which alone negotiatons were possible. Supremacy, as Chamberlain said, was not justified in logical terms. Attention was now seemingly focused on it, but such attention had not been reached by the process of reasoning and cool understanding which Chamberlain had originally tried to promote. For this reason, it was especially doubtful whether popular support would be lasting, however much Chamberlain was confident that people understood the issues involved. Only if a convincing ultimatum was framed could their understanding be put on a surer foundation.

It was at this point, shortly before news came that the Boers had withdrawn the Smuts proposals, that Salisbury suddenly wrote to Lord Lansdowne, belittling the significance of the South African question and casting the blame for the present situation upon Milner 'and his jingo supporters. And therefore I see before us the necessity for considerable military effort – and all for people whom we despise, and for territory which will bring no profit and no power to England.'[43] While to account for Salisbury's attitude is not to detract from the strength of his criticism of Milner, it needs to be pointed out that this was nevertheless an uncharacteristic utterance, hardly in keeping with the letter which he had written to calm his Chancellor on the same day.[44] Seen in the light of Salisbury's long and active commitment to a favourable solution of the South African problem, this represented neither a sudden change of mind nor a view of the quesiton fundamentally different from that of Chamberlain himself. Indeed, since July he had been pressing the Portuguese to prevent arms imports into the Transvaal, and on the day of his letter to Lansdowne threatened, in the face of their constant refusal, to act in such a manner as to raise the question of her position in Mozambique under the Anglo-German agreement.[45] The Prime Minister's wish to be done with the

Transvaal for good was as strong as ever, and in a sense he was giving vent in his letter to the frustrations which almost all the members of his Cabinet felt. At the same time, in his capacity as Foreign Secretary and just as had happened in the spring of 1897, Salisbury was once more afraid of the possible repercussions of a persistent forward policy in South Africa on British interests elsewhere, particularly in the East.[46] Germany again was suspect here for, despite the agreement, she had recently encouraged Portuguese resistance to Britain's requests. Although he would not have accepted the label of the intellectual in politics, it is the case that Salisbury saw too many sides to the question for any one course of action to be comfortable. This time, however, the option of a conciliatory policy was not open. Salisbury found himself in a position akin to that in which Chamberlain had been over the Anglo-German negotiations the previous year. The Prime Minister did not like the Uitlander case as an issue on which to fight, not least because it made Britain's position appear an offensive one and its handling did not appeal to his preference for discreet diplomacy; yet he could see no alternative. Perhaps he wished that this clarity of vision had been his in May when the Cabinet, for want of any other policy, took up the grievances question as the one way which then lay to hand of teaching the Boers that Britain was 'Boss' in southern Africa.

His mood lasted for a few days, and gave rise to a similar outburst of feeling during preparations for the Cabinet meeting called to discuss Chamberlain's latest memorandum.[47] Chamberlain now pressed for the immediate despatch of troops and for the final formulation and raising of Britain's demands which Salisbury had envisaged in his speech to the House of Lords a few weeks previously. The Prime Minister sharply denied ever having advocated raising Britain's demands while peace lasted; such a move would 'widely extend the impression of our bad faith which, unfortunately and most unjustly, prevails in many quarters abroad, and has been of much value to the Boers'.[48] This fear of his was certainly grounded in the problem of which Chamberlain was also aware, namely that while the Cabinet understood the link between Uitlander grievances and the idea of British supremacy, the formulation of this connection in a convincing ultimatum was an extremely difficult task. Nevertheless, Salisbury had to be made to face up to the situation.

Chamberlain's terse reaction to the Prime Minister's memorandum was to write on his own copy Salisbury's words in Parliament on 28 July, and then to compose yet another memorandum himself on 'The South African Situation', for discussion alongside the others.[49] In this, he outlined yet again the way in which the existence and behaviour of the Transvaal was undermining the allegiance to Britain of South Africans, both Britons and Dutchmen, and concluded that 'it depends upon the action of the British government now whether the supremacy which we have claimed so long and so seldom exerted is to be finally established or for ever abandoned'. Rehearsing the course of recent negotiations and emphasising the stages of the British Government's commitment since May to intervention in the interests of obtaining a final and just settlement, Chamberlain argued that the practical necessities of the case and Ministerial utterances made an advance in the British claims essential. Past publicity, notably Chamberlain's own but also, recently, that of his colleagues, now seemed to make it impossible to stand still, let alone retreat.

The differences between the Colonial Secretary and the Prime Minister, however, were now as before essentially tactical ones, not ones of broad principle. 'We have not always seen "eye to eye" . . . in this business, though on the broad lines we have been agreed', was Goschen's way of describing the Cabinet's relations with Chamberlain in the summer of 1899.[50] The coming of autumn had not changed the British Government's consciousness that room for manoeuvre in South Africa was diminishing. Alternatives were few and small, and both Salisbury and Chamberlain had experienced the frustration of seeing only one unpleasant path for them to follow. Salisbury had few suggestions to make not only because he often felt that they were not required, but also because few alternatives existed. Perhaps his illness hampered him and made him more irritable, but it is difficult to believe that, even given better health, his over-all leadership on South African questions could have been firmer and productive of a more imaginative solution. Salisbury, Chamberlain, and their colleagues saw that war might come and disliked the idea. Early in September this led Hicks Beach to question many of the details of Chamberlain's proposals,[51] but most Ministers even then were prepared to put constant pressure on Kruger to achieve their end, whether peacefully or not.

The main difference among them lay in the speed at which they thought that pressure should be applied. Salisbury, anxious about the adverse effect of war on foreign and home opinion, wished to minimise that effect by moving fairly slowly. Others agreed with him especially if it gave the Boers another chance to give way completely. Chamberlain sympathised with this desire, but had little hope left of its leading to results. At the same time he was far more confident of the public response and, seeing this as something likely to mute foreign criticism, therefore favoured moving ahead rather faster.

Cabinet discussion on this occasion produced several results. Ministers accepted Chamberlain's view that opinion in the country was behind them, and for that reason authorised the despatch of ten thousand troops to South Africa. However, in the light of the failings in War Office organisation and delayed military preparations, the feeling that the slow approach was essential won the day. An interim reply was therefore sent to the Boers on 8 September.[52] At the same time the difficulties of the ultimatum to the Boers were fully realised. The Cabinet found itself facing the same dilemma which had led Balfour towards arguments in support of using overwhelming force in each individual case of unsatisfied grievances in the Republic. Such a course was quite obviously impossible; continuous military expeditions were sheer fantasy, and unless a complete change of policy was secured in the Transvaal, a permanent and very large garrison might yet have to be maintained in South Africa 'at great expense to the British taxpayer and involving the utter disorganization of our military system'.[53] On the other hand, the necessity for insistence on the detailed observance of the Conventions had already marked a decline in British power in South Africa, and recent controversies had only worsened relations all round, creating the situation in which the use of force had now to be contemplated.

It was quite possible to make out a case for suzerainty based on the Conventions, to prove breaches of those Conventions, and to insist on their correct observance in future, as had been shown in the case of the Aliens Legislation and Article IV. Such a case was legally possibly – if also legally disputable – and could command a substantial political support. The grievances question, however, arose out of a situation never envisaged at the time when the Conventions were drafted. It was also true that the Conventions had been the outcome of circumstances in which Britain really was paramount, or at least able to be 'magnanimous'. This together with compromises designed to achieve a settlement with the Boers had so affected their drafting that, at a later date, it was extremely difficult to connect British indignation at grievances – fundamentally questions of internal administration – with the right to compel good behaviour by the Boers, in a way that would gain wide support. This problem had been further complicated by Chamberlain's and Milner's handling of the conflict with the Transvaal. For a long time insistence on grievances and the letter of the Convention had rooted the dispute in details of practical administration. If Britain's final demands were so formulated as to secure British supremacy as something distinct from the simple observation of the existing Conventions, an outcry might be the result both at home and abroad.

The Cabinet found it impossible to come to a decision, and so the question was temporarily adjourned. As friends of the Transvaal made frantic attempts to reopen negotiations, Chamberlain became more and more worried that the Boers would find some way of avoiding any direct answer to Britain; this danger in turn made the possible fragility of the public mood both at home and in South Africa an additional source of worry. He had already telegraphed to the Governor of Natal his hope that 'nothing will now be done by the loyal colonists which might alienate public feeling in this country',[54] and it was to keep opinion in line that he laid a Blue Book before the Commons on 9 September. It contained two remarkable despatches from Milner, stressing the dedication of the loyalists and attempting to link the question of the franchise with supremacy sufficiently to satisfy the waverers. Pinpointing the desire of the loyalists to see the dreadful uncertainty 'terminated at any cost', Milner explained how

> the purport of all the representations made to me is to urge prompt and decided action; not to deprecate the further interference on the part of Her Majesty's Government. British South Africa is prepared for extreme measures, and is ready to see the vindication of British authority. It is prolongation of the negotiations, endless and indecisive of result, that is dreaded.

In the other, he emphasised how the franchise proposals at Bloemfontein had been generally misunderstood. 'A particular proposal put forward by me . . . with regard to a single question, has been treated as if it were by itself not only a panacea for the grievances of the Uitlanders, but a settlement of all the questions at issue between Great Britain and the South African Republic.' In fact, he said, there are many other issues which the latest Boer proposals try to ignore, but without solution of which there can be no satisfactory settlement.[55] There could have been no greater condemnation of Milner's whole management of the confrontation with the Boers than that implicit in these last sentences. Having purposely swung the terms of the controversy towards the single issue, and away from Chamberlain's broader approach, in order to capture public support and comprehension, and having in the process made genuine negotation impossible, he was now trying to transfer the onus for this back to his opponents, in the interests of maintaining that same public backing and of disparaging all recent offers which the Republic had made on the franchise issue. Nevertheless, the move was an astute one, for the Blue Book created a sensation. Gell told Milner that even the *Westminster Gazette* approved his despatch of 23 August. 'In fact I should say that the British Public have now "got the hang" of Kruger & Transvaal Statecraft much more acutely than the Cabinet *appears* to have. They have become impatient of the Diplomatic rejoinders in wh. the Official Politicians have become enmeshed.'[56]

This was less than fair to the Cabinet, whose problems were very real. Although Salisbury and Balfour allowed the military considerations to weigh more heavily than did Chamberlain, who felt that Milner and the military authorities exaggerated the risks and dangers involved, they had not given up trying to solve the ultimatum difficulty. Beach was unsure of any solution being reached, and had already given his opinion that the best way out of the impasse, from Britain's point of view, would be for the Boers to take up the offensive.[57] Salisbury wrote to Chamberlain explaining what he wished to do.

> I want to get away from the franchise issue which will be troublesome in debate – & to make the break on a proposal to revise the Convention of 1884 on the grounds that it has not been carried · out as we were promised: and because it has been worked to benefit not the people of the Transvaal ... but a very limited minority of them who are hostile to the rest.[58]

A 'majority of underdogs' would hold considerable appeal at least to the British public. Salisbury wished to manoeuvre in a way similar to that of January 1896, except that this time the Conventions were to be got finally out of the way to free the British Government for making the demands envisaged in his two Memoranda put to the Cabinet early in September.

Prolonged discussion and some delay during September thus helped to solve some of the difficulties surrounding the ultimatum. At the same time it re-emphasised the basic community of intent which existed within the Unionist Cabinet. Hicks Beach wrote to Lady Londonderry 'I am sure that none of us (except possibly J.C. though I am by no means sure about him) likes the business. But we all feel that it has got to be done – . . .'[59] Balfour made the same point at greater length.

> As not uncommonly happens in difficult circumstances, we – the Government and the people of this country – have got to find not the course which is best, but the best which is least bad. I am afraid this will involve a military expedition: I am still sanguine enough to hope not a *war* . . . few of us, I should think, are sufficiently self-satisfied to be absolutely confident that a particular course we may happen to recommend is beyond all question the right one – yet in this case I feel little doubt.[60]

Before very long Salisbury himself was again taking a more forthright line than Chamberlain in the Cabinet discussions, apparently re-echoing his words to Selborne on the eve of the July debate. He was 'prepared to face war sooner than not get out of Kruger terms that will secure good government at Johannesburg and make the Boers feel that we are & must be the paramount power in S. Africa'.[61]

This community of approach appears in the comments of Ministers on the draft ultimatum at the end of September. In reply to the Boer refusal of their proposals set out in their despatch of 8 September, yet another had been sent which, while giving the Boers time for further thought, stated that Britain was now considering terms for a final settlement.[62] Copies of a draft ultimatum were then circulated. The problem of popular support for such a document was evident to them all, and Hicks Beach concentrated on opinion at home.

> I think it important to bring out the fact that the Boers have themselves stamped the franchise law of 1889 as inadequate, by proposing a better one . . . the fewer our demands are in number, the fewer are the points on which we shall be open to attack. . . . Our

strong point, both for Parliament and for the future of South Africa, seems to me ... the repeal of all legislation affecting the rights and privileges of the Uitlanders since 1881, with a provision as to any necessary safeguards in view of the increase of population since that time, but *with the equality of the white races as its basis*. This last principle ... would really secure all we can desire, viz. British predominance.

Chamberlain not surprisingly sympathised with this approach, but felt that even if it widened the scope for their critics there was an irreducible minimum of demands, essential to 'cover a just settlement'. The franchise alone was not enough, and he felt that the question of foreign relations could not be omitted.[63] Goschen's view was one with a wider perspective:

> ... I fear the admission that the real issue is different and far wider than the points on which we have been negotiating, will lead to the exclamation from sceptical Europe etc. 'We knew it! We said so! The British Government have meant all along much more than they confessed to!'
> The whole difficulty of the despatch is to make the *transition* as natural and as little open to attack as possible.[64]

Devonshire, Lansdowne, and Balfour had little to say except to approve, although the latter was of the opinion that the independence of the Judicial Bench should be insisted upon.[65] Chamberlain agreed; Britain's position in the conflict had, in his opinion, to be associated as far as possible with the cause of civilisation.[66] One other modification Chamberlain accepted in his plans: whereas he would have preferred to meet the Transvaal with the proviso that both she and Britain should limit their forces in future, the Cabinet, apparently at Salisbury's suggestion, insisted that the Transvaal alone should disarm.[67]

While these final terms were debated, Chamberlain was still uncomfortable about the talks going on between the Boers, the Cape Dutch and President Steyn of the Orange Free State. He felt that any suggestions which might issue from these could not be refused, and it was also true that the passage of time allowed Britain's military preparations to move ahead; but there was danger that 'these communications may lead to some offer of a compromise, which public opinion might require us to accept, though in reality unsatisfactory ...'[68] To keep the pot simmering, the Colonial Secretary turned again to the press for publication when a Blue Book was impossible. He had already given Milner's version of the Smuts–Greene exchanges to the papers in response to the appearance of the Boer account. The Boers then published the British Cabinet's reply of 8 September, and on 19 September the Colonial Office in its turn released the Boer answer rejecting its terms. The exchange of telegrams between Milner and President Steyn appeared on 22 September, and four days afterwards the British Government's despatches of the 22nd were also published, stating that the ultimatum was now under consideration.[69] This was done as soon as they reached the Boers, in an attempt to sustain public belief in Boer obstructiveness and British good faith, to ensure that the British side of the case had a full hearing. Chamberlain also kept up his concern for those lesser groupings which went to make up the public as a whole; he confessed, for example, that he would like to put into the ultimatum 'the removal of religious disabilities, as it is the existence of these which keeps the support of many R[oman] Catholics . . . & Jews'.[70]

The great problem now was to prevent delay from destroying that state of public preparedness which could alone make possible, it was thought, a settlement satisfactory to Britain – whether by a complete Boer retreat or a successful war. In this respect the problem was now one equally for Chamberlain and the other Ministers, and on the eve of the war Selborne, acutely conscious of this, wrote again to the High Commissioner.

> You cannot realize the enormous difficulty we have had with public opinion at home. We have only now got 4/5th of the nation behind us because of the infinite patience we shewed, because of our hesitancy (militarily almost criminal) in making adequate preparations early enough, & because they believe that there is *now no more openings for negotiation*. . . . But, if Steyn had got Kruger this week to offer us your Bloemfontein terms, we could not have rejected them! That I believe to be literal fact. Far the best thing from the home point of view is that the Boers should this last week or the coming week, & before they receive our proposals, commence the war by invading our territory.[71]

Selborne's final comment showed how the Cabinet, though decided on their ultimatum, were still less than happy about the conviction its terms would carry with the public they now believed sympathetic. However, the day for its despatch was nearing. 'I think it must go on Monday or Tuesday. We cannot meet Parliament without showing our hand & unless the Boers take the offensive in the meanwhile we have to allow some days for delivery & printing of Blue Books' wrote Chamberlain to a colleague not normally bothered by this kind of consideration.[72] Milner meanwhile was more sanguine than those at home. Even he now felt that as far as 'home opinion is concerned the management of the controversy has been perfect. Seeing how hopelessly people were dead to the real issues 4 months ago, it is wonderful where they stand today.'[73] He admitted that the formulation of Britain's final demands posed a problem, as well he might: for it had been the continual effort to win over public opinion that had led to the introduction into the debate of terms which, while they provided admirable focal points, finally allowed of no compromise unless the Imperial Government was prepared to accept a complete loss of face. The progressive simplification of the controversy in the interests of publicity which first he, and then Chamberlain, had striven for, was largely responsible for making further plausible negotiations impossible. 'Ultimatum has always been great difficulty, as unless we widen issue there is not sufficient cause for war, and if we do so, we are abused for shifting our ground and extending our demands.'[74] Milner's activity of course had been consistently designed to make negotiation impossible; British demands were to be met, not negotiated upon. He was not prepared, therefore, at the last moment to rush ahead again by sending the ultimatum, and thereby risk further delay, even failure. Now more confident of his achievement, for once he advocated delay, advice finally justified by the delivery of the Boers' own ultimatum on 9 October.

No action of Milner ever consolidated the British as did this declaration of war, which at the same instant removed any necessity to deliver Britain's final demands. 'This great slow nation *has* woken up at last', announced George Wyndham.[75] Chamberlain too expressed his relief and his conviction when Parliament reassembled to grant the necessary finance and powers for the conduct of the war.

> With that great instinct of the British people in all times of crisis, the man in the street has put aside technicalities and legal subtleties and has gone to the root of the question. He knows perfectly well that we are going to war in defence of principles – the principles upon which this Empire has been founded and upon which alone it can exist.[76]

Those principles, as the Colonial Secretary explained, were

essentially the maintenance of peace and good government, and protection of the rights of British subjects, above all in an area such as South Africa where Britain's paramount position imposed additional responsibilities. What he did not mention was the necessity of preserving Britain's control over a region in which lay one of the traditional lynch-pins of the Empire, the necessity to put an end to foreign intrigues in a part of the imperial back-yard, the need to see that if the Transvaal became the most powerful region in southern Africa it should do so under British auspices. These were matters for Cabinet consideration and for Foreign Office negotiation, the realities of imperialism able to fascinate and inspire the few rather than the many. It was as a fig-leaf to cover their nakedness, as a concession to the priorities of the many who now held effective political power, that Uitlander grievances had eventually become important for the few. Salisbury announced as much when he thankfully observed in a statement the implications of which went far beyond the question of the undelivered ultimatum, that the Boers, by their declaration of war, 'liberated us from the necessity of explaining to the people of England why we are at war'.[77] Yet in one sense only was this true. For Chamberlain that explanation had been in progress for more than four years. While he had had no wish himself to be responsible for causing and for coping with a war, it was for just such a crisis that he had set out to prepare the country when he took the Colonial Office. Whether the instruction of the British public would stand the strain of a war, finally lead to a solution of South African questions, and play its part in an even grander imperial reorganisation, had yet to be decided.

Conclusion

I

'History consists, for the greater part, of the miseries brought upon the world by pride, ambition, avarice, revenge, lust, sedition, hypocrisy, ungoverned zeal, and all the train of disorderly appetites .... These vices are the *causes* of those storms. Religion, morals, laws, prerogatives, privileges, liberties, rights of men, are the *pretexts*. The pretexts are always found in some specious appearance of a real good.'[1] No doubt Burke would have felt his judgement amply borne out by the way in which 'grievances' and then 'the franchise' became bound up with the defence of British supremacy in South Africa. In Chamberlain's mind, however, there was only considerably pleasure at what he felt was the extent of his success. As he told Milner

> our policy of extreme patience, coupled with full explanation of the issues, has been thoroughly successful, and ... the country now understands the South African question as they have never done before.
>
> . It was all very well for you and for me to know, as we did, what a tremendous issue was behind such questions as franchise and alien immigration; but the public did not. They could not see that the things that we were contending for were worth a big war, nor were they particularly pleased with the clients on whose behalf we appeared to be acting. There was too much 'money bags' about the whole business to be agreeable to any of us.
>
> Fortunately, as the argument developed and especially owing to the diplomatic mistakes made by Kruger, the country became alive to the intolerable position into which we were settling. Even some of our strongest opponents were at last awake to the intentions of the Transvaal government, and ... see that if we had gone on in the old rut for a year or two longer, nothing could have saved South Africa to the British Crown.[2]

Chamberlain felt his belief that the nation would understand the issues if given the opportunity had been vindicated, and in the House of Commons he was perfectly sincere in defending his 'open diplomacy' and plain speaking as becoming in one who was the representative of the people.[3] However much this claim may smack of political rhetoric, there is no doubt that it reflects a fundamental line of thought in Chamberlain's whole approach to Empire and diplomacy. He did not ask himself whether the judgement of the public on the South African question was really more sound than its earlier approval of the person of Gladstone. For him the answer was as inevitable as the question was absurd. The education of public opinion which he had attempted was both a process of giving the public the 'right' views, and of helping people to formulate what he believed were their own often incoherent inclinations or beliefs. Thus the 'representative of the people' had also to fulfil the functions of a leader. Although in theory this might be a clear conception, its practical application, as has been seen, and as Chamberlain always acknowledged, was fraught with difficulties. In his own plan for diplomatic success in South Africa and for the future of the Empire, the public, in its widest sense as the electorate, had a dual role to play. A general education on imperial questions would provide a wide body of opinion sufficient to ensure the continuation of a coherent imperial policy. People would see the importance of the Empire and wish to preserve it. At the same time this groundswell of opinion would, given a little extra prompting in times of crisis, enable the Government to achieve its aims through a truly national show of determination, without squandering its resources by resorting to force. These were the lines upon which Chamberlain worked from 1895, and which gave the consistency to his, and increasingly that also of his staff's, concern with public opinion. These were also the assumptions which led Chamberlain to try to use the force of public opinion as a counter in the diplomatic game, particularly early in 1896, in 1897, and again through 1899. There were great technical problems in such an approach, not least those owing to the limited means at Chamberlain's disposal, and the liability of public attention to be distracted by other questions. This played a considerable part in his inability to make much of the South African question late in 1897 and in 1898. None the less, Chamberlain's efforts, together with those of Milner, achieved a remarkable degree of concentration on the issues they selected. Grievances and the franchise remedy were particularly successful through being very positive and constructive issues. In the House of Commons, Conservatives thought chiefly of a suzerainty or paramountcy flouted by the oppression of British subjects, while the Opposition dwelt on that traditionally liberal solution, the extension of the franchise. Evidence of popular meetings in the country suggests that they too for the most part accepted the gist of Chamberlain's arguments.

Although he was aided by propaganda from other sources, this was a very considerable success when, as Chamberlain was fully aware, the public with which he was concerned was so diverse in its composition. For a concise statement of what was in effect Chamberlain's approach to the problem of public support, the historian can scarcely do better than turn to E. D. Morel, at the point where he defined the nature of the appeal required to launch his own Congo Reform Association in 1903. Having stressed the impracticability of leading a crusade by invoking any one particular sentiment, Morel went on

> if it [the Congo Free State] were to be struck down the appeal must be varied and widened in character, and forces other than humanitarian must be brought into play. There must be appeal to national honour, which meant that the Public, and especially the philanthropic and religious Public ... must be vividly reminded of the very special national responsibility which rested upon England and Englishmen in the matter. There must be appeal to the Imperial side ... [by this he meant the dangers of arming and unrest to contiguous British territory]. There must be appeal to the commercial side. ...[4]

Although written some years later, this description could apply word for word to Chamberlain's handling of imperial affairs in general and of the South African question in particular. His attempt to present the basic issues clearly, but with as much illustrative detail as possible, was a consistent feature of his publicity. Boer arming and the danger to the other British colonies, the national responsibility, the Boer attack on legitimate trading interests, appalling misgovernment of Africans as of Europeans, the taxation without representation of Britain's kith and kin who were often poor working men – all were points in his case for grievances, selected as much for the width of their appeal at home as for their truth or importance in South Africa, and were essential, Chamberlain felt, if public enthusiasm was to be awakened and sustained.

Two modifications only did the Colonial Secretary make in his campaign. The first was in his almost total abandonment of the non-white peoples in the white South African territories, as distinct from Basutoland, Bechuanaland, and the lands of the British South Africa Company, all of which lay ultimately under imperial control. This was important in that it showed how Chamberlain was brought increasingly to realise the significance of white South African opinion in any future settlement. As has been seen, it was in the first half of 1899 that this problem reached its climax, when events and opinion in South Africa set the pace and Chamberlain followed as best he could. In these circumstances, responsibility was surrendered more and more to Milner, a development intensified by changes at home, where hostility towards Chamberlain increased as the conflict deepened. In an attempt to avoid the undermining of his campaign by efforts to discredit him personally, Chamberlain passed the initiative to the High Commissioner at the time of the Bloemfontein Conference. Although he and the Cabinet later reassumed control, this move resulted in the final abandonment of his pet scheme for an Uitlander municipality on the Rand. The franchise issue was Milner's contribution to the debate on South Africa, an issue which he took up less for its potential as a means of bringing down Kruger peacefully than for its attractions as something which could be projected to the public. As a practical remedy for grievances it appeared to command support in South Africa, and was able to attract the same in England. For this reason it could be easily accommodated in Chamberlain's campaign to win over the British people to the cause of Empire.

Campbell-Bannerman was very shrewd in his appreciation of this aspect of the crisis.

> If you ask my opinion, I hold this 'franchise' movement as the biggest hypocrisy in the whole fraud. It was designed in order that:–
> (a) Kruger, seeing the real drift of it, might refuse it, and supply a direct ground of quarrel;
> (b) If he accepted it, it would mean that not being able to get in by the front door they would get the area gate opened and get possession in this way of the country.
> (c) The innocent Briton would be gulled by the flavour of legality and of civilized progress in the word 'franchise'. But this is only my view of it, and practically they are dropping it because the Outlander does not care about it and would not use it if he might.[5]

In common with many other people, however, the Liberal leader showed less insight in his understanding of the relations of Milner and Chamberlain.[6] In Liberal eyes the Colonial Secretary was always the arch-villain, and yet Campbell-Bannerman's own feelings on the general question were hardly different from those of the Unionist Cabinet, Chamberlain included. In the same letter to Harcourt, he explained that

> as to the general power or responsibility of this country, it is no doubt vague, but I think it is substantial. As a matter of fact the two races in the Colony, Natal, and for that part of it, Free State, are hindered from forgetting their differences by this quarrel in the Transvaal. The sooner it is settled the better in the interest of S. Africa generally. Therefore we have a stronger inducement or title to intervene than if it was merely the ill-treatment of some Englishmen at Calais.
>
> It is analogous, surely, to the right of the Powers of Europe to try and stop misgovernment in Turkey, which endangers general peace. ... It is a question of 'tua res agitur' intensified by our undoubtedly predominant position, which carries with it responsibility, and responsibility gives a right which, if not technically and legally definite, is yet, as I said, substantial.

Chamberlain would have accepted this, and it formed part of the reasoning behind his early approaches to the Republic, notably his adoption of grievances early in 1896. He was unwilling to abandon this early stand, or his 'municipality' solution when Milner wished to raise the franchise; his confidence in the Uitlander was not overwhelming, and he had no wish suddenly to introduce into the discussion a new subject which he felt sure would confuse the public at home. Milner, by his manoeuvring in South Africa, left Chamberlain with no choice but to take up the franchise.

The possibility that this might lead to war held no terrors for the High Commissioner. The rapidity with which he came to believe – as he told Fitzpatrick – that war was the only way out of the situation created by Boer intransigence, the way in which he attempted to force the pace of the diplomacy, his relief when war came, and his immediate consideration of plans for the future, all confirm this view. Milner may have been a man of some vision when it came to thinking of the Empire as a whole, but this is certainly not the case in his pre-war approach to South African problems. Desperately busy and enormously hardworking, he kept his nose to the grindstone; rarely allowing himself much time for reflection or relaxation, he also kept a narrow circle of acquaintances. Eye trouble, weariness, and tension were increasingly his lot. In short, he lived at the Cape under conditions which were in no way conducive to largeness of feeling or thought, and which only accentuated his tendency to be narrowly single-minded and inflexible. Such rigidity was possibly one way in which the burden of work could be kept within bounds, and at times certainly contributed to the air which Milner for long had of a man bent on war. War, it came to seem, would soon provide the *tabula rasa* upon which Milner the administrator might work to fashion the new South Africa.

Although it was a widely held British view that the war would be short, in this respect too Milner's approach differed very markedly from that of Chamberlain. As a politician, Chamberlain was more aware of the problems a war would create as well as those which it might solve. In May 1896, when he expressed his feelings as to the gravity of any war in South Africa, he was only echoing words of his own uttered nearly fifteen years before.[7] For him justification of the Empire was bound up with justification of a war as this latter became increasingly necessary in the summer of 1899. Milner had no such problems. Singleminded in his belief that the Empire and British customs embodied the highest of civilised values, even though practice might occasionally leave much to be desired, he was incapable of understanding those who in any way thought otherwise. Devotion to the Empire was for him the test of friend or foe, and from the time of his speech at Graaff Reinet, Milner was concerned to separate the two. Not that the two were respectively or exclusively British or Dutch; the bogey of a pan-Afrikaner conspiracy was something in which neither he nor any other British statesman believed or professed belief until very late in the day.[8] Even in May 1899, it was one of Milner's aims in not taking Schreiner to Bloemfontein to keep him and others like him under British influence,[9] and only in the last months before war broke out did the High Commissioner begin to talk of 'British' South Africa without qualification. It was the Boer ultimatum, the support given to the Transvaal by the Orange Free State, and the revolt of the Cape Dutch, which progressively gave substance to that particular cry. Nevertheless, Milner's belief in war as the outcome involved the assumption that two irreconcilable sides already existed. In setting out to force those two sides into the open, Milner did more than anyone to create them. His concern with English opinion at home was secondary, but grew as he realised the necessity of awakening it to force the British Government into action, or at least enable it to move. This two-sided process affected his diplomacy more noticeably than, but in ways similar to, that of Chamberlain. He thought that exaggeration and over-simplification were required to make the British Government and people see the situation in South Africa as starkly as he did himself. They were needed too to convince South African 'loyalists' that their predicament was known, and that they would not be ignored.

The importance of 'public opinion' and the effects of publicity on the course of Anglo-Boer relations in these years can therefore hardly be exaggerated. Such considerations affected the issues taken up by Chamberlain and Milner, the way in which they were developed, and contributed largely to the impossibility of successful negotiation. A mixture of diplomacy and propaganda was created in which the demands of publicity and the need to avoid losing face led constantly to the simplification of issues involved, and to the premature adoption of firm positions. It was because they both saw their public as of fundamental importance, rather than a simple result of personal exasperation with Boer long-windedness and lack of response, that Chamberlain, and especially Milner, felt that matters had to be constantly pushed forward. It was finally the propaganda rather than the diplomacy which was successful.

II

The historian must however resist the tendency of con-temporaries and of many subsequent historians to attribute sole responsibility for the war to particular British officials. One can certainly say that Milner's machinations did much to bring about the war he thought inevitable, and that Chamberlain became in many respects the victim of his methods by getting a war he did not want. Yet ultimately responsibility lay with the British Government. Salisbury and his colleagues may have acted reluctantly, yet they still went ahead, and insufficient recognition has been given to the importance of the Prime Minister's and other Cabinet Ministers' attitudes in prompting, not delaying, a confrontation with the Boers. Although Chamberlain was, by virtue of his Cabinet post, the chief articulator of British policy, his feeling in 1895 that by choosing the Colonial Office he was taking the ground on which he had most in common with his colleagues was amply borne out by events. The wish to maintain what they thought should be British paramountcy in South Africa was shared by all members of the Cabinet. Fundamental agreement on the objectives of South African policy meant that discussion of principles was minimal: the questions raised by the South African situation became the question of the extent to which basic aims in South Africa should be subordinated to the achievement of British aims elsewhere. This was above all a consideration which affected Salisbury and Balfour, and was one which prevailed strongly with all Ministers both after April 1897, and at the time of the Anglo-German negotiations in 1898. On the third occasion, when Salisbury expressed some doubts as to the wisdom of a forward policy in August 1899, he was overborne by the rest of the Cabinet. In 1897, Chamberlain, who was naturally able to give less consistent attention to diplomacy and general foreign policy, accepted Salisbury's reservations with respect to the European situation. In 1898, he was quite clearly brought round by Balfour, and late in 1899 his views were also shared by the majority of his colleagues. It is no easier to see Chamberlain as the creator of a strong forward policy in South Africa, relatively unchecked by the rest of the Cabinet, than it is to see him unscrupulously choosing a policy which was from the start 'arrogant in conception and crude in execution'.[10] Even on more purely technical or tactical questions his views were frequently rejected, either by Salisbury or by the Cabinet as a whole. On all points even remotely involving foreign powers, Salisbury was firmly in control; the response to the Kruger Telegram, the protests over the Aliens legislation, the observance of Article IV, and the negotiations after May 1899, were none of them left for Chamberlain to manage alone. On occasions when Chamberlain suggested direct approaches to those other nations involved in South Africa, he met little positive response. At other times, the Colonial Secretary's attitude was thought insufficiently forward, for example on the observance of Article IV, or in his readiness to accept the revised franchise proposals in July 1899. Not only did considerable fundamental agreement exist in the Cabinet, but one is not even confronted with a situation in which the Cabinet wished to move consistently more slowly than the Colonial Secretary.

For the Cabinet as a whole, it was the elimination of the possibilities of a satisfactory solution involving the European elements in the South African situation which was crucial. Having realised this, they turned, in May 1899, to the one remaining opportunity for making it clear to the Boers and to South Africa that Britain was 'Boss', that opportunity created by Chamberlain in the shape of grievances and brought further forward by Milner after his visit to England. It was in his publicity rather than his strictly diplomatic actions that Chamberlain was unchecked, and it was in taking up the issues thus aired that the Cabinet came to see a means of salvation for British supremacy. Given what was widely believed to be the choice between a loss of prestige, perhaps even the 'loss' of South Africa, and a war, the Cabinet was prepared to face a war rather than give the impression that the Transvaal had got its way, or that Britain was powerless in the face of the Republic. For this reason, successive Boer proposals were found unsatisfactory, the British Government persisted because on this issue it felt that public opinion would be behind it, and Milner received a viscountcy rather than due correction.

One of the most alarming features of the handling of South African diplomacy in these years is the uncritical nature of the thought given to the wider aspects of British interests in that part of the world. Vaguely stated claims to supremacy and statements of the need to preserve it, an awareness that Germany and possibly France were trying to undermine British influence, a conviction of the strategic importance of the region's harbours, a feeling that British dominance in southern Africa was essential to a consolidation of the Empire which was in its turn required for the defence of Britain's future in a hostile world, – these were all present to the official mind. The truth of them was taken for granted, and alternatives hardly discussed. Britain was a great power, and had traditionally dominated South African affairs; this was the day of empires, as Chamberlain never tired of asserting, and retreat was not to be countenanced especially when Kruger's republic was ultimately the only nigger in the woodpile. The British Government never considered the virtues of withdrawal in these years; perhaps this was too much to expect of a party with a strong tradition of criticism directed at Liberal 'weakness' in this respect, and apt to be described as very 'anti-Boer'. Nor did it consider the dangers inherent in the publicity that was so much a part of Chamberlain's tactics; apart from the desire where possible to avoid rubbing Chamberlain up the wrong way, there was apparently no real awareness among Ministers that significant dangers existed. Instead, in the context of the prevailing scepticism about the effect of popular feeling in the realm of foreign policy, there was a willingness in the early summer of 1899, when all other British moves in South Africa had produced negative results, to accept the Chamberlainite assumption that victory might be achieved peacefully by taking up the Uitlander Petition. The combination of widespread popular support, evident in South Africa and anticipated at home, with the Imperial Government's determination was likely to be a winning recipe, or at least worth trying as a last resort. A war against the Boers would be small one, but in any case it was unlikely to come to that. The lessons of South African history and straight common sense suggested that the Boers would give way in the face of determination, military preparations, and the weight of popular disapproval. This was not the last occasion when an imperial government failed entirely to understand how its actions appeared to those on the receiving end, or to appreciate the nature of local nationalism.

Reluctant to reconsider assumptions either about Britain's place in South Africa or about the Boers, the British Government moved from expedient to expedient as new hopes of a favourable solution appeared. It was a policy not of drift but of opportunism, in which general assumptions went unquestioned and were often pushed into the background, and practical day-to-day details became all. The Cabinet failed to see what their High Commissioner fully appreciated and exploited, that the publicity and popular support which gave the case for grievances its strength, as well as adding strength to its arm, could become a straitjacket, putting an end to diplomatic flexibility and changes of course which might be fatal if the Boers failed to behave as officials in Britain expected.

III

Historians are now generally agreed that the maintenance of British supremacy together with the ultimate intention of pro-moting federation were the local objects of British endeavours in South Africa. Yet this by itself leaves unanswered the question why the diplomacy of imperialism in South Africa was conducted in the manner set out in the preceding pages. Contemporaries were convinced that there was a very marked difference between the conduct of imperial affairs under Chamberlain, and their conduct under his mid-century predecessors. He was both praised and criticised for the publicity which he gave to his actions, as for the financial outlay which many of his schemes involved. All the evidence seems to point to the fact that in South Africa the ends of policy remained largely unchanged. Only the diplomacy by which the ends were to be reached altered. The historian must ask why, for in much previous writing the question has been either ignored or swept aside.

In their references to the significance of 'public opinion' for late nineteenth-century British imperial policy, historians have, broadly speaking, taken up one of two positions. The older tradition, following closely on the heels of many contemporary critics of Empire, is reflected in Elie Halévy's assessment of the general attitude towards the Boer War.

> The British were practically unanimous in their belief that they were waging a just war to liberate their fellow countrymen oppressed by an oligarchy of corrupt and stupid peasants. . . . But what need to say more? To attempt to analyse a fit of patriotic frenzy would be a thankless task.[11]

This was given further support by Ensor in his contribution to the *Oxford History of England*, and later detailed studies such as that by W. L. Langer tended to demonstrate that official policy mirrored this generally popular bellicosity and expansive urge.[12] As late as 1964, Richard Koebner and H. D. Schmidt, while attempting the analysis Halévy had felt unnecessary, came to similar conclusions, and spoke of 'the waves of imperialism', 'of militancy and assertive spiritedness' which 'engulfed the English-speaking world . . . between 1897 and 1899'.[13] Public opinion and official policy were wholly at one with each other; South African policy appeared to be the direct offspring of the general mood, for, as Koebner remarked, 'Milner and Kruger personified rather than caused the struggle'.[14]

The second line of thought has more recent origins, following for the most part from R. E. Robinson's and J. Gallagher's analysis of African partition and British expansion in *Africa and the Victorians*. Not only did rational strategic considerations lie at the heart of the matter, but in any case 'British opinion restrained rather than prompted ministers to act in Africa'.[15] Halévy has been stood on his head. Any analysis was likely to be still a thankless task for the imperial historian, not now by reason of the obvious congruence of policy with popular passion, but rather because the influence of any public opinion – or, indeed, of domestic issues – was negligible. This argument for the lack of such constraints on the 'official mind' has lately been given apparent additional weight by conclusions arrived at as a result of work on the attitudes of the British working class at the turn of the century. Official failure to be influenced by other than traditional concepts was, it seems, paralleled by a great weight of apathy and unconcern in the nation at large.[16] Thus were the arguments for the existence of an excited populace and an aggressive, expansive policy countered with others which envisaged a government working steadily on traditional lines, able to ignore vociferous economic or humanitarian groups who were rendered ineffective by their lack of basic popular support.

It is not the fact of conflict between these two positions so much as the underlying similarity of approach, which needs to be examined. Despite the fact that British politicians were having to operate within a reasonably democratic political system, it seems to have been commonly assumed that the feelings of 'the electorate', the state of 'public opinion', left governments with a free hand. No evidence is offered to suggest that officials responsible for policy-making ever felt the necessities of policy would be in conflict with what their public would allow. Official assumptions could govern the general conduct of policy and the demands made by overseas crises might fairly be met, because governments and a majority of their people were not pulling in opposite directions. Conditions were imposed, if at all, from the periphery, never from the seat of empire.[17] Public agitation or opinion may or may not have been an element in the total situation, but at no point did it exercise a compelling force; statesmen were never forced to do things against their will.

Robinson and Gallagher suggested that because the basic principles of imperial policy remained unchanged, being officially adapted only locally to meet new crises arising in more or less distant parts of the Empire, the impotence of public opinion was therefore demonstrated and the continuity of mid- and late-century imperialism an inevitable conclusion. This was a view challenged by Stengers who asserted that, beginning with the affair of Brazza and the Congo in 1882, there began

> en matière coloniale, la série des mouvements d'opinion publique de la fin du XIXe et du début du XXe siècle. Il faut parler au pluriel, de mouvements et non d'un mouvement, car il ne s'agira jamais là d'une de ces passions, comme on en connaît en politique, qui s'emparent littéralement des esprits et les dominent de manière durable. C'est par à coup, de manière sporadique, que vont se succèder, dans un pays puis dans un autre, des flambées d'enthousiasme colonial. Elles seront séparées souvent par des périodes de quasi-indifférence, dont les champions de la cause coloniale se désoleront.[18]

However, while suggesting that the existence of these waves of opinion was one of the distinguishing features of late-century imperialism, he does not argue that in their effects they were ever more than an incidental characteristic of the age. Reintroducing the element of popular feeling only to dismiss it again – along with, it would seem, the anxieties of imperialists – as of relatively superficial significance, Stengers preferred to argue as the point of fundamental importance the fact that

> dés l'instant où l'on entamait la pénétration économique du continent noir, la tentation était forte, irrésistible même, de se réserver d'une manière ou d'une autre certains avantages dans les régions où l'on pénétrait. La marche vers l'intérieur devait être presque nécessairement synonyme, dans beaucoup de cas, d'acquisition de privilèges économiques.[19]

Just as Stengers left the assumptions as to the relation between policy-makers and their public unexamined, so too recent analysts of Anglo-South African relations have allowed them to remain intact. Marais, Wilde, Drus and Van der Poel all saw the diplomacy and the resulting war as the personal responsibility of Chamberlain and Milner. Public opinion is something they only briefly refer to, something given marginal consideration only when a British use of force against the Boers became a possibility in the summer of 1899.[20] Robinson and Gallagher adopt a similar interpretation. Again their concern is with the statesmen involved, and those statesmen are, as always, remarkably unencumbered with problems on the home front. Domestic considerations do not seem for a moment to have narrowed their room for manoeuvre. The one recent discussion of the origins of the war of 1899 which allows for the significance of any 'public opinion' in contributing to that disaster, has produced little more than a gloss on the then contemporary criticisms of the new imperialism.[21]

It is also the burden of Robinson's and Gallagher's analysis that the issues which did have popular significance, Uitlander grievances and the franchise, were brought to the fore because the imperial government perceived the necessity of cultivating a community of 'collaborators' in South Africa, who would with their economic and political weight more than counterbalance Afrikaner nationalists hostile to the British presence, and, with their 'loyalty', uphold the imperial connection and interest, whether economic or strategic. In much of the above, arguments and evidence have been put forward which suggest that such a formulation ought to be modified, that imperial statesmen saw in South Africa a more complex situation. They were prevented from believing in the possibility of any straightforward re-arrangement of South African supporters and opponents of the imperial connection, both by the presence or initiatives of European competitors and by their own doubts as to the Uitlanders' ultimate value as collaborators. In various ways, through their diplomatic bargaining with the European powers, in Chamberlain's reluctance to go beyond a municipality, in Milner's final lack of belief in the franchise and his feeling that war would bring down Kruger's republic and re-establish imperial supremacy, the response of imperial officials showed that there were severe limits to their acceptance either of the idea that Boer hostility was their only problem, or of 'collaboration' as the complete or only answer. However, in addition to this, both the issues developed and the style of the diplomacy owed much to the relationship between imperial policy-makers and metropolitan public opinion.

It has been one of the purposes of this book to suggest that in the case of South Africa the relation between 'public opinion' and other factors affecting the making of imperial policy is far from being either unimportant or as simple as is sometimes imagined. Public opinion in so far as it affects the formulation of policy is not necessarily an objective, active or narrowly definable reality which politicians have freely chosen either to ignore or to take into account. It is also unhelpful to treat it as something of which politicians were either the living expression or passive instrument. Without doubt, anxiety as to the interests and inclinations of the rest of their countrymen was very marked on the part of those responsible for making policy decisions; the problems and circumstances of the day, together with the personal characteristics and situations of certain politicians, were sufficient to elevate the state of public opinion for consideration, setting it alongside other factors often in a position of decisive importance. It was not simply the *fact* of 'quasi-indifférence' noted by Stengers which caused 'les champions de la cause coloniale' to despair; nor did their depression lift entirely with the rekindling of 'les flambées d'enthousiasme colonial'. It was as much the unpredictable and seemingly unthinking alternation of popular interest and unconcern which worried imperialists. In Britain, certain imperialists were not prepared to accept the continuing necessity for such anxiety and actively sought a cure for this malady which they associated with the nature of democratic politics. In that cure, their handling of the South African question was designed to play a large part.

Problems related to the conduct of foreign policy within a parliamentary or democratic system of politics had long been faced by statesmen, whether kings or ministers.[22] However, as was argued above, these were felt to be changing rapidly in the later nineteenth century. In the Introduction to his *English Constitution*, written in 1872, Walter Bagehot was at pains to offer advice to statesmen in a period 'when ignorance has an unusual power in public affairs'. 'What is mostly needed', he thought, 'is the manly utterance of clear conclusions; if a statesman gives these in a felicitous way . . . he has done his part. He will have given the text, the scribes in the newspapers will write the sermon.'[23] He specifically warned against assuming 'a pedantic and *doctrinaire* tone with the English people'.[24] Many, however, were not inclined to heed his suggestions, least of all with respect to imperial and foreign affairs. Sir Stafford Northcote for example remained characteristically patrician. He told a Scottish audience

> I think I may say this in regard to the general attitude which the people in this country hold with regard to foreign policy – as a rule they do not understand it. (A voice, 'A thousand times better than the Government.') I say that not by way of reproach to the people of this country, I say it merely as a metter of fact, and because it is almost impossible that it could be otherwise.[25]

These were early days; subsequently, experience of extended

democracy together with a growing apprehension of foreign rivalry caused many people to change their tune. Chamberlain's handling of the South African question showed just how different their key was in the last decade of the century. His prolonged and consistent response to public opinion, or, rather, to the absence of the kind of opinion and understanding he wished for, the kind of issues he selected, the gulf between the ostensible cause and the issues which statesmen admitted privately to be at stake, the size of the audience which Chamberlain was trying to capture for the future, all set him apart from his predecessors and many of his milder contemporaries.

In some ways it is tempting to dismiss all this as the indulgence of a private whim by the new Colonial Secretary, or to see it as his attempt to satisfy some temperamental necessity. Certainly there is evidence that Chamberlain liked to feel the public with him, and he was conscious that his political position depended in large part on the votes which he was felt to command. Such a position had to be maintained, and popular support was a good counterweight to the hostility which Chamberlain knew many among the ruling classes felt for him. But it is difficult to credit this as the sole or even principal spur to his persistent efforts to involve the public in South African affairs despite the problems which this created for him. There are difficulties too in the suggestion that his dedication to the cause of Empire was alone sufficient to sustain such a campaign; it is possible to argue that Chamberlain might have had his success, and even rehabilitated himself in many people's eyes, by paying no attention to the public at all.

Perhaps, it may be suggested, this was a style of diplomacy attributable simply to the presence of new men, business men and others, in the forefront of British politics. Certainly, if one takes account of all those Members of Parliament who were committee members of the ISAA during this period, and therefore approved of Chamberlain's activities, this can be quite strongly supported.[26] On the other hand, it is not true that these were his only supporters, even if they were some of the most active. Nor were they the most numerous or influential within the parties of the day. While their age and occupations may have gone hand in hand with temperaments which predisposed them to approve of Chamberlain's plain-speaking and open diplomacy, this was not a mode of procedure which they backed indiscriminately. A number of the ISAA's members also belonged to the group of Parliamentarians especially interested in Chinese affairs; yet on this more traditionally foreign than imperial subject, they did not attempt propaganda on anything like the same scale.[27] Furthermore, there is no evidence to suggest that Chamberlain was in any way giving special encouragement to the Association, or that he felt any special affinity with its members.

There are more fundamental and less personal reasons for the new approach. On the one hand, there was that awareness in the late century of the increasingly complicated international situation, in which it was thought that the preservation of the Empire was the key to survival as a Great Power. On the other, social and constitutional developments were taking place inside Britain. Together, these circumstances raised for large numbers of people the problem as to how a successful imperial and foreign policy could be developed in a democratic system of politics. Involvement in this unprecedented debate, or at least a sharing of the preoccupations which gave rise to it, was something which united late Victorians far more widely and in greater numbers than any grouping by age or occupation. At the same time, the question of the British position in South Africa was one upon which many men, well beyond the confines of the ISAA, were agreed. British rule in South Africa was something upon which there could be no yielding. It was this relatively new and increasingly uncertain situation, and the consequent awareness amongst statesmen and others, which did much to set the imperialism of the 1890s apart from that of the mid-Victorian period, adding greatly to its sense of pessimism and haste. Fears at the top, rather than increased public excitement over aspects of imperialism for their own sakes, were responsible for the fact that there developed, in the case of South Africa at least, a new relationship between policy-makers and their public.

This new relationship was above all the creation of Joseph Chamberlain. His response to the situation, based on ideas developed slowly over more than a decade, was apparent from the moment of his arrival at the Colonial Office. His initiatives in the nine months after June 1895, during which time it was South Africa's misfortune to be brought fully into the limelight by the Jameson Raid, set the tone of imperial diplomacy for the next four years. His initiatives and methods were ones which he and many others felt to be a necessity; they were a response to a general narrowing of the possible alternatives for action. Opposition to the South African policies of Chamberlain and Milner finally developed, especially in the summer of 1899, as a result of the ultimate failure by them and many others to solve what for years had been seen as a growing problem, the reconciliation of the needs of Empire and the problems of democracy. At that time, however, the defection of liberal intellectuals, whether as defenders of a free press or of honest, open government, was relatively insignificant, and there was as yet no sense of failure; on the contrary, a solution had at last been attempted. In 1895, the situation was such that Chamberlain felt that he had to use whatever issues came to hand in his attempts to counter the bad effects of democratic politics on imperial policy. It was widely felt that the choice of alternatives was small, with the result that with Chamberlain in office secret diplomacy was largely abandoned; the way in which imperial affairs were handled became one with the process of publicising the value and aims of Empire. It was thought that only if such a campaign was conducted could the more mundane economic or traditional strategic necessities be maintained. It was, however, not appreciated that for those like the Boers, faced with trying to negotiate for the protection of their own interests, this created an impression of total insincerity on the part of the British Government, and thus, contrary to the expectations of British politicians, threatened constructive diplomacy from the outset.

Chamberlain was the only man who combined the possession of effective power, the temperament and willingness to take risks, and the previous radical experience which helped him to respond constructively to the new situation. His predecessors had either not felt the problems to be so pressing, or had failed to see their way to a solution. His successors, whether at the Colonial Office or the Foreign Office, lacked even in office the political power and temperament to carry out a similar campaign. In any case, Chamberlain himself was from 1903 waging the battle on a different front. 'Make a mistake in your Imperial policy – it is irretrievable', he warned his Birmingham audience as he demanded an inquiry into the question of Tariff Reform.[28] Thus the Colonial Secretary set out on the second stage of his long campaign to make sure that no more mistakes should be made by an 'ignorant' populace, to instil into the electorate and its representatives an informed determination to protect imperial interests. The first stage, dominated ultimately by the South African question, was brought to an end by the war; as Chamberlain realised, the principles he had spelt out between 1895 and 1899 were inevitably tarnished by 'methods of barbarism' and the experience of a long bitter struggle. The fight for Tariff Reform, however, also ended in defeat and disappointment. The imperial theme was submerged, and Chamberlain himself was doomed to live out a period of years, as long again as his Colonial Secretaryship, under the shadow of the stroke which effectively removed him from public life. For Milner too the defeat of Tariff Reform and his experience of Reconstruction brought great disappointment.

For a time, some of the aims lived on, albeit often in different guises.[29] From Birmingham, Austen Chamberlain inherited his father's mantle, and in it the ghost was sometimes seen to walk.

> I am deeply impressed by our undeserved good fortune in carrying our people so unanimously with us. There had been nothing beforehand in official speeches or in official publications to make known to them the danger that we ran or to prepare them for the discharge of our responsibilities and the defence of our interests. Those who knew most were silent: those who undertook to instruct the mass of the public were ignorant, and our democracy, with its decisive voice on the conduct of public affairs, was left without guidance by those who could have directed it properly, and was misled by those who constituted themselves its guides.
>
> You may say that all this is past; but I think it has a very serious bearing upon the present and even more upon the future. Now is the time, when people will read and ponder over these things, to form an enlightened public opinion which will support the Government through whatever sacrifices are needed in the weary months of war and will uphold them in insisting upon stable terms of peace. Now is our opportunity to lay the foundations in the minds of the public of a wise, responsible, & consistent foreign policy after the war is finished[30]

Thus wrote the son soon after his father's death and in the first months of the First World War. Yet times were by then changing fast; democracy was becoming familiar, the shape of the world was beginning to alter, and history was not to repeat itself.

Notes

Notes to Chapter I *(pp. 1–26)*

[1] T. Baines, 'Democracy and foreign affairs', *Quarterly Review* (January 1899), 241.

[2] J. Holland Rose, *The Rise and Growth of Democracy in Britain* (1898), Intro.

[3] *Ibid.*, 10.

[4] P. Lyttelton Gell to Milner 1 Feb. 1901, Gell MSS.

[5] *Ibid.*, 14 March 1901.

[6] Salisbury to Sir E. Baring 22 Dec. 1888, *CHBE* III, 163.

[7] G. F. Wilson to Milner 22 June 1899, J. G. Maydon to Milner 11 Aug. 1899, MP 15 ff.66–70, 32 f.135.

[8] To Milner 27 June 1891, Wrench, 119–20.

[9] Milner to Goschen 18 Feb. 1885, *ibid.*, 74.

[10] Milner to G. Parkin 13 Sept. 1901, *ibid.*, 228–9.

[11] See for example D. P. Crook, *American Democracy in English Politics 1815–1850 (Oxford, 1965).*

[12] K. Bourne, *The Foreign Policy of Victorian England 1830–1902* (Oxford, 1970), 3 and *passim*; A. P. Thornton, *The Imperial Idea and Its Enemies* (1959); Robinson and Gallagher, *Africa and the Victorians*; G. Martin, 'Empire federalism and imperial parliamentary union, 1820–1870', *HJ* 16 (1) (1973).

[13] D. C. M. Platt, *Finance, Trade and Politics in British Foreign Policy, 1815–1914* (Oxford, 1968).

[14] R. A. Jones, *The Nineteenth-Century Foreign Office: An Administrative History* (1971), 41–64; Z. S. Steiner, 'The last years of the old Foreign Office 1898–1905', *HJ* 6 (1) (1963), 60.

[15] Sir R. Peel to J. W. Croker 23 March 1820, P. Fraser, 'Public petitioning and Parliament before 1832', *History* XLVI (1961), 196.

[16] S. Lambert, 'A century of diplomatic Blue Books', *HJ* 10 (1) (1967), 125–31.

[17] P. J. V. Rolo, *George Canning* (1965), ch. 1; S. G. Checkland, *The Gladstones: A Family Biography 1764–1851* (Cambridge, 1971) esp. 99–117.

[18] *Ibid.*, and Rolo 180–1; H. W. V. Temperley, *The Foreign Policy of Canning 1822–1827* (1925), 32–42, 235–8.

[19] *Ibid.*, 512–13 for a list of such speeches; for an exception, Canning's speech at Harwich 11 Feb. 1823, 78–82.

[20] *The Journal of Mrs Arbuthnot*, I, 275, 304, entries for 18 Nov. 1823 and 22 Apr. 1824.

[21] Canning to Lord Granville (Ambassador at Paris) 24 Jan. 1826, Granville MSS PRO 30/29/8/9 f.1107.

[22] *The Journal of Mrs Arbuthnot*, I, 221–7, 292; Duke of Wellington to Lord Liverpool 5 March 1824, cit. C. Webster and H. W. V. Temperley,

'British policy in the publication of diplomatic documents under Castlereagh and Canning', *Cambridge Historical Journal*, I (1924), 166; Temperley, 83–6, 118–21; Canning to Bagot 14 July 1823, J. Bagot, *George Canning and His Friends* (2 vols, 1909), II, 180.

  . [23] A. G. Stapleton, *George Canning and His Times* (1859), 377–9.

  [24] *Ibid.*, 379.

  [25] A. Aspinall, *Politics and the Press c. 1780–1850* (1949), 186, 200–1, 213–14; Temperley, 297–307.

  [26] Lord Dalling, *The Life of Henry John Temple Viscount Palmerston*, (3 vols, 1870–4), I, 138–41; also E. Ashley, *The Life of Henry John Temple Viscount Palmerston 1846–1865* (2 vols, 1876), I, 129.

  [27] Ashley, II, 189–92.

  [28] Palmerston to W. Temple 19 April 1827, Dalling, I, 186–90.

  [29] Dalling, III, 112–13; J. Prest, *Lord John Russell* (1972), 225.

  [30] J. Ridley, *Lord Palmerston* (1970), 99.

  [31] 14 June 1829, Dalling, I, 333–7.

  [32] Sir C. Webster, *The Foreign Policy of Palmerston 1830–1841* (2 vols, 1951), I, 31–41; Palmerston to Granville 5 June 1838, Dalling, II, 266.

  [33] Webster, I, 40; Duke of Argyll, *Autobiography and Memoirs* (2 vols, 1906), II, 47–9.

  [34] Palmerston to Russell 11 Sept. 1864, comparing contemporary Cabinets with those of Pitt and Peel, Ashley, II, 257–8.

  [35] 12 Aug. 1831, *HPD* 3rd (v) 1290–6; Ridley, 153–4.

  [36] Webster, I, 45–54 and *passim*; Ridley, 114–17 and *passim*.

  [37] Webster, I, 60–2.

  [38] *Ibid.*; Temperley, 32, 88–9, 306–7.

  [39] 14 Nov. 1842, Dalling, III, 117.

  [40] Sir H. Maxwell, *The Life and Letters of George William Frederick Fourth Earl of Clarendon*, (2 vols, 1913), I, 213; D. Southgate, *The Most English Minister* (1966), 135–6.

  [41] Palmerston to Normanby 7 May 1847, Ashley, I, 29.

  [42] Clarendon to Granville 18 Nov. 1841, Maxwell, I, 222.

  [43] Palmerston's Diary 21 Aug. 1844, Dalling, III, 153; Palmerston to Normanby 20 Nov. 1846, *ibid.*, 322–3; Clarendon to Brougham 13 Nov. 1846, Maxwell, I, 270–5; cf. Charles Greville's view in 1839, *ibid.*, 159.

  [44] V. Cromwell, 'The private member of the House of Commons and foreign policy in the nineteenth century', *Liber Memorialis Sir Maurice Powicke. Studies Presented to the International Commission for the History of Representative and Parliamentary Institutions* (Dublin 1963); V. Cromwell, 'The administrative background to the presentation of parliamentary papers on foreign affairs in the mid-nineteenth century', *Journal of the Society of Archivists* II (1960–4), 302–15.

  [45] B. K. Martin, *The Triumph of Lord Palmerston* (1924), 52–8.

  [46] B. Connell, *Regina v. Palmerston: The Correspondence between Queen Victoria and her Foreign and Prime Minister* (1962), 46–50; Southgate, 195; Ridley, 324–7.

  [47] 25 June 1850, *HPD* 3rd (cxii) 380–444.

  [48] Palmerston's letters to Normanby and W. Temple, 29 June and 8 July 1850, Ashley, I, 224–5.

  [49] His Tiverton election speech in 1841, for example, Southgate, 167;

Dalling, II, 93, 105; Ashley, II, 103, 189.

[50] Cromwell, 'Private member', 204–13.

[51] Cromwell, 'Administrative background', 307, 311.

[52] Clarendon to Hammond 2 July 1860, Hammond MSS FO 391/3.

[53] Memo by Palmerston 5 Jan. 1860, Ashley, II, 174–80.

[54] Earl of Malmesbury, Memoirs of an Ex-Minister (2 vols, 1884), II, 339; Ridley, 526.

[55] Cromwell, 'Administrative background', 304–5, 308–9.

[56] To Palmerston July 1853, Ashley, II, 28–9.

[57] Malmesbury, II, 191–2.

[58] Maxwell, I, 257, 292.

[59] Clarendon to his wife 27 Sept. 1853, ibid., II, 30; and to E. Hammond 5 March 1856, 30 Sept. 1867, and passim, Hammond MSS FO 391/4.

[60] To Lord Howden 23 Dec. 1856, Maxwell, II, 136.

[61] Clarendon to the Duchess of Manchester 6 Nov. 1858, A. L. Kennedy, My Dear Duchess: Social and Political Letters to the Duchess of Manchester 1858–1869 (1956), 33; Clarendon to Hammond 6 and 27 Feb., 28 May 1868, Hammond MSS FO 391/4; Hammond to Layard 14 Apr. 1862, Layard MSS Add. MS 38591 f.50.

[62] Clarendon to Hammond 27 Feb. 1868, Hammond MSS FO 391/4.

[63] H. J. Hanham, Elections and Party Management: Politics in the time of Disraeli and Gladstone (1959), 112–13.

[64] To Granville 10 Dec. 1875, A. Ramm ed., The Political Correspondence of Mr Gladstone and Lord Granville 1868–1876 (Camden Society Miscellany, 3rd series lxxxi, lxxxii, 1952), 476.

[65] See the correspondence between Granville and F. Hill, Editor of the Daily News, covering the period 1870–85, Granville MSS PRO 30/29/426A. Lord Salisbury's early links were also well known.

[66] E.g. Granville to J. Walter, proprietor of The Times, 29 May 1885, Lord E. Fitzmaurice, The Life of Lord Granville 1815–1891 (2 vols, 1905), II, 444.

[67] E.g. Lord E. Fitzmaurice to Granville 14 Oct. 1884, Granville MSS PRO 30/29/195.

[68] See the exchange between Gladstone and Granville 31 Oct., 1 Nov. 1880, A. Ramm ed., The Political Correspondence of Mr Gladstone and Lord Granville 1876–1886 (2 vols, Oxford 1962), 213–14; Fitzmaurice, II, 132.

[69] Memo by Staveley 6 Feb. 1863, cit. Cromwell, 'Administrative background', 305, gives twelve daily papers; the list for 1889 in FO 83/1106 gives twenty-one.

[70] Sir W. Langley (private secretary to Parl. Under-Secretary) to J. Turner (Gallery Reporters' Committee) 27 Jan. 1883, Langley MSS FO 800/29, f.261. Such was the volume of work that this generated, that a typist was employed for the purpose in 1896, ibid., f.385.

[71] E.g. Lord Derby to Lord Wilton 1 July 1877, H. St C. Cunningham, 'British public opinion and the eastern question 1877–1878', unpub. D.Phil. thesis (Univ. of Sussex 1968), 220. I am most grateful to Dr Cunningham for allowing me to quote from his thesis.

[72] Rose to Corry 11 Jan. 1877, ibid., 210; Rose was formerly Conservative Party agent, Corry Disraeli's private secretary.

[73] Lady G. Cecil, Life of Robert Marquess of Salisbury (4 vols, 1921–32), III, 196.

[74] Cit. C. J. Lowe, *The Reluctant Imperialists: British Foreign Policy 1878–1902* (2 vols, 1967), 11–12.

[75] Derby to Hammond 17 Nov. 1876, Hammond MSS FO 391/27; W. F. Monypenny and G. E. Buckle, *The Life of Benjamin Disraeli Earl of Beaconsfield* (6 vols, 1910–20), VI, 83, 194 and *passim*; R. Blake, *Disraeli* (1966), chs. 15, 16.

[76] Letters to Lords Carnarvon and Lytton in 1877, Cecil, II, 130–66.

[77] Cecil, II, 285–9, 296.

[78] Speech 8 Apr. 1878, House of Lords, *HPD* 3rd (ccxxxix), 799–800.

[79] 29 Aug. 1886, Cecil, IV, 2–3.

[80] 9 Nov. 1887 at the Guildhall, Cecil, IV, 80.

[81] Dalling, II, 103 fn; Ashley, II, 278, suggested that not only were certain personal traits required, but 'such circumstances of comparative freedom to act without check or interference as can hardly be the lot of any minister, however able, now-a-days, when foreign matters are made as familiar to the peasant, if he can only read, as aforetime to the prince. . . . the activity which characterised the Foreign Office under the Palmerstonian régime is a thing of the past'.

[82] *The Shorter Oxford English Dictionary* conveniently gives 1877 for this usage.

[83] See G. Carslake-Thompson, *Public Opinion and Lord Beaconsfield 1875–1880* (2 vols, 1886); R. T. Shannon, *Gladstone and the Bulgarian Agitation 1876* (1963).

[84] Fitzmaurice, II, 166–71; A. Ramm, 1876–86, II, 1061, 1135, 1309, 1502.

[85] Article in the *Quarterly Review*, Oct. 1883, reprinted in P. Smith ed., *Lord Salisbury on Politics* (Cambridge 1972), 335–76.

[86] Cecil, II, 240–1, 346.

[87] Minute, November 1878, FO 83/591.

[88] Granville to Gladstone 4 May 1879, Ramm 1876–86, I, 148. There was an element of continuity here, Gladstone having complained in 1877 at the presentation of large Blue Books without an index which made them impossible to use at all easily – cutting from *The Times* 24 Mar. 1877, FO 83/591. Temperley and Penson, 251–2, also argue that as a result of their large size, their worst deficiencies passed unnoticed.

[89] In 1882, see Ramm 1876–86, I, 788, 790, 809, 817.

[90] Cecil, IV, 23–4.

[91] As suggested by H. W. V. Temperley, 'British secret diplomacy from Canning to Grey', *Cambridge Historical Journal* 15 (1938), 12–14.

[92] E.g. A. H. Layard to Tenterden 29 Jan. 1879, critical of the Liberal Party, FO 363/2 f.199–200.

[93] Cecil, III, 131–2.

[94] For the Venezuela Crisis, see minutes by E. Barrington (Salisbury's Private Secretary) 4 Mar. 1896, T. H. Sanderson (Permanent Under-Secretary, Foreign Office), and Salisbury, March and April 1896, FO 83/1623. For Fashoda, Grenville, *Lord Salisbury*, 227–8. Salisbury to Chamberlain concerning despatches about Siam and the Niger, 7 June, 17 Sept., 23 Oct. 1897, JC 5/67/78, 81, 82.

[95] Minute, April 1892, FO 800/34 f.27, concerning W. J. Lawrence's question 11 Apr., *HPD* 4th (iii) 1108–9.

[96] The Russian Ambassador quoted Salisbury on the source of the latter's

weariness in 1889 as being due to 'La nécessité de parler constamment en public . . . que . . . ne date d'une époque récente. Lord Salisbury l'attribue à l'initiative de M. Gladstone. . . .', *Correspondance Diplomatique de M. de Staal, 1884–1900*, ed. A. Meyendorff (2 vols, Paris, 1929); also Cecil, IV, 393–5, for his Guildhall speech in November 1891.

[97] Cecil, IV, 161–2.

[98] Cecil, IV, 41–2, 44–5.

[99] Cecil, III, 270, IV, 165–6, 310.

[100] P. Smith, Introduction, *passim*.

[101] To Sir H. Drummond Wolff 17 July 1899, Midleton MSS PRO 30/67/4 ff.80–3.

[102] Minute by Salisbury 14 July 1899, *ibid.*, f.78.

[103] Salisbury to Cranbrook 19 Oct. 1900, A. E. Gathorne Hardy, *Gathorne Hardy First Earl of Cranbrook: A Memoir* (2 vols, 1910), II, 374.

Notes to Chapter II (pp. 27–48)

[1] Garvin, I, ch. xix, esp. 420–9.

[2] *Ibid.*, 316–17.

[3] *Ibid.*, 377.

[4] A. J. Balfour, *Chapters of Autobiography*, ed. B. E. C. Dugdale (1930), 220–1, and Garvin, II, 191.

[5] To Earl Grey 21 Aug. 1896, Grey MSS.

[6] Salisbury to Balfour 29 Mar. 1886, Cecil, III, 297; cf. his view expressed some years before, that 'it may be said that the best form of Government (setting aside the question of morality) is one where the masses have little power, and seem to have a great deal', cit. P. Smith, 47.

[7] Chamberlain to Capt. O'Shea 17 Apr. 1882, J. Chamberlain, *A Political Memoir*, ed. C. H. D. Howard (1953), 35.

[8] Chamberlain to W. E. Gladstone 7 Feb. 1885, *ibid.*, 116.

[9] Cf. n. 4 above.

[10] Speech delivered 5 Jan. 1885, cit. Boyd, I, 134–6.

[11] See above, 1–6.

[12] Chamberlain to H. Labouchere 20 Oct. 1885, A. Thorold, *The Life of Henry Labouchere* (1913), 240. For another example at the same time, D. A Hamer, *Liberal Politics in the Age of Gladstone and Rosebery* (Oxford 1972), 96, n. 2.

[13] Garvin, I, 412.

[14] Disraeli to Lady Bradford 20 Aug. 1880, Monypenny and Buckle, VI, 588. A century later, the epithet would have been rendered, less poetically, as 'grocer'.

[15] 24 Feb. 1883, *The Diary of Sir Edward Walter Hamilton 1880–1885*, ed. D. Bahlman (2 vols, 1972).

[16] Michael Hurst, 'Joseph Chamberlain and West Midland politics, 1886–1895', *Dugdale Society Occasional Papers no.15* (1962), and 'Joseph Chamberlain, the Conservatives, and the succession to John Bright', *HJ 7* (1) (1964), 64–93.

[17] Chamberlain to Dr R. W. Dale 30 Mar. 1885, Garvin, I, 569.

[18] Speech in Birmingham Town Hall, 29 Jan. 1885, Boyd, I, 152.

[19] To W. T. Stead 10 Aug. 1878, JC 6/4k/24 cit. Cunningham, 97.

[20] Strauss, 54; cf. M. Hurst, 'Joseph Chamberlain and late Victorian liberalism', *Durham University Journal* 66 (1973), 60–75.

[21] Schreuder, *Gladstone and Kruger, passim*; Garvin, I, 439–40, 488 *et seq.* For the texts of the Conventions, the legal basis of Britain's relationship with the Transvaal, see Eybers, *Documents*, 455–63, 469–74.

[22] Garvin, I, 494. Seeley's *Expansion of England* was first published in 1883; Dilke's *Greater Britain* Chamberlain had re-read in 1881, S. Gwynn and G. M. Tuckwell, *The Life of the Rt. Hon. Sir Charles W. Dilke,* (2 vols, 1917), I, 501.

[23] Strauss, 118 n. 13, for Chamberlain's use of Benjamin Kidd's writings to support his arguments for imperial expansion. Cf. Chamberlain's views on expansion south of the Zambezi in 1888, cit. Galbraith, *Crown and Charter* (1974), 25.

[24] Sept. 1884, Gwynn and Tuckwell, II, 83.

[25] *Ibid.*, II, 205.

[26] Speeches at Birmingham 5 Jan., and to the Eighty Club 28 Apr. 1885, Garvin, I, 542–3, 573; Chamberlain even suggested Canadian troops for use in the Sudan, *ibid.*, 568.

[27] Letter in *The Times* 8 May 1886, Strauss, 50.

[28] Speech delivered 8 July 1886, Boyd, I, 278.

[29] Garvin, II, 191.

[30] Boyd, I, *passim*, but especially speech to the Devonshire Club 9 Apr. 1888; Garvin, II, chs. xxxvi, xl.

[31] Garvin, II, 338, 347.

[32] Hurst, *HJ* (1964).

[33] 20 Mar. 1893 in the House of Commons, Boyd, I, 351, and *HPD* 4th (x) 602.

[34] Speech at Lambeth 4 Nov. 1885, Cecil, III, 263–4.

[35] E.g. speech in Birmingham 11 Oct. 1894, Garvin II, 607–9.

[36] J. Chamberlain, *Memoir*, 278.

[37] 20 Mar. 1893 in the House of Commons, Boyd, I, 342–4, and *HPD* 4th (x) 594, 593.

[38] Speech at Liverpool 12 Jan. 1888, Cecil, IV, 165–6.

[39] Chamberlain to Salisbury 15 Nov. 1894, Garvin, II, 617.

[40] Hamer, 261–2.

[41] Salisbury and Balfour agreed on this in 1886, Cecil, III, 297.

[42] Cecil, III, 301. P. Smith, 94.

[43] 13 Apr. 1895, SP 5 ff.21–4. The most serious and bitter of these local disputes occurred at Hythe and Warwick and Leamington. For a full recent account of the strained relations between the two parties, Peter Marsh, *The Discipline of Popular Government: Lord Salisbury's Domestic Statecraft, 1881–1902* (1978), esp. 235–41.

[44] Salibury to Balfour 22 Apr. 1895, BP 49690.

[45] Salisbury to Selborne 13 and 20 Apr. 1895, SP 5 ff. 21–8.

[46] Balfour to Salisbury 24 July 1892, B. E. C. Dugdale, *Arthur James Balfour* (2 vols, 1939 edn.), I, 160.

[47] 18 and 22 Dec. 1894, Strachey MSS. Strachey was editor of the Liberal Unionist party paper, and the *Cornhill Magazine*, before becoming editor of the *Spectator* in 1898.

[48] *Ibid.*, 26 Dec. 1894.
[49] Garvin, II, 617–32.
[50] To Selborne 13 Apr. 1895, SP 5 ff. 21–4.
[51] To R. H. Hutton, 1 Apr. 1895, JC 6/40/2.
[52] To the Duke of Devonshire 19 Apr. 1895, B. H. Holland, *Life of the Duke of Devonshire 1833–1908* (2 vols, 1911), II, 267–9. Garvin, II, 617–32.
[53] Garvin, III, 9.
[54] S. H. Jeyes, *Joseph Chamberlain* (1898), ch. 8.
[55] Fraser, *Joseph Chamberlain*, 144–5.
[56] Chamberlain had already developed this idea in the detailed context of Old Age Pensions, in evidence to the Royal Commission of 1893, *PP* (1895) XV, 657–7, 693–704. E. E. Gulley, *Joseph Chamberlain and English Social Politics* (New York 1926), 271.
[57] At Birmingham, Walsall, and Selly Oak, *The Times* 11 July 1895, 7; 16 July, 10; 20 July, 7: see also speech 23 May 1895, Fraser, *Joseph Chamberlain*, 166.
[58] Garvin, II, 621.
[59] Garvin, II, 345.
[60] Chamberlain to Strachey 12 Aug. 1887, Strachey MSS. Balfour to Salisbury 24 July 1892, Dugdale, I, 161.
[61] *The Times* 11 July 1895, 7.
[62] P. Fraser, 'The Liberal Unionist alliance: Chamberlain, Hartington and the Conservatives, 1886–1904', *EHR* lxxvii (1962), 53–78.
[63] Fraser, *Joseph Chamberlain*, 166–7.
[64] Hamer, 221–3, 261.

Notes to Chapter III (pp. 49–94)

[1] To Selborne 30 June 1895, SP 5 ff.31–2.
[2] 'Some memories and reflections in my old age', SP 191, 76–7.
[3] Liberals 177, Irish Nationalists 82, Conservatives 341, Liberal Unionists 70, giving a majority of 152; Chamberlain had forecast one of 70, Garvin, II, 641.
[4] Speech at the Birmingham Conservative Club, *The Times* 3 Aug. 1895, 6.
[5] Nov. 1895, Garvin, III, 28.
[6] Speech 22 Aug. 1895, *HPD* 4th (xxxvi) 640–5; reply to West Indian deputation, *The Times* 24 Aug. 1895 and Garvin, III, 20.
[7] *The Times* 26 Aug. 1895, 4.
[8] See above, Ch. II, 32.
[9] Sir H. MacDonell [Minister at Lisbon] to Kimberley 5 Apr. 1895, FOP 6773, and to Salisbury 27 July 1897, *ibid.* 7031.
[10] MacDonell to Salisbury 6 Apr. 1897, *ibid.* 7128.
[11] Sir H. Loch [High Commissioner in South Africa] to Lord Ripon 18 Dec. 1894, *ibid.* 6773. The Marquis of Ripon was Colonial Secretary in the Liberal Government, Aug. 1892 to June 1895.
[12] MacDonell to Salisbury 21 Feb. 1896, *ibid.* 6910.
[13] CO to FO 26 June 1895, and R. Casement [Consul at Lourenço Marques] to Salisbury, 28 Nov. 1895, *ibid.* 6773.
[14] Casement to Salisbury 4 Aug. 1896, *ibid.* 6975. For the Netherlands

Railway Company, and the grounds for British fears about its association with German interests, see Van-Helten, 'German capital'.

[15] CO to FO 10 Oct. 1895, ibid. 6773.

[16] Ibid., 6 Dec. 1895.

[17] Casement to Salisbury, 16 Nov. 1895 recd. 10 Dec., ibid. This, the Katembe concession, belonged to F. R. Eiffe who also had Transvaal support; it became a source of continual worry to Britain: below, 126, 137, 152, 177 and Marais, 153–5, 216.

[18] FOP 6773, passim.

[19] Gosselin to Salisbury 18 Nov. 1895, ibid.; Garvin, III, 64.

[20] 25 Sept. 1894, Af.(S) 483. Ripon's reference to a 'treaty' illustrates a common uncertainty about the Transvaal's status. Increasingly British ministers appealed to Article IV of the London Convention as proof of her subordinate position; this read 'The South African Republic will conclude no treaty or engagement with any State or nation other than the Orange Free State, nor with any tribe to the eastward or westward of the Republic until the same has been approved by Her Majesty the Queen'.

[21] MacDonell to Sir P. Anderson 26 Aug. 1895, to Salisbury 31 Aug., and subsequent correspondence, FOP 6773.

[22] MacDonell to Salisbury, tel. 6 Nov. 1895, ibid. In 1889 Portugal had seized the Delagoa Bay Railway, and claims for compensation were referred to the Berne Tribunal which began proceedings in 1892. That Portugal would have to pay was never in doubt, but the scale of compensation was a matter for speculation. After lengthy proceedings, the award of just less than £1,000,000 was made against Portugal in 1901. Until that date the prospect of payment, for long thought imminent, aggravated her financial situation and hence the vacillations of her policy under pressure from the Great Powers.

[23] Chamberlain to Salisbury 4 Sept. 1895, MSP.

[24] Memo by G. V. Fiddes 11 Oct. 1895, Af.(S) 508. Fiddes, a first-class clerk, joined Milner's staff as Imperial Secretary in 1897.

[25] Selborne to Chamberlain 7 Sept. 1895, SP 8 ff.52–5.

[26] Robinson to Chamberlain 5 and 13 Oct. 1895, C. 8474 nos. 2, 3, PP (1897) LXII. Sir Hercules Robinson was reappointed Governor of the Cape Colony and High Commissioner to succeed Loch, in February 1895.

[27] Memorandum on the Drifts Question by Selborne, 15 Oct. 1895 SP 15 ff.3–5. It concluded '16.10.95. I showed this copy to Lord Salisbury after dinner in the Library at Hatfield today and he accepted it, so far as it concerned himself, as correct.'

[28] Lascelles to Salisbury 28 Dec. 1895, FOP 6773; Salisbury to Chamberlain 30 Dec. 1895 JC 5/67/35, and Drus BIHR (1952), 36. Sir Frank Lascelles, British Ambassador at Berlin.

[29] Devonshire to Salisbury 30 Dec. 1895, MSP.

[30] Sir E. Ashmead Bartlett, 6 Feb. 1895, HPD 4th (xxx) 137.

[31] H. O. Arnold-Forster, ibid. 161–3.

[32] S. Buxton, ibid. 145–56.

[33] Reply to Ashmead Bartlett 28 Feb. 1895, ibid. (xxxi) 37.

[34] Supply Debates, 29 Mar. and 30 May 1895, HPD 4th (xxxii) 495–7, (xxxiv) 709–13; C. 7780 'Correspondence relating to certain native territories situated to the north-east of Zululand', presented on 27 June, PP (1895)

LXXI, 571.

[35] Clark [MP for Caithness and one time Consul General for the Republic], 6 Feb. 1895, *HPD* 4th (xxx) 158; criticism by Dr R. Macgregor, 29 Mar., *ibid.* (xxxii) 493; papers promised by Ripon, 28 Feb., *ibid.* (xxxi) 1–2.

[36] Debate on Swaziland, 14 Mar. 1895, *ibid*, 1068.

[37] C. 7611 respecting the Affairs of Swaziland, presented 5 Feb. 1895, *PP* (1895) LXII; *HPD* 4th (xxx) 141–5, (xxxi) 1064–79, (xxxii) 490–3.

[38] Marais, chs. 1–2; also Gordon, *Growth of Boer Opposition*.

[39] R. Meade [Permanent Under-Secretary at the CO] to Ripon, 9 Oct. 1894, Ripon MSS 43558 f.12. Meade retired at the end of February 1897.

[40] 30 May 1895, *HPD* 4th (xxxiv) 709–13.

[41] To Ripon about 17 June 1895, Ripon MSS 43558 f.136.

[42] 30 May 1895, *HPD* 4th (xxxiv) 706.

[43] C. 7878 relating to Certain Native Territories situated to the North-East of Zululand, *PP* (1895) LXXI.

[44] Arnold Forster and Ashmead Bartlett, 14–30 May 1895, *HPD* 4th (xxxiii) 63, 1338, 1339, 1600, (xxxiv) 109, 452, 463, 630; Buxton's replies, 20, 28 and 30 May, *ibid.* (xxxiii) 1600, (xxxiv) 452, 463, 630.

[45] Enquiries announced 16 Aug. 1895, *HPD* 4th (xxxvi) 171; *The Times* 30 Aug., 7, 10.

[46] C. 7911 relative to the Grievances of Her Majesty's Indian Subjects in the South African Republic, presented 4 Sept. 1895, *PP* (1895) LXXI; minute by Fairfield [Assistant Under-Secretary at the CO], 7 Aug. 1895, CO 417/150/13615.

[47] Minute on Robinson to Chamberlain, 12 Oct. 1895, CO 417/151/19491.

[48] For correspondence between the Wesleyans and the CO, CO 417/158 and 159, *passim*. At this time the Transvaal region was the scene of rapidly expanding missionary activity by the Wesleyans; see *Wesleyan Methodist Missionary Society Annual Report 1896*, 6–7.

[49] See ch. 4 (vii), 114–21.

[50] Letter in the *Daily Chronicle*, 1 Aug. 1895.

[51] Minute by G. V. Fiddes, CO 417/158/13419; Uitlander Association press extracts recd. 7, 19 Aug. 1895, with minutes on *ibid.* 13712 and 14547.

[52] H. Hess to Chamberlain 16 Aug. 1895, JC 10/2/4B/2; also 7 and 18 Dec. 1895, CO 417/159/21993, 22596.

[53] *The Times*, 5 Dec. 1895, 9; *The Economist*, 7 Dec. 1895, 1584; see also Kubicek, *Administration of Imperialism*, esp. chs. 4, 6: H. A. Will, 'Colonial policy and economic development in the British West Indies, 1895–1903', *Economic History Review* 23 (1970), 129–47.

[54] *The Anti-Slavery Reporter*, Sept.–Nov. 1895, 168–75. He had associated himself since the 1880s with the Rev. J. Mackenzie's attempts to extend imperial authority for the protection of African interests in Bechuanaland.

[55] Porter, *JICH* (1972).

[56] Generally on this point, A. N. Porter, 'Iain Macleod, decolonization in Kenya, and tradition in British colonial policy', *Journal for Contemporary History*, 2 (Bloemfontein 1975), 37–59.

[57] For exhaustive treatment of the available evidence on these lines see Van der Poel, *Jameson Raid*; Drus, 'A report on the papers of Joseph Chamberlain', *BIHR* XXV (1952); Drus, 'The question of imperial

complicity', *EHR* LXVIII (1953); Drus, 'Select documents from the Chamberlain papers', *BIHR* XXVII (1954); Wilde, *AYB*; Marais ch. 4. For an account sympathetic to Chamberlain, Pakenham, *Jameson's Raid*; see also Butler, *Liberal Party*. Current debate about the Raid centres on the participation and motives of the goldmining firms: see Bibliography for works by Blainey, Jeeves, Kubicek, Mendelsohn, and Phimister.

[58] See Stokes, 'Milnerism'; Le May, *British Supremacy*; Jeeves, 'The Rand capitalists'.

[59] Cf. Robinson and Gallagher, 426–7.

[60] Drus *BIHR* (1952), 46.

[61] 28 Mar. 1895, *HPD* 4th (xxxii) 431–3; Butler, *Liberal Party*, 37–43.

[62] MSP and Garvin, III, 78.

[63] Galbraith, *Crown and Charter, passim*; Flint, *Cecil Rhodes*.

[64] 30 Dec. 1895, Drus, *BIHR* (1952), 36–7.

[65] 20 June 1895, Cab 37/39/36. For the detailed history of the railway, see Maylam, *Rhodesian History* (1977).

[66] Lockhart and Woodhouse, *Rhodes*, 279.

[67] Chamberlain to Earl Grey 13 Oct. 1896, Drus, *BIHR* (1952), 55.

[68] The interviews took place at the Colonial Office on 1, 13 and 20 August; B.S.A.Co. to CO 21 Aug. 1895, CO 879/44 n. 38.

[69] CO (E. Fairfield) to B.S.A.Co. 30 Aug. 1895, CO 879/44 n.57.

[70] Telegrams received and sent 20 Aug. 1895, *ibid.*, nos. 33, 34, 35.

[71] October is mentioned in both the descriptions to Rhodes of the interview with Chamberlain on 1 August (Lockhart and Woodhouse, 485–7), and the Company's formal letter to the CO dated 21 Aug.

[72] Lockhart and Woodhouse, ch. 16 *passim*, 276–7.

[73] Sir H. Robinson to Chamberlain 9 Oct. 1895, CO 879/44 n.121.

[74] *Ibid.*, telegram recd. 9 Sept. 1895, CO 879/44 n.77. See the useful account of these negotiations with the Tswana in Dachs, *Rhodesian History* (1971), 5–9.

[75] CO 879/44 nos. 77, 79, 81, 100, 103, 105, 108, 109, 111; cf. Van der Poel, 33–4.

[76] Van der Poel, 34.

[77] For the details of the settlement, correspondence 7–9 Nov. 1895, CO 879/44 nos. 128–32, and E. Fairfield to Chamberlain 4 Nov. 1895, quoted in full by Van der Poel, 45–7.

[78] Garvin III, 70–1, 111–12; Van der Poel, 48, 66.

[79] Chamberlain to Meade 18 Dec. 1895, Garvin, III, 72; Van der Poel, 68–71. Cf. Salisbury to Chamberlain 30 Dec. 1895, Drus, *BIHR* (1952), 36–7.

[80] Chamberlain to Grey 13 Oct. 1896, Garvin, III, 115–6 and Drus, *BIHR* (1952), 54–6.

[81] *Ibid.*, 51.

[82] For the Enquiry, see below, 133–5.

[83] E.g. Marais, 82–3. An example of the interpretations to which this approach has given rise is the construction placed upon Fairfield's letter to Chamberlain on 4 November 1895. This was written to give Chamberlain the results of Fairfield's day of negotiations with Dr Harris, designed to pave the way for the final settlement with the Company and the Chiefs. Read out by Chamberlain to the Select Committee of Enquiry into the Raid in 1897, it has been subject to much subsequent comment, especially its

second sentence: 'Rhodes having accepted the responsibilities imposed on him, is naturally keen to get the Protectorate question settled, and has been telegraphing all day to this end.' This has been understood as referring to the responsibilities Rhodes had undertaken in regard to events in the Transvaal, and the letter therefore seen as confirmation of Colonial Office foreknowledge of Rhodes' plans. This is the conclusion of those concerned to illustrate the extent of Chamberlain's attempts to obscure issues in 1897, to challenge the Select Committee's exoneration of the Colonial Secretary, and to reveal Garvin's unwillingness fully to explore Chamberlain's role; it is a conclusion assumed to back up the case of indicting Chamberlain on two counts – guilty knowledge and provocative involvement in Rhodes' schemes in 1895. Yet this is to clutch at straws, straining both the meaning of the printed word and the context of the letter. In view of the above account, it seems quite as likely that this is a reference to the fact that Rhodes, having on this day at last given way and accepted the conditions set by the Colonial Office for the transfer to him of Protectorate territory, now wanted the settlement finally agreed at once with the Chiefs.

⁸⁴ Memo by Chamberlain 12 June 1896, or his letter to Grey 13 Oct. 1896, Drus, *BIHR* (1952), 46–51, 54–6.

⁸⁵ Grey to Hawksley 12 June 1896, Grey MSS. It is worth recording here that the files of the Director of Public Prosecutions, recently opened at the Public Record Office, throw no new light on the Raid; see Trial of Dr L.S. Jameson, DPP 1/2/1 to 4.

⁸⁶ Woodhouse, 'Missing telegrams.'

⁸⁷ Chamberlain to Salisbury 4 Jan. 1896, MSP and Garvin, III, 95–6.

⁸⁸ Goschen to Salisbury 7 Jan. 1896, and Salisbury's reply 8 Jan. MSP.

⁸⁹ Queen Victoria to Salisbury 8 Jan. 1896, Goschen to the Queen, 10 Jan., QVL 3rd ser., III, 13, 16.

⁹⁰ Lascelles to Salisbury tel. 6 Jan. 1896, Salisbury to Lascelles, 7 Jan., FOP 6910.

⁹¹ Dugdale, I 225; cf. Marais, 98–100, who seems unaware of the Salisbury–Hatzfeldt exchange.

⁹² Fiddes, for example, appeared to attribute the interpretation to Lord Salisbury, minute 28 Feb. 1896, CO 417/179 f442.

⁹³ C. 7933 on the subject of the recent Disturbances in the South African Republic, presented 11 Feb. 1896, *PP* (1896) LIX, 18, 50, 83.

⁹⁴ Memo 5 Jan. 1896, JC 10/1/24 and Drus, *BIHR* (1952), 42.

⁹⁵ Minutes by Selborne, 6 Feb. 1896, CO 417/198, and Fairfield, 13 June 1896, CO 417/177 f.116–17.

⁹⁶ Tel. 30 Jan. 1896, JC 10/3/27 and Af.(S) 505. Some of Chamberlain's correspondence confirmed this view: from Sir J. Puleston, 5 Jan., 6 Feb. and Feb. n.d., JC 10/4/2/3, 4, 7; also from the Governor of Natal, 11 Apr., JC 10/7/25.

⁹⁷ Chamberlain to Robinson tel. 1 Feb. 1896, Af.(S) 505; *The Times*, 1 Feb. 1896, 5.

⁹⁸ Minute 4 Apr. 1896, CO 417/180 f.225. Frederick Graham, Principal Clerk and head of the South African department; Fairfield's retirement saw him promoted to Assistant Under-Secretary in March 1897.

⁹⁹ C. 7933, *PP* (1896) LIX.

[100] Diplomaticus, 'The struggle for African supremacy', *Fortnightly Review* (Aug. 1899), 340; 'Mr. Chamberlain's mistakes', *ibid*. (Oct. 1899), 707.

[101] C. 7933 nos. 185 and 203, from Johannesburg residents, referred to in Chamberlain to Robinson, 20 Feb. 1896, Af.(S) 505.

[102] To Meade 27 Jan. 1896, Austen Chamberlain MSS AC 2/1/2/5.

[103] Buxton to Ripon, 17 Feb. 1896, Ripon MSS 43555 ff.19–22. Chamberlain to R. B. Brett (Lord Esher), 1 Feb. 1896, *Journals and Letters of Reginald Viscount Esher*, ed. M. V. Brett (4 vols, 1934–8), I, 193–4.

[104] Butler, *Liberal Party*, 181.

[105] *The Times*, 1 Feb. 1896, 5: '... while Mr. Chamberlain does not consider that they [anonymous telegrams] give a true picture of the state of affairs at Johannesburg, he has thought it prudent to send telegraphic instructions to the British Agent at Pretoria to proceed to Johannesburg and report on the state of affairs, and, if he finds any immediate grievances capable of redress, to draw the attention to them of the Government of the South African Republic ...'.

[106] Minute 11 Mar. 1896, CO 417/179 f.408.

[107] Minute by Meade, *ibid*. See despatch from residents in Johannesburg, C. 7933 no. 203.

[108] Robinson to Chamberlain 7 and 10 Feb. 1896, published as telegrams nos. 8 and 10 in C. 8063 relating to Affairs in the South African Republic, presented 30 Apr. 1896, *PP* (1896) LIX.

[109] To Brett, 27 Mar. 1896, JC 5/6/24.

[110] Drus, *BIHR* (1952), 38–9; Marais, 110–12; Wilde, 24–30.

[111] Garvin, III, 109.

[112] At Manchester 15 Jan. 1896, *The Times*, 16 Jan., 10.

[113] Printed article on South Africa, May 1896, Arnold-Forster MSS 50356 ff.162–9.

[114] Draft reply to the Editor of *Country Life*, late Jan. 1896, referring him to the forthcoming Blue Book, CO 417/195/1893. Indian Papers reviewed on 8 Feb. 1896 (Minute on CO 417/152/22358) were presented on 11 Feb. as C. 7946 relating to the Grievances of Her Majesty's Indian Subjects in the South African Republic, *PP* (1896) LIX.

[115] C. 7933, C. 7946, C. 7932 relative to the Transfer of British Bechuanaland to the Cape Colony, on 11 Feb. 1896, and C. 7962 relative to the visit to this country of the Chiefs Khama, Sebele, and Bathoen, and the future of the Bechuanaland Protectorate, on 17 Feb., *PP* (1896) LIX.

Notes to Chapter IV (*pp. 95–121*)

[1] MacDonell to Salisbury 25 Feb. 1896, FOP 6910.

[2] MacDonell to Salisbury 5 Mar. 1896 and *passim*, *ibid*; memo by Fairfield 29 Feb. 1896, JC 7/3/20/1.

[3] Memo by J. Seear in CO to FO 31 Mar. 1896, FOP 6910.

[4] MacDonell to Salisbury 27 Oct. 1896, FOP 6975, 29 Mar. 1897, *ibid*., 7031.

[5] MacDonell to Salisbury 17 Feb. 1897, *ibid*.

[6] MacDonell to Salisbury 23 Apr. 1897, *ibid*.

[7] Memo 23 Feb. 1897, *ibid*.

[8] 23 Mar. 1896, MSP/A/92/12, and Robinson and Gallagher, 434–7.

[9] Selborne to Chamberlain 18 Oct. 1897, JC 10/1/71.

[10] Garvin, I, 439.

[11] Chamberlain to Selborne 14 Oct. 1896, SP 8 f.101.

[12] Salisbury to Selborne 24 Mar. 1896, SP 5 ff.39–40.

[13] FO to CO 20 and 21 Jan. 1896, Af.(S) 505.

[14] Correspondence on the Interpretation of the Convention, 1894–1899, can be found in FOP 6971 and 7365.

[15] Correspondence relating to Kruger's visit, Af.(S) 514 and Cab 37/42/45.

[16] FO to CO 11 Feb. 1896, with CO minutes, CO 417/187 ff.314–349; CO to FO 23 March, 11 April 1896, and Law Officers to CO 27 April, holding that H.M.G's approval had to be sought before ratification of the treaty by the assemblies of the respective countries, Af.(s) 505.

[17] Chamberlain to Robinson 20 Mar. 1896, Af.(S) 505.

[18] FO to CO 9 May 1896, Af.(S) 516.

[19] Correspondence between Foreign and Colonial Offices July 1896, Chamberlain to Goodenough 11 Aug. (tel.), Robinson to Chamberlain 14 Oct., Chamberlain to Robinson 25 Nov. (tel.), Af.(S) 516. General W. H. Goodenough was commander-in-chief of the British forces in South Africa.

[20] FO to CO 12 Dec. 1896, FOP 6971. Cf. Marais 121–4.

[21] 27 July 1896, Af.(S) 518.

[22] R. Casement to Salisbury 4 Aug. 1896, FOP 6975.

[23] Memo 10 Nov. 1896, Cab 37/43/45.

[24] Chamberlain to Meade 30 Oct. 1896, Austen Chamberlain MSS AC 2/1/2/21.

[25] 13 Feb. 1896, HPD 4th (xxxvii) 331–2; The Times, 6 Jan., 7.

[26] Marais, 110–12, Wilde, 28–32.

[27] Minute by Graham 3 Feb. 1896, CO 417/201 f.52.

[28] Buxton to Ripon 17 Feb. 1896, Ripon MSS 43555 ff.19–22.

[29] Telegram, 4 Feb. 1896, Af.(S) 505. Chamberlain had had doubts about this invitation some time before, telegrams 21 and 25 Jan. 1896 in C. 8063 relating to Affairs in the South African Republic, PP (1896) LIX, and minute by Fairfield, CO 417/179 f.94.

[30] Above, 91–2.

[31] 13 Feb. 1896, HPD 4th (xxxvii) 283.

[32] Ibid., 381.

[33] 14 Feb. 1896, ibid., 382–3.

[34] Harcourt, ibid., 365–8; Balfour, ibid., 377–9; Curzon's reply to T. Gibson Bowles, 13 Feb., ibid., 225.

[35] T. G. Bowles, 14 Feb., 1896, ibid., 386–9; J. M. Maclean, ibid., 394–5.

[36] 27 Jan. 1896, C. 8063 no. 3, PP (1896) LIX.

[37] Robinson to Chamberlain 3 Mar. 1896 enclosing Kruger's reply, C. 8063 no. 20, PP (1896) LIX.

[38] Cf. Marais, 118, Wilde, 34.

[39] Minute by Chamberlain 5 Apr. 1896, JC 10/1/35 and Wilde, 35.

[40] 17 Mar. 1896, JC 10/2/4B/9 and Marais 117.

[41] Minute 8 Apr. 1896, JC 10/1/36 and Drus, BIHR (1954) 160–2.

[42] Chamberlain's replies to Ashmead Bartlett 10 Mar. 1896, HPD 4th (xxxviii), 612, and Wyndham 13 Apr., ibid. (xxxix), 748.

[43] Selborne 31 Mar. 1896, noted that Robinson 'never gives us any

information of the state of public opinion in the Cape Colony, Dutch or English', CO 417/181 f.54; possibly for this reason, Fairfield and Chamberlain welcomed the likelihood of an Uitlander Association in London, 27 and 29 Jan. 1896, CO 417/205 f.112.

[44] Montague White [Transvaal Agent in London] to CO 30 Mar. 1896, Af.(S) 514; the invitation to Kruger was withdrawn on 27 Apr., C. 8063 no. 32.

[45] 22 Apr. 1896 at the Constitutional Club, 21 May at the South African Dinner, J. Chamberlain Foreign and Colonial Speeches (1897), 206–7, 208, 212, and House of Commons 8 May, HPD 4th (xl), 910–11, 925.

[46] 8 May 1896, ibid., 925, 916–17.

[47] The Times, 1 May 1896, 10.

[48] Annual Report 1899–1900, 3, gives figures for 1896–7; George Wyndham, MP was its Chairman and organising spirit.

[49] C. 8063, PP (1896) LIX.

[50] The Times, 14 May 1896, 7; 20 May, 7.

[51] Supply Debate, HPD 4th (xl), 884–975.

[52] 8 May 1896, ibid., 920.

[53] Above, 105–6.

[54] Rosebery, 11 Feb. 1896, HPD 4th (xxxvii), 35–8; Stanmore, ibid., 9–10.

[55] Ripon to Meade 8 Feb. 1896, Ripon MS 43558 f.146. Sir Edward Hamilton, who confided most things to his diary and was no lover of Chamberlain, far from disapproving, thought that the Rand solution which it advocated very important, Diary 8 Feb. 1896, Add. MS 48668 ff.105–6.

[56] 14 Feb. 1896, HPD 4th (xxxvii), 365–77.

[57] Ibid., 377–84.

[58] R. Blennerhasset, 'Our relations with Germany', Quarterly Review, Apr. 1896, 568–9.

[59] G. R. Parkin, 'The imperial note in British statesmanship', National Review (May 1896), 399–400, 394.

[60] 13 Feb. 1896, HPD 4th (xxxvii), 332.

[61] House of Commons, 8 May 1896, ibid. (xl), 936.

[62] The Times, 16 Apr. 1897, 4.

[63] Chamberlain's minute 29 May 1896, CO 417/182 f.199. More particularly, the acting High Commissioner's reply to the British Agent at Pretoria was to be published at the Cape; its object was 'to influence Dutch opinion there & not English opinion at home', according to Chamberlain, minute 30 May, ibid., f.238.

[64] Marais, 118.

[65] C. 8159 relating to the Commandeering of British Subjects in the South African Republic in 1894, and the Visit of the High Commissioner to Pretoria, presented on 23 July 1896, PP (1896) LIX.

[66] F. M. Mackarness, 'The rights and duties of Great Britain in South Africa', Edinburgh Review (April 1896), 286–7; another of his exceptions was the Drifts Crisis, which also formed the substance of a Blue Book in 1897.

[67] 30 June 1896, Ripon MS 43558 ff.220–1.

[68] In reply to J. H. Dalziel 23 Apr. 1896, HPD 4th (xxxix) 1535.

[69] Ripon to Fairfield, and Fairfield's reply, both 1 July 1896, Ripon MS 43558 f.222–4.

⁷⁰ *Ibid*. In the Blue Book itself the reference to Ripon's congratulatory telegram is no. 16 p. 12, indicating one further excision between proof stage and printing; but I found nothing to suggest that this was of particular significance.

⁷¹ Report from the *Cape Times* 16 July 1894, C. 8159, 41–53, *PP* (1896) LIX.

⁷² Minutes by Chamberlain 30 July 1896, and Fairfield's minute of 9 Aug. noting that Chamberlain decided against publication on 4th August, both on Robinson's despatch of 27 June, CO 417/182 f.546; the despatch was however kept in mind, and appeared later in C. 8423, 39.

⁷³ E.g., L. J. Maxse, 'Mr Rhodes' Raid', *National Review* (July 1896), 719–36; B. C. Skottowe, 'Mr Chamberlain', *ibid.*, (Aug. 1896), 771–82; Edward Dicey, 'Boers and Uitlanders', *Quarterly Review* (Oct. 1896), 241–67.

⁷⁴ H. M. Bourke [Secretary to the S.A. Association] to Chamberlain 15 Oct. 1896, JC 10/5/1/25.

⁷⁵ Sir J. Bramston, 'The Colonial Office from within', *The Empire Review*, I, (1901), 279–87, gives figures for each decade which suggests a doubling of business during Chamberlain's tenure of office.

⁷⁶ Sir H. F. Wilson, 'Joseph Chamberlain as I knew him', *United Empire*, viii (Feb. 1917), 102–11.

⁷⁷ 28 Feb. 1896, CO 417/195/4350; the London correspondent of this Transvaal Dutch paper wished to clarify a case of the misreporting of his paper's views.

⁷⁸ *Neues Wiener Tagblatt*, 7 May 1897, CO 417/235/9483.

⁷⁹ Letters and minutes Nov. 1897–June 1898, JC 6/4g/1, 4, 5.

⁸⁰ Approach by Reuter in May 1897, minute by Selborne 30 June, Chamberlain's decision 16 Nov. JC 6/4m/1-6.

⁸¹ Minutes by Meade and Fiddes 9 Mar. 1895, CO 417/158/4266.

⁸² Minute by Lambert 1 Feb. 1897, CO 417/214 f.37. H. C. M. Lambert joined the Office in 1892, and was promoted to the rank of First Class Clerk in November 1898.

⁸³ Minutes by Fairfield and Graham 21 July 1896, CO 417/183 f.130; by Fiddes, 'Mr Weinthal, as usual, lies', 12 Mar. 1897, CO 417/215 f.440.

⁸⁴ By Graham 14 May 1896, CO 417/181 f.622; H. F. Wilson discovered that Weinthal, editor of *Die Presse*, corresponded for both, 2 Feb. 1897, CO 417/214 f.499. Wilson was one of Chamberlain's Private Secretaries.

⁸⁵ Minutes by Fairfield 17 and 16 Jan. 1896, CO 417/177 ff.613, 537.

⁸⁶ Minute by Lambert 23 June 1899, CO 417/262 f.886.

⁸⁷ Below, Chs. 5–8, and Porter, *HJ* (1973).

⁸⁸ One exception is in minutes written in Feb. 1897, CO 417/214 f.531.

⁸⁹ Above, 62–3.

⁹⁰ Minute by Fiddes 3 Apr. [?] 1896, CO 417/180 f. 347; R. Lucas, *Lord Glenesk and the Morning Post* (1910), 374, and W. Hindle, *The Morning Post 1772–1937* (1937), 226–7.

⁹¹ Minutes Dec. 1896 and Jan. 1897, CO 417/185 ff. 424, 446, 450; minute by Fairfield 9 May 1896, CO 417/196 f.76.

⁹² Minutes on CO 417/159/20478.

⁹³ Lord Glenesk to Salisbury 14 Jan. 1896, MSP.

⁹⁴ Robinson to Chamberlain tel. no. 4 of 7 Feb. 1896, CO 417/179 f.481, to the press; telegram no. 1 of 10 Feb. withheld, with minute, *ibid*, f.518.

⁹⁵ J. M. Le Sage to Chamberlain 2 Mar. 1896, and the reply, JC 6/4e/2.

⁹⁶ Lord Ampthill [Chamberlain's Private Secretary] to Chamberlain 21 Aug. 1899, minutes 22, 23 August, S. H. Jeyes [Editor of the *Standard*] to Ampthill 23 Aug., JC 6/4p/1–3.
⁹⁷ Steiner, *HJ* 6 (1) (1963), 66.
⁹⁸ Minute by Graham 7 Apr. 1897, CO 417/236/5996; Marais, 146. E. H. C. Moberley Bell, *Flora Shaw* (1947), 174–95, 226–9.
⁹⁹ Milner to Chamberlain 18 Apr. 1899, with minutes by Just, Graham, Selborne and Chamberlain, 30 and 31 May, CO 417/260 ff.676–7.
¹⁰⁰ G. E. Buckle [Editor of *The Times*] to Chamberlain 25 Mar. 1897, with Ampthill's minutes, JC 6/4q/7, 8.

Notes to Chapter V (pp. 122–51)

¹ 11 July 1896, JC 10/7/34.
² R. A. Huttenback, *Gandhi in South Africa* (1971), chs. 2 and 3.
³ Minute by Fairfield 31 July 1896, CO 417/204 f.122.
⁴ Minute 18 May 1897, CO 417/233/9380.
⁵ Minute 19 May 1897, *ibid.*
⁶ Salisbury's comment on military campaigns against Africans, 9 Nov. 1888, Cecil, IV, 135.
⁷ Minute 20 May 1897, CO 417/233/9380 and despatch to Milner 28 May, Af.(S) 536.
⁸ Minute 6 Feb. 1897, CO 417/203 f.32.
⁹ Chamberlain to Sir G. Sprigg [Prime Minister, Cape Colony] 23 Nov. 1897, JC 10/6/4/9.
¹⁰ South African Association to CO 21 Dec. 1897, enclosing 'The Chieftainess and Indunas of the Secoecoeni Tribe Versus The Native Commissioners', and minutes Jan. 1898, CO 417/223 ff.98–114.
¹¹ May 1899, CO 417/254/17432; Wingfield 14 Mar. 1899, CO 417/259 f.527.
¹² CO 417/280 ff.350–5.
¹³ 19 and 25 Oct., *HPD* 4th (lxxvii) 271–2, 678.
¹⁴ Minutes by H. W. Just, on Fiddes to Chamberlain 10 Nov. 1897, CO 417/223 f.124, and 13 March 1899, CO 417/259 f.527. Just was Principal Clerk in the South African department at the CO.
¹⁵ Meade to the FO 12 Dec. 1896, with minutes, FOP 6971.
¹⁶ Chamberlain to Salisbury 11 Dec. 1896 with draft reply, MSP. Salisbury to Chamberlain 13 Dec., JC 5/67/56; FO to CO 13 Dec., Af.(S) 516.
¹⁷ Porter, *JICH* (1972), 7.
¹⁸ MacDonell to Salisbury 17 Feb. 1897, FOP 7031.
¹⁹ Rosmead to Chamberlain 2 Feb. 1897, sent to the FO 13 Mar., *ibid.*
²⁰ MacDonell to Salisbury 6 Feb. 1897, and CO to FO and 20 Mar., *ibid.*
²¹ 29 Jan. 1897, *HPD* 4th (xlv) 802–8. He also presented a Blue Book on the continued imprisonment of two Reform prisoners, Sampson and Davies, on 18 Feb., C. 8346, *PP* (1897) LXII.
²² Minute by Chamberlain 23 Oct. 1896, CO 417/198 f.471.
²³ Butler, *The Liberal Party*, 132.
²⁴ Minute 12 Jan. 1897, CO 417/185 f.427.

25 29 Jan. 1897, *HPD* 4th (xlv) 802–8.

26 Minutes by Chamberlain 24 and 28 Feb. 1897, CO 417/214 ff.350, 327.

27 13 Mar. 1897, cit. Marais, 150–1.

28 To Salisbury, 19 Dec. 1896, MSP; Goschen, writing to Sir T. H. Sanderson, later referred to the Foreign Office and the Colonial Office 'who pressed for the demonstration', [copy] 14 Apr. 1897, FO 63/1341.

29 Cit. Marais, 150.

30 Goschen to Salisbury 22 and 23 Dec. 1896, MSP; minute by Salisbury on Admiralty to FO 28 Dec. 1896, FO 64/1403 f.384; FO to Admiralty 1 Jan. 1897, and reply 13 Jan., FO 63/1340.

31 *The Times*, 23 Apr. 1897.

32 Minutes by Chamberlain and Selborne 23 Feb. 1897, CO 417/214 ff.324–5.

33 Memo 22 Mar. 1897, JC 10/4/2/21.

34 18 Mar. 1897, cit. Wilde, 56–7.

35 Minute 28 Feb. 1897, CO 417/214 f.327.

36 Memoranda by Selborne and Graham 22 Mar. 1897, JC 10/4/2/20 and 21. Chamberlain's letter to Greene, 13 Mar., had concluded 'I hope the Transvaal Government will draw the proper conclusion and will understand that while we desire above all things friendly relations with them, we will not suffer our rights to be impaired', cit. Wilde, 57. Also Director of Military Intelligence to CO 2 Mar., Af.(S) 532.

37 Chamberlain to Salisbury 8 Apr. 1897, MSP.

38 Note by Chamberlain on Selborne's letter to him, both 3 Mar. 1897, SP 8 f.161.

39 Below, 133–4.

40 To Salisbury 9 Apr. 1897, MSP.

41 *Ibid.* 13 Apr. 1897, MSP and part cit. in Lord Newton, *Lord Lansdowne: a Biography* (1929), 144–5.

42 Memo by Balfour, 10 Apr. 1897, and cit. D. Judd, *Balfour and the British Empire* (1968), 162.

43 C. 8423 relating to Affairs in the South African Republic, *PP* (1897), LXII.

44 22 Jan. and 2 Mar. 1897, *HPD* 4th (xlv) 287–8, (xlvi), 1444.

45 *The Times*, 29 Mar. 1897, 8; Sir E. Hamilton's Diary, 27 Mar., Add. MS 48671 ff.18–19; Headlam I, 35. Selborne added his mite in South Wales a little later, *The Times*, 4 May, 6.

46 See his replies concerning the Cape Report on the Raid, 28 Jan. and 26 Feb. 1897, *HPD* 4th (xlv) 679, (xlvi) 1264. The Boer claim for an indemnity arising out of the Raid was read in answer to a question in the House on 18 Feb., the day after details arrived, *ibid.* 726.

47 Minute on High Commissioner to Chamberlain tel. 7 Apr. 1897, CO 417/217 f.154. Question by J. P. Smith, later Chamberlain's private secretary, 12 Apr., *HPD* 4th (xlviii) 956.

48 Extracts in *The Times*, 26 Apr. 1897, 10, *Manchester Guardian*, 26 April, 6.

49 Minutes 30 Mar. 1897, CO 417/233/6619.

50 *The Times*, 27 Mar. 1897; minutes March and April 1897, CO 417/216 f. 320, 417/233/6636, 6826, 7528.

51 Minutes 10 and 12 May 1897, CO 417/217 f.268.

52 Minutes of Evidence, 7 May 1897, questions 7425–31, HC 311-II, *PP*

(1897) IX. Also Chamberlain's examination of Schreiner, 26 Mar. 1897, questions 4303–4, 4433–59.

⁵³ Second Report from the Select Committee on British South Africa, x, xi, xvi, HC 311-I. See e.g. Chamberlain's questions, nos. 7442–50, HC 311-II.

⁵⁴ Monson to Salisbury 15 Apr. 1897, FOP 7031, and 17 Apr. enclosed in FO to CO 24 Apr., Af.(S) 532.

⁵⁵ 16 Apr. 1897, JC 5/67/77, and Garvin, III, 141.

⁵⁶ 21 Apr. 1897, Newton, 145–6.

⁵⁷ Monson to Salisbury, 22 Apr. 1897, sent to CO 24 Apr., Af.(S) 536; Sir T. H. Sanderson to Salisbury, 25 Apr., MSP.

⁵⁸ Acting High Commissioner to Chamberlain tel. 27 Apr. 1897, Af.(S) 532.

⁵⁹ Chamberlain to Salisbury 19 Apr. 1897, MSP; CO to FO 4 May, and Salisbury to Monson 11 May, FOP 7031.

⁶⁰ Grenville, 182–5.

⁶¹ Memo by Selborne 15 Mar. 1897, JC 7/3/2D/12.

⁶² MacDonell to Salisbury 5, 6, and 23 April 1897, FOP 7031.

⁶³ Memoranda of Chamberlain's Interviews with Soveral 10 May 1897, Cab 37/44/19, 29 May, 18 June, JC 7/3/2B/4, 5; Chamberlain to Salisbury 29 May, MSP.

⁶⁴ Note by Salisbury 18 June 1897, FO 63/1359.

⁶⁵ MacDonell to Salisbury 27 July 1897, and Salisbury's reply 3 Aug., FOP 7031.

⁶⁶ MacDonell to Salisbury 13 July 1897, and CO to FO 19 July, FOP 7031.

⁶⁷ Milner to Chamberlain 19 July 1897, Af.(S) 532.

⁶⁸ To Earl Grey (copy) 5 Apr. 1897, SP 15 ff.102–4.

⁶⁹ Headlam, I, 63, 69–70, 102–3.

⁷⁰ Milner to Selborne 2 June 1897, ibid., 105; Milner to Chamberlain, 5 Oct., CO 417/254/7529.

⁷¹ 29 Sept. 1897, Headlam, I, 180.

⁷² Selborne to Earl Grey (copy) 5 Apr. 1897, SP 15 ff. 102–4.

⁷³ H.S. Wilkinson to Milner 10 July 1897, MP 31 pt.1, f.165.

⁷⁴ 26 July 1897, HPD 4th (li) 1176–7.

⁷⁵ Minute for consideration by Selborne, Graham and Wingfield, 2 Aug. 1897, JC 10/4/2/36. Edward Wingfield succeeded Meade as Permanent Under-Secretary in March 1897.

⁷⁶ A. R. D. Elliott, 'Public opinion and South Africa', Edinburgh Review (July 1897), 245–73. The author was reviewing Parliamentary Papers for 1896–7, the Report of the Cape Committee of Enquiry into the Raid, a biography of Rhodes, and F. R. Statham's South Africa As It Is (1897).

⁷⁷ Ibid., 245, 261, 271.

⁷⁸ Ibid., 269–70. The Edinburgh Review was not the only one writing in this vein; 'A colonial chronicle', National Review (Sept. 1897), p. 149 et seq., was positing the idea of class dispute rather than mass Uitlander grievances.

⁷⁹ Minutes 29–30 Aug. 1897, JC 10/4/2/37.

⁸⁰ Cf. Marais, 195–200, Wilde, 69–74.

⁸¹ Chamberlain to Milner 16 Oct. 1897, delivered at Pretoria 6 Dec., C. 8721, 18–22, PP (1898) LX.

⁸² Minute 9 Jan. 1897, CO 417/185 f.305.

⁸³ 29 June 1897, CO 417/219 f.232.

[84] Chamberlain to Milner 11 Dec. 1897, Af.(S) 499.

[85] Milner to Chamberlain 18 May 1897, Af.(S) 532, and 21 July, Af.(S) 536.

[86] Milner to Grey 6 June 1897, Grey MSS.

[87] Milner to Chamberlain 10, 16, 30 Aug, 22 Sept. 1897, Af.(S) 536, 6 Nov 1897, Af.(S) 543; Milner to Greene 6 Dec. 1897, Headlam, I, 137.

[88] General Goodenough's memo on Milner's arrival, 5 May 1897, Headlam, I, 48.

[89] Milner to Chamberlain, 11 May 1897, JC 10/9/3.

[90] Milner to H. H. Asquith, 18 Nov. 1897, Headlam, I, 177–80. For discussion of Milner's views on this question, see Butler, 'Sir Alfred Milner on British policy'.

[91] Milner to Chamberlain, telegrams 15 and 18 May 1897, Af.(S) 532.

[92] Milner to Hely Hutchinson 20 June 1897, and to Chamberlain 25 May, Headlam, I, 53, 63–5.

[93] Milner to Chamberlain, 15 Dec. 1897, 14 Jan. 1898, Af.(S) 543.

[94] Ibid., tel. 18 Feb. 1898, Af.(S) 557.

[95] Ibid., 6 Nov. 1897, Af.(S) 543.

[96] To Greene, 11 Feb. 1898, MP 6 f.240: final word missing.

[97] Earl Grey to C. J. Rhodes, 10 Dec. 1897, Grey MSS.

[98] C. 8721 relating to Affairs in the South African Republic, presented 8 Feb. 1898, PP (1898) LX.

[99] 18 Feb. 1898, HPD 4th (liii) 1052.

[100] Milner to Chamberlain 1 Mar. 1898, Af.(S) 543; Marais, 203–4.

[101] Milner to Greene 18 Feb. 1898, MP 6 f.244.

[102] Fitzpatrick to Alfred Beit 4 Mar. 1898, in Duminy and Guest, Fitzpatrick, 143–7. This corrects the version referred to by J. P. R. Wallis, Fitz: the Story of Sir Percy Fitzpatrick (1955), 69. Fitzpatrick's employers, H. Eckstein and Co., were managers of Wernher Beit and Co.'s Transvaal interests; Fitzpatrick headed the Intelligence Department, and was shortly to become a partner.

[103] 18 Feb. 1898, MP 6 f.244.

[104] 4 Mar. 1898, MP 5 f.40.

[105] Text of the speech, Headlam, I, 243–6.

[106] 18 Feb. 1898, Headlam, I, 216. Sir Walter Hely-Hutchinson, Governor of Natal.

[107] Milner to Chamberlain 9 Mar. 1898, Af.(S) 543.

[108] Notes by P. L. Gell of conversation with Milner 19 Nov. 1898, Gell MSS. The Bond member of the ministry was Dr Te Water, Headlam, I, 260–1.

[109] Fitzpatrick, Lord Milner and His Work. This is central to the interpretation of Milner's entire pre-war career advanced in Duminy, Sir Alfred Milner and the outbreak of the Anglo-Boer War.

[110] 23 Feb. 1898, Headlam, I, 221.

[111] Milner to Miss B. Synge 27 Feb. 1898 [copy], MP 8 f.13. H. M. Stanley was now a member of the ISAA, and speaking on its platforms.

[112] Milner to Chamberlain 23 Feb. 1898, Af.(S) 543 and Headlam, I, 218–20.

[113] The Times' correspondent G. H. Wilson, then on the staff of the Cape Times, tells the story in his book, Gone Down The Years (2nd ed. Cape Town 1947), 45–6. C. D. Don, reporting the event for the Argus, gives a similar account, And Having Writ (Cape Town 1942), 241.

[114] Milner to Chamberlain 15 Mar. 1898, Headlam, I, 226.

[115] Milner's Diary 6 Mar. 1898, MP 261; Milner to Chamberlain, 16 Mar., Af. (S) 557.
[116] *The Times*, 29 Mar. 1898.
[117] Minutes 22 and 23 Mar. 1898, CO 417/242 f.542.
[118] Minutes 28 and 29 Mar. 1898, CO 417/243 f.40.
[119] Chamberlain to Milner 16 Mar. 1898, Headlam, I, 227–9.

Notes to Chapter VI (pp. 152–74)

[1] Memo by F. Bertie [Assistant Under-Secretary, FO] 10 Jan. 1898, JC 7/3/2C/8; Grenville 187.
[2] F. Graham to Milner 25 Feb. 1898, MP 5 f.41.
[3] Correspondence in FOP 7213, *passim*.
[4] Memo by H. Lambert Jan. 1898, Af.(S) 548; MacDonell to Salisbury, 16 Apr. 1898, FOP 7213.
[5] Memo by T. H. Sanderson [Permanent Under-Secretary, FO] 21 Mar. 1898, JC 7/3/2C/9; by Bertie 1 May, BDI, 65; Bertie to Salisbury, 24 May, FO 63/1359.
[6] Memo by Chamberlain 15 June 1898, JC 7/3/2C/10.
[7] Minute 14 June 1898, FO 63/1359.
[8] Milner to Chamberlain 6 and 17 May 1898, Af.(S) 557.
[9] Salisbury to Gough [Chargé d'Affaires at Berlin] 17 and 21 June 1898, Cab 37/47/45, 46.
[10] Salisbury to Lascelles, 11 May 1898, reporting a conversation with Hatzfeldt, G. S. Papadopoulos, 'Lord Salisbury and the projected Anglo-German alliance of 1898', *BIHR* XXVI (1953), 214–18.
[11] MacDonell to Salisbury 22 June 1898, FOP 7213.
[12] Memo by Chamberlain 6 July 1898, JC 7/3/2C/14.
[13] Minute by Chamberlain 4 July 1898, FO 63/1359.
[14] Salisbury to MacDonell 13 July 1898, Cab 37/47/53; memo by Chamberlain 15 July, JC 7/3/2C/15; Salisbury's denial, Grenville, 193.
[15] Lascelles to Salisbury 23 July 1898, FOP 7303; Salisbury to Gough with Hatzfeldt's proposals 23 June, *ibid.* and Cab 37/47/47.
[16] Memo by Chamberlain 23 July 1898, JC 7/2/2A/10.
[17] Chamberlain to Salisbury 25 July 1898, MSP.
[18] Chamberlain to Balfour 16 and 17 Aug. 1898, JC 5/5/75, 77 and BP 49773.
[19] Balfour to Chamberlain 18 Aug. 1898, JC 5/5/32 and MSP A/96/37.
[20] Cabinet Memo by Balfour 5 Sept. 1898, Cab 37/48/71 and MSP A/96/63; memo 17 Aug., BP 49773; Dugdale, I, 269.
[21] Chamberlain to Balfour 19 and 23 Aug. 1898, JC 5/5/78, 80 and MSP A/92/45; texts of the agreements, BDI, 90 and 91.
[22] Balfour to Salisbury 30 Aug. 1898, MSP.
[23] Cf. Grenville 177–98.
[24] Above, 150–1.
[25] H. M. Bourke [ISAA Secretary] to CO 21 Dec. 1897, CO 417/223 ff.115–16.
[26] *Letters of George Wyndham*, ed. G. Wyndham (2 vols, Edinburgh 1915), I, 386; H. O'K. Webber, *The Grip of Gold* (1936), 95.

[27] *South African Association Second Annual Report, 1897–8*, pub. May 1898, *passim*.

[28] *British, Natives and Boers in the Transvaal; the Appeal of the Swazi People* (1894), two editions in that year; *The Transvaal Crisis: the Case for the British Uitlander Residents in the Transvaal* (1896) went into three editions in twelve months, the third being expanded from 40 to 84 pages, a cheap and readable size.

[29] H. W. Lucy, *A Diary of the Unionist Parliament, 1895–1900* (Bristol 1901), 19.

[30] Bartlett to Chamberlain 7 Nov. 1897, CO 417/234/24462.

[31] Compiled early in 1898, revised in May and finally printed in Dec. 1898 as Af.(S) 561, CO 600/12 f.540.

[32] Aug. 1898, CO 417/244 ff.761–3.

[33] 2 July 1898, CO 417/250/14704.

[34] Minutes 23 June 1898, CO 417/244 f.685. C. 9093 'Report on the trade commerce and gold mining industry of the South African Republic, for the year 1897', presented on 26 Oct. 1898, finally published 25 Nov., *PP* (1899) LXIV.

[35] Minute 25 May 1898, CO 417/250/11301.

[36] Minutes 20–3 June 1898, CO 417/244 ff.685–7, and 8 Jan. 1899, CO 417/247 f.586.

[37] Minute [?] 21 October 1898, CO 417/245 f.17.

[38] Headlam, I, 223.

[39] Milner to Miss B. Synge 20 Apr. 1898 [copy], MP 8 f.23.

[40] 9 May 1898, Headlam, I, 232–5.

[41] Greene to Milner 25 Mar. 1898, MP 5 f.57.

[42] 22 Mar. and 28 June 1898, Headlam, I, 229–30, 236.

[43] Fitzpatrick to Beit 4 Mar. 1898, Duminy and Guest, 143–4.

[44] Cf. Duminy, *Sir Alfred Milner*, 1–15.

[45] P. L. Gell to Milner 22 July 1898, MP 31 f.91; Milner to Gell 28 July, Gell MSS.

[46] Milner to Goschen 3 May 1898, MP 8 f.33.

[47] Greene to Milner 29 July 1898 from London reporting Bell, Manager of *The Times*, MP 5f.110; Headlam, I, 237 n.1.

[48] Milner to Greene 17 Aug. 1898, Headlam, I, 237.

[49] Greene to Milner 25 Mar. 1898, MP 5 f.57.

[50] Milner to Selborne 13 Oct. 1897, Headlam, I, 100.

[51] This is set out fully in Porter, *HJ* (1973).

[52] Milner to Miss B. Synge 14 Sept. 1898 [copy], MP 8 f.28.

[53] G. Wyndham to Milner 5 Oct. 1898, MP 5 f.135.

[54] Greene to Graham 28 Oct. 1898, and to Selborne 6 Nov., Af.(S) 557.

[55] Milner to Selborne 9 May 1898, Headlam, I, 232–5.

[56] Milner to Chamberlain 4 May 1898, Af.(S) 543.

Notes to Chapter VII *(pp. 175–202)*

[1] Marais, 140–4.

[2] Minutes 4 and 25 Nov. 1898, CO 417/255/24350.

[3] To Selborne 18 June 1897, SP 14 f.201.

[4] Memo by Bertie 17 Nov. 1898, FOP 7303.

[5] Correspondence Jan. and Feb. 1899, FOP 7646 *passim*.

[6] Minute 26 Jan. 1899, CO 417/271 f.407.

[7] Memo by Bertie 17 Nov. 1898, FOP 7303.

[8] MacDonell to Salisbury 9 Jan. 1899, FOP 7303; 5 Jan. 1899, and FO to CO 8 Mar., *ibid*. 7646.

[9] FO to Consul Ross, 25 Mar. 1899, *ibid*. 7326.

[10] To Salisbury 18 July 1899, *ibid*. 7326.

[11] Minute 9 Mar. 1899, CO 417/271 f.649.

[12] Thornton to Salisbury 30 Sept. 1898, and *passim*, FOP 7303.

[13] MacDonell to Salisbury 2 Mar., 28 Apr. 1899, FOP 7646; and 17 Apr., *ibid*. 7326.

[14] Howard to Salisbury 9 May 1898, Monson to Salisbury 23 July, FOP 7365.

[15] FO to CO 30 July 1898, *ibid*.

[16] Minute by Bertie 10 June 1898, initialled by Salisbury, and correspondence *passim*, FO 2/265 ff. 70–106.

[17] Minute by Bertie 3 Mar. 1899, ff. 38–9, and correspondence *passim*, esp. ff. 50–3, FO 2/266.

[18] Milner to Fiddes 23 Dec. 1898, Headlam, I, 299.

[19] MP 261 and 262, *passim*.

[20] For the mining houses' attitudes, and the role of the press in their own plans, see Jeeves, 'The Rand capitalists', and Duminy, *The Capitalists*.

[21] Samuel Evans to W. T. Stead 7 July 1898 [copy], MP 9(3) ff. 213–14.

[22] Correspondence in MP 9(3) ff.210–14.

[23] 5 Dec. 1898, Gell MSS.

[24] 3 Jan. 1899, Gell MSS.

[25] Milner's Diary, MP 261 and 262 *passim*.

[26] 30 Nov. 1898, Headlam, I, 298.

[27] Milner to Fiddes 25 Nov. and 23 Dec. 1898, Headlam, I, 299–300.

[28] Milner to Selborne 23 Jan. 1899, Wrench, 196–7.

[29] Milner to Fiddes 31 Jan. 1899, Headlam, I, 301–2.

[30] Butler to Chamberlain 25 Jan. 1899, Af.(S) 572.

[31] 12 Feb. 1899, MP 13 f.47.

[32] Fiddes and O. Walrond [Milner's private secretary] to Milner both 28 Dec. 1898, MP 31 ff.69, 200.

[33] To Milner 30 Dec. 1898, MP 5 f.145.

[34] To Selborne 18 June 1897, SP 14 f.202.

[35] Greene to Graham and Selborne 28 Oct., 1 and 6 Nov. 1898, CO 417/255/24630.

[36] Chamberlain's reply 7 Mar. 1899, *HPD* 4th (lxviii) 28; Chamberlain to Milner, tel. 11 Mar., Af.(S) 571. This phrase was omitted in the printed Blue Book version, C. 9345 no. 49, *PP* (1899) LXIV.

[37] Chamberlain to Butler 13 Jan 1899, Af.(S) 571.

[38] Minute by Graham 17 Jan. 1899, CO 417/247 ff.603–4.

[39] Chamberlain to Butler 22 Jan. 1899, Af.(S) 572; minute by Milner, Jan. n.d., CO 417/259 ff. 141–2.

[40] Milner to Chamberlain 4 Mar. 1899, Af.(S) 572.

[41] Chamberlain to Milner tel. 9 Mar. 1899, Af.(S) 572.

[42] Chamberlain's opinion noted by Wingfield, 24 Apr. 1899, CO 417/260

f.264.
[43] Minutes by Chamberlain 14 Mar. 1899, CO 417/259 f. 628, and 15 Mar., SP 9 f.35.
[44] 20 Mar. 1899, *HPD* 4th (lxviii) 1376–80.
[45] Milner to Chamberlain 25 May 1897, Headlam, I, 63–5.
[46] Wrench, 186.
[47] To Chamberlain 11 Mar. 1899, Af.(S) 572.
[48] To Moberley Bell 2 May 1899, Times Archives.
[49] Greene to Milner 7 Mar. 1899, Headlam, I, 340, and 10 Mar., MP 13 f.128.
[50] *Ibid.* 17 Mar. 1899, MP 13 ff.194–202.
[51] Milner to Greene tel. 20 Mar. 1899, MP 13 f.203.
[52] Diary 24 Feb. 1899, MP 262.
[53] 10 Mar. 1899, MP 13 f.128–33.
[54] To Moberley Bell 20 Mar. 1899, Times Archives. Cf. Walrond to Graham, 30 Aug. 1899, 'The Boers are like the Arabs and Turks. They have a large strain of Kaffir in them', CO 417/266 f.227.
[55] Greene to Milner tel. 21 Mar. 1899, MP 13 ff.216–18.
[56] To Milner 17 Mar. 1899, MP 13 ff.194–202.
[57] *Ibid.*
[58] Minute by Selborne 7 Apr. 1899, CO 417/259 f.584.
[59] To Chamberlain 4 Apr. 1899, Af.(S) 572.
[60] C. 9345 relating to the Complaints of British Subjects in the South African Republic, 216–18, *PP* (1899) LXIV. For the divisons amongst the capitalists, see Duminy, *The Capitalists*, esp. 27–30.
[61] Fiddes to Selborne 14 Mar. 1899, SP 14 f.57.
[62] To Chamberlain 27 Mar. 1899, MP 13 ff.272–3 and Af.(S) 572.
[63] To Milner 28 Mar. 1899, MP 13 ff.366–73.
[64] Diary, MP 262. Fitzpatrick described the meetings in his letter to J. Wernher, 6 Apr. 1899, Duminy and Guest, 202–6. Fitzpatrick's version of how he arranged publication occurs in his *South African Memories*, 175–9.
[65] 7 Apr. 1899, MP 12 f.25.
[66] Milner to Fiddes 1 Apr. 1899, Headlam, I, 331.
[67] 3 Apr. 1899, Headlam, I, 345–6.
[68] Fiddes to Milner 28 Mar. 1899, MP 13 ff.366–73.
[69] 7 Apr. 1899, MP 12 ff.6–8.
[70] Milner to Greene 15 Apr. 1899, Headlam, I 332.
[71] 25 Apr. 1899, SP 14 ff. 73–4.
[72] Quoted in Fitzpatrick to Wernher, 6 Apr. 1899, Duminy and Guest, 204.
[73] 4 Apr. 1899, Af.(S) 572.
[74] Minutes Apr. 1899, CO 417/260 f.262.
[75] Minutes on Milner to Chamberlain, 26 Apr. 1899, CO 417/260 f.780.
[76] 5 Apr. 1899, Headlam, I, 348. For the Lombaard incident, concerning the Johannesburg police and the pass laws, Marais, 234–7.
[77] Minute by Graham 16 Apr. 1899, CO 417/260 f.209.
[78] Minutes by Graham 24 Apr., and Just. 26 Apr. 1899, CO 417/260 ff.263, 769.
[79] 24 Apr. 1899, *HPD* 4th (lxx) 490; Greene to Milner, 27 Apr. MP 13 f.453.
[80] Minute 1 May 1899, CO 417/260 f.617.
[81] Minutes Aug. 1899, on E. Fitton to CO, CO 417/281 f.499.

[82] *Ibid.*
[83] Minutes 25–8 Apr. 1899, CO 417/279 f.205–20.
[84] Selborne to Milner tel. 28 Apr. 1899, Af.(S) 572.
[85] To Selborne 2 May 1899, MP 14 ff.2–4.
[86] Selborne to Milner 20 Apr. 1899, MP 14 ff.105A–105C.
[87] Milner to Greene 1 May 1899, MP 14 f.6; to Miss B. Synge 26 Apr., Headlam, I, 336; and to Selborne, 3 May, *ibid.*, 344.
[88] 8 May 1899, Af.(S) 572.
[89] Milner to Greene 15 Apr. 1899, Headlam, I, 332.

Notes to Chapter VIII (pp. 203–33)

[1] Salisbury to Chamberlain 16 Apr. 1897, JC 5/67/77.
[2] Chamberlain's memo for the Cabinet 29 Apr. 1899, Cab 37/49/28.
[3] Cabinet memo by Balfour 1 May 1899, Cab 37/49/29 cit. Drus *BIHR* (1954), 173–5; there were in fact no reliable census figures to enable such an assertion to be made without reservation.
[4] Cabinet memo by Chamberlain 6 May 1899, Cab 37/49/33, and despatch drafts in CO 417/260.
[5] To Chamberlain 6 May 1899, Drus *BIHR* (1954), 175.
[6] *Ibid.*
[7] G. R. Askwith, *Lord James of Hereford* (1930), 257.
[8] 9 May 1899, Cab 41/25/10.
[9] *Ibid.*
[10] Milner to Chamberlain tel. 10 May 1899, Af.(S) 572.
[11] Milner to Greene 12 May 1899, Headlam, I, 378.
[12] Milner to Chamberlain tel. 15 May 1899, Af.(S) 572.
[13] Garvin, III, 401.
[14] 24 May 1899, Headlam, I, 378, and Garvin, III, 402.
[15] Minute by Chamberlain 15 May 1899, CO 417/261 f.208.
[16] Minute 25 May 1899, CO 417/261 f.539.
[17] Sir E. Hamilton's Diary, 25 March, 25 Apr., 14 July, Add. MSS 48674, 48675.
[18] T. Baines,'Democracy and foreign affairs', *Quarterly Review* (Jan. 1899), 241–65. See also F. Greenwood, 'Public opinion in public affairs', *Macmillan's Magazine* (Jan. 1899), 161–9.
[19] E.g. Sir H. Campbell-Bannerman, 7 Feb. 1899, *HPD* 4th (lxvi) 94.
[20] C. 9317 relating to the Explosives Monopoly in the South African Republic, *PP* (1899) LXIV, presented to House of Commons 18 May and finally released on 2 June, to include the Boer reply of 22 May which asserted that HMG had no right to intervene on this question, CO 600/13 f.149.
[21] Monypenny to Walrond 14 May 1899, MP 12 ff.30–1; Greene to Milner 28 Apr., *ibid.* 13 ff.466–9; Monypenny to Moberley Bell, 2 May, Times Archives.
[22] Greene to Milner 12 May 1899, MP 14 ff.56–8. This was a reply to Milner's letter of 6 May which Greene destroyed as asked; even Milner, unusually for him, did not keep a copy of this particular missive.
[23] Vice-Consul at Johannesburg (Evans) to Walrond 15 and 19 May 1899,

MP 6 ff.16, 17.
[24] 18 May 1899, MP 14 f.63.
[25] 6 May 1899, MP 14 f.167.
[26] P. L. Gell to Milner 25 May 1899, MP 32 f.46.
[27] For the Bloemfontein Conference, C. 9404 *PP* (1899) LXIV; Marais, 280–4.
[28] To Milner 2 June 1899, Gell MSS.
[29] To Selborne 27 June 1899, SP 14 ff.90–5.
[30] Tel. 7 June 1899, CO 417/262 f.34.
[31] Chamberlain to Milner, tel. 5 June 1899, Af.(S) 572, and minute 4 June, CO 417/262 ff.12–13.
[32] To Milner 18 May 1899, MP 14 f.63.
[33] Minutes, CO 600/13 f.151. C. 9345 relating to the Complaints of British Subjects in the South African Republic, *PP* (1899) LXIV.
[34] Minutes on CO 417/261 ff.245, 258–9, 312; CO 417/279 ff.277–8, 281–95.
[35] Sir E. Hamilton's Diary 9 and 14 June 1899, Add. MS 48675.
[36] E. T. Cook, Editor of *Daily News*, to Milner, 16 June 1899, cit. E. Stokes, 'Milnerism', *HJ* 5 (1) 1962, 58–9.
[37] 16 June 1899, MP 15 ff.42–5.
[38] Salisbury to Queen Victoria 13 and 20 June 1899, QVL 3rd III, 382, 384.
[39] To H. Fowler 28 June 1899, BP 49853.
[40] Salisbury in conversation, reported in G. E. Buckle to A. F. Walter [Proprietor of *The Times*] 13 June 1899, Times Archives.
[41] To Milner 25 June 1899, Headlam, I, 445.
[42] To Chamberlain tel. 20 June 1899, Af.(S) 572.
[43] Marais, 279.
[44] Chamberlain to Milner 21 June 1899, Af.(S) 572.
[45] A. Rothschild to Chamberlain 12 June 1899, JC 7/2/2C/4, 9.
[46] Garvin, III, 417–18.
[47] To Chamberlain 23 June 1899, JC 10/4/2/45.
[48] G. Wyndham to Milner 1 July 1899, MP 15 f.167.
[49] To Chamberlain 3 July 1899, JC 10/4/2/47. G. C. T. Bartley, MP for Islington North.
[50] To Gell 18 June 1899, Gell MSS.
[51] To Milner tel. 18 July 1899, Af.(S) 572; *The Times*, 19 July.
[52] 19 July 1899, JC 5/67/114.
[53] Chamberlain to Salisbury 20 July 1899, MSP.
[54] Marais, 296.
[55] C. 9404 relating to the Bloemfontein Conference, presented 20 July; C. 9415 relating to Proposed Political Reforms in the South African Republic, presented 25 July; *PP* (1899) LXIV.
[56] Chamberlain's draft despatch Cab 37/50/46, with comments by Salisbury and Long, 21 and 22 July 1899, JC 10/4/2/50, 48. Long was President of the Board of Agriculture.
[57] Comments all 21 July 1899, JC 10/4/2/49, 51, 53, 54. Henry Chaplin was President of the Local Government Board; C. T. Ritchie, President of the Board of Trade.
[58] Minute 22 July 1899, CO 417/264 ff.45–6; Marais, 303.
[59] Lucy, 303.
[60] Lord Camperdown to Milner 1 Aug. 1899, MP 32 ff.6–7.

⁶¹ 28 July 1899, *HPD* 4th (lxxv) 661–4.
⁶² Selborne to Milner 27 July and 11 Aug. 1899, MP 16 (1) ff.87–96, (2) ff.196–7.
⁶³ Diary, 7, 11, 18 July 1899, MP 262.
⁶⁴ *Ibid.*, Headlam, I, 469, 471.
⁶⁵ 25 June 1899, Headlam, I, 445–6.
⁶⁶ 14 July 1899, MP 16 (3) f.53.
⁶⁷ 13 July 1899, MP 16 (3) f.30.
⁶⁸ 20 July 1899, MP 32 f.15.
⁶⁹ 14 July 1899, MP 32 ff.50–1.
⁷⁰ Milner to J. Rendel 21 July 1899, Headlam, I, 473.
⁷¹ Milner to Chamberlain 5 July 1899, Af.(S) 600; cf. Headlam, I, 456–7.
⁷² Milner to Selborne 12 July 1899 [copy], MP 8 f.25.
⁷³ 5 July 1899, Spender MSS 46391 f.36.
⁷⁴ 12 July 1899, *ibid.* ff.37–8.
⁷⁵ 17 July 1899 [copy], MP 8 ff.4–5.
⁷⁶ P. L. Gell to W. T. Stead, 21 July 1899, Gell MSS; A. Weston Jarvis, *Jottings from an Active Life* (1928), 116.
⁷⁷ Tel. 16 July 1899, Af.(S) 572.
⁷⁸ Milner to J. Rendel 5 Aug. 1899, Headlam, I, 355–6.
⁷⁹ Tel., 26 July 1899, Headlam, I, 471.
⁸⁰ 17 May 1899, Headlam, I, 384.
⁸¹ Chamberlain in the House of Commons, 28 July 1899, *HPD* 4th (lxxv) 697–716.
⁸² C. 9507 relating to the Status of the South African Republic, *PP* (1899) LXIV, was presented on 11 Aug., but unfortunately delayed at the printers until 22 Aug., CO 600/13 f.152.

Notes to Chapter IX (pp. 234–57)

¹ To Salisbury 15 Aug. 1899, MSP.
² Salisbury to Chamberlain 16 Aug. 1899, JC 5/67/115.
³ Memo by Wolseley 17 Apr. 1899, Cab 37/50/52.
⁴ Goschen to Salisbury 18 Aug. 1899, MSP.
⁵ 23 Aug. 1899, St Aldwyn MSS PCC/83.
⁶ Milner to Chamberlain tel. 15 Aug. 1899, Af.(S) 572.
⁷ To Salisbury 16 and 18 Aug. 1899, MSP.
⁸ Lansdowne to Wolseley 20 Aug. 1899, Cab 37/50/53, 54.
⁹ M. White to F. Reitz 28 Aug. 1899 [copy], MP 19(3) ff.29–30.
¹⁰ To Milner tel. 16 Aug. 1899, Af.(S) 572.
¹¹ Hicks Beach to Salisbury 24 Aug. 1899, MSP part cit. Lady V. Hicks Beach, *Life of Sir Michael Hicks Beach* (2 vols, 1932), II, 107.
¹² To Salisbury 23 Aug. 1899, SP.
¹³ To Hicks Beach 30 Aug. 1899, St Aldwyn MSS PCC/69.
¹⁴ To Lady Elcho 27 Aug. 1899, cit. K. Young, *Arthur James Balfour* (1963), 185.
¹⁵ To Wolseley 27 Aug. 1899, Cab 37/50/57.
¹⁶ CO 600/13 f.162. C. 9518 relating to Proposed Political Reforms in the South African Republic, *PP* (1899) LXIV.

[17] Garvin, III, 438–9.
[18] To Salisbury 31 Aug. 1899, Hicks Beach, II, 104–5.
[19] 28 July 1899, Headlam, I, 472–3.
[20] G. Drage [MP for Derby and ISAA Chairman] to Milner 12 Aug. 1899, MP 16(1) f.225.
[21] To Milner 18 Aug. 1899 (only completed and sent mid-Sept.), ibid. 16(1) ff.117–28.
[22] Minutes in July 1899, CO 417/263 ff.681–2, CO 417/264 f.100.
[23] Minutes early Aug. 1899, CO 417/263 f.249.
[24] C. 9521 relating to Political Affairs in the South African Republic, presented 9 Sept., and C. 9530, with same title, presented 12 Oct., PP (1899) LXIV.
[25] Minutes Aug.–Nov. 1899, CO 417/264 ff.89, 129, 289, 311, 414, 463, 533 and CO 417/266 f.147.
[26] To J. Rendel 21 July 1899, Headlam, I, 473.
[27] To Strachey [Editor of the Spectator] 24 Aug. 1899, Strachey MSS; Diary, 16 Aug., 6 Sept., MP 262.
[28] Obituary of L. J. Maxse by F. Grigg, National Review, Feb. 1932, 140.
[29] 2 Sept. 1899, Headlam, I, 525–8.
[30] 28 July and 25 Oct. 1899, HPD 4th (lxxv) 686–97, (lxxvii) 684–91.
[31] Manchester Guardian, 18 July 1899, 7; 21 July, 6; 4 Sept., 9; 5 Sept., 7; 22 Sept., 6.
[32] J. Holland Rose, The Rise and Growth of Democracy in Britain (1898); ISAA Pamphlet, Speech by G. Drage MP, given at Derby 7 Dec. 1899; Memo for the Cabinet Defence Committee by E. A. Altham, 'Military needs of the Empire in a war with France and Russia', 10 Aug. 1901, 30–1, Cab 37/40.
[33] See H. S. Wilkinson, Thirty-Five Years 1874–1909 (1933), 238.
[34] Well over four hundred reaching the Office and passed before the outbreak of war are preserved in CO 417/277 and 278; another two hundred different resolutions were reported in The Times and the Manchester Guardian between 1 Sept. and the war.
[35] ISAA Annual Report for 1899–1900, 3–4.
[36] J. A. Spender, Life, Journalism and Politics (2 vols, 1927), I, 86; H. O'K. Webber, The Grip of Gold (1936), 102–3.
[37] To Milner 27 July 1899, Headlam, I, 473–4.
[38] Ibid.
[39] 9 Oct. 1899, CO 417/278.
[40] Manchester Guardian, 19 July 1899, 4–5.
[41] 'A symposium of the Transvaal crisis', 'By a Wanderer in the Slums', ibid., 3 Oct. 1899, 5.
[42] 2 Sept. 1899, MP 8 f.44. An extract is printed by Headlam, I, 525–8, with no indication of omissions, particularly a long passage following the words 'for I take no account of the Labouchere and Scott section' (p. 526 para. 1); also Garvin, III, 457–9.
[43] Newton, 157.
[44] Above, 236–7.
[45] Salisbury to MacDonell 30 Aug. 1899, FOP 7630.
[46] Salisbury's views as reported by W. St J. Brodrick in Gell to Milner 21 Sept. 1899, cit. Stokes, 57; also Gell to Earl Grey, 19 Sept., Grey MSS.

[47] Memo by Chamberlain 5 Sept. 1899, Cab 37/50/63.
[48] Memo by Salisbury 6 Sept. 1899, Cab 37/50/64.
[49] Memo by Chamberlain 6 Sept. 1899, Cab 37/50/70.
[50] To Milner 28 July 1899, Headlam, I, 472.
[51] See his pencillings on Chamberlain's 6 Sept. Memo, St Aldwyn MSS PC/PP/75.
[52] Garvin, III, 442–3.
[53] Memo by Chamberlain 6 Sept. 1899, Cab 37/50/70.
[54] To Hely Hutchinson 4 Sept. 1899, Af.(S) 572.
[55] To Chamberlain 31 and 23 Aug. 1899, C. 9521, 51, 60–4, PP (1899) LXIV.
[56] 15 Sept. 1899, MP 32 ff.58–63.
[57] Sir E. Hamilton's Diary 9 Sept. 1899, Add. MS 48675.
[58] 19 Sept. 1899, Drus BIHR (1954), 181.
[59] 30 Sept. 1899, cit. Hicks Beach, II, 108.
[60] To Bryce 2 Oct. 1899, BP 49853.
[61] Sir E. Hamilton's Diary 6 Oct. 1899, Add. MS 48675.
[62] 22 Sept. 1899, Garvin, III, 447–8.
[63] Hicks Beach to Chamberlain 29 Sept. 1899, Drus BIHR (1954), 187; Chamberlain to Hicks Beach 29 Sept. 1899, St Aldwyn MSS PCC/86.
[64] Goschen to Chamberlain 29 Sept. 1899, Drus BIHR (1954), 186–7.
[65] Ibid.
[66] Chamberlain to Balfour 3 Oct. 1899, BP 49773.
[67] Garvin, III, 464.
[68] Minute by Chamberlain 23 Sept. 1899, CO 417/267 f.4.
[69] Chamberlain to Milner tels. 5 and 6 of 22 Sept. 1899, C. 9530 nos. 12, 13, PP (1899) LXIV.
[70] To Hicks Beach 29 Sept. 1899, St Aldwyn MSS PCC/86.
[71] 7 Oct. 1899, MP 17 f.233.
[72] To Hicks Beach 7 Oct. 1899, St Aldwyn MSS PCC/86.
[73] Milner to Chamberlain 27 Sept. 1899, Headlam, I, 546–7.
[74] Ibid. 29 Sept. 1899, JC 10/9/76.
[75] To Milner 13 Oct. 1899, MP 17 f.238.
[76] 19 Oct. 1899, HPD 4th (lxxvii) 266.
[77] 17 Oct. 1899, ibid. 16–22.

Notes to Conclusion (pp. 258–76)

[1] E. Burke, Reflections on the Revolution in France (1825 ed.), 196.
[2] 6 Dec. 1899, JC 10/9/82.
[3] 25 Oct. 1899, HPD 4th (lxxvii) 645–7.
[4] E. D. Morel's History of the Congo Reform Movement, eds. W. R. Louis and J. Stengers (Oxford, 1968), 63–4.
[5] To Sir W. V. Harcourt 10 Oct. 1899, cit. J. A. Spender, The Life of the Right Hon. Sir Henry Campbell-Bannerman G.C.B. (2 vols., 1923), I, 246–7, and J. Wilson, C.B. A Life of Sir Henry Campbell-Bannerman (1973), 312.
[6] Even J. C. Smuts, in a letter to Hofmeyr on 13 June 1899 following the Bloemfontein Conference, confessed himself undecided whether Milner was the mouthpiece of Chamberlain or 'a very naughty proconsul who is only concerned to make the idea of an "independent South Africa" give

way to that of imperialism . . .', *Selections from the Smuts Papers*, eds. Sir K. Hancock and J. Van der Poel (7 vols., Cambridge 1966–73), I, 245–50.

[7] Chamberlain to R. W. Dale, 14 Sept. 1882, JC 5/20/40 and in part Garvin, I, 489.

[8] See for example chs. IV and VI above.

[9] Fiddes to Selborne 29 May 1899, SP 14 ff.84–9.

[10] E. Drus, 'Chamberlain and the Boers', *JAH* (1963), 144.

[11] E. Halévy, *A History of the English People in the Nineteenth Century*, 5 (2nd ed., 1951), 93–4.

[12] R. C. K. Ensor, *England 1870–1914* (Oxford 1936), 250–1; W. L. Langer, *The Diplomacy of Imperialism, 1890–1902* (New York 1935).

[13] R. Koebner and H. D. Schmidt, *Imperialism, The Story and Significance of a Political Word, 1840–1960*, (Cambridge 1964), 212–16.

[14] *Ibid.*, 235–6.

[15] Robinson and Gallagher, 462.

[16] H. Pelling, *A Social Geography of British Elections 1885–1910* (1967); H. Pelling, *Popular Politics and Society in Late Victorian Britain* (1968), ch. 5 'British labour and British imperialism'; R. Price, *An Imperial War and the British Working Class* (1972); P. Smith, Introduction to the *Unionist Campaign Guide* for the Election of 1895 (Harvester Press reprints, forthcoming).

[17] Robinson has developed this argument further: 'Non-European foundations of European imperialism: sketch for a theory of collaboration' in R. Owen and B. Sutcliffe, eds., *Studies in the theory of imperialism* (1972).

[18] J. Stengers, 'L'impérialisme Colonial de la fin du XIXe siècle: Mythe ou Réalité?', *JAH* III (1962), 486.

[19] *Ibid.*, 490.

[20] Marais, 69, for example, asserts that Chamberlain 'knew also how to make use of the press, including the halfpenny popular press, to enhance his influence'. This is neither substantiated nor shown to be of any significance.

[21] Garson, *South African Journal of Economics* (1962). He refers to 'a general climate of imperialism that should not be ignored. It meant that the views of Chamberlain and Milner were backed by a powerful sanction that they could bring into play by focusing the unspecific elements of popular imperialism on to the particular issue of South Africa.' There was apparently no difficulty in creating an 'appeal of political grandeur' which would attract the support of 'the newly enfranchised, the newly literate and the politically inarticulate among the inhabitants of the towns'. Garson fails however to explain why such focusing was needed, makes no suggestion of the difficulties which Chamberlain or Milner saw, and provides no hint that attention to the widest possible public was more than a flash in the pan, still less that it fundamentally affected the nature of the issues at stake in negotiations with the Boers.

[22] See M. A. Thompson 'Parliament and foreign policy, 1689–1714', and G. C. Gibbs, 'Parliament and the Treaty of Quadruple Alliance', in *William III and Louis XIV. Essays 1680–1720 by and for M. A. Thompson*, eds. R. Hatton and J. S. Bromley (Liverpool 1968), pp. 130–9, 287–305. For these references I am indebted to Prof. P. J. Marshall.

[23] W. Bagehot, *The English Constitution*, Introduction 1872 (Nelson's ed., n.d.), 21.

[24] *Ibid.*

[25] Speech at Edinburgh, 16 Sept. 1876, cit. H. Jephson, *The Platform Its Rise and Progress* (2nd ed., 2 vols, 1892), II, 499.

[26] Of a total of 62 MPs (50 Conservatives, 11 Liberal Unionists, 1 Liberal) only some 9 or 10 Conservatives seem to have had even predominantly landed interests. Their average age was 45 years 8 months, 33 being aged 45 or younger; more than one third – 22 – were below 40, and these included, perhaps not surprisingly, the most active members. Compare this with an estimate of a 30% landed interest for the whole Conservative party in 1900, by J. A. Thomas, *The House of Commons 1832–1901. A Study of its economic and functional character* (Cardiff 1939), 20; the average age of MPs in 1899, based on the 648 whose age is given in *Dod's Parliamentary Companion*, was 51 years 8 months.

[27] Members of the China Committee included E. W. Beckett, E. A. Goulding, A. S. T. G. Boscawen, and R. A. Yerburgh; see A. S. T. G. Boscawen, *Fourteen Years in Parliament* (1907), 135, and N. A. Pelcovits, *Old China Hands and the Foreign Office* (New York 1948), 205–59 *passim*.

[28] Speech at Birmingham, 15 May 1903, Boyd, II, 140.

[29] See for example J. O. Springhall, 'Youth and empire: A study of the propaganda of imperialism to the young in Edwardian Britain' (unpub. D.Phil. thesis, University of Sussex, 1968); G. R. Searle, *The Quest for National Efficiency* (Oxford 1971); J. E. Kendle, *The Round Table Movement and Imperial Union* (Toronto 1975).

[30] Austen Chamberlain to F. Acland, 7 Dec. 1914, cit. C. Hazlehurst, *Politicians at War, July 1914 to May 1915. A Prologue to the triumph of Lloyd George* (1971), 163.

Select bibliography

It has been necessary to confine items listed here to the principal manuscript sources used, and to a selection of secondary works bearing directly on the origins of the war. Many other works are cited in the footnotes where appropriate.

Official sources

Public Record Office, London

Cabinet Records
Cab 37	1894–1899	General Papers
Cab 38	1888–1904	Committee of Defence
Cab 41	1894–1899	Prime Minister's letters to the Queen

Colonial Office
CO 417	1894–1901	South Africa Original Correspondence
CO 537	1895–1899	Supplementary Correspondence
CO 600	1895–1899	Printing Registers
CO 879	1894–1900	Confidential Print

Director of Public Prosecutions
DPP/1/2/1–4   The Trial of Dr L. S. Jameson and Others

Foreign Office
FO 2	1895–1899	Africa General Correspondence
FO 63	1895–1899	Portugal
FO 64	1895–1899	Germany
FO 83	1825–1898	Miscellaneous (Parliamentary and Domestic)
FO 881	1894–1900	Confidential Print

War Office
WO 32	1895–1899	Miscellaneous Correspondence

Private papers

Public Record Office, London
Sir J. Ardagh
Earl of Clarendon
Earl Granville
Baron Hammond
Earl of Midleton
Lord John Russell
Sir T. Sanderson
Baron Tenterden
Lord Howard de Walden

Miscellaneous, in FO 800/1–4, 25–30, 34, 229–31, 382.

British Library
H. O. Arnold Forster
A. J. Balfour
T. H. S. Escott
F. E. Garrett
Sir E. Hamilton
E. B. Iwan Muller
Marquess of Ripon
J. A. Spender

Bodleian Library, Oxford
Viscout Milner
Lord Monk Bretton
Earl of Selborne

Rhodes House, Oxford
Sir G. Bower
Sir F. Hamilton
C. J. Rhodes

University of Birmingham
Joseph Chamberlain
J. Austen Chamberlain

County Records Office, Gloucester
Earl St Aldwyn (Sir M. E. Hicks Beach)

Commander C. H. Drage, 38 Sheffield Terrace, London W8
G. Drage

Hopton Hall, Wirksworth, Derbyshire
P. L. Gell

University of Durham
Albert, 4th Earl Grey

Hatfield House, Hertfordshire
Marquess of Salisbury

House of Lords Record Office
J. St Loe Strachey

New Printing House Square, London
Archives of *The Times*

Army Museums Ogilby Trust, London
H. S. Wilkinson

The papers of George Wyndham were discovered in the possession of the Duke of Westminster, but were not available for examination.

Secondary works

A. Atmore and S. Marks, 'The imperial factor in South Africa in the nineteenth century: towards a reassessment', *JICH* III (1) (1974), 105–39.

E. Axelson, *Portugal and the scramble for Africa 1875–91* (Johannesburg 1967)

J. O. Baylen, 'W. T. Stead and the Boer War', *Canadian Historical Review* XL (1959)
——, 'W. T. Steads's *History of the Mystery* and the Jameson Raid', *JBS* 4 (1) (1964), 104–32.

M. F. Bitensky, 'The South African League' (unpub. M.A. thesis, University of the Witwatersrand, 1951)

R. W. Bixler, *Anglo-German Imperialism in South Africa 1880–1900* (Baltimore 1932)

G. Blainey, 'Lost causes of the Jameson Raid', *Economic History Review* 18 (1965), 350–66

C. W. Boyd ed., *Mr Chamberlain's Speeches* (2 vols., 1914)

J. Butler, *The Liberal Party and the Jameson Raid* (Oxford 1968)
——, 'Sir Alfred Milner on British policy in South Africa in 1897', *Boston University Papers on Africa I* (Boston 1964), 243–70.
——, 'The German factor in Anglo-Transvaal relations', in P. Gifford and W. R. Louis eds., *Britain and Germany in Africa* (1967), 179–214
——, 'Cecil Rhodes', *International Journal of African Historical Studies* 2 (1977), 259–81.

T. C. Caldwell, *The Anglo–Boer War. Why was it fought? Who was responsible?* (Boston 1965)

A. J. Dachs, 'Rhodes's grasp for Bechuanaland, 1889–1896', *Rhodesian History* 2 (1971), 1–9.

T. R. H. Davenport, *The Afrikaner Bond. The History of a South African Political Party 1880–1911* (Cape Town 1966)
——, *South Africa: a Modern History* (1977)

D. Denoon, *A Grand Illusion. The failure of imperial policy in the Transvaal Colony during the period of reconstruction 1900–1905* (1973)
——, 'The Transvaal labour crisis, 1901–6', *JAH* VII (3) (1967), 481–94
——, ' "Capitalist influence" and the Transvaal Government during the Crown Colony period, 1900–1906', *HJ* 11 (2) (1968), 301–31

E. Drus, 'A report on the papers of Joseph Chamberlain relating to the Jameson Raid and the Inquiry', *BIHR* XXV (1952), 33–62
——, 'The question of imperial complicity in the Jameson Raid', *EHR* LXVIII (1953), 582–93
——, 'Select documents from the Chamberlain papers concerning Anglo-Transvaal relations, 1896–99', *BIHR* XXVII (1954), 156–89
——, 'Chamberlain and the Boers', *JAH* IV (1) (1963), 144–5

A. H. Duminy, *Sir Alfred Milner and the outbreak of the Anglo-Boer War* (Durban 1976)
——, *The Capitalists and the outbreak of the Anglo-Boer War* (Durban

1977)

A. H. Duminy and W. R. Guest, eds., *Fitzpatrick South African Politician. Selected Papers 1880–1906* (Johannesburg 1976)

G. W. Eybers ed., *Select Constitutional Documents illustrating South African History, 1795–1910* (1918)

J. P. Fitzpatrick, *The Transvaal from Within* (1899)
——, *Lord Milner and His Work* (Cape Town 1925)
——, *South African Memories* (1932)

J. E. Flint, *Cecil Rhodes* (Boston 1974)

M. Fraser and A. H. Jeeves, eds., *All that Glittered: Selected Correspondence of Lionel Phillips, 1890–1924* (Cape Town 1977)

P. Fraser, *Joseph Chamberlain. Radicalism and Empire, 1868–1914* (1966)

J. S. Galbraith, *Crown and Charter. The Early Years of the British South Africa Company* (Berkeley 1974)
——, 'The pamphlet campaign on the Boer War', *Journal of Modern History* 24 (2) (1952), 111–26
——, 'The British South Africa Company and the Jameson Raid', *JBS* 10 (1) (1970), 145–61

N. G. Garson, 'The Swaziland question and the road to the sea 1887–1895', *AYB* (1957) (2)
——, 'British imperialism and the coming of the Anglo-Boer War', *South African Journal of Economics* 30 (2) (1962), 140–53.

J. L. Garvin and J. Amery, *The Life of Joseph Chamberlain* (6 vols., 1932–69)

A. M. Gollin, *Proconsul in Politics. A Study of Lord Milner in opposition and in power* (New York 1964)

C. F. Goodfellow, *Great Britain and South African Confederation 1870–1881* (Cape Town 1966)

C. T. Gordon, *The Growth of Boer Opposition to Kruger, 1890–1895* (Cape Town 1970)
——, 'Aspects of colour attitudes and public policy in Kruger's republic', *St Antony's Papers 21* (Oxford 1969), 92–112

J. A. S. Grenville, *Lord Salisbury and Foreign Policy* (rev.ed., 1970)

V. Halperin, *Lord Milner and the Empire: the evolution of British imperialism* (1952)

R. J. Hammond, *Portugal and Africa 1815–1910. A study in uneconomic imperialism* (Stanford 1966)

C. Headlam ed., *The Milner Papers. South Africa 1897–1905* (2 vols., 1931–3)

J. A. Hobson, *The War in South Africa: its Causes and Effects* (1900)
——, *The Psychology of Jingoism* (1901)

——, *Imperialism* (1902)

R. J. S. Hoffman, *Great Britain and the German Trade Rivalry 1875–1914* (Pennsylvania 1933)

M. G. Holli, 'Joseph Chamberlain and the Jameson Raid: a bibliographical survey', *JBS* 3 (2) (1964), 152–66

A. H. Jeeves, 'The Rand capitalists and the coming of the South African War, 1896–1899', *Canadian Historical Association Papers 1973* (Ottawa 1974), 61–83
——, 'The control of migratory Labour on the South African gold mines in the era of Kruger and Milner', *JSAS* 2 (2) (1975), 3–29

D. Judd, *Radical Joe. A Life of Joseph Chamberlain* (1977)

R. V. Kubicek, *The Administration of Imperialism: Joseph Chamberlain at the Colonial Office* (Durham, N.C. 1969)
——, *Economic Imperialism in Theory and Practice. The Case of South African Gold Mining Finance 1886–1914* (Durham, N.C. 1979)
——, 'The Randlords in 1895: A Reassessment', *JBS* 11 (2) (1972), 84–103
——, 'Finance capital and South African goldmining 1886–1914', *JICH* III (3) (1975), 386–95

G. H. L. Le May, *British Supremacy in South Africa 1899–1907* (Oxford 1965)

J. G. Lockhart and C. M. Woodhouse, *Rhodes* (1963)

R. I. Lovell, *The Struggle for South Africa 1875–99. A study in economic imperialism* (New York 1934)

A. F. Madden, 'Changing attitudes and widening responsibilities, 1895–1914', *CHBE* III (Cambridge 1959) 339–405

J. S. Marais, *The Fall of Kruger's Republic* (Oxford 1961)

J. Marlowe, *Milner. Apostle of Empire* (1976)

A. A. Mawby, 'Capital, government and politics in the Transvaal 1900–1907: a revision and a reversion', *HJ* 17 (2) (1974), 387–415

P. R. Maylam, 'The making of the Kimberley–Bulawayo railway: a study in the operations of the British South Africa Company', *Rhodesian History* 8 (1977), 13–33.

R. Mendelsohn, 'Blainey and the Jameson Raid: the debate renewed' (Institute of Commonwealth Studies. Collected Seminar Papers, Societies of Southern Africa, vol. 8, London 1977)

G. Monger, *The End of Isolation: British Foreign Policy 1900–1907* (1963)

E. Pakenham, *Jameson's Raid* (1960)

I. Phimister, 'Rhodes, Rhodesia and the Rand', *JSAS* 1 (1) (1974), 74–90

A. N. Porter, 'Lord Salisbury, Mr Chamberlain and South Africa, 1895–9', *JICH* I (1) (1972), 3–26
——, 'Sir Alfred Milner and the press, 1897–1899', *HJ* 16 (2) (1973), 323–39

——, 'In memoriam Joseph Chamberlain: a review of periodical literature 1960–1973', *JICH* III (2) (1975), 292–7

——, 'Joseph Chamberlain: a radical reappraised?', *JICH* VI (3) (1978), 330–6

B. J. Porter, *Critics of Empire. British Radical attitudes to colonialism in Africa 1895–1914* (1968)

R. N. Price, *An Imperial War and the British Working Class* (1972)

G. B. Pyrah, *Imperial Policy and South Africa, 1902–1910* (Oxford 1955)

T. O. Ranger, 'The last word on Cecil Rhodes?', *Past and Present* 28 (1964), 116–27

D. Rhoodie, *Conspirators in Conflict. A Study of the Johannesburg Reform Committee and its role in the conspiracy against the South African Republic* (Cape Town 1967)

R. E. Robinson and J. Gallagher, *Africa and the Victorians. The Official Mind of Imperialism* (1961)

R. E. Robinson, 'Imperial problems in British Politics', *CHBE* III (Cambridge 1959), 127–80

D. M. Schreuder, *Gladstone and Kruger. Liberal Government and Colonial 'Home Rule'* (1969)

B. Semmel, *Imperialism and Social Reform. English social-imperial thought 1895–1914* (1960)

Z. Steiner, *The Foreign Office and Foreign Policy, 1898–1914* (Cambridge 1969)

W. L. Strauss, *Joseph Chamberlain and the Theory of Imperialism* (New York 1942, rep. 1971)

M. Streak, *Lord Milner's Immigration Policy for the Transvaal, 1897–1905* (Johannesburg 1969)

E. Stokes, 'Milnerism', *HJ* 5 (1) (1962), 47–60

——, 'The British moment in South Africa', *JAH* VII (3) (1966), 528–30

C. A. Thompson, 'The administration of Sir Henry Loch as Governor of Cape Colony and High Commissioner for South Africa, 1889–1895' (Duke University, Ph.D., 1973; repr. Ann Arbor and London 1978)

L. M. Thompson, 'The origins of the South African War', *JAH* II (1) (1962), 148–50

——, 'Great Britain and the Afrikaner Republics', in M. Wilson and L. Thompson eds., *The Oxford History of South Africa* II (Oxford 1971)

J. Van der Poel, *Railway and Customs Policies in South Africa, 1885–1910* (1933)

——, *The Jameson Raid* (Cape Town 1951)

J-J. Van-Helten, 'German capital, the Netherlands Railway Company and the political economy of the Transvaal 1886–1900', *JAH* XIX (3) (1978),

369–90

——, 'British capital, the British State and economic investment in South Africa 1886–1914' (Institute of Commonwealth Studies, London. Societies of Southern Africa, Seminar Paper 13, 1977)

——, 'Milner and the mind of Imperialism' (*ibid.*, Seminar Paper 5, 1978)

E. B. Van Heyningen, 'The relations between Sir Alfred Milner and W. P. Schreiner's Ministry, 1898–1900', *AYB* (1976)

E. A. Walker, *A History of South Africa* (3rd ed. 1957)

——, *CHBE VIII. South Africa* (2nd ed. Cambridge 1963)

——, 'Lord Milner and South Africa' *Proceedings of the British Academy* 28 (1942), 155–78

P. R. Warhurst, *Anglo-Portuguese relations in South Central Africa 1890–1900* (1962)

R. H. Wilde, 'Joseph Chamberlain and the South African Republic 1895–1899', *AYB* (1956) (1)

C. M. Woodhouse, 'The missing telegrams and the Jameson Raid', *History Today* XII (1962), pt. 1 395–404, pt. 2 506–14

J. E. Wrench, *Alfred Lord Milner. The Man of No Illusions 1854–1925* (1958)

Index